PHILOSOPHY

Mirrors of Human Nature

JOSHUA LOTT

Kendall Hunt
publishing company

Cover image © Shutterstock.com

Kendall Hunt
publishing company

www.kendallhunt.com
Send all inquiries to:
4050 Westmark Drive
Dubuque, IA 52004-1840

To Dad.

I wish you were still here to see the afterglow
of your love and labor.

Contents

Philosophy of Human Nature and The Uncanny

Take a moment and contemplate the room around you. If you are not inside a room, then observe your surrounding area. Place this book aside and take it all in. What did your external senses reveal? If you are in a room, perhaps you noticed several familiar items of an everyday sort. Perhaps you saw painted walls, finished floors, furniture such as desks and chairs, couches, a bed if you're in a bedroom, in addition to some modern equipment designed to make our lives easier and more luxurious, such as a smart TV, a mobile phone, and a computer of some sort, as well as the buzzing of an air conditioning unit. For those of you who are outdoors, I'll hazard a guess that you saw the grass, the open sky, buildings, vehicles parked in a nearby lot, and other people, some of whom maybe exercising their pet dogs. More than likely, you can feel the gust of the wind and hear buzzing of the insects and chirping of the birds around you, among various other sensory effects of the modern world. Suppose now that you reach for that mobile phone beside you, but alas, it does not work as usual. Perhaps the device is locked pending the removal of malware, or somehow the circuitry became damaged. Can you restore it? Do you even know what caused the malfunction in the first place? After all, it is an item of your property that you use effortlessly every day. Who knows more about it than you? Can you remember a time when you didn't have it? If not, what will your life be like without it? Consider also the possibility of a less "technical" gadget malfunctioning, such as the zipper on your jacket, or on your bag. Do you even know how a zipper works? What about the leg of the chair on which you now sit? How about the door of the room in which you might be at this moment? Suppose you get up out of your chair and attempt to leave that room, but the door will not open. Now what? Or maybe you are outside in a park, and when you return to your vehicle it will not start.

So, what is the meaning of this thought-experiment? *The greatest mysteries of life are usually concealed behind a very thin veil of familiarity.* That is, people tend to know much less about the seemingly familiar world around them and the items that populate the world than they think they do. Most of us drive cars every day, but how many of us truly understand how they work and could repair them if they were to break down? Every working house has appliances such as refrigerators, microwaves, ovens, and various entertainment systems. But if such things ceased to function, the illusions of their familiarity fall before our eyes only to be replaced by the dreadful mystery of just how life could possibly go on without such essential items. We take for granted the world around us. Fortunately, there are individuals who provide services in the repair and restoration of such necessities, and we may call upon them in such times of crisis. But the irony is that it perpetuates the illusion of our knowledge of the commonplace, forever looping us within a cycle of complacency, dread, temporary relief, and ultimately a shared false sense of security. Those things that are within arm's reach are, in a sense, light years removed from us.

Human beings, thus, could be described as strangers on their own planet, where even a seemingly simple task such as eating dinner is shrouded in mystery. How so? Suppose that you are invited to a friend's house to a cookout on Saturday, September 22, 2018 that will begin around 6:00 p.m. Your friend is someone that you presumably know very well. You will drive to the destination in your vehicle. Since you visited said friend's house before, you are aware of the neighborhood and the house itself, its size, its model, where the rooms are located, and the various furniture and devices within it. You will be sitting at a table of some kind, and, as indicated, you will most likely be eating hamburgers, hot dogs, and chicken, presumably with your choice of toppings. Now, consider the same scenario described in a slightly different way. On a Saturday, when the earth is roughly three-quarters through its 265th rotation on its axis during its 2018th revolution around the sun since the beginning of the Common Era of history, you will leave your domicile, get into a motorized carriage that operates on petroleum fluid and travel down a formerly wooded area that is now cleared and paved with concrete to another domicile constructed primarily of tree parts, concrete, and steel in order to participate in a ritual gathering with other members of your species in order to ingest the body parts of dead pigs, cows, and chickens. Sound strange? But isn't something that you do quite often?

However, the greatest irony of all is not that the world which we inhabit and navigate every day lends itself as an enigma, but that *we in fact created such a world*! This world and the lives we lead, our activities of duty and leisure, are the culmination of thousands of years' progressive and industrious labor to change the world around us, in effect, assuming control of nature. But in humankind's quest to control nature, the world we built in its place now has us under its control. It remains *uncanny*.[1]

The uncanniness of the world causes both physical and mental discomfort, forcing our minds to take measures simultaneously to ease our pain and structure the world of our experience into a more sensible, familiar, and comfortable framework, assuaging the angst conjured by our confrontations with the mysterious and affording us the blissful

---

[1] The following example constitutes another way to understand the term "uncanny." Suppose you are enrolled in philosophy course at your college or university. You would likely become accustomed to seeing your professor two or three times per week, dressed in his or her work clothes, and lecturing about a topic pertinent to that course. Now, imagine seeing that professor dressed more casually at a sporting event, such as a football game, or at a supermarket with their spouse and children. Your experience can be described as uncanny, because you are encountering something familiar, but in an unfamiliar context, just as when a familiar device such as your mobile phone ceases to work, the situation is less familiar, and the mystery of that item comes hurtling to the surface of everyday life.

harmony achieved by escaping such a harsh reality. The human brain, for instance, allows us to construct patterns of meaning in the world where there may be no such patterns. Inkblots on a Rorschach test perfectly illustrate such an attempt to fill-in-the-gaps left by the world around us. A random splash of ink takes on the form of a horse, or a bird. Why? So we can make sense of the world around us, so that it becomes less mysterious and vague, and easier for us to control.

In addition, the brain will often filter out bits of information received through the senses. For example, you may be, at this precise moment, sitting at your desk on the first floor of your home, so focused on reading this book that you might not notice if a friend dressed as a giant chicken is standing outside the window directly beside you. Such a situation, however, is quite startling, and, potentially, can lead into grave danger. Suppose that while you're distracted, it is not a friend invading your privacy, but a drifter with ill-intentions who wishes to do you harm. Again, irony abounds, since the very same instinctive process whose intent is to provide us with security also leaves us vulnerable to harm.

As I am preparing the manuscript for this book, the Halloween season approaches. John Carpenter's classic movie of the same name illustrates how easily one can be deceived by the agency of familiarity. The film's opening credits sequence convey its intent to subvert its audience's expectations. It consists of a slow track-in to a gaping, glowing jack-o'-lantern, a symbol of the film's titular holiday, and one that is itself shrouded in lore half-forgotten by the vast majority of the human race. Jack-o'-lanterns have come to symbolize an innocent ritual associated with childhood, in which children disguise themselves and visit houses begging for candy, another of humankind's efforts to disguise their fears. So accustomed are we to this ritual that only faint resonances remain of the memory of the use of such a figure to ward off evil spirits wishing to do us harm. Just as the camera pans into the eye of the smiling, glowing pumpkin, the light that burns within it is extinguished, foreshadowing the fate of the oblivious characters in the film, who fail to discern a dangerous killer lurking in their homes before it is too late.

The setting of the movie is within a very familiar environment—a small, Midwestern suburban neighborhood, the fictional Haddonfield, IL, where seemingly no violent or horrific act is possible. Many of us live or have lived in very similar environments. The film's first few moments place the audience in the point of view of a killer preparing to murder an intended victim, a victim who is apparently a teenaged woman. The killer methodically procures a large kitchen knife, walks upstairs and dawns a mask whose narrow viewpoint is portrayed on the screen, reflecting the very confines of the assumptions of the audience about the world around them and, perhaps, of the killer himself, who stabs the woman several times, and only seconds later is revealed to be a 6-year-old child named, Michael Myers. The mask is ripped from the killer's face just as rapidly as the audience is pulled outside of the killer's perspective in this brilliantly deflating frame-shifter. That such violence would be possible within a seemingly docile community is less a strain on one's credulity than the idea that such a young child would be capable of it.

After being incarcerated for 15 years, Michael escapes and returns to the scene of his previous violence to relive the event. He becomes fixated on a high school student, Laurie Strode, and her two friends, Annie and Linda. Several times during the day, Laurie suspects that someone is watching her. Michael, for instance, stares at her through a window from across the street of her high school, and then again from the backyard of her neighbor's house. But Laurie convinces herself that she's only imagining the whole process, partly because Michael, a character with a supernatural edge, seems to vanish almost as quickly as Laurie spots him. Later that night, while Laurie is babysitting Tommy Doyle, Tommy frequently sees a mysterious figure that he believes to be the "Boogeyman" lurking in the neighborhood.

But Laurie dismisses Tommy's complaints, never believing that any such danger could be present in her own neighborhood. Of course, when she visits the home at which Tommy claims to have seen this ominous figure, her worst nightmares become real, as she finds three of her friends murdered, her world literally turned upside-down as she is knocked from the staircase by Michael Myers, whose signature white mask appears as a silhouette out of the darkness, covering the face of a now full-grown killer. In his elegant and erudite article on the film, Telotte wrote that *Halloween* lends itself as "a beneficial investigation of the nature of our conventional manner of seeing" that can lay bare what lies "beneath the surfaces" of ourselves and our world in order to achieve "a new level of awareness"[2] that will enable us to avoid both the treachery of the commonplace[3] and the perception of reality dictated by the prejudices of human cognitive biases. Telotte's citation of Blake's *Auguries of Innocence* concisely underscores the illusions constructed by human perception.

> This life's five windows of the soul
> Distort the heavens from pole to pole,
> And leads you to believe a lie
> When you see with, not thro' the eye.[4]

Blake's musings of the distortion of the world via human perception describes a process attributable to *human nature*, and for most persons walking the earth, reality comprises a mirror of their very nature. The question of human nature is a *philosophical* question, and two of the primary goals of the discipline called philosophy are to understand what is meant by human nature and avoid its various tendencies for error, the consequences of which range from harmless to fatal.

---

[2] Telotte, J. P. "Through a Pumpkin's Eye: The Reflexive Nature of Horror," p. 116.

[3] See Sirridge, Mary. "The Treachery of the Commonplace," in Hunt & Carroll (Eds.) *Philosophy in The Twilight Zone*, Wiley-Blackwell, 2009, pp. 58–76. I believe Ms. Sirridge deserves credit for coining this term, whose basic meaning aligns with the general capacity of people to be easily deceived by that which is familiar.

[4] In Telotte, p. 114.

These tendencies for error can be described as what Francis Bacon deemed the "idols which beset men's minds," of which he listed four: Idols of the Tribe, Idols of the Cave (or Den), Idols of the Marketplace, and Idols of the Theater.

The Idols of the Mind: An Exposition

The first type of errors that concerned Bacon, the Idols of the Tribe refer to tendencies for misjudgment and errors for which all human beings are susceptible. Such errors arise from the basic constitution of people naturally. Bacon believed that the human mind resembled a crooked mirror that can easily produce a false image of reality. He describes Idols of the Tribe in the following way:

> For man's sense is falsely asserted. . . to be the standard of things: on the contrary, all the perceptions, both of the senses and the mind, bear reference to man and not to the universe; and the human mind resembles those uneven mirrors, which impart their own properties to different objects... and distort and disfigure them.[5]

Bacon seemed to have in mind three sorts of errors: errors of sensation and perception, errors based on anthropomorphic projections, and errors based on general psychological propensities. Optical and various perceptual illusions illustrate the first sort of error. Try to remember the last time you placed a straight stick in water. From your perspective, it almost certainly appeared bent. Consider also the following illusion:

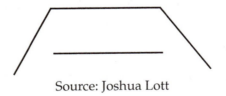

Source: Joshua Lott

---

[5] *Novum Organum*, cited in Will Durant, *The Story of Philosophy*, Pocket Books, Simon & Schuster, New York, NY: 2006, p. 165.

Which line appears to be longer? The line at the top, or the line in the middle? They are both the same length, but the top line probably appears to be longer. If you were to make such a judgment, your error would constitute an Idol of the Tribe, based entirely on the capacity of your brain to impose on sensory data an order or form that does not reflect reality.

To understand the second sort of error that constitutes an Idol of the Tribe, it is necessary to understand the meaning of the term "anthropomorphic." The English word comes from the Late Latin word "anthropomorphous," which traces back to two Greek terms, "anthrop," meaning human being, and "morphous," meaning form or structure. Hence, the term anthropomorphic means something that has human form or human structure. For example, an anthropomorphic animal would be an animal with human properties, such as a duck that wears clothes and talks, as in cartoons. An anthropomorphic deity, moreover, is a god that has human properties, such as a human body. An image or an idea, thus, is anthropomorphic if such an image or idea ascribes human attributes to non-human things. An anthropomorphic error occurs when human qualities are falsely attributed to non-human items. Bacon himself gave examples of such errors where he wrote, "the human understanding, from its peculiar nature, easily supposes a greater degree of order and regularity in things than it really finds."[6] One example of such fictions is the belief that the motions of the planets form perfect circles, or, an idea that greatly perturbed Bacon, the belief that everything in nature acts with a purpose, or to achieve a goal. Because human beings behave with purpose and intent, it is within their nature to assume that everything else does.

In addition, those Idols of the Tribe that arise from general psychological propensities are not unrelated to anthropomorphic tendencies.

---

[6] Ibid, p. 166.

One such propensity is the capacity for the defense mechanisms that psychologists refer to as projection, the tendency to read one's own character traits into other people. For example, a person who is very proud might find other people to be insufferably arrogant. Or, an individual who is overly sensitive might judge that others possess that very same quality. Another such propensity, also a defense mechanism, is illustrated by the tendency to deny established facts and cling irrationally to those ideas and values that one holds dear. An individual who discovers evidence that his spouse may be having an affair with his best friend, for instance, might pretend that such evidence does not exist, and seek out his own evidence that confirms that his wife is loyal, thereby resolving the mental discomfort and dread brought about by the very thought of betrayal. As another example, imagine a religious student who is exposed to the theory of evolution for the first time. Having been taught her whole life that Earth was created in exactly 6 days somewhere between 4,000 and 6,000 years ago, and that all human beings, herself included, occupy a distinctively special place in creation, made in the image and likeness of a God who "has a plan" for each and every person in that creation, the idea that the entire human race is a glorious accident, the product of several billion years of evolution that gradually progressed from simpler to more complex life forms according to a completely impersonal process of natural selection simply is unacceptable! This theory and all its supporting evidence most certainly is the work of Satan testing her faith!

The cases described above constitute Idols of the Tribe because they arise purely based on natural tendencies shared by all human beings. Since human beings are rational creatures, incongruity between one's accepted beliefs and new, opposing information is the source of mental disharmony called cognitive dissonance. To resolve such a conflict, most people tend to deny the opposing information and seek out any information to confirm what they already accept, twisting their experiences to accommodate the prejudices of their prior beliefs and accepted theories. Bacon's description of the process is similar: "Having first determined the question according to his will, man *then* resorts to experience; and bending her into conformity with his placets, leads her about like a captive in a procession."[7] Ultimately, "what a man would rather were true, he more readily believes."[8]

Since Idols of the Tribe provide the opportunity for the most general types of errors in judgment that people make, the other idols listed by Bacon may be described as very broad illustrations of his Idols of the Tribe, including Bacon's second class of errors, the Idols of the Cave. While Idols of the Tribe comprise mostly general tendencies shared by all people, including the capacity for the additional Idols, Idols of the Cave[9] are errors specific or unique to an individual: "For every one. . . has a cave or den of his own which refracts and discolors the light of nature."[10] Idols of the Cave can be illustrated by the errors in judgment that a specific individual is prone to based on either his or her personal agenda, prejudices, personality, or education. Such idols may also be described as the product of both nature and nurture, the products of an individual's education and socialization. For example, a person raised in a Catholic household may believe that all people should convert to Catholicism, just as people raised in a democratic society most likely will believe that democracy is the best form of government. Additional examples of Idols of the Cave can be illustrated by errors that arise from personal preferences or agendas. For example, if a young woman has an affinity for

---

[7] Ibid.

[8] Ibid, p. 167.

[9] The question will arise as to whether Bacon intended to reference Plato's allegory of the cave when developing his conception of Idols of this type. While he most certainly seemed to have Plato in mind, Plato's allegory of the cave is broader and more complex than Bacon's Idols of the Mind. I address this question in more detail in Chapter 1 of this book.

[10] In Durant, p. 167.

surreal art, such as paintings by Dali or Picasso, she may not approve of your home decorations if you included no such paintings. Furthermore, recall the previous example of the Rorschach test, in which indeterminate inkblots are shown to patients and they report what they see. If a patient happens to have an affinity for dogs, then such a patient will likely see dogs in the picture. On the other hand, if a patient happens to be an equestrian, then the individual will probably report images of horses.

The same may be said about the judgment that there should be one, universal religion for all people. Such a judgment may be wrong, but determining whether it is requires a more complex investigation of the doctrines of the religion in question, and how said religion compares to all others, etc. Each of the examples above reflect *the capacity for error that may arise due to Idols of the Cave*. For instance, imagine a homicide detective who has, without a doubt, witnessed the very worst and most reprehensible acts that human beings can commit. Such a person would most likely believe the worst about people, and perhaps be unduly suspicious of everyone with whom he or she comes into contact. At the opposite end of the spectrum, a more sheltered person, raised by charitable law-abiding citizens would most assuredly assume the very best about people even when there may be reason to think otherwise. Notice that each of these cases reflect both general and specific tendencies for error. The general tendency in each case is illustrated by the capacity to be influenced by the world around us, to construct a model of reality based on personal experience. The specific tendency in each case is illustrated by the content of each model. The first tendency is facilitated by the Idols of the Tribe, whereas the model of reality one creates reflects the Idols of the Cave.

The Idols of the Marketplace, a third source of errors and according to Bacon the most troublesome of all, arise from communication between people. More specifically, Idols of the Market-place comprise errors made based on confusion over the meaning of words. In Bacon's own words,

> Idols of the Marketplace arise from the commerce and association of men with one another. For men converse by means of language; but words are imposed according to the understanding of the crowd; and there arises [from] a bad and inapt formation of words, a wonderful obstruction to the mind.[11]

Bacon seemed to be concerned primarily with terms used by the academics and the great theoretical thinkers of his time, especially religious authorities. For example, a medieval theologian might talk about God as being "infinite" and as being the "first cause" or the "unmoved mover." However, the meanings of such terms are never made precise, nor are the terms themselves used with any great degree of precision. Given their vagueness, people are left to their own devices to imagine what they might mean. And given that every individual has a "cave or den" of their own, perhaps no two people will agree on the meaning of such terms. Moreover, the individuals who express such words seem to use them only as a mask for their ignorance. Words, thus, become masks of wisdom and knowledge that further obstruct people from the truth about reality.

To elaborate, more general examples of Idols of the Marketplace include what philosopher Gilbert Ryle called "category mistakes."[12] For instance, consider the word "university." Suppose you visit the campus of a college for a tour. Your tour guide walks you through various buildings. You see several classrooms, offices, and lounges. You learn to distinguish between academic buildings, administrative buildings, and recreational facilities. You walk down several different

---

[11] Ibid, p. 168.

[12] Ryle, Gilbert. *The Concept of Mind*, University of Chicago Press, 1949, p. 16. Ryle seems to coin this term in the context of a criticism of Cartesian dualism, a topic that I address in Chapter 4.

paths. You see the athletic field and various parking lots. Perhaps you visit the cafeteria at lunch time. Now suppose that at the end of the tour someone asks the guide, "Where exactly was the *university* on this tour?" Clearly, this person had a different understanding of the term "university" than everyone else. This individual probably believed that the "university" was an individual building, a specific, concrete, indivisible entity. The term itself, however, corresponds to multiple individual realities, including the network of people who study and work at the institution. To assume that the term "university" refers only to one specific building would, in Ryle's terms, constitute a category mistake. And it is this very sort of mistake that Bacon had in mind when he referred to Idols of the Marketplace.

Why exactly did Bacon believe these types of errors to be the most troublesome? Certainly, everyone knows what is meant by "university." How could anyone possibly ever make such a mistake? While it is not very likely that a person would be confused over the meaning of "university," consider the following terms: "substance," "soul," "the Form of the Good," "the self," "human nature," "virtue," "justice." These terms are not so easy to define. And the discipline called philosophy is replete with such terminology. Many disagreements arise because individuals attempt to communicate but only succeed in talking past each other due to the vagueness of terms. Even more problematic is the fact that words can exercise power over people. Words represent beliefs, ideas, and values. Many ideas and beliefs are sacred to people, such as religious beliefs. When those beliefs, ideas, or values are threatened, people might respond violently. Words can also be used to incite people to support a cause when they appeal to cherished values and ideas. Hence, the rectification of terms and precision in their usage can be a very efficient source of conflict resolution and avoidance.

The final category of errors Bacon calls Idols of the Theater, which can be described concisely as mistakes in judgment that arise from worldviews or schools of thought that contain numerous errors and should either be fixed or rendered defunct. Bacon describes them thus:

> Lastly, there are idols which have migrated into men's minds from the various dogmas of philosophers, and also from wrong laws of demonstration. These I call *Idols of the Theatre*, because in my judgment, all the received systems of philosophy are but so many stage-plays, representing worlds of their own creation after an unreal and scenic fashion. . . .And in the plays of this philosophic theatre you may observe the same thing which is found in the theatre of the poets, that stories invented for the stage are more compact and elegant, and more as we would wish them to be than true stories out of history.[13]

The classical Aristotelian/scholastic worldview that dominated the Middle Ages[14] comprised Bacon's primary concern. However, there seem to be two types of general errors that may be classified as Idols of the Theater. First are beliefs that arise from adherence to ideas or schools of thought that are outdated or discredited. For instance, suppose a person believes that Earth is at the center of the solar system, and all the planets and the sun revolve around it. This belief adheres to the geocentric model of the solar system, which was rejected roughly 500 years ago. Such an error could be deemed an Idol of the Theater. But an error does not have to emerge from worldviews that are known to be false to constitute an Idol of the Theater, which leads to the second sort of error, that may be grouped under this category: beliefs that may be true or false, but that emerge from mere dogmatic adherence to any school of thought. By dogmatic, I mean an uncritical, unreflective acceptance of ideas or principles. For example, Christianity, a religion with many denominations and literally billions of practitioners, does not constitute a worldview whose doctrines are

---

[13] In Durant, pp. 168–169.

[14] This worldview is described in more detail in Chapter 3 of this book, with emphasis on the ideas of St. Augustine and St. Thomas Aquinas.

known to be false, even though its doctrines are, at the very least, debatable. But suppose that a Christian insists that all homosexuals are sinners and will be punished in the afterlife if they do not repent. Suppose also that said Christian holds this belief solely because the Bible says so, or solely because their pastor told them so. Such a belief may be called an Idol of the Theater.

As indicated, one of the primary goals of philosophy is to aid in the avoidance of these errors, errors that arise due to the very nature of human beings. But very little has been said about just what philosophy is and what constitutes the study of human nature. The remainder of this introduction will be devoted to a more general description of both philosophy and the study of human nature as it will be approached in this book.

The Study of Philosophy and Human Nature

The main problem in defining both philosophy and human nature is simply that *too many* definitions of both have been offered throughout the last two and a half thousand years. There are, however, two pitfalls to avoid in defining philosophy. From the outset, it would be a mistake to think of philosophy merely as a container of unique knowledge, separate and distinct from all others. In fact, it would be mistaken to conceive of any academic discipline in such a way. The natural sciences—physics, chemistry, and biology—do not each exist in vacuums. Each discipline builds on the other, and, thus, they overlap. Physics consists of the study of the laws governing the most basic and fundamental components of the physical world. Chemistry consists of the study of the synthesis (putting together) and analysis (taking apart) of those physical elements. Hence, chemistry is, in many ways, an extension of physics. Biology applies the principles of both chemistry and physics to living organisms. And all three of these disciplines rely heavily on a general understanding of mathematics. The study of genetics, for instance, requires an understanding of ratios, and it would be completely futile to attempt to study chemistry without a basic understanding of algebra, just as it would be to attempt to learn physics without the knowledge of geometry and trigonometry. A similar assessment can be made about the relationship between the events of history and many of the great works of literature, which often coincide with each other. Certainly, the major religious traditions of the world connect in very substantial ways with both history and literature. The basic point is that all disciplines of learning overlap in some way. And philosophy is unique in that it overlaps with *all* of them because philosophers address the most basic and fundamental questions about the nature of reality, knowledge, morality, and the meaning of human life.

The second pitfall one must avoid is the exaggerated claim that there simply is no such thing as philosophy whatsoever, and that any claim that there is such a discipline is a logical fiction. Truly, philosophy may not be a "thing" in the sense that the table at which I now sit is a thing, or it may not be a "thing" in the sense that the laptop on which I now type is a "thing." In addition, "philosophy" is not a "thing" in the sense that it is a "container of knowledge" isolated from all others. Were one to make such a claim about philosophy, the same may be said about all other disciplines as well, since they are all related in some way. Simply because items overlap with or connect to each other does not warrant the dismissal of their existence!

So, how shall we define this term, "philosophy?" I prefer to begin at the beginning, and examine the roots of the word, which derives from two Greek words, "philo," meaning "love," and "sophia," meaning "wisdom." Hence, the English word, "philosophy", literally means "love of wisdom." This expression has two connotations. First, philosophy consists in a *passionate longing*, comparable to the love that characterizes many human relationships. Second, the term "wisdom" connotes a very basic kind of knowledge, an understanding of fundamental truths. So, philosophy can be defined, provisionally as a passionate longing for an understanding of fundamental truths. But such a longing is not merely passive. Rather, it consists in an active quest, a pursuit of answers to very basic, general questions. And if such answers cannot be found, at the very least, such a quest improves the seeker's understanding of such questions and of the seeker's own basic beliefs.

Ultimately, philosophy refers to a way of living and a way of thinking. Philosophical thinking has three central features. First, as previously implied, philosophical thinking consists in the use of logic, reason, and experience to resolve, or at least improve people's understanding of certain intellectual problems that resist easy solution, as opposed to attempting to resolve such problems and the questions they pose based on divine revelation and/or appeals to authority. Such intellectual problems can be expressed as questions about basic or fundamental truths. Examples of such questions include, but are not limited to, the following:

a. Is the physical world all that exists? If not, what else could there be?

b. Does a "God" exist? If not, then are there any transcendent absolutes?

c. Why does anything exist at all? That is, why is there *something* rather than *nothing*?

d. What is a human being? A body, a soul, or a combination of the two?

e. Are human beings basically good or basically evil?

f. Do human beings have free will, or is everything they do determined?

g. What is knowledge? Moreover, what is it possible to know?

h. When are we justified in believing something? Are we ever justified in believing anything?

   i. What is the difference between right and wrong? Moreover, what is the meaning of "good" as opposed to "bad"?

   j. If there is a difference between right and wrong, how can we know this difference?

  k. Do human beings have any "rights"? If so, what are they and how do we even find them?

   l. What is the best way to govern human beings? Should people be expected even to live under a government?

  m. What does it mean to be beautiful? Are there absolute standards for this concept?

  n. What is the meaning of life?

Questions (a)–(d) and (f) are usually grouped under the category of Metaphysics, a branch of thought that addresses questions about the basic nature of reality. Questions (g) and (h) are usually filed under the category of Epistemology, the study of the basic nature of knowledge, truth, and belief. Questions (e), (i), and (j) are usually grouped under the category of Ethics, the study of the basic nature of right and wrong, good and evil, and the standards that distinguish these terms. Questions (k) and (l) are usually classified under Social and political philosophy, which emphasizes the justification of government and the study of the nature and origin of basic human rights. Question (m) is usually categorized under Aesthetics, the study of the standards that distinguish beauty from ugliness, and of the nature of art. Question (n) is one of the broadest philosophical questions and I will develop it further in later chapters. The greatest problem with these questions is not that they have no answers, but, like the definition of "philosophy," that there are vastly many answers.

The second feature of philosophical thinking is that it is *theoretical*, which means that it includes the use of *models*. Simply put, a model is an item that represents another item. Typically, models represent "the real thing." That is, a model car resembles a real car, but is smaller and, thus, easier to comprehend. In the same way, a model of the human body makes it much easier for medical students to learn human anatomy and physiology, in addition to the procedures involved in operations, rather than starting with actual, living human beings. Hence, models are useful in that they make difficult things easier to understand. They are especially useful when one needs to represent something much broader and more abstract than any concrete item such as a car or the human body. Try to remember the first time you learned about our solar system. I'm guessing that you did not learn about it by getting in a space ship and visiting every planet that comprises it. More than likely, you learned about it from sketches in a book, or smaller physical representations. Typically, the answers to philosophical questions are parts of much broader answers which may be called theories, which consist of models. Throughout this book, several theories and the models comprising them will be examined.

Lastly, what very well may be the most distinctive feature of philosophical thinking is that it is not only *radical*, but the *most radical of* all the academic disciplines. The process of philosophical thinking is radical because it subjects all beliefs to critical scrutiny, even those that seem obviously and indubitably true. This process of thinking is far different from what may be encountered in a course in the natural sciences. In a physics course, for instance, the existence of the physical world would never be subject to question, otherwise the practice of physics itself would not be possible. The same applies to the elements of the periodic table in a chemistry course, as well as to the anatomy and physiology of the human body that is presupposed in a biology course. Likewise, in a course on Christian Theology, the existence of God must be assumed so that the material of the course can be conceived in any relevant way. However, the existence of the physical world, the human body, and God are, or at least were at some point, topics of impassioned debate in philosophical circles. The 18th century thinker, Bishop George Berkeley, for instance, argued that physical matter does not exist, and that only minds and sensible but non-physical objects are ultimately real. We will explore thinkers with similar ideas, in addition to those who believed the exact opposite.

But what about the topic about which this book is written, human nature? Why focus an introductory philosophy book on this topic? Primarily, the reason for doing so is that it is virtually impossible to separate philosophy from human nature. Human beings are both naturally inquisitive and rational creatures. Instinctively, they ask questions not only about what happens, but also about why things happen as they do. Moreover, even if satisfactory answers can be found to their questions, the "whys" continue. And even if satisfactory answers cannot be found, the very process of inquiry itself is tantamount to the augmentation of rationality. Just as the body requires physical exercise, the mind requires intellectual exercise lest it atrophy. Hence, to live completely meaningful and fulfilling lives, it is necessary for human beings continually to examine their lives as well as the lives of others and the reality of the world around them.[15]

But an additional reason is that an individual's assumptions and beliefs about human nature influence virtually all their other beliefs. For instance, suppose a person believes that people are basically good. Such an assumption will likely lead this individual to believe that all people, regardless of what they have done, deserve a "second chance," or an opportunity for redemption, given that it is their basic nature. In alignment with such a view is the idea that all alleged criminals are "innocent until proven guilty," and that reasonable doubt about accusations made against a person should be carefully weighed in making a judgment about that individual. Hence, an optimistic view about

---

[15] For a brief but excellent account of the value of the study of philosophy, see Wall, T. F. *On Human Nature: An Introduction to Philosophy*, Belmont, CA: Wadsworth, 2005, pp. 7–8. A classical account of the value of philosophy can be found in Russell, Bertrand. *Problems in Philosophy*. New York: Galaxy, 1959.

human beings would likely influence one's opinions about the sorts of laws that should govern our country, presumably, those that grant individuals as much freedom as possible in addition to due process in legal matters. Such an assessment of people is sometimes called *liberal*. An individual with a more *conservative* view, on the other hand, would not be so inclined, and would more likely estimate the general disposition of most people to be selfish, cynical, and unreliable. Hence, such an individual would more likely believe that anyone accused of a crime most probably is guilty of the alleged offense, and laws should be in place not only to account for that fact, but to coerce people into effectively abiding by strict rules for fear of the consequences. In short, since everyone's assumptions about human nature influence what they think, believe, do, and how they treat people, it is beneficial to investigate the concept of human nature thoroughly. Fortunately, there exists a wide variety of contributions on the topic from many learned thinkers.

So just what exactly is human nature? *Is* there even such a thing? You most probably read or heard someone's behavior referred to as merely a manifestation of this elusive "nature" at some point. For instance, when a person exacts revenge by murdering a rival over a long-standing grudge, the perpetrator's actions may be assessed as merely "human nature." That is, revenge is merely a result of human nature, a term whose use in this sense connotes that the action or actions in question are self-explanatory, that the reasons for the behavior are self-evident. The question of the meaning of "human nature" is complicated by the fact that there are cases in which actions or general behaviors of the opposite sort may be explained as merely the product of human nature. For instance, if an individual passing by a burning building were suddenly to run inside, putting his or her own life at risk, and pull out the occupants, saving their lives in the process, this person's behaviors might be explained as the result of human nature, as would the actions of someone who instinctively reaches out to grab someone falling from a cliff, or someone who instinctively dives into a river to save a drowning child. How can the same term explain such diverse actions? The answer seems to be that it does not explain such behavior. Rather, the theory of human nature to which one subscribes influences how one conceives of people in general. The problem is determining which theory is the best one. And it is the goal of this enterprise to survey and assess many well-known theories of human nature proposed in the history of thought.

A pioneer in the study of human nature, Leslie Stevenson provided a very useful and efficient way to analyze theories of human nature.[16] According to Stevenson, theories of human nature include references not *only* to human beings, but encompass the following:

1. A general theory of reality or of the universe.
2. A theory of humanity and of its place in the universe.
3. A diagnosis of the primary flaw of people and of the human condition.
4. A prescription to remedy that flaw.

The first two components of each theory may be called *factual* and *descriptive*—focusing on what is the case, what in the universe exists, what human beings are, what human beings do, and why they do what they do—whereas the second two may be called *normative* and *prescriptive*, emphasizing standards, ideals, and what people ought to do.

The first aspect of each theory may be stated as a question: What is the nature of the universe? There are two basic answers to this question. The first answer is that the universe is the product of an all-powerful creator generally known as God. Typically, those who subscribe to this answer refer to the conception of God associated with Judaism, Christianity, and Islam, in which God created the universe, the world,

---

[16] Stevenson, Leslie. *Twelve Theories of Human Nature*. 6th ed., New York: Oxford University Press, 2013, pp. 1–2.

and human beings within 6 days, and that all of creation is roughly 4,000 to 6,000 years old. This answer may be called *theistic*. There are non-religious variations of this answer. Plato, for example, held that ultimate reality is made possible by non-personal, transcendent realities called Forms, although he maintained that the universe was created by a being he called the demiurge. His successor, Aristotle, argued that a Prime Mover must exist to account for motion. Later thinkers, such as the Islamic philosopher, Averroes, and the Christian philosopher, St. Thomas Aquinas, identified Aristotle's Prime Mover as the God of their respective religions. The second answer is that the universe and all that exists within it are the product of a series of glorious accidents beginning with the "big bang," which led to the creation of Earth, and billions of years of subsequent evolutionary processes from which human beings and all other living things emerged. According to this answer, the universe is roughly 13 to 15 billion years old, and Earth is roughly 4 to 5 billion years old. This answer may be called *secular*, or *naturalistic*.

In addition, this aspect of each theory will usually characterize reality in one of three ways, each of which correlates with either the theistic or naturalistic answer. First, *materialism* is the idea that reality consists solely of physical substances, such as matter and energy. This answer correlates most closely with the naturalistic position. The theories of David Hume, Charles Darwin, and contemporary evolutionary biologists, Karl Marx, Sigmund Freud, and Friedrich Nietzsche all illustrate this position. Second, *idealism* is the view that physical matter is somehow less real than non-physical, spiritual substances. Finally, *dualism* is the idea that reality consists of both physical and non-physical substances. These last two views correlate most closely with the theistic answer, as well as with its many variations. For example, Plato's view may be called idealistic, whereas the views of Aristotle, the Christian philosophers such as Aquinas, Descartes, and, to a tentative extent, Kant may be called dualistic.

The second aspect of each theory may be stated as answers to three separate questions: (a) What are human beings? (b) Do human beings have free will? and (c) What is the meaning of death? The answers to (a) usually match up with the positions described in the previous paragraph. The first, materialism, is the idea that human beings are basically highly evolved animals, and that the extent of their being consists solely of their physical bodies. Typically, proponents of this view embrace determinism, the idea that human beings lack free will in any meaningful sense, since they are the products of forces beyond their control. The physical world and everything in it, including human beings, are governed by the indifferent laws of nature. On this basis, death is the cessation of human consciousness and the only afterlife that exists is the fact that upon death, our bodies are recycled into the earth. The second answer, dualism, theorizes that human beings are both body and soul, hence, part physical and part spiritual. Since part of our being is not governed by the laws of nature, we have at least some free will, the capacity to make our own choices and determine our own destinies. Usually, this response leaves room for an afterlife of some kind. The best known such conception is that of Christianity, in which the blessed and the righteous live an existence of eternal bliss in Heaven, while the sinners and the damned experience everlasting torment in Hell. This concept of the afterlife is given similar expression in Islam. Not all dualistic theories, however, profess the immortality of the soul. Aristotle, for instance, held that while there is a spiritual aspect of humanity—the passive intellect—the only entity that is immortal is the Prime Mover. The least adapted contemporary view, idealism, supposes that persons, in effect, have no bodies, since physical matter is not truly "real" on this theory. But, the theories of Plato, Augustine, and Descartes are closely aligned with this theory, since all the three thinkers maintained a hierarchical conception of reality, insisting that the best and most real of things are non-physical.

The third and fourth aspects of each theory are closely related to the first two. Basically, each of these aspects attempt to answer the questions of (a) what human beings should do so that they may live happy, meaningful lives, and (b) why they often fail to do so. One's conception of reality influences one's conception of humanity, and one's conception of humanity gives rise to the idea of what's required for human fulfillment and happiness. In short, the naturalistic answers typically manifest a theme of resignation and acceptance. That is, since humanity occupies no special place in creation and exists on a continuum with all other animals, organisms, and natural objects, people should stop thinking themselves superior to the rest of creation, take comfort in the fact that they are not answerable to any "God" at the end of their lives, and appreciate the fact that when they die, they will make more room for their species. To do the opposite is the source of abject misery and irrationality. On the other hand, the theistic answers view humanity as occupying a special place in creation, either created in the image and likeness of God (Christianity), or extensions of an immaterial, ethereal, eternal substance whose source is perfect goodness (Plato). Moreover, human beings are inherently rationalistic creatures, unlike all other animals, their rationality a testament to their divinity. To live deeply fulfilling and meaningful lives, human beings must develop this facet of their being by living in accordance with the dictates of their creator and the moral principles that govern the universe. To focus only on carnal, physical desires and appetites and to use others merely as means to our own selfish ends not only will not result in happiness, but also will serve as chief causes of abject misery and unhappiness.

The chapters that follow will have the following pattern: (1) a presentation of background material relevant to the thinker in question; (2) a concise overview of the theory of the thinker in question; and (3) an assessment of that thinker's theory in terms of Bacon's four Idols of the Mind by estimating (a) whether and to what extent the thinker's theory addresses each of Bacon's four idols, and (b) whether and to what extent the thinker in question avoids each of these idols.

Introduction Worksheet

1. Try to describe a normal event in your life that exposes the uncanny element of it, like the author's account of the barbecue on page 3.

2. Watch a movie or a television show of your choice and try to find ways in which the concept of the uncanny, the treachery of the commonplace, and/or Bacon's Idols of the Mind are illustrated by it.

3. Think of how you made errors that correspond to each of Bacon's four Idols of the Mind.

4. Does the author commit any of Bacon's Idols of the Mind?

5. Consider the model for theories of human nature developed by Leslie Stevenson. How do you answer each of these four questions: (a) What is the nature of reality? (b) What is the nature of humanity? (c) What is the primary flaw of human beings? (d) What is the remedy for that flaw?

Plato—The Ascent out of Darkness

Alfred North Whitehead once wrote that the entire history of western philosophy consists in a series of footnotes to Plato[1]. Hence, it is appropriate to devote suitable attention to Plato. Whitehead's reflection notwithstanding, there exist several 100 years of philosophical thought prior to Plato's birth, and to develop a complete understanding of his theory as it is traditionally understood, it is necessary to understand Plato's "footnotes" to his past. There are three basic influences on Plato's thought: (1) the Pre-Socratic thinkers, (2) the Sophists, and (3) Socrates. A presentation and assessment of Plato's theory will follow an overview of the highlights of these sources.

Plato's Footnotes to the Past—The Pre-Socratics, the Sophists, and Socrates

The Pre-Socratics: The first western philosophers are sometimes called the Pre-Socratic philosophers (so named because their work predates that of Socrates), the first of whom, Thales, became active in Greece in roughly 585 B.C.E. The significance of these thinkers is that they were the first in recorded history to propose *naturalistic*, or *scientific*, explanations for observable phenomena rather than defaulting to the popular *mythological* ones. An example of mythological explanation is found in the story of how the seasons change. Persephone, daughter of Demeter – the Goddess of the Earth – was responsible for sowing seeds so that plants would bloom. But she was kidnapped by Hades, the lord of the underworld, and a deal was struck, the

---

[1] Alfred North Whitehead, *Process and Reality*, Tampa, FL: Free Press, 1979, p. 39.

terms of which were that each year, Hades would keep her in the underworld for six months, and Persephone could return to the surface of the Earth for the remainder of the year. Early Greeks also believed that Poseidon, was responsible for controlling the ocean, that Apollo's chariot dragged the sun and moon across the sky each day, and that Zeus, king of the Gods, also controlled thunder and lightning.

The Pre-Socratics, thus, represent a paradigm shift in Greek thought, the transition from religion to an early form of natural science. The primary goal of each thinker in this tradition was to discover an underlying foundation for all things that exist, an *arche*. Such a substance would provide a basis for understanding how so many various, diverse items still manage to be part of the same world. More specifically, the substance they sought would provide an understanding of what unifies and brings order to diversity[2].

Thales proposed that everything is a form of water, quite a reasonable proposal, given that all living things need water to survive. Moreover, water is capable of existing either as a liquid, as a gas (steam), or as a solid (ice). On this basis, all gases are forms of steam, whereas all solid objects are forms of ice. Furthermore, water can account for how things move, since rivers, streams, and the tides of the ocean are all capable of moving on their own. However, his associate and student, Anaximander felt that water was far too limited to explain everything in existence, as would be any physical item. He proposed that *apeiron* (the unlimited, or boundlessness) was the foundation of everything. Believing Anaximander's proposal to be a regression into the mythological way of thinking, Anaximenes synthesized his predecessors' theories, suggesting air as the unshakable foundation of all things, a substance less limited than water, but still a natural item. Next, a mathematician, Pythagoras, proposed that numbers and

---

[2] For a more thorough introduction to the Pre-Socratic thinkers, see the chapter devoted to the subject in R.C. Sproul's *The Consequences of Ideas* (Wheaton, IL: Crossway, 2009).

mathematical form are the basis for all things, since everything in the universe conforms to mathematical rules and ratios. While this view elevates the naturalism of the previous thinkers into the realm of the abstract, and perhaps even the mystical, explanations in terms of numbers and ratios are not inherently mythological either.

The two dominant positions of this tradition, however, were those of Heraclitus and Parmenides. Heraclitus conceived of reality as constantly in a state of flux, constantly changing. For this reason, Heraclitus maintained that, "No one can step twice into the same river." Since change requires the dynamic of contraries to perpetuate it, Heraclitus claimed that war, conflict, is the father of all things, quite an ingenious idea. Consider the political metaphor in which two countries engaged in war leads to the birth of a new country, a new nation. Often, the suffering and struggles involved in one's daily life can allow one to become a different person. The pain of exercise can transform a person's body, just as the confusion one experiences in solving a difficult intellectual problem can enhance one's intelligence. On the other hand, without struggle, without conflict, life seems to lapse into a state of inertia and boredom. Practically no one wishes to engage in tasks that are too easy, at least, not for very long. The thrill of gambling, for instance, loses its luster if one wins constantly. And with such inertia, the meaning of one's existence is lost, lest one expose oneself to more difficult, productive tasks. As a metaphor for the strife of reality, Heraclitus proposed fire as his *arche*.

The ideas Heraclitus put forth have their basis in sensory observation, as did those of Thales and Anaximenes. Parmenides of Elea is known as a *rationalist*. That is, he privileged the principles of logic and the use of reason over sense-experience. Whereas Heraclitus insisted that reality constantly changes, Parmenides reasoned that change is impossible! Being, Parmenides maintained, is absolute: "Whatever is, is." This idea combined with the following principles supposedly render change impossible: (1) the law of non-contradiction which states that nothing can simultaneously exist and not exist at the same time in the same capacity; and (2) the law that something cannot come from nothing. Consider the first principle. If something were to change, it would have to become something else. But in that state of becoming, it would have to simultaneously exist and not exist at the same time. And even if violating this first law were possible, for one item to turn into something else, how would that second item emerge? From where, exactly, did it come? If it really is different than the original item that supposedly changed, it must have come from nothing, which is impossible. There are two consequences of Parmenides's conclusion. First, any appearance of change is just that, mere appearance, an illusion. When a caterpillar transforms into a butterfly, for instance, there is no actual change. Rather, there only appears to be one. The butterfly and the caterpillar are, in effect, the same thing, and have always been so. This consequence is closely connected with the second, which is the idea that all people are impenetrably trapped within their own sphere of subjectivity. What I experience is fundamentally different from and irreconcilable with the experiences of another. Everyone has a uniquely different perspective of reality, which is ultimately changeless, motionless, and eternal.

Parmenides had several followers, known as the Eleatic Rationalists. One such follower was Zeno, who used several paradoxes from mathematics to defend Parmenides. Others, however, found his conclusions to be patently absurd. In the view of these critics, Parmenides's conception of reality conflicts too severely with common-sense for it to be true. One such thinker was Empedocles, affirming that change is confirmed by experience. Reverting to the naturalistic empiricism of earlier thinkers, he deduced that four elements serve as the source of all reality – Earth, air, fire, and water. Everything is combination of these elements. Moreover, there exist two forces that govern the universe in Empedocles's worldview – love and hate. Love mixes things and hate segregates things.

Empedocles seemed to think that reality consisted of a perpetual cycle of creation and destruction, implying what a later thinker called "the eternal return of the same," and what forms the basis of modern thermodynamics.

Anaxagoras also rejected the rationalism of Parmenides, although the starting points of the two thinkers are quite similar. Anaxagoras conceived of reality as, one, big interconnected mass. But something called nous (Mind) separated everything. As a result, everything that exists has a bit of everything else in creation mixed in with it. The individual concrete items making up reality Anaxagoras called *spermata* (seeds).

Democritus and Leucippus capped off the pre-Socratic tradition by proposing an early version of atomic theory. Like earlier thinkers, they seemed to synthesize competing views, suggesting that reality consists of indivisible atoms, invisible to the naked eye. Hence, they produced a naturalistic theory that accounts for change, but ultimately described reality as a bunch of tiny Parmenidean-type beings.

This tradition of thinkers culminated with the ideas of those inspired by Parmenides, who maintained that reality is permanent, stable, and unchanging, and those who were more inspired by Heraclitus, whose conception of reality as unstable, constantly in a state of flux, was best exemplified by the atomists. But startlingly, both positions had something in common: *they both contradicted common-sense experience.* On the one hand is the idea that change is impossible, and, thus, the experience of change is an illusion. On the other hand is the view that reality is in a constant state of change due to endless collisions between tiny, indivisible atoms, and so the appearance of solid point masses and objects that continue to exist over time are also illusory. This impasse led to the development of the mantra that the pursuit of ultimate truth is futile, and that instead we should live only be appearances, and attempt to cultivate a life of comfort and luxury. The *Sophists* embraced this worldview.

The Sophists[3]*:* Prominent between 460 and 380 B.C.E., there were two major groups of Sophists. The early sophists consisted of thinkers such as Gorgias, Prodicus, Protagoras, and Hippias. The later sophists consisted of thinkers such as Thrasymachus, Antiphon, and Critias, Plato's uncle. Due to the controversies that arose from the work of the pre-Socratics, the sophists wanted to replace natural philosophy and the search for objective truth with *subjectivism*, the view that truth is merely a matter of individual opinion. That is, whatever an individual believes is true for that individual, and vice versa. Protagoras's claim that "Man is the measure of all things" constitutes the most famous example of such relativism. And if truth is only a matter of opinion and personal preference, then so are moral and ethical standards. Whatever an individual believes is right for that individual. Protagoras himself ultimately held that people generally ought to abide by the laws dictated by their culture. However, the later sophist, Thrasymachus, however, saw the much more dangerous implication of relativism, the idea that might makes right, or, in his own words, "Justice is the will of the stronger."

In keeping with their general mantra of subjectivism, the sophists championed the art of rhetoric, a form of speaking whose chief goal is to persuade an audience to adopt one's view rather than discover truth. Subsequently, the sophists became the first individuals who received money to teach, and primarily they taught the art of persuasive speaking, a valuable skill that can lead to success in both law and politics, and success in both fields leads to the accumulation of wealth and power. Typically, the sophists would travel to

---

[3] For an excellent introduction to Socrates and the Sophists, see the first chapter of Louis Pojman's *Who Are We? Theories of Human Nature* (Oxford University Press, 2005). Chapter 2 of Donald Palmer's *Looking At Philosophy: The Unbearable Heaviness of Philosophy Made Lighter* (New York: McGraw-Hill, 2013) also provides a thorough and accessible introduction to the sophists and the themes in the teachings of Socrates.

different cities to offer their expertise in exchange for a price. In some cases, they would be hired to give speeches on behalf of politicians, not unlike modern day motivational speakers or hostage negotiators. Not everyone, however, was privy to the ideas perpetuated by the sophists, and during his life, Socrates became their chief antagonist.

Socrates: One word that summarizes the life and teachings of Socrates is *irony.* Socrates is one of, if not *the* most, famous western philosophers in history, yet he claimed that the only thing he knew for sure was that he knew nothing at all! Nonetheless, in a famous story, an associate of Socrates, Chaerephon (whose name literally means "bat boy"!) visited the temple of the Oracle at Delphi and asked if there was anyone wiser than Socrates, and the Oracle answered in the negative, that there was no one wiser than Socrates. Astounded, Socrates began to test this claim by seeking out and challenging the teachers of his time, in addition to those who claimed to have any kind of special expertise.

Typically, an exchange between Socrates and one of his interlocutors had the following pattern. Socrates would pose a question to his interlocutor. The interlocutor would then confidently provide a quick and ready answer. Socrates, next, would expose flaws in the interlocutor's answer. The process of this exchange would continue until the interlocutor admitted ignorance on the topic in question, and both he and Socrates mutually agree to engage in a more genuine, active pursuit of objective truth. This procedure is sometimes called the Socratic Method[4]. More generally, it is known as *dialectic.* The most interesting feature of Socrates's practice of dialectic is that making the interlocutor aware of his own ignorance would frequently augment his true desire to learn. And ultimately, Socrates came to understand why the

---

[4] Palmer presents a similar account of the Socratic Method in chapter 2 of his *Looking at Philosophy*, but for a more detailed introductory analysis of the method, see David Melling's *Understanding Plato* (New York: Oxford University Press, 1987), pp. 58–59.

Oracle proclaimed that there were none wiser than he: at the very least, Socrates knew that he was ignorant, whereas others thought themselves to be truly wise.

As an example, take the idea of subjectivism, the idea that truth is relative to the individual. Imagine that Socrates confronted Protagoras, the chief proponent of subjectivism, with the following analysis. If truth really is relative to the individual, then two individuals might hold completely opposite beliefs. Person A might believe that Earth is flat, whereas Person B might believe that Earth is a sphere. Yet according to subjectivism, they are both right! But that cannot possibly be! In addition, anyone who maintains that "all truth is relative" must at least admit to one universal, objective truth: the truth of relativism itself! Hence, the idea is a complete self-contradiction. Now, imagine that you are the famous teacher, Protagoras, and that when your students see this exchange happen, they abandon you to follow Socrates instead. This scenario is the equivalent of a person walking into a modern-day college classroom and making the professor appear to be a total buffoon! If you were in the position of Protagoras, how would you feel? And more importantly, how would you react, especially if you had the power to do so?

Ultimately, Socrates agitated more people than only his interlocutors. His followers, many of whom were quite young, began to challenge the authority of their parents, in addition to the customs of Athens. He earned the nickname of the "Gadfly of Athens." Eventually, the Athenian government brought Socrates to trial on the charges of impiety (since he frequently referred to Gods not in the Athenian canon) and corrupting the youth. While he argued valiantly at his trial, the jury found him guilty and sentenced him to death by hemlock, a poison. Even though Socrates had the opportunity to escape, he remained in prison and accepted his fate. He acknowledged that he did, in fact, break the law and wanted to accept the punishment.

Before his death, Socrates professed a thesis referred to by one author as the maxim of the *invincibility of goodness*, a dual notion implying that (1) no one can harm the soul of a just person, and (2) to commit an injustice harms the soul of the perpetrator more than his victim. This Socratic maxim links the notion of justice to the human soul, and, thus, to human nature in that the good is good for a person, and the bad is bad for a person. But understanding why and how means understanding the good itself and the human soul.

Plato and the Legacy of Socrates

As a student of Socrates, Plato bared witness to the arguably unjust circumstances of his death and found it inspiring that a man would die for his beliefs. But the influence of Greek philosophy on Plato extends beyond Socrates. From the pre-Socratics, Plato adopted the ideas that (1) for change to occur, something must remain permanent, and (2) the visible world does not present a complete picture of reality. From the sophists, Plato learned that education must have some value. And from Socrates, Plato learned that the value of learning must be tempered by a view toward that which is truly good for the soul. But the questions of just what *the good* and the nature of the human *soul* are must be answered. Moreover, providing an answer on Plato's behalf is complicated by the fact that he elaborates his "theory" in no one place[5]. Socrates never wrote anything, as he believed that writing things down would lead to the deterioration of the memory. In his view, conversation was the key to uncovering truth. Plato's works, however, are written in the form of dialogues. That is, they consist of conversations between different characters, most of whom are based on historical figures, with Socrates usually serving as the chief speaker, although in the later dialogues he is mostly in the

---

[5] Some question whether Platonic philosophy contains any "doctrines" at all, which I take up in my assessment of Plato.

background. In doing so, Plato seemed to achieve a compromise in that he wrote, but in the form of conversation. But what makes matters even more complicated is that Plato, himself, never shows up in his own work to apprise the audience of his thoughts! I will address the following topics of Platonic philosophy: (a) the theory of the forms; (b) the recollection argument and the immortality of the soul; (c) the emergence of justice in the soul; and (d) the challenge of the ring of Gyges.

The Theory of the Forms: For Plato, it seems that the theory of the Forms is the resolution to the problem of change and permanence that confronted the pre-Socratics. Before elaborating the theory, consider the following example. The world we inhabit is filled with imitations. These imitations include photographs taken by cameras, in addition to sketches and paintings created by artists. Other works of art include sculptures and statues. There are also children's toys, such as action figures, and puppets. Most of these objects are used for the purposes of entertainment, but in other cases they make a complex item easier to understand by reducing and then presenting it in a more simplistic way. If these imitations exist, then it is reasonable to ask whether the items which they imitate are themselves copies of something. Plato seemed to think that concrete items in the real word are just that – copies of something else, imitations of something greater. The things of which concrete, physical items are copies Plato called *Forms.* Even though Plato did not elaborate this doctrine in any one dialogue, it is possible to reconstruct it by elaborating what the forms are, what the forms do, and analogies used to explain them in Plato's most famous dialogue, *The Republic.*

First, the clearest and most concise description of what the Forms are is that they are *universal*, *immaterial*, *transcendent*, and *eternal*. Each of these terms will be explained in turn. To begin with the universality of the forms, they are not spatially located in any one place, but rather exist at any place at which they are manifested by a concrete object. To illustrate, consider a dog. There are individual dogs, and there is the essence of Dog, including the attributes of what makes a dog a dog. For instance, the essence of Dog would include the attributes of being a natural creature that is a mammal, walks on all four legs, barks, chases squirrels, buries and eats bones, is carnivorous, wags its tail, etc. Each individual dog is a concrete, physical embodiment of the essence of Dog in that it manifests such properties. Hence, whereas an individual dog is located only in one place at a time, the essence, or form of "Dog-ness" is instantiated by all dogs. While the form of Dog-ness is exemplified by all dogs, it is not itself a physical dog. That is, the form is not composed of physical matter. It is thus, immaterial. Because the form is not material, it is indestructible. Hence, it is eternal, perpetually in existence. Lastly, the form is transcendent, meaning that it is above and beyond anything within the observable universe. That it is transcendent connotes superiority, the standard by which all items of its kind are to be judged. In this case, the form of Dog-ness would be the ideal Dog, the most perfect and complete Dog.

Plato's theory of the forms has several aspects, each of which accounts for the functions the forms serve[6]. First, the forms supposedly make concrete objects possible. That is, physical items – whether they be dogs, trees, tables, chairs, or human beings – eventually perish. They become old and dysfunctional. But the Forms of such things remain longer after their concrete, individual manifestations cease to exist. Hence, whereas physical items undergo change and decay, the Forms remain permanent as the source of those things that change. A connected function the Forms serve is the stipulation of aesthetic standards.

---

[6] Parts of my overview of the theory of the Forms are comparable to Stevenson's in *Twelve Theories of Human Nature*, pp. 81–85, although I go into more details about the analogies of the Divided Line and the Allegory of the Cave.

That is, they are conditions for the possibility of beauty. Just as there are individual dogs distinct from Dog-ness itself, there are individual beautiful items distinct from the beautiful itself. The theory of the Forms lends itself as Plato's solution to the impasse between the rationalist followers of Parmenides and the atomistic descendants of Heraclitus. The fact that physical items constantly undergo change points to a transcendent world that remains permanent and the ground of reality.

Second, the Forms make knowledge possible. For Plato, true knowledge cannot derive from sense-experience, which consists merely of the data of the physical world, which constantly undergoes change and is fleeting. The possibility of knowledge requires the ability of the mind to grasp that which does not change. Consider the example of the dog again. Dogs come in many shapes and sizes, and in many different breeds. There must be some general concept in virtue of which one can recognize an individual dog as a dog. That is, one must be able to distinguish the German Shepard in front of him from the Black Labrador at the other end of the street, but still recognize both as being dogs. Since they are numerically different, and have distinctly different features, the knowledge that they are both dogs must come from the idea, essence, or form of Dog-ness itself.

Closely related to this function is the third, the idea that the forms are conditions for the possibility of the use of general terms. For instance, I can apply the word "dog" to several different dogs of the same type. I can refer to a Labrador, a Dalmatian, a St. Bernard, a German Shepherd, a Golden Retriever, and a Dachshund as dogs. Since each individual thing, again, is numerically different, the term "dog" refers not individual, concrete things, but to the idea of Dog-ness itself. This function reinforces the status of the forms as somehow possessing more reality than concrete physical items. That is, they are *more real* than physical items.

Fourth, and finally, the forms provide *moral standards*, and are the basis for our general awareness of them. That is, it is via the forms that we can understand the difference between right and wrong. Moreover, the same moral standards will apply regardless of one's situation, time, or place. In that sense, moral standards are universal and eternal, each of which is made possible by the forms. For Plato, the forms dictating moral standards are the form of the Just and the form of the Good. This aspect of the theory is inextricably linked with its metaphysical aspect, since it is the form of the Good that makes it possible for individual things and people to be good, just as it is the form of the Just that makes possible individual just actions.

The exact way in which the forms fit into Plato's general conception of reality is illustrated by the analogy of the Divided Line, which occurs in *The Republic*. Socrates draws this line in the sand to illustrate Plato's conception of reality. The line is divided into two sections. The bottom half of the line represents the visible world, the natural, physical, concrete state of existence, whereas the top half represents the intelligible world. Each section is further subdivided into additional sections. The bottom half of the visible realm consists of shadows, reflections, and images, the imitations of the visible world. The upper half of the visible realm consists of actual, concrete physical objects – trees, mountains, lakes, rivers, dogs, etc. The bottom half of the intelligible realm consists of concepts, scientific hypotheses, and mathematical truths. Their position on the line indicates that they are not part of the visible world, but, nonetheless, are not "forms," either. Essentially, concepts exist in the mind of the individual. The top half of the intelligible realm represents the forms themselves, which transcend mere human conceptions.

Corresponding to each section of the line is a mental state. For instance, the mental state correlated with the section of shadows, images, and reflections is called imagining (*eikasia*). These are of the line characterizes the mental state of the individual viewing a mere imitation, or perhaps putting forth a theory that is totally conjectural, and without proof or justification. The mental state corresponding to the section of concrete physical objects is called belief (*pistis*). That is, the mental state of belief characterizes that of the individual observing a visible object. The next level of the line, the lower half of the intelligible division, corresponds to the mental state of understanding or thinking (*dianoia*). For instance, when a person considers a mathematical truth such as the Pythagorean theorem, one is in the state of understanding. The same applies to a person who is aware of a generally accepted scientific theory, such as the theory of evolution in our own time. At the next level of awareness, at the level of the forms themselves, one achieves knowledge (*episteme*). Another term for the level of awareness one achieves at this stage of the line is noesis, or noetic insight, which constitutes a complete and intuitive understanding of the form in question along with how it is interconnected with all other things. The difference between knowledge at this level and the previous level is that at this stage one achieves direct acquaintance with the form in question, completely divested of earthly attachments. Mathematical theorems, for instance, typically rely on visible diagrams for their application, as do scientific hypotheses, which require empirical observations and experiments for confirmation. At the highest level, one achieves insight into the unity of seemingly disparate ideas. For instance, at the highest stage of the line, one discerns how mathematics, the natural sciences, art, morality, and politics all converge in the Good itself. That is, each craft contributes to the good of all by increasing humanity's understanding, health, general well-being, and aesthetic pleasure.

The following example illustrates the difference between each mental state at every level of the line. Consider an apple. A picture of an apple, or a model of an apple would exist at the lowest level of the line, and one would be in a state of imagining were one to observe such an item, as it would constitute an imaginary apple. One is in the mental state of belief when observing a real, tangible, edible apple. Moreover, at this stage of awareness, one can group together items that share the same observable qualities. That is, one can group together many items that are called apples. At the third level, the stage of understanding, one can give an account of what exactly an apple is, perhaps by providing a thorough definition of the substance. At the highest level, however, of noetic insight, one does not merely know what an apple is, but has complete and direct intuitive acquaintance with Apple-ness itself, and, thus, understands the interconnection of all apples with everything else in the scheme of all things in creation. One understands apples in such a way that unifies biological science (apples as an organisms), mathematics (apples as having a spherical shape), and the good of humanity as whole (eating them keeps us healthy and, thus, enable us to live happy meaningful lives).

At this point, it is useful to establish that Plato considered all the forms to be unified in one, supreme form, the Form of the Good, or Goodness itself. Ultimately, Plato's conception of the Good and its place at the top of the line is *teleological*. That is, everything that exists, particularly in the natural world, serves some purpose. To the extent that an item serves its purpose or fulfills its natural function, it may be called good. For instance, a tool or an instrument is "good" insofar as it does what it is supposed to do, insofar as it works. Moreover, by fulfilling its natural function, an item approaches direct acquaintance with the form of the Good itself. Goodness is conferred upon those items that participate in it. Or, more concisely, if a thing does good, it becomes good. How does this idea apply to the example of the apple? Basically, noetic insight with respect to Apple-ness, as such, means understanding completely and intuitively the *good* of all apples in the order of creation, which goes beyond apples themselves. For instance, apples provide nutrition, which is good for the human body, and with that nutrition, human beings can perform their function within creation.

An additional analogy used to elucidate further this conception of the Good is the sun. Just as humanity's sense of vision requires the sunlight to illuminate the natural world to see, so the mind requires illumination from Goodness itself to possess genuine knowledge. In keeping with the example of the apple, noetic insight into the apple is made possible by the form of the Good, just as the ability see in the natural world is made possible by the light of the sun. Moreover, it is the light of the sun that makes growth possible, since plants convert sunlight into nutrition. Living things also depend, fundamentally, on the sun, since the temperatures on Earth throughout the seasons could not sustain life without it. The following diagram illustrates the Divided Line and its corresponding mental states:

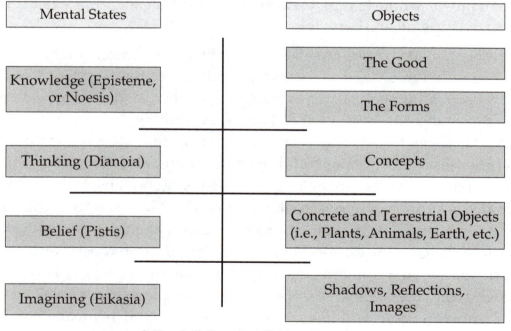

© Kendall Hunt Publishing Company

While the theory of the forms and the analogy of the Divided Line comprises Plato's general metaphysical theory, an final analogy helps to illustrate the humanity's place in this order of being – the Allegory of the Cave. Socrates asks his audience to imagine an underground structure in which several people are chained to a wall in such a way that they cannot turn their heads and, hence, can see only straight ahead. Above the heads and behind these prisoners burns a fire. In front of the fire stand several roadway puppeteers, projecting shadows of models of animals, humans, and natural artefacts. The prisoners can see only the shadows, but as they spent the entirety of their lives in this position, the shadows are all that they ever experienced. As far as they know, all of reality consists of the shadows on the wall. However, imagine that one of these prisoners manages to free himself somehow. This prisoner would be able to observe the show on the stage behind the other prisoners but would not quite be able to discern what the puppets represent, as he knew only their shadows before now. Eventually, this man escapes the cave completely, but cannot at first observe the world around him, since the sun blinds his eyes. Ultimately, his eyes adapt to the light and he can see the artefacts of the natural world around him, and finally, he can see the sun itself. This man returns to the cave to alert the others of his discoveries. Unfortunately, the returned escapee voices them in such a way that his fellow prisoners are unable to comprehend them, and they think him a fool.

The implications of this analogy coincide with the simile of the Divided Line and the theory of the forms. The allegory of the cave seems to suggest that all people begin life like the prisoners in the cave. The "shadows" of our experience correspond to what we are told by our parents, teachers, and various other authority figures sanctioned by social institutions. The clearest parallel on the line is the very bottom. Next, people start to think independently. The discovery that different authorities disagree with each other usually triggers autonomous thought, compelling people to seek things out on their own and form their own opinions, which has its parallel to the second part of the bottom half of the line, which corresponds to natural artefacts. Typically, this stage would involve learning by trial and error in addition to creativity. During this process, one must break free of old patterns of thinking and adapt to those that are both meaningful to others and anchored to reality. At the next stage, people have formulated a general understanding of reality and can impart a fully constructed theory to others, the first section of the top half of the line. Lastly, the vision of the sun itself corresponds to complete intuitive insight into the whole system of reality, how one's theory is interconnected with all others and what good it can do for both individuals and the lives of others.

Of course, in Plato's allegory, the escapee returns to the cave but is unsuccessful in imparting to them the knowledge he acquired. The general admonition implied by this scenario is that a uniquely and independently formulated worldview will likely encounter resistance, especially if one's worldview contradicts a far more familiar and palatable status quo. Imagine a physician telling you that you will have to relinquish your current lifestyle, that you can no longer eat your favorite foods, that instead your diet will consist of practically tasteless and unfulfilling items, and that you will have to exercise twice as frequently to reduce your bodyweight, but that these prescriptions, ultimately, will be better for you, and that as a result you will feel better and live longer. Despite the goal of these prescriptions, you would likely have a very difficult time assimilating this advice, and you would find it even more difficult in practice. It is always more comfortable to believe that others are wrong[7].

Recollection and the Immortality of the Soul: If Plato's theory of the forms is accepted, then the primary goal of human life should be to escape the realm of the shadows and discover ultimate truth. But on what basis should the theory of forms be accepted at all? The exposition of Plato's conception of reality thus far consisted mostly of analogies,

---

[7] See Chapter 10 of Melling's *Understanding Plato* for a more thorough account of the theory of the Forms and its nuances than I can provide here. For a very illuminating account of the allegory of the cave and the metaphor of the sun, see Chapter 1 of Nalin Ranasinghe's *The Soul of Socrates* (New York: Cornell University Press, 2000).

such as the Divided Line and the Allegory of the Cave, neither of which guarantees the truth of the doctrines that they are intended to support. The clearest argument in favor of the doctrine of the forms is the argument from recollection. For Plato, learning is recollection, or remembering. The items remembered are, supposedly, from previous lives. That is, everyone has lived before and learned all that there is to learn in their past lives. The processes of learning included direct acquaintance with the eternal, unchanging forms, which comprise the standards for making judgments about reality, knowledge, morality, aesthetics, and the meaning of life in general. Since we all encountered the forms in our previous states of existence, they are obviously real. An exposition of this argument gives rise to Plato's conception of the human soul.

The recollection argument goes as follows. True knowledge cannot come from sense-perception, since sense-perception is always of the constantly changing world of flux. The seasons change just as do people, animals, and the natural artefacts of the visible world. Sense-perception can never provide a general, universal, unchanging principle. If knowledge equated to perception then the relativism espoused by Protagoras would be correct, in which case everything would appear to each person as he or she perceives it. But if everything is for each person as he or she perceives it, each person is infallible, in which case there is no basis for challenging anyone's judgments about their perceptions. Moreover, no two people would have anything in common. Hence, there could be no *standard* of comparison between the two to determine the accuracy of one's perceptions compared to another. Making judgments requires standards that cannot come from the senses alone, since they have no perfect manifestation in the visible world. An example of such a standard is Equality. Often, it is possible to judge items in the world as being "equal" to each other. But no two items in the world are perfectly equal. That is, nothing in the world of sense exemplifies "Equality itself." Imagine two sticks.

By glancing at them and even measuring them, you may be able to determine that they are, in fact, the same length. However, one of the sticks may be slightly bent. The other may have some chips in its bark. One may have a slightly pointed edge, while the other may be slightly rounded off. The two sticks, thus, may be equal in length, but they are not equal as such. The idea of Equality itself, thus, cannot have derived from our experiences within the visible world. The only way in which any of us could come to understand this concept is by direct acquaintance with it in the intelligible realm during a previous phase of existence.

The argument of the previous paragraph occurs in a dialogue called *Phaedo*. An earlier dialogue, *Meno*, offers a different proof of the recollection thesis. Socrates interacts with a teenager working on an estate. He asks the youth if he can solve a difficult geometry problem. Ultimately, with some slight suggestions from Socrates, the youth discovers the answer to the problem without having to be directly told. Since this youth had no prior training in geometry, the conclusion must be that he acquired the information in a previous life, in a transcendent realm.

While the recollection thesis certainly supports the theory of the forms, it has significant implications for the nature of the human soul. Specifically, it implies that after death, the soul flees its current body and later occupies a new one. This idea lends itself as the basis for a dualistic conception of the human person. That is, a person is a soul trapped inside of a body. Plato seemed to maintain that the body is an earthly prison for the soul. But since the soul is capable of existing apart from the body, it is certainly distinct from the body. While the body is a physical thing, the soul is non-physical. Since the soul is non-physical, it cannot be destroyed. The soul is, thus, *immortal.*

Justice in the Soul: So, there is a human soul, and it is indestructible. But two additional topics remain to be addressed: (1) the specific nature of the soul; and (2) the purpose of the soul, what it needs to achieve. As for the second item, Plato held that the purpose of the soul is to achieve justice. And the nature of justice is inextricably linked to the nature of the soul itself, and Plato again uses his most famous spokesperson to construct an analogy after which it is modeled in *The Republic*.

Early in the dialogue, Socrates and his chief interlocutors, Glaucon and Adeimantus, mutually agree that the individual soul is comparable to a city. Conversely, the city is the "soul writ large." They seem to agree on this point because people are naturally social creatures, and the city they construct emerges from two basic principles of human nature. First, everyone, even the most introverted of people, rely on others to some extent. To buy food, we must interact with cashiers at the grocery store. And there would be no food in those stores if not for farmers. To wear clothes, we rely on the people who make those clothes, and still on the stores that sell them. If we get sick, we rely on healthcare professionals to cure us. If our vehicles break down, we rely on auto-mechanics to fix them. But even if a person would prefer not to interact with other people, that individual must learn how to provide for himself, in which case he would at the very least have to read books written by other people! Furthermore, Socrates, Glaucon, and Adeimantus mutually seem to agree that there is a natural division of labor between people, the idea that people are naturally suited to perform different tasks. Some people are naturally skilled at farming, those who have a "green thumb," perhaps. Other people are naturally suited to architecture and building. Some may be better suited to medicine. It follows that all human beings not only rely on others to meet their basic, rudimentary needs, but also rely on performing the role or roles to which they are best suited to live meaningful and fulfilling lives.

Since the city is a larger version of the individual soul, the three interlocutors construct the ideal city from the ground up to obtain a model by which to countenance the faculties of the individual soul. The city they design has three classes. The first is the artisan *class*, the workers. This class would consist of farmers, toolmakers, people to build and maintain shelters, people to make clothing, and physicians, primarily. But a city consisting solely of workers would be insufficient. Imagine a small rural community stripped of all modern conveniences attempting to survive. Such a group of people would likely have to expand beyond their boundaries to obtain necessary resources. In so doing, they are likely to encounter danger, most likely from the members of other communities who lay claim to the same available resources. The arrangement of a trading agreement is also likely to develop. Moreover, once the community becomes more luxurious and sophisticated, they are likely to become a target from fringe groups, who would want to steal their resources.

For these reasons, the need for a class of protectors, or *guardians* emerges. The people in this class will need a specific kind of education. Obviously, they will require physical training, as they may have to engage in combat. Moreover, they should have a musical regimen to temper their moods properly. They will have to address the concerns of the citizens in addition to dealing with potential threats. Each scenario dictates a specific frame of mind, and they must be capable of shifting between them. Furthermore, they should be educated in philosophy, since through philosophy they will learn to distinguish appearance from reality. They will need to know the difference between their friends and their enemies and will require the ability to detect deceit and treachery. Socrates suggests the image of the dog as the animal that represents this class. Dogs are friendly to those they know, but harsh toward those they do not, just as the guardians must be. In this sense, dogs are philosophical animals, since they love what they know, and hate what they do not know. Lastly, the guardians should have no private property, since their lives should be devoted to serving the good of the community. As such, it is decided that they should have their own common living quarters.

Finally, as with all groups, there must be people in charge, rulers. The question is, how should such people be chosen? The leaders of a community must act always for the good of the community itself, rather than for their own selfish good. Moreover, these leaders would be responsible for developing rules which everyone, including the guardians, must follow. These rules are designed primarily for the protection of the community. Since the guardians dedicate their lives to protecting the community, it is determined that the best of the guardians should be chosen as the rulers.

These are the classes of the city. The city can only become just, however, if each class develops a specific virtue, a trait of character. It is determined that the ruling class must have wisdom, or prudence, since this class must have knowledge of what is best for everybody and how to achieve it. Such knowledge would include the highest level of understanding humanly possible, knowledge of the Good itself, which implies knowledge of how all elements of the city function in unison. Since the guardian class must protect the city, the guardians will require courage. Courage should not be understood merely as the absence of fear, but rather the ability to carry out one's duty in the presence of fear. In this sense, the virtue of courage functions as a safeguard against abandoning one's duty out of fear alone. Furthermore, not only will the guardians protect the city, but they must enforce the laws created by the rulers. On this basis, courage is not merely a safeguard, but is directed toward the Good itself, since making these laws requires a basic understanding of the Good. All the classes, including the artisan class, require moderation, or self-control. That is, each class must focus on its specific contribution to the community. A person who is more naturally suited to designing buildings should not be put in charge of creating rules for an entire community. Moreover, a person who is better suited to lead should not spend his entire life manufacturing farming equipment. The right people must rule over the city, and each person must focus on the development of his or her unique craft. Justice emerges when each class achieves its specific virtue. Justice, that is, is a holistic virtue, arising from a combination of the previous three.

The next step is to determine whether the human soul has the same faculties as this city. Typically, the dynamic of a conflict implies the presence of more than one entity. Recall the law of contradiction, typically expressed as something cannot both be and not be in the same respect at the same time. Applied to the search for the nature of the soul, it follows that no person would experience competing desires if human nature were fundamentally a unified whole. Moreover, the Heraclitean maxim that conflicts gives rise to all things may be applied metaphorically in this instance, since the presence of conflict within an individual can give birth to an illuminating understanding of the human soul. Hence, conflict within people leads to the discovery of the soul's faculties.

In its most basic form, conflict occurs between what people *want* to do and what they *ought* to do. For instance, a person might have chores to do, but he would rather laze about on his couch watching television. Or a student might have a major assignment imminently coming due even though she would prefer to attend the birthday party of her closest friend. The person in each case experiences a conflict between *reason*, on the one hand, and pure *appetite* on the other. Another common thread between each scenario is that if these two people constantly appease the desires of the appetite but neglect the dictates of reason, the results would most likely consist of short-term gains but long-term losses. If the man in the first scenario never gets around to cleaning his house, he may enjoy a few relaxing weekends, but his house will become increasingly unsanitary, filthy, and germ-infested. If the young woman in the second scenario continually shirks her project and defers her academic activities, she may enjoy a few fun nights with her friends, but she will likely fail her course, and if she subsequently becomes demoralized she may withdraw from the university altogether. On the other hand, each case seems to raise a paradox: If you do only what you want, you'll get the exact opposite of what you really want! The distinction between long-term desire and immediate, momentary, fleeting, selfish desire resolves this paradox. Each case really establishes a natural order of desires in addition to the link between reason and human fulfillment. In neither case do these two individuals do anything reprehensible. Neither relaxation, nor celebrating with friends poses any inherent harm. But the task of keeping a tidy household and the responsibility to become an educated citizen must each be completed first, lest one be even less content.

Briefly recall the major subdivisions of the city. Reason corresponds to the ruling class of the city, while appetite corresponds to the artisan class. Imagine if a butcher became a lawmaker. Would that really be best for the citizens? Such an individual would likely be much more hardened by his work than others, and as a result would be more harsh than necessary. The laws made by such an individual would likely fall short of fairness. For instance, this butcher might be more willing to torture or kill a citizen for a minor offense, such as cursing in public. Or perhaps this butcher, out of bias in favor of his field, will decree that all people should become butchers, thereby neglecting other facets of the city. For laws to be fair, just, and enforceable, they must be made by those best suited to do so, those with the knowledge of what is best for all and how to implement them. Just as the butcher should not be the ruler of the city, appetite should not rule the human soul.

Now the third faculty of the soul must be located, the aspect corresponding to the guardian class. Since conflict between the two revealed reason and appetite, the third element would conflict with both. That is, an element that conflicts both with reason, what a person ought to do, and appetite, a person's immediate desire. The following scenario seems to illustrate the possibility of such a faculty. Suppose that a doctor recently worked a 16-hour shift at a hospital, but that on his way home he passes by a burning building with several people trapped inside. This doctor needs sleep, having been awake for more than 16 hours. Moreover, he is not a trained firefighter, and does not have adequate knowledge of the protocols for dealing with the present situation. If he enters the building, he could die. Hence, he should not go inside it. That is, it is not truly in his best interest to do so. Moreover, given his condition and the circumstances, he certainly does not desire to enter the building, at the very least, not in the same way that he desires a good night's sleep after a very long day. Nonetheless, he experiences a sudden burst of energy, allowing him to rush into the building and pull the occupants to safety. Given his medical acumen, he can also resuscitate any of them if necessary. In this scenario, the doctor acts in a way that conflicts with both reason (his need for sleep and the preservation of his life) and pure appetite (his desire simply to return home and get his much-needed rest). It could be said that he acts purely out of *spirit*, the third faculty of the soul which corresponds to the guardian class. Notice that in this scenario, the doctor acts as a protector, as a soldier would.

Finally, how does the soul achieve justice? Remember that in the city, the ruling class needed wisdom, while the guardian class needed courage, and all three of the classes, including the artisans, needed moderation. Once each class procured its virtue, justice emerged. Applied to the soul, reason requires wisdom, knowledge of human nature, the Good, and what is best for the individual. Spirit requires courage, the capacity and willingness to do the right thing regardless of fear or the preference to pursue one's immediate, selfish desires. And all three faculties, including appetite, requires moderation, self-control. In terms of this tripartite model of soul, self-control means that the correct faculty must control the others. The desires of the appetite and the passion of spirit must abide by the dictates of reason. When this balance is achieved, the individual soul becomes just. Just as a balanced body is healthy, a balanced soul is just.

While the scenarios of the lazy man and procrastinating student addressed why appetite must obey reason, consider courage. Many people conflate courage with brashness, or with the sort of individual who is short-tempered. For instance, suppose that a bully calls a trained martial artist a name. In his fury, the martial artist then strikes and kills the bully. Such an action cannot truly be called courageous, since it defies reason. The martial artist acted more from a purely appetitive desire rather than from a goal to achieve what is best for himself and others. Even though the bully's behavior in this scenario is contemptible, he certainly did not deserve to be injured or killed! Consider also the long-term repercussions of the martial artist's behavior. He would likely face severe consequences for his actions, including the possibility of life imprisonment, another example of short-term gain with long-term loss. But what if such a person faced no consequences for his actions? That is, what if an individual could commit heinous crimes with complete and total immunity? The fable of the ring of Gyges, introduced in Book II of *The Republic*, addresses such a scenario[8].

The Fable of the Ring of Gyges: In this fable, a shepherd in Lydia, Gyges, finds a ring in an underground cave. When he dawns the ring, he discovers that by turning the ring inward toward his palm, he can make himself invisible. In the story, Gyges uses the ring to seduce the queen of Lydia and then kill, and overthrow the king, becoming the king himself. This fable poses a challenging question: If an individual can commit a grave, reprehensible crime and get away with it, why should that individual behave in a just manner at all? While Gyges literally made himself invisible, the metaphorical applications of it raise the very same sort of problem. For example, a criminal mastermind could engineer a bank robbery, managing to steal millions of dollars. This

---

[8] The account of the soul I provided here is based mostly on Books II and IV of *The Republic*. The first three chapters of Jeffrey Tiel's *Philosophy of Human Nature* (CenterSpace Independent Publishing Platform, 2012) gives a similar but more detailed account of these sections of *The Republic*.

criminal could then frame an innocent person for the crime, call in an anonymous tip to the authorities, and then live a long and fruitful life. Since there is a patsy to go down for it, the mastermind need not worry about his actions being discovered. Moreover, his associates in the criminal underworld can help him launder the money, so that his riches appear legitimate. He can even become a bona fide hero to the public by donating a substantial portion of his wealth to various charities. He becomes a famous and beloved philanthropist, while the innocent man he framed suffers a destroyed reputation, living in squalor and infamy as he pays for a crime he did not commit. Suppose that you could be this criminal. Why should you not behave in the same way if you can profit from doing so, just as he did?

The short answer is because even though it *seems* that such a criminal suffers no consequences for his actions, as the Platonic model of the soul suggests, there are always consequences for our actions. Maybe there are not always external consequences for our actions, such as punishments sanctioned by a judicial system or rightful authority, but what a person does inevitably affects his soul, for better or for worse. Specifically, the challenge posed by ring of Gyges scenarios fails for two reasons: (1) acts of injustice are harmful to the individual soul, and (2) goodness has intrinsic value.

To illustrate the first reason, recall briefly the example of the rash martial artist. Assume that the exchange between him and the bully happened in a vacant parking lot in the dead of night with no witnesses. Basically, these conditions allow the martial artist literally to get away with murder. And people tend to be creatures of habit. If a person resorts to violence once, he is much more likely to do so a second time, and perhaps when that second time comes, he may react violently over a much less severe infraction. Maybe on the next occasion, someone merely need to look at him the wrong way, without saying anything at all. As a creature of habit this man will acclimatize quickly. Eventually, he might not even wait for someone to offend him at all.

By this point, his propensity for violence drives him to seek out people to hurt, just as drug addicts go to great lengths to obtain their poison of choice. But in this case, the poison harms not the man's body but his soul. It may cause him momentary pleasure due to the power he has over others, but eventually he will grow bored of this pleasure. He will have to find some other means to satisfy his appetite. Perhaps he will have to orchestrate an act of violence and destruction on a larger scale. He may have power over others, but he has no power over himself. Just as poison disrupts the health of the body, acts of injustice disrupt the health of the soul, especially since, by the analogy through which the faculties of the soul were revealed to us, humans are social in nature. By harming others in any way, we also harm ourselves. Can such an individual truly be described as "happy?" Is this man "better off" for getting away with his actions? Were such a man truly happy, he likely would not resort to violence in the first place. More than likely, his proclivity for violence and aggression emanate from his attempt to find something that he lacks. What he lacks is a just soul, and each subsequent action only makes him more prone to such actions, thereby bending the soul away from the dictates of reason.

To illustrate the second point, the reintroduction of the criminal mastermind will be useful. What would happen if somebody exposed this man? The outrage against him would likely reach biblical proportions. The reason that the public would likely have such a response runs parallel to the reason that they embraced and adored him in the first place: People value justice for its own sake. This criminal would never gain any recognition or admiration as a hero if people did not attach some value to the good that he did. In the same way, people tend to revile acts of injustice. We admire the acts of those who risk their own lives and well-being for the good of others, such as the valiant doctor of the previous example who risked his own life to save people from a burning building. Admiration typically is also felt for those who struggle against their own capacity for selfishness and injustice. There is a reason why soldiers often suffer from PTSD, and it is not only because of the horrors they experienced, but from those they had to dole out to others in carrying out their orders.

If the challenge of the ring of Gyges fails for these reasons, then there is a deeper reality that lies beyond the visible world, a reality that makes justice in the human soul possible, and that reality is the Good itself. If the goal of human life is to obtain a just soul, then that goal begins by looking beyond the mere shadows of blind desire and seeking out the good itself guided by reason.

Plato and Bacon's Idols of the Mind

The case can be made that Bacon outright plagiarized Plato in the development of his conception of some of the idols of the mind, especially his Idols of the Cave. Plato most assuredly had the same kinds of concerns in mind, albeit he expressed them in a much different way and in an obviously different historical context. Whereas Bacon's primary concern lay with revolutionizing the sciences and shifting away from the worldview perpetuated during the middle ages, each class of Idols can be applied across a much broader spectrum.

Plato and Bacon's Idols of the Tribe: To begin with Bacon's Idols of the Tribe, recall that idols of this class refer to errors that arise from universal tendencies shared by all humans. These are errors based on human nature itself. The two most discernible ways in which Plato addresses idols of this class are through (1) his theory of the forms in connection with the recollection thesis, and (2) his assessment of the effects of injustice on the soul. Plato's theory of forms constituted an effective synthesis of the worldviews of both Heraclitus and Parmenides, reconciling change with permanent realities. The items of the physical world change, whereas the forms are eternal and immutable. The implication of this theory is that the visible world is not ultimately real, that reality lies beyond what can be readily observed with the naked eye. In that sense, we all begin like the prisoners in the cave, seeing only the "shadows" of ultimate reality. Moreover, our physical bodies place constraints on the ability of our minds to grasp the forms fully. In our mortal lives, we have only vague recollections of these ideas. One of the main lines of argument in Phaedo is that death is a blessing, since it frees the soul of the individual to experience the eternal and immutable truths of the forms. Hence, not only does Plato provide an explanation as to why people are subject to errors such as the idols of the tribe, but his central metaphysical and epistemological doctrines convey precautions against making hasty judgments about what can be seen or known.

As for the second way, Plato's conception of the soul often strikes first time readers and students as counter-intuitive. Plato seemed to maintain the Socratic notion that it is better to suffer injustice than it is to commit it, since injustice harms the soul of the perpetrator more than it does his victim. Plato's model of the soul provided the foundation for this claim. Since the soul needs justice in the same way that the body needs nutrition, to commit acts of injustice are harmful to the individual. Such actions may often result in short-term gains, but in virtually every scenario have long-term deleterious effects. The reason I list this Platonic notion as a way in which Plato addresses idols of the tribe is that most people are prone to taking shortcuts to reach their goals believing that it is really in their best interest to do so. In multiple dialogues, most notably *Meno* and *Gorgias*, Socrates often claimed that no one does wrong willingly. Rather people only do wrong on the presumption that they will obtain something *good* by doing so. That is, people do wrong only out of ignorance about the consequences of their actions, primarily, ignorance about the effect such actions will have on them.

Plato and Bacon's Idols of the Cave: Plato's model of the soul is also, surprisingly, the primary way in which he addresses the sorts of errors that emerge from the idols of the cave. I maintain that it is surprising because one would think that the allegory of the cave would address the idols of the same way. The allegory of the cave, however, is much broader. It seems to address all four of Bacon's idols in some way. Since it is connected to the theory of the forms and the admonition to seek reality beyond mere appearances, it addresses the idols of the tribe. It served as Bacon's inspiration for his conception of idols of the cave. Specifically, since the cave comprises the entire world of the prisoners it holds, the worldview imparted them would reflect their general dispositions, preferences, and biases. Hence, they cannot comprehend the seemingly outlandish suggestion by the returned escapee that there is a completely different world beyond the walls of the cave. I address the cave in connection with the idols of the marketplace and theater below.

More specifically, Plato's tripartite division of the soul emerged by analogy with the ideal city, which itself grew from a natural principle about the human division of labor. For such a city to be just, everybody must remain in their place and fulfill a specific role for which they are naturally suited. A person naturally suited to the role of farming should not be forced into a life devoted to mortal combat, just as a person who is best served and best serves others working as a butcher should not create the laws that govern the city. Beyond the context of Plato's analogy between the just city and the just soul, one should always keep a keen eye on how one's inclinations affect the judgments they make about the world and others. The butcher should not assume that everyone wants to be a butcher. The soldier should not assume that everyone wants to be a soldier, or that everyone thinks like a soldier. Just as important is that the ruler should not assume that other people want to be lawmakers, or that they are even capable of carrying such a burden.

Plato and Bacon's Idols of the Marketplace: Bacon's idols of the marketplace refer to errors that arise due to miscommunications between people or confusion over the meanings of words. Plato seems to address these types of errors in four ways. First, his theory of the forms contains an aspect that accounts for the use of general terms. That is, the words we use refer not to the fleeting, ephemeral realities of the visible world, but to eternal ideas. This theory, thus, attempts to provide a firm foundation for the words that we use.

A second connected way Plato addresses these idols is through the allegory of the cave, especially in the way that the story ends. Remember that upon the return of the liberated prisoners, none of the others believe him. That is, he voices his discovery in a way unfathomable to the rest of the prisoners. Being imprisoned in a cave since birth, they never so much considered any other possibilities. The exchange plays out the same way that an exchange between people from different cultures who do not understand each other's language probably would. More than likely, the "outsider" in this exchange would be persecuted, injured, or perhaps even killed. Notice also the parallels between the allegory of the cave and the fable of the ring of Gyges. If you were wrongly accused of a crime, how would you react? You would likely assert your innocence in such an aggressive manner that people would be even less likely to believe you based on your defense alone. The point is that the way in which people try to communicate always influences the intended message.

Third, Plato did not write treatises. That is, he did not produce a systematic exposition of his doctrines. He wrote dialogues, usually with Socrates as the primary speaker. This methodology signifies Plato's way of adapting the Socratic method to his own purposes. Recall that the Socratic method began with Socrates asking his interlocutor a question, which the interlocutor would then readily and confidently answer. Then, Socrates would expose flaws in the answer, forcing the interlocutor to amend his position. This process would continue until the interlocutor is forced to admit ignorance, and he and Socrates mutually agree to continue pursuing the truth. Socrates's intentions were linked with his own self-professed ignorance, his awareness that he did not know with certainty fundamental truths about the nature of reality, knowledge, or the meaning of human existence, except for his insistence that the unexamined life is not worth living and his remarks about justice and morality. Thus, he wanted to bring his interlocutors to realize their own ignorance about the topics on which they claimed to be experts, thereby augmenting their interest in seeking out the true answers. Plato's depiction of this dialectical method in his dialogues seems to serve a similar purpose. That is, he wanted to display to his readers that having true knowledge is not merely a matter of understanding what words mean, just as having genuine courage is not merely a matter of knowing the definition of the word courage. Words are, after all, transmitted to us through various media of the physical world, either via sounds or written language. The earliest forms of language were pictorial, such as the Egyptians' use of hieroglyphics. Words, thus, keep us tethered to the realm of illusions and shadows. Through dialectic, we ascend closer to the realm of eternal truth.

Fourth, Plato's concerns with the sophists coincide with the very sorts of errors to which the idols of the marketplace give rise. The sophists wanted to replace philosophy with rhetoric, which is primarily the art of persuasive speaking. The sophists knew that words can have power over people. Words can incite people to take up arms in war, and they can soothe turbulent emotions. Plato did not want to the power of rhetoric used irresponsibly. The clearest example of his critique of rhetoric occurs in the dialogue, *Gorgias*. In this dialogue, Socrates converses with three interlocutors, Gorgias, a famous teacher and sophist, and two of his students, Polus and Callicles. I cannot go into the details of the dialogue here, but in short, Gorgias is forced to bear witness to the contradictory and implausible implications of his teachings as Socrates humbles his two students. The point is that a teacher must be responsible for his students, and that if a teacher is as powerful as Gorgias claimed to be, then he would be able to impart his knowledge to his students without the fear that they would misunderstand or abuse the subject. The dialogue, in fact, can be read as the punishment of Gorgias through his students[9].

Plato and Bacon's Idols of the Theater: The last of Bacon's idols to which Plato seemed pointedly attuned, Idols of the Theater consist of errors that arise due to false teachings and sophistry. Plato's misgivings with the sophists apply here as well, especially since Bacon, specifically listed "sophistry" as one of the chief forms of such idols, but the previous paragraph addressed that topic. His famous allegory of the cave, furthermore, consists of something quite like a theatrical play (except that the audience consists of prisoners), but this concept too has been discussed at length. The only aspect of Plato's thought not yet considered that is also relevant to the idols of the theater is his condemnation of poets of and artists. Plato wanted to ban most artists from his ideal city for many reasons, but all his objections to art and artists had a common theme: Art and artists distract individuals from ultimate reality. Since artists create imitations in the form of statues, sculptures, and paintings, they create illusions, and as such they draw attention away from the realm of the forms and the truth emanating from them. Moreover, artists appeal primarily to human passions and appetites, hence, pave the way for the corruption of reason, the emergence of injustice within the soul.

Critical Assessment: Does Plato *himself* avoid these idols? It is very difficult, if not impossible, to determine whether Plato avoided the idols of the tribe and the cave, as one would have to know an individual personally to make such a determination. Nonetheless, Plato's suspicions

---

[9] For a very thorough and compelling reading of the dialogue Gorgias, see Nalin Ranasinghe's *Socrates in the Underworld* (St. Augustine Press, 2009). This book is quite advanced but written in a very engaging style.

about the corrosive effects of art and sophistry may reflect idols of the cave on his own part, personal biases that do not stem from an entirely rational basis. The same may be said about his insistence about the distinction between the realm of the visible and the realm of the forms, in addition to his doctrines of recollection and the immortality of the soul. During his youth, Plato closely adhered to the doctrines of Pythagoras, a mathematician, so it is not surprising that he emphasized a mathematical concept such as form over matter. The idea of reincarnation also has its roots in the Pythagorean school of thought. With respect to idols of the marketplace, much criticism can be made of Plato's theory of the forms and his ontological stratification of reality depicted through the analogy of the divided line. For instance, if a form is both abstract and an entity, then how is a form different from some other concrete object? The quick and easy answer is that such an entity is immaterial, and thus not subject to the laws governing physical objects. But still, such entities must be located somewhere. And there are not very compelling reasons for thinking that in such a place there would be no space-time continuum. Hence, the eternal realm of the forms seems not to be all that different from the mortal realm of the concrete, except that it is invisible to the human eye and non-physical. Moreover, the analogy of the line presents a hierarchical conception of reality, implying that some things are "more real" than others. As we will see, this idea influenced many later thinkers, but such a notion is excruciatingly difficult to grasp. What exactly does it mean to say that object X is "more real" than object Y? Prima facie, it seems to violate the law of contradiction, since nothing can simultaneously be and not be. Does it mean that some things are more powerful than others? Even so, how is the more powerful thing more real than the less powerful thing? Plato himself recognized many difficulties with his theory of the forms and attempted to address them in a later dialogue, *Parmenides*. As for idols of the theater committed by Plato, it is possible that given the numerous difficulties with his metaphysical outlook, such a worldview may be seriously flawed, even if not all its aspects are erroneous. Of utmost interest on Platonic idols of the theater, though, is Plato's conception of the human soul. Since Pythagoras heavily influenced Plato's conception of the soul's immortality, Plato himself may have fallen victim to a false worldview, rather than creating one. But the idol that Plato possibly created arises in *The Republic*. Recall that the subdivisions of the soul were discovered based on an analogy that Socrates and his interlocutors tentatively agreed exists between the individual and the city. But is there any real basis for accepting such an analogy? Only because human beings rely on others and seem naturally suited to perform specific jobs does not entail the analogy the interlocutors draw. Such a city consisted of many individuals following the dictates of one ruler, the best person who fits such a role. But within the individual soul, every individual must be his own ruler, and as such, every individual must know what is best for himself. It seems as if the analogy of the city were real, the individual soul as Plato describes it would not be possible. On the other hand, if every individual can in fact rule over himself, then the model of the city from which it emerged could not exist. Furthermore, on what basis should the natural division of labor be accepted? Human beings are exceedingly adaptable creatures, capable of learning multiple tasks and applying what they learn in a variety of ways. And if everyone were devoted to only one task, how can anyone achieve the intuitive insight of the Good that is supposedly all-encompassing? It seems that such a feat would be impossible.

But perhaps Plato never intended his audience to ascribe any doctrines to his teachings at all, and thus, to prevent his work from becoming a theater of false dogmas. It is entirely possible that Plato wrote in dialogue and frequently displayed Socratic dialectic to allow his audience to realize independently the shortcomings of the worldview a mere surface reading of his work entailed. Plato's goal just might have been to avail his readers the opportunity to realize on their own the eternal truths that cannot be done justice by human language, and which can only be drawn out through the admission of one's own ignorance[10]. Only then can one ascend from the darkness of illusions to the natural light of truth.

---

[10] For a unique and intriguing examination of this topic, see Francisco Gonzalez's *Dialectic and Dialogue: Plato's Practice of Philosophical Inquiry* (Northwestern University Press, 1998). As with some other sources I recommended, this book is very advanced, and should only be approached after gaining familiarity with the primary sources of Plato himself (especially *The Republic*, *Meno*, and *Phaedo*) in addition to the traditional interpretation of his work.

Chapter 1 Worksheet

1. Which theory of the pre-Socratics makes the most sense to you and why?

2. What is the connection between Protagoras's famous claim that "Man is the measure of all things" and Thrasymachus's conception of justice as "the will of the stronger?"

3. How would you respond to the basic teaching of the sophists that philosophy should be replaced with rhetoric, since only the latter has real value? What value is to be gained from philosophy?

4. While the author claimed that Socrates was the chief antagonist of the sophists, in what way would they agree with each other, especially in terms of Socrates's paradoxical assertion that he knew only his ignorance?

5. Do you think that Plato's theory of the forms is plausible? Is there a better way to account for how different things share characteristics in common? For instance, if the theory of the forms is erroneous, then how can many individual dogs still all be "dogs" in some sense?

6. Think of at least three different ways that Plato's allegory of the cave can be interpreted. How does this concept apply to your life? Has it changed the way you view your life.

7. Do you think that the Platonic notion that learning is recollection and is plausible? How is this notion different from something like déjà vu? Does it really entail that the soul is immortal?

8. Is Plato's account of the soul complete? That is, do you think that there might be other parts that he left out? Why or why not?

9. Think of at least three different scenarios that illustrate the fable of the ring of Gyges. Do you accept the implications of this fable? That is, do you believe that doing bad things really harms the perpetrator more than his victims?

10. Watch a movie or a television show of your choice and try to find any three Platonic themes that it illustrates.

Aristotle—Back to Earth!

It is often said that a picture is worth one thousand words. Raphael's famous painting, *The School of Athens*, in one image, conveys the major differences between the thought of Plato and Aristotle. The painting shows Plato and his most famous student, Aristotle, walking side by side. Plato, on the left, has his right hand raised toward the sky, whereas Aristotle, on the right, has his right hand extended toward the ground in front of him. What is the significance of these gestures? Recall Plato's insistence that the visible, material world is not truly "real," but only consists of copies of transcendent and eternal realities, the Forms. Hence, for Plato, reality is not what can be readily seen. On the other hand, Aristotle's gesture toward the world of sense indicates his chief disagreement with his mentor: Reality is indeed right in front of us, in the visible, material world. In *The Cave and the Light: Plato Versus Aristotle, and the Struggle for the Soul of Western Civilization*, Herman crafted an entire book based on the implications of Raphael's masterpiece. In Herman's own words, his book "tells the story of how everything we say, do, and see has been shaped in one way or another by two classical Greek thinkers, Plato and Aristotle."[1] He summarizes the influence of both where he writes,

> Far from being "dead white males," [Plato and Aristotle have] been powering the living heart of Western culture from ancient Greece to today. Their influence extends from science and philosophy and literature, to our social life and most cherished political institutions – and not just in the West but increasingly in the rest of the world, too, including the Muslim world. And

---

[1] Richard Herman, *The Cave and the Light: Plato Versus Aristotle and the Struggle for the Soul of Western Civilization*, New York, NY: Random House, 2014, p. ix.

at the center of their influence has been a two-thousand-year struggle for the soul of Western civilization, which today extends to all civilizations: a struggle born from an act of rebellion.[2]

Born in Stagira to a family of physicians in 384 B.C.E., the philosopher known as Aristotle arguably had intellectual prejudices in favor of a form of naturalism based solely on his heritage. He entered Plato's Academy at the age of 17. Even though he was an exceptional student, Plato refused to name Aristotle as his successor. The latter subsequently fled to Macedonia and became the tutor of Alexander the Great. He returned to Athens in 335 B.C.E. and founded his own university, The Lyceum. In 323 B.C.E., he was brought to trial and fled Athens, hoping to avoid the fate of Socrates. The next year, he died of illness. Given that Plato was Aristotle's teacher, and that both Plato and Aristotle shaped the course of the western intellectual tradition that followed, it will be useful to compare and then to contrast the ideas of the two thinkers.

Plato and Aristotle[3]

Points of Agreement between Plato and Aristotle: Despite their differences, the philosophies of Plato and Aristotle had much in common. First and foremost, both affirmed that reason is the most distinctive human faculty. Plato's tripartite conception of the soul seated reason atop the faculties of spirit and appetite, while Aristotle acknowledged that reason distinguishes the human soul from those of plants and animals.

Secondly, in connection with the first, both believed in the necessity of philosophy. Since human beings are rational creatures, they have needs that go beyond those of all other terrestrial creatures, and human fulfillment requires the appeasement of this rationality. In short, both

---

[2] Richard Herman, *The Cave and the Light: Plato Versus Aristotle and the Struggle for the Soul of Western Civilization*, New York, NY: Random House, 2014, p. ix.

[3] For an alternative, but efficient comparison between Plato and Aristotle, see Louis Pojman's *Who Are We? Theories of Human Nature*, Oxford University Press, 2005, pp. 57–59.

believed, like Socrates, that the unexamined life is not worth living, but moreover, that such a life is not even fully human, since it would fail to augment the most distinctive aspect of humanity's being. The very first line of Aristotle's *Metaphysics* reads, "All men by nature stretch themselves out toward knowing."[4] Such a desire, however, constitutes not merely the drive to discover information, but the drive to live one's life in meaningful ways by asking and understanding the importance of life's deepest questions. In addition, Aristotle once even proposed an argument on the necessity of philosophizing that ran as follows: Either we ought to philosophize, or we ought not. If we ought, then we ought. But if we ought not, then we still must philosophize in order to justify why we ought not to philosophize.[5]

Thirdly, both authors would be considered virtue ethicists by modern standards. That is, both authors maintained that morality is achieved through the development and perfection of character traits called virtues rather than through either merely following rules, or by acting on the basis what one presumes will yield the best consequences. Instead, everyone should focus on becoming a good person, and in so doing, one will be prepared to address adequately any situation that arises in one's lifetime.

Fourth, both authors affirmed a doctrine of teleology. That is, they maintained that everything has a purpose or goal to which it is naturally suited. In other words, everything has a function that it performs better than anything else, and a thing may be called good insofar as it performs that function. For Plato, the purpose of the human soul is to achieve the virtue of justice, and all the forms are unified in the Form of the Good, which is a teleological concept, since everything

---

[4] Joe Sachs (Translator), *Aristotle's Metaphysics*, Santa Fe, NM: Green Lion Press, 2002, p. 1. Sachs's translation of this first line contrasts with Ross's "All men by nature desire to know."

[5] Aristotle makes this argument in a lost work called *Protrepticus*, of which all that remain are fragments. It is a work that encourages youth to study philosophy. A recent attempt at a reconstruction of this work is D.S. Hutchinson and Monte Ransom Johnson's 2017, *Protrepticus or Exhortation to Philosophy*.

participates in the form of goodness insofar as it does what it is naturally suited to do. Plato's use of natural imagery in the analogies of the Sun, the Line, and the Cave also testify to his affirmation of natural hierarchical order of being. Aristotle argues in a similar way, suggesting that the natural purpose of a thing is inextricably linked with the sort of soul by which the thing is constituted. Aristotle's argument on this matter will be elaborated below.

Fifth, both authors assumed that human beings are basically social creatures. The development of the ideal city of *The Republic* emerges from the principles that human beings rely heavily on each other to meet their needs, and that each person is suited to a specific task according to a natural division of labor. Like his mentor, Aristotle insisted that human beings are inherently social creatures. While he gives more than one argument for this doctrine, the primary reason for holding it is linked to his conception of teleology, since he insisted that all human beings are inclined by nature to congregate with others and construct cities. He went so far as to claim not only that human beings are "political animals," but that the city is the natural end of humanity and necessary for complete and total fulfillment.

Lastly, both Plato and Aristotle affirmed the existence of a reality beyond the physical world. For Plato, such realities consisted of the Forms and the Demiurge, the latter of which constitutes the deity which Plato suggested created the universe. Aristotle, however, argued for the existence of a Prime Mover, which later Islamic and Christian thinkers identified as God. The details of Aristotle's argument are addressed below.

Points of Disagreement between Plato and Aristotle: Since the focus of this chapter is Aristotle, it will be helpful to outline the ways in which he differed from his mentor as well. The most pronounced difference in the thought of the two thinkers concerns the doctrine of the Forms. While Aristotle provides several arguments against this doctrine, his primary reason for rejecting it seemed to be based on a paradox that it poses. For instance, according to Plato, the dog wagging its tail in front of me is less real than the abstract idea "Dog." That is, the essence of the dog is not within the dog, but in something else, the form "Dog." One of Plato's primary reasons for holding this view was that it seemed to resolve the problem of change and permanence left over by the pre-Socratics, since the visible dog changes, while the idea of Dog remains eternally. However, in Aristotle's view, this resolution only raises a further problem: The visible dog is somehow both a dog and not a dog! How could it be a dog if its essence is not contained within it? An equally problematic question concerns how a form can simultaneously exist both within the thing that represents it and apart from it. Moreover, there must be something in virtue of which we are able to recognize Plato's forms. That is, there must be some way that I can recognize the form "Dog" as being that very form. But I would not be able to do so unless I already knew what a dog generally looks like. But to make such a recognition requires the use of one's visible senses, which, according to Plato, cannot yield true knowledge. One possible solution is that there is some third item in virtue of which the form can be recognized. But this solution only leads to an infinite regress, since there must be some additional fourth thing in virtue of which the previous item can be recognized!

Instead, Aristotle substitutes a more commonsensical theory to serve as a resolution to the problem of change and permanence. Change always takes place within a subject. Such a subject can exist independently even though it contains properties that undergo change. A subject that can exist independently is a *substance.* Substances are objects that have both matter and form, which can be separated by the mind, or in thought, but not in reality. The properties of a substance are called *accidents,* so named because they are parasitic on substances, while substances can exist without them. For example, an individual man or woman is a substance. But the color of their skin, the color of their hair, and their height are each accidental, as they are subject to change. Moreover, without the individual man or woman, there would be nothing to possess skin, hair, or height. Aristotle, thus, focused more heavily on the natural world than did his predecessor.

A second point of divergence between the two thinkers is Aristotle's conception of the human soul. Ultimately, Aristotle rejected both Platonic doctrines of the immortality of the soul and recollection. Below, I will elaborate further on Aristotle's conception of the soul. As for the Platonic doctrine of recollection, since Aristotle focused more on nature than did Plato, he embraced a form of empiricism and common-sense realism. That is, he insisted that all knowledge derives from sense-experience and the items of our experience accurately constitute reality. Hence, there is no distinction between the visible world and the transcendent, intelligible world as can be found in Plato. As such, no one is born with any innate ideas acquired from such a realm. Learning consists predominantly in the construction of knowledge from experience.

Third, while Aristotle and Plato both may be considered virtue ethicists, Aristotle's conception of virtue differs markedly from Plato's. Recall that Plato maintained that justice is a holistic virtue that is achieved when each faculty of the soul achieves a specific virtue. Reason requires wisdom, while spirit requires courage, and the appetite requires moderation. Once each part of the soul has its virtue, it becomes just, in the same way that a body is healthy when it is balanced. Aristotle was convinced that Plato misunderstood the concept of justice, which should not be treated as a virtue of character. He also provides a more comprehensive list of character virtues than is found in Plato.

Lastly, in connection with Aristotle's different account of virtue, he insisted that virtue does not equate to happiness. A person may be morally righteous, possessing all the virtues of character listed by Aristotle, but may still lack happiness. Aristotle's conception of happiness is a common translation of the term *eudaimonia*. Etymologically, this term means "good spiritedness." So, a more literal translation of the term would mean, "being possessed of a good indwelling spiritedness." Perhaps the most useful translation of the term in this context is total, complete overall flourishing, which Aristotle insisted is the "final cause" of humanity. Understanding just what exactly he meant by final cause requires an exposition of his account of causality.

Aristotle on Nature, Humanity, and the Meaning of Life

The Four Causes: In our own time, the term "cause" tends to be used in two related senses. First, "cause" might mean an immediate precipitating event or circumstance that brings about some other event, such as in a chain depicting the process or sequence by which something happened. To illustrate, imagine a row of 10 dominoes, perfectly lined up on a table. In this scenario, a person pushes over the first domino which sets off a chain reaction until the final domino falls. The "cause" of the 10th domino falling is the 9th, the cause of the 9th, the 8th, etc. In connection with the first, the second sense of "cause" typically refers to the force or agent that produces something. In the scenario with the dominoes, this such cause is the person who pushed the first domino, setting off the sequence. For Aristotle, each of these scenarios depict only one type of cause, of which there are four: material, efficient, formal, and final. A complete account of any substance demands an explanation of its being in terms of each of these causes.

The material cause of an object is basically the physical matter of which it is comprised, the tangible "stuff" that a thing has that makes it a "thing." The efficient cause of an object is depicted by the scenario above, the immediate force or agent that produced a thing. The formal cause of an object is the essence of the object, the type of thing that the object is. Lastly, the final cause of an object refers to the end or purpose of a thing, why the thing exists in the first place. As an example, consider a table. The material cause of the table consists of the table's wood, nuts, bolts, steel, plastic, and any other items used to construct it.

The efficient cause of the table would be the carpenter who processed the various pieces of wood and assembled them into the shape of the table. The formal cause of the table would be the blue-print used as a guide regulating the construction of the table. And the final cause of the table consists in the purpose for building the table in the first place – so that items may be placed on top of it.

There is a sense in which each of the previous three causes serve the final cause of an object. Since the purpose of the table is to hold items, the material chosen to hold said items must be sturdy and relatively thick. The individual who constructed the table must have adequate knowledge of how to build the table so that it will serve its purpose. Specifically, the agent serving as the efficient cause of the table must know the proper form of a table in order to build it correctly. More-over, if the table is not shaped properly, then it cannot serve its purpose of holding up other items. If one of its legs is too short, the table will slant, and the objects resting on it will slide off. There is a sense in which if the table cannot serve its purpose, thus, it ceases to be a true table.

Each of the four causes help to explain the nature of a thing. "Nature" in this sense derives from the Greek word *phusis*, which literally means "to develop out of oneself." It may also be translated as "growing" or "becoming," understood via analogy with plant and animal development. Ultimately, the nature of a thing, the process by which it grows and develops, its matter, where it came from, and the sort of thing it is, dictate its *purpose*. On this basis, Aristotle's conception of human nature can be understood in terms of the material, efficient, formal, and final causes of humanity.

Aristotelian Human Nature: Heraclitus remarked that "nature loves to hide," since the nature of a thing is internal. Human nature, thus, is internal, and what is internal to a thing designates its patterns of growth and development in addition to its needs and goals. In this sense, the nature of a thing always shines through in its actions.

A table made from trees, for instance, is much more likely to give birth to another tree, rather than a table. A tree can be shaped into a table, but that does not change the nature of the wood from which the table is fashioned. Moreover, if the wood from which the table was made were not solid and sturdy, the wood could not be fashioned into a suitable table. In a similar way, the actions of humanity reveal their nature, and the prescriptions for human fulfillment are not merely matters of opinion or choice but have as their source the nature of humanity.

The material cause of humanity, the physical "stuff" of which a human is made, is simply the matter comprising the human body, including the skin, tissues, bones, and organs that make up the human animal. The efficient cause of a human being, the force or agent that produces a human being, quite simply is a person's parents. The formal cause of humanity is the human soul. As noted above, Aristotle's conception of the soul differs remarkably from Plato's. Not only did Aristotle dispense with the doctrines of immortality and recollection, but he also rejected the notion that the soul is the efficient cause of a person, as Plato implied. But if that were the case, then it would be extrinsic to its effect, as parents are to their children, rather than contained by the body. Before explaining the "final cause" of humanity, Aristotle's conception of the soul requires further elaboration.

Aristotle's understanding of the human soul is intimately connected with its meaning as designated by the Greek term "psuche," from which the English word "psychology" derives. Literally, "psuche" means "life principle." Hence, a thing's soul, is the principle that gives rise to life within the thing. In Aristotle's own words, the soul is "the first grade of actuality of a natural body having life potentially in it."[6] This definition may also be stated, "the first act of a living body that has life potentially." Notice that the way Aristotle defines the soul

---

[6] From Aristotle, "*De Anima*," in Wall, Philosophy of Human Nature, p. 122.

establishes an inextricable link between the soul and the body. The two are related as act and potency are related. That is, the material of which a thing's body is comprised constitutes its potency, or its potential for life. A pile of flesh accompanied by yet another pile of bones with some organ meat on top of it is not a human being. All that exists in these random piles are, at best, the potential for human life. The soul, as the formal cause of human being, is what allows for the material of the body to function as a living organism, just as the shape of the table allows it to function properly as a table. Or, in other words, a thing's soul comprises the total set of a thing's abilities based on the sort of organism that it is. Thus, it simply makes no sense to say that a soul can exist apart from a body. It would be just as nonsensical to say that a human being can survive without a heart! In short, the human soul is the ability to have abilities.

A couple of analogies help to illustrate Aristotle's conception of the soul. The soul basically activates the body by making it alive, but why would Aristotle call it the "first act" of a living body? A similar relationship exists between having a mind and knowing. In order to have knowledge, one must first have the potential to know, which means that one must have a mind. And in order to apply one's knowledge, one must first have knowledge. Imagine that your car breaks down. You would not requisition a dog or a cat to fix it, as such animals lack even the potential to do so, since they cannot possibly acquire the knowledge necessary. Moreover, you cannot simply ask any human being to fix the car either. Even though all human beings have the potential to do so, only some have the actual knowledge, the first act. Fixing the car, in this case, cannot be the first act, since one must possess the knowledge first. Hence, the relationship between the mind and knowing is analogous to the relationship between the body and the soul. Just as the first act of the mind is the possession of knowledge, the first act of a body is possessing life, or being alive. And just as the ability to fix a car cannot be separated from the knowledge of how to fix a car, the soul cannot be separated from the body. A second helpful analogy consists of the relation between the eye and the power of sight. Simply having the physical organ, the eye, constitutes the potential for seeing. And before one can use that organ to see, it must have the power to see. Hence, the power of sight cannot be the second act of the eye, just as the soul cannot be separated from the body.

Basically, anything that's alive has a soul, or "life principle," and anything that moves based on the power of its own life principle is alive. Aristotle distinguishes three types of souls, or three types of "life principles." First is the vegetative soul. These souls have the power of growth and reproduction, but not much else. These forms of life are basically plants. While they can "move" in terms of growing, they lack locomotion in any other sense and lack the capacity for sensation. Second is the sensitive soul, the souls of non-human animals. While such animals have locomotion and are sentient, they lack the ability to think in any deep or reflective capacity. Third is the rational soul, the human soul.

While the human soul is rational, it also contains a non-rational component, which houses the virtues of character. The rational component houses the intellectual virtues. Aristotle distinguishes theoretical intellectual virtues from practical intellectual virtues. The theoretical intellectual virtues are called *sophia* and *techne*. Recall from the introduction that "sophia" means "wisdom." In the context of Aristotle's conception of the soul, "sophia" consists in academic knowledge. To illustrate, consider a young surgeon who recently graduated from medical school, but has very little experience working with patients. Such a person would possess a vast amount of knowledge of surgery, but still may not know how to apply that knowledge perfectly. On the other hand, "techne" translates into "art," or "craft," and the etymological root of the English terms "technique," "technical," and "technology." In contrast with the young medical school graduate, consider a nurse, not an M.D., who spent several decades working in an emergency room triage unit, who also assisted with many surgeries. Suppose that a patient with a knife impaled in his leg comes into the emergency room on the shift of both the nurse and the young surgeon. Whereas the young surgeon possesses knowledge of the injury sustained by the patient and perhaps can give an erudite explanation of why the impaled knife should not be removed, the nurse, although lacking the same eloquence and knowledge, knows not to remove the knife simply based on her experience, and knows how to perform a procedure to keep the patient alive until the knife can be removed safely.

The practical intellectual virtue Aristotle ascribes to the soul he calls *phronesis*. While it is very difficult to describe just exactly what phronesis consists in, it seems to encompass intuitive wisdom applicable to many situations. The individual who possesses such wisdom may be called the *phronemos*. In some ways, it is comparable to techne, but transcends its limits, since techne refers to knowledge of skills within a specific field demanding a level of precision and expertise. And it certainly differs from sophia, not only in terms of scope but in terms of the kind of knowledge it is. The intellectual virtue of sophia refers primarily to academic knowledge that, like techne, applies to a specific field. As an example of a *phronemos*, imagine a man of advanced age who is not especially learned in any specific field, but who has amassed a vast amount of experience in life and can provide advice on many different issues. Suppose that this person is the next-door neighbor of a young couple experiencing marital problems. Based on his experience, the two might seek his counsel to preserve their marriage, as this man once saved his own from divorce. Such knowledge cannot be obtained from a book, nor is it merely procedural, but applies to a more general life problem whose resolution demands experience.

The final cause of humanity is eudaimonia, or total overall fulfillment, more commonly referred to as "happiness." This condition constitutes the goal that all human beings naturally strive to achieve. Everything a person does, ultimately, is so that they can be happy. If a stressed college student were asked why he or she subjects himself or herself to such stress, the student in question will most likely reply that it is so that they may obtain a good job once they graduate college. If pressed further, the student will likely say that they want a good job so that they can make enough money in order to provide for themselves and their family. If asked why they want families in the first place, they would likely say that they desire companionship, and others to share their lives with, as well as children who can carry on their legacy after they die. Moreover, they might say that they want the respect of others, and to be truly valued. That is, everyone wants to be *wanted*. At last, if they were asked why they want any of this at all, they will finally assert that it so they can be happy!

Ironically, while everyone instinctively pursues happiness, very few ever achieve it. Part of the reason so many people fail to achieve happiness is that most people are inclined to believe that happiness is totally subjective. That is, many people believe that happiness is whatever they want it to be. But recall that, for Aristotle, the final cause of thing, the end or purpose of thing, is determined by the sort of being that thing is. Since human beings are rational creatures, human happiness, complete and total flourishing, will require some exercise of rationality. A more important reason that it is so difficult is that the pursuit of happiness is analogous to the attempt to hit a very small target from very far away. Doing so not only requires much trial and error, but much time. Doing so demands not only effort, but the resilience and determination to continue trying even after failure. How can such a condition be achieved?

Aristotle on "Happiness:" All human beings naturally seek happiness, which seems like a truism, and thus, trivial. However, the "happiness" that is the final cause of humanity is quite distinct from the general meaning attached to the term's ordinary usage. Aristotle's conception of happiness is attached to the best possible human life that can be lived. That is, one becomes happy when one lives the best possible life. Such a life must fit several criteria.

First and foremost, the best possible life must involve the use of *rationality*. Since human beings possess the rational soul, rationality is the feature that distinguishes them from all other animals. Human happiness cannot consist in the exact same conditions as those that would make a dog, or any other animal happy. Closely connected with this criterion is the second, the fact that happiness must consist in an *activity* of some kind. No one can be happy if no one ever actively pursues of one's goals. A person who never leaves his or her sofa for fear of missing out on the latest TV series to binge watch will never achieve the life of happiness prescribed by Aristotle. And since happiness also must include rationality, the activity in which happiness consists must be a *rational activity*.

Next, happiness cannot be merely temporary. It lasts a lifetime and it takes a lifetime to achieve. It is, thus, continuous. Happiness, therefore, is not merely the end of life's journey, but consists in the journey itself. The fact that it takes so much time implies the demand of the exertion of effort and the possibility of failure. It implies that one will experience doubt and uncertainty in the struggle to fulfill one's purpose. Just as "Rome wasn't built in a day," happiness cannot be achieved quickly. Development over the course of one's journey toward happiness occurs slowly, but consistently. And the longevity of one's pursuit enhances one's integrity and resilience. Conversely, a life lived without struggle, without uncertainty, without the exertion of effort can never lead to happiness, but perhaps only to momentary gratification. Consider two different meals. On the one hand, a person can spend several hours carefully marinating and tenderizing a pot roast, carefully cutting fresh vegetables, and even preparing appetizers and a desert. On the other hand, when one becomes hungry, one may simply visit the nearest McDonalds or Burger King and purchase a couple of quarter pounders, or whoppers, thereby taking the easier path from hunger to the sating of one's appetite. But, when the day is done, who truly had the better meal? Who had the better experience? Which of these two is better off for their efforts? I'm willing to wager that most readers will vote that the first of these two people enjoyed the better meal. Moreover, even if one were to object that an item from the menu of a McDonalds or a Burger King tastes better than one's own cooking, one forgets that the more practiced one is in the culinary arts or any field, the better one will become at it. The process of development will take time and effort. Mistakes will most likely be made, but one can always learn from one's mistakes and be all the better for them. In addition, clearly the nutritive value of the first meal is superior to the second, so even if the first meal does not taste as good, it is still the better meal. Just as nutrition is not merely a matter of what a person happens to believe is nutritious, happiness is not a matter merely satisfying one's appetite.

So far, there are three criteria for happiness, the best possible life. Such a life consists in the *continuous* development of a *rational activity*. A fourth criterion is that this life must be pursued with *virtue*. That is, there is a correct way to pursue the life of happiness. It must be pursued with skills that demand the refinement of both the intellectual virtues of sophia and techne, but also the virtues of character. Quite simply, developing the virtues of character means that one becomes a "good person." But what does it mean to be a "good person?" And what are the virtues of character? Aristotle lists 11,[7] but what will be more helpful here is a general explanation of Aristotle's conception of virtue and an example from his list. Aristotle conceives of a virtue as "a trait of character that is manifested in habitual action and is the mean between two extremes." The fact that virtue is habitual coincides with the lifelong development demanded by the life of happiness.

---

[7] For the sake of brevity, I will list Aristotle's virtues here: courage, moderation, liberality, magnificence, pride, patience, truthfulness, wittiness, friendliness, modesty, and righteous indignation, as stated in his *Eudemian Ethics*. Pojman provides this list in his *Who Are We? Theories of Human Nature*, p. 69. For Aristotle's account of Virtue, see the *Nicomachean Ethics*, Book II.6.

Just as happiness requires effort and dedication, so does the development of virtue, which is a necessary condition for happiness. But why is virtue so difficult to achieve? Quite simply, because it is a *mean* between two extremes. Or, virtue may be thought of as the "Goldilocks position," the one that's "just right." Discovering such a position is akin to finding a proverbial needle in a haystack, a very difficult, arduous task, but with perseverance and a keen mind, it can be found. Moreover, it can be found more easily if one knows where *not* to look. And when it comes to the haystack in question, the more exposure one has to it, the more places one has looked, the closer one gets to procuring the needle. By comparison, the more exposure one has to situations that demand virtue, the more likely one is to develop virtue.

Each virtue Aristotle lists applies within a specific sphere of action or feeling. In life, for instance, our choices, especially our moral choices, do not occur in a blank, vacant space disconnected from the world and other people. It is only within a specific situation confronted by both circumstances and the emotions that they trigger within us that we will have to decide how to act. Some situations provide the opportunity to feel fear or confidence, whereas others provide the opportunity to experience pleasure or pain. Some situations trigger our anger, while others ignite our desire for honor, respect, and the esteem of our peers. In each situation we encounter, there are three basic ways we can act in response to both the situation itself and the emotion it elicits from us: (1) out of excess, (2) out of deficiency, or (3) toward the mean. As an example, imagine that you're walking home one night, and on your way, you see a person being held at gun point, presumably, so that the assailant can steal his victim's belongings. Suppose that this situation triggers the emotion of fear within you. If you were to run away because of that fear, you would be acting from cowardice, which is a vice of deficiency. Imagine, however, that you have the opposite reaction, in which you don't feel fear so much as you feel *confidence*. Perhaps you feel a bit overconfident. Based on this feeling, you rush over to confront the assailant and are shot. You survive, however, as a nearby witness saw the events unfold and alerted EMS just in time. In this scenario, you act from a vice of excess – rashness. Notice that in each case, something vital was absent. In the first case, you lacked the appropriate amount of confidence to temper your response, whereas in the second, you lacked the appropriate amount of fear to more cautiously address the situation at hand. Imagine now a third scenario that unfolds after the second. Suppose that months have passed and you're recovering from your gunshot wound. You're walking along the same street and once again, you observe the same assailant, still at large, perpetrating another crime against a different victim. You still feel confident, but based on your experience, you also feel a cautious apprehension, much more fear than you did the first time around. But this time, you address the situation more carefully, and, thus, you find a way to disarm the assailant without suffering any further injury, alert the police, and he is taken into custody. In this third scenario, you displayed the virtue of courage, the mean between the vices of cowardice and rashness. On the seesaw that is life, you found your way, through trial and a near fatal error, to the middle ground on which to balance yourself. Similar scenarios apply to each of the virtues Aristotle lists. Like with Plato, the common thread between them is moderation, since the development of each virtue demands that we find the mean between extremes. Moreover, one cannot be virtuous without exposure to the situations that present the opportunity to act from the emotions within the domain of each virtue. That is, without the opportunity to be courageous, without the feelings of fear and confidence that such situations evoke, you will never have courage. And without continuous exposure to such situations and the exercise of rational deliberation within each of them, you can never be truly happy.

Virtue itself, while a necessary condition for happiness, is not enough to achieve happiness. There are two additional criteria yet to be addressed, each of which concerns the *specific activity* in which one must engage to live the best possible life. So far, the criteria for the best possible life are that it must be a continuous, rational activity done with virtue. But what is the activity? If this activity really equates to the best life possible, then it must be *ultimate*. That is, it cannot merely be a means to some other end. It must be the sort of activity that one undertakes for its own sake. Lastly, since this activity is not merely a means to some other end, it must be *self-sufficient*, making life worth living in and of itself. If one engages in this activity, then one needs nothing else. Aristotle considers several options.

The first option to consider is pleasure. This option is plausible in at least one way, since pleasure seems to be an end-in-itself. It is never a *means* to some other end. People engage in activities simply because of the pleasure such activities afford them. Eating, drinking, dancing, spending time with one's friends or romantic partner, viewing one's preferred medium of entertainment, reading literature, perusing art, and listening to music, for instance, all are done simply for the pleasure they evoke. However, pleasure fails to accommodate nearly all the other criteria on Aristotle's list. In the first place, pleasure is only temporary, fleeting. That is why the activities that cause pleasure must constantly be repeated. And the repetition of these activities can result in boredom, which results in the loss of the pleasure associated with them. If your favorite food is pizza, for instance, you would likely not enjoy it so much after eating it for 7 days in a row. Hence, not only does pleasure fail to meet the continuity criterion, but it is insufficient for human happiness. Moreover, the pursuit of some pleasures or pleasant activities requires no use of rationality. Thus, the pursuit of pleasure is not a distinctively human activity. Non-human animals experience pleasure, too. Lastly, pleasure can be pursued without virtue. In fact, some activities that evoke pleasure constitute the very *opposite* of virtue. Serial killers derive pleasure from stalking and murdering their victims. Rapists derive pleasure from dominating and controlling people weaker than them. Neither of these two groups constitute Aristotelian virtue. So, happiness does not consist merely in the pursuit of pleasure.

The next plausible option is the life that consists of the pursuit of wealth, or money. Some unspecified amount of money is most probably the first item anyone would wish for if given the opportunity. Contrary to popular opinion, money is not intrinsically a bad thing. Much good can come from the use of money. Money enables us to eat, live in nice homes, and maintain our health. Money may also be donated to charities to help those less fortunate, those who run the risk of death by disease and malnutrition simply because they lack money. But money is not intrinsically good either. It can be used to do bad things and it can be acquired unjustly. A person might become wealthy by robbing a bank, or once wealthy, a person can use their wealth to harm or oppress others. More importantly, money is only a *means* to some other end. It is primarily a medium of exchange. Thus, it is not ultimate. Furthermore, wealth, like pleasure, is only temporary, so, it is not self-sufficient. Wealth once accumulated can be lost. Thriving businesses fail and economies crash. Currencies can lose their value. And even if wealth lasts over one's lifetime, millionaires commit suicide on occasion.

To illustrate, consider an early episode of *The Twilight Zone* called, "A Nice Place To Visit." In this episode, a small-time thief named Henry Francis Valentine, who prefers to call himself "Rocky," is apparently shot and killed while fleeing a crime scene. When he awakes, a rotund white-suited man named Pip introduces himself to Rocky as his guardian angel. Skeptical at first, Rocky follows Pip to a lavish hotel room where he can apparently have whatever he desires simply by asking for it. He has an endless supply of clothes, money, women, and cars. He has the best food and finest wines he ever tasted. At a local casino, he always wins, regardless of the game. Rocky naturally draws the conclusion that he died and went to heaven. But after a while, Rocky's newfound good fortune begins to weigh on him, precisely because he has no idea what he did to deserve such an embarrassment of riches in the afterlife. He spent his entire life as a criminal and always figured that he belonged in "the other place." When he makes a trip to Hall of Records with Pip, Rocky's records reveal that he slaughtered animals as a child, and at the age of 8 organized a street gang. In Rocky's own words, "[He] just can't figure it." He resolves that at some point he did something very good that made up for all the bad in his life, and that "If it doesn't bother [God], it doesn't bother [him]." After a month passes, Rocky becomes increasingly frustrated and irritable. There is just simply no excitement in his life. He calls upon Pip, demanding to be sent to "the other place," at which point Pip, laughing maniacally, reveals to Rocky that "This *is* the other place!"[8]

While the events and dialogue of this episode carry many implications, their relevance to the topic at hand is clear: Money and wealth alone cannot provide happiness. In fact, they can be used to provoke the greatest state of unhappiness, since this "other place" is presumably an eternal hell. Moreover, what first provokes Rocky's agitation is that he "just can't figure" why he would ever go to heaven. And when he finally comes apart at the seams in the episode's final act, his frustration emanates from a lack of meaningful interactions and activities in what Pip describes as "[Rocky's] own private domain...created especially for him."[9] When Rocky asks if he can meet with some of his old friends, he is summarily rebuffed. Rocky, thus, deduces that the women, food, and various luxuries he now enjoys are merely "props." When he finally lashes out over his boredom he complains that "I never thought I would get bored with beautiful dames," and that even though he enjoys gambling, "...when you win *every* time, that's not gambling, it's charity!"[10] When Pip suggests that Rocky engage in a simulation of

---

[8] "A Nice Place to Visit," *The Twilight Zone,* written by Charles Beaumont, directed by John Braham, CBS, April 15, 1960.

[9] Ibid.

[10] Ibid.

his old vocation, Rocky rejects the prospect of such an escapade, since there is not much of a risk that he will be caught, unless of course Pip orchestrates his capture from the outset! The lack of meaning and utter ennui that settles into Rocky's own private hell establishes that without a goal that it is itself, sufficiently and ultimately meaningful, money not only fails to provide happiness, but also can prevent it.

The third option many people would not contest as an ultimate good, the life devoted to honor and achievement. Such things must be earned. As social creatures, one of the most basic desires people have is to be valued by others. And what better way is there to be valued than to earn recognition and status in the eyes of others through one's actions? Very few people would deny themselves the opportunity to be viewed by others as a hero. According to this life option, happiness can be achieved through some combination of good deeds for others and/or service to a government or institution, for which a reward is conferred upon the doer. A soldier who earns the Congressional Medal of Honor would qualify as making a special achievement. A philanthropist recognized as "Man" or "Woman of the Year" for their charity would also qualify, as would a professor at a university who earns the title of being "Distinguished" in some way. So, the sorts of people who are happy are those who earn distinctive achievements. The main problem with this sort of life is that it is always possible that one may be worthy of such an honor but not receive it. Conversely, one may not truly deserve such recognition, but get it anyway. That is, receiving an award, an honor, or some title of distinction, often depends more on the person or group of people who bestow them, rather than on those who receive them. Recall the fable of the Ring of Gyges from the previous chapter. It is entirely possible for a criminal to appear worthy of some honor. But what's more important is that an individual be virtuous and worthy of such distinction. Virtue should be pursued even if it does not, alone, equate to happiness. Moreover, if one truly is vindictive and treacherous, simply having recognition in the eyes of others will not make one happy. If a brilliant mastermind organizes a scheme to frame an innocent person for a crime and forge himself as a hero, then in order to maintain his cover, no one can ever truly know. That is, no one can ever truly recognize his brilliance! And if a person does nothing and receives an honor or distinction merely because those who bestow it are prejudiced in his favor, then such an honor is about as meaningful as the luxuries in Rocky Valentine's world. Hence, honor and distinction are not truly adequate for happiness. In addition, such honors and distinctions are temporary. There is always the possibility that they may be stripped away, and that their luster can fade away with time.

That leaves only one option, the life devoted to contemplation, the life devoted to pure, intellectual reflection. This option differs from the others on this list in that it is not an obvious choice. Pleasure, wealth, and honor or recognition many people will instinctively agree lead to ultimate happiness. When people think about the best possible life, the life of happiness, typically they think of life in which they have the resources to engage in the most pleasant activities and enjoy esteem and recognition by others. But as we have seen, there are many reasons why each of these items is insufficient for happiness. Why is the life devoted to contemplation the best life possible? There seem to be at least three reasons. First, such a life consists in the perfect augmentation of rationality. In that way, it is the most distinctively human. Human beings are the only animals capable of deep, abstract thought, the only animals who ponder the question of what it truly means to exist. Humans are the only animals, in fact, capable of considering what happiness is, in addition to the possible ways to achieve it. Furthermore, in order to be happy, one must be able to make sense of the reality of the world around them. In virtue of our rationality, we demand reasons for what happens. If an unfortunate event happens to one of us, we are naturally inclined to ask, "Why?" Why did burglars choose to rob *my* house? Why do *I* have this painful illness? Why did *I* lose my job? Why did the bank foreclose on *my* parents' house? Indeed, such questions demand answers, and the failure to obtain answers devastates contentment. What first provoked Rocky Valentine's frustration, remember, was a lack of understanding. And when he failed to understand his situation, everything became meaningless. In order to make peace with one's circumstances, one must understand why and how they came about. But such understanding requires the augmentation of reason by contemplation, whereby one thinks beyond one's mere situation and in terms of the broader reality of the world around them. Often, the shock of horrific and traumatic circumstances snap people out of their everyday, mundane attitudes and reveal to them how precious life is. In crisis situations, many people find themselves capable of feats of which they never thought themselves capable. Through contemplation, one becomes aware of the value of one's life and how all of one's experiences run together in a meaningful way. The discovery of such meaning allows one to live a truly happy life, since through such contemplation one will be able to deal effectively with anything thrown their way.

There is one additional reason, however, that Aristotle seemed to maintain that the life of contemplation is the best life possible. Such a life, Aristotle thought, is comparable to the life of God himself. Recall that Aristotle referred to the God of his system as the Prime Mover, or the Unmoved Mover. In his argument for the existence of a Prime Mover, Aristotle insists that both time and change are imperishable. That is, if time "begins," there would be time prior to its existence, just as if time "ends," there would be time after. Moreover, time is measured through change. Hence, the two exist eternally. Since time is measured through change, and since we notice change through motion, though, motion must be eternal as well. But whatever is in motion must have a cause. Hence, the cause of all motion must itself be eternal. And since such a being is eternal, it must be immaterial. So, it must be able to cause motion without physically interacting with any of the things that it moves. But the only way such a thing could move other things without making physical contact is if such a thing *draws everything to itself by acting as an object of desire, or a final cause.* Therefore, there exists an eternal, immaterial being that is the first and unmoved cause of all motion. It moves everything by acting as an object of desire, the final cause of all things. But since such a being is completely immaterial yet engaged in an activity of some kind, the only possible activity that it can be engaged in is pure thought. Aristotle, in fact, describes the Prime Mover as thought thinking itself.[11]

In terms of human happiness, since the Prime Mover is the best and most blessed thing that there is, and its activity consists purely of thought, the life devoted to pure contemplation imitates the divine. Such a life engages in the very activity that the Prime Mover uses to draw everything toward itself. Hence, to engage in contemplation is not only to be happy, but to approximate a way of living that potentially transcends life itself![12]

Aristotle and Bacon's Idols of the Mind

As with Plato, Aristotle's various works predated Bacon's conception of the Idols of the Mind by over 1,000 years. However, he seemed to address himself to the concerns raised by Bacon's idols in the construction of his philosophy. First, I will examine how Aristotle's philosophy addresses each of Bacon's idols, and then I will consider the extent to which Aristotle avoids such tendencies for error himself.

Aristotle and Bacon's Idols of the Tribe: Aristotle's philosophy seems to address Bacon's idols of the tribe in at least three ways. First, Aristotle's

---

[11] For an accessible but more thorough account of this argument, see Mortimer Adler's *Aristotle For Everybody: Difficult Thought Made Easy*, New York, NY: Touchstone, 1997.

[12] A good place to find accessible selections from Aristotle himself is Wall's *On Human Nature*. For passages on Airstotle's conception of the soul, see the selections from Ross's translation of *De Anima*, specifically pp. 119–121, which focus on the mind, and pp. 122–125, which discuss soul more generally. The selections from *Nicomachean Ethics* are taken from Book I, the subject of which is the Good (pp. 125–129), Book II, the subject of which is Moral Virtue (pp. 129–133), and Book X, the subject of which is Contemplation (pp. 133–136).

conception of learning emphasizes realism and the improvement of understanding, the process by which one moves from confusion to distinctness. In so doing, people come to understand that which is less known through that which is more known, or that which is unfamiliar through that which is more familiar. For example, imagine learning the meaning of a new word. Typically, you would discover the meaning of such a word in a dictionary. But what do dictionary definitions do? They provide more familiar terms by which you can understand new ones. Moreover, Aristotle created the first sophisticated system of logic, contributing the concept of the syllogism to logic. Hence, he established logic and reasoning as a science, the primary tools by which to avoid Bacon's idols.

Second, Aristotle's distinguished both the mind from the soul and sensation from thinking. Recall that for Aristotle, the human soul is mortal, it is, like other souls, a set of abilities or capacities, the form of the body. However, as rational creatures, humans have both the power of sensory cognition and intellectual cognition. The former, for Aristotle, always reflects the reality of the world that is sensed. Basically, reality is the world that can be readily observed. Sensory cognition breaks down into two categories – external and internal. Through external sensation, one receives the form of the object sensed without the matter. Furthermore, Aristotle carefully distinguishes the objects of sensory cognition. Those items that can be perceived by only one sense he terms the *proper objects* of sensation. For instance, only the sense of sight can perceive colors. For hearing, the proper objects are sounds. For the sense of smell, the proper objects are aromas or odors. For the sense of taste, the proper objects are commonly referred to as olfactory senses, which are the tastes of food – sweetness, sourness, bitterness, and saltiness. For the sense of touch, the proper objects are primarily textures (roughness and smoothness), temperatures (heat and cold), and how wet or dry something is. The *common objects* of sensation may be perceived by more than one sense. These include shape, size, and location. For instance, to know the shape of an object, one may merely look at the object, or one may feel it. Lastly, an incidental object of sensation refers to the total object that is sensed – a red ball, a blue square, etc.

As for the internal senses, Aristotle lists four: memory, imagination, common-sense, and estimative sense. The internal sense of memory consists in the recall of a previous experience, an event that, in fact, happened. One has a sensation of the event but in the absence of the physical trigger. Imagination consists of an experience that one makes up, or invents, although the products of the imagination are always based on real experiences. The common-sense functions as a coordinator between the five external senses and the other internal senses. For instance, suppose that you hear a faint chirping emanating from outside your bedroom window. You remember from a previous experience that only a pigeon chirps in such a way. Hence, you deduce that there is a pigeon outside your bedroom window. Your external sense of sound coupled with your internal sense of memory came together allowing you to make a judgment. When you reason in this way, you use the faculty of common-sense. Finally, the estimative sense enables us to make judgments of value. Notice that the term "estimate" is part of the word. When one estimates, one merely takes a guess at how much or how little of something there is without knowing, precisely. The estimative sense allows us to make educated guesses about the value of our experiences. For example, suppose that you are taking a philosophy course, and that your professor devotes 50 out of 75 minutes focusing on a specific topic, such as Aristotle's theory of virtue. You judge that since your professor spent so much time on the subject, that questions about the topic will likely appear on the midterm exam. Your estimative sense allowed you to make such a judgment. The same sense also allows us to make judgments about danger and safety. For example, if you are walking down a dimly lit street late at night, you would likely deem that it is unwise to walk on the side next to an even darker alley, as there may be Vandals lurking. Again, the estimative sense facilitates such a judgment.

Whereas sensory cognition is responsible for the perception of items that frequently change, intellectual cognition is the process by which we perceive universal, or essences, that which remains permanent. Recall that Aristotle rejected Plato's theory of the forms, believing that form cannot be separated from matter in physical reality, but only in thought. Intellectual cognition allows the mind to do just that. Moreover, it is for this reason that Aristotle believed the human intellect to be fully spiritual, but nonetheless mortal![13] He seemed to believe this idea because while each sense has a very limited range (hence, the proper objects of external sense), there is nothing that the intellect cannot think about. For instance, it is possible to correlate sounds with visual imagery depicting different frequencies. Moreover, colors can become associated with temperatures, in which red signifies hot, blue, cold, and green, a lukewarm temperature. In addition, if one overstimulates any one sense, such overstimulation becomes obstructive. If light is too bright, it is impossible to see clearly. However, understanding a concept too clearly certainly does not obstruct one's understanding! Lastly, the mind is capable of abstracting from a singular, concrete object, since it can grasp essences or forms apart from matter. Each of these instances mark a difference between intellectual cognition and bodily senses, implying that the mind is, in fact, distinct from the body. However, since the mind remains a part of the soul, and since the soul is mortal, the human mind is mortal as well.

The final way in which Aristotle seems to address himself to Bacon's idols of the tribe is through his account of happiness. He makes it clear that happiness is not merely a matter of personal preference, but that objective conditions must be fulfilled to live the best possible life.

---

[13] Aristotle's term for the human intellect is the passive intellect, which contrasts with the active intellect. The difference between the two is that the latter can effectively create the reality that it thinks.

Failure to do so results in one's unhappiness. In connection with Aristotle's account of happiness is his doctrine of the mean, and his insistence that living a totally fulfilling life is a continuous process of development involving much trial and error, practice, and habituation. In this way, Aristotle suggests that happiness requires the proper training, the same sort of training that enables people to avoid the tendencies for error built into the very fabric of their nature. Just as it is human nature to seek happiness, it is also within human nature to try to find the quick and easy paths of least resistance to it. Ironically, as we learned from Rocky Valentine's trip to "the other place," human nature leaves those who take such routes forever empty and trapped in cycles of repetition devoid of meaning.

Aristotle and Bacon's Idols of the Cave: The most obvious way in which Aristotle recognizes these sorts of idols is through his account of happiness and the best life, but since I treated this concept in the previous section, I will here focus on two additional ways in which Aristotle addresses idols of the cave. Recall that idols of the cave refer to errors that arise from personal preferences and biases. Aristotle's doctrine of the mean seems specifically to address such tendencies for error. If one is too rash, or short tempered, for instance, or if one frequently overindulges oneself, such tendencies will likely transfer to the judgments one makes about the actions of others. To the rash person, the patient, calculating, and deliberate individual will likely be judged a coward. At the other extreme, the coward may judge a person who displays true courage as a fool who should have run the other way. To the individual who imbibes alcohol excessively, an individual who restricts their intake of the substance to one or two drinks may be judged as a prude who needs throw caution to the wind. Once again, at the other extreme, to the individual who never drinks, even the most modest drinkers may seem no better than full-blown alcoholics.

In connection with his doctrine of the mean, Aristotle's life options reflect different types of preferences and modes of living. There are people who devote themselves entirely to the pursuit of physical plea- sure – eating, drinking, having sex, and various other distractions from the stress of daily life. Even though such a life is not necessarily intrin- sically bad, ultimately it amounts only to a prolonged form of distrac- tion from that very stress, and from the struggle to be truly happy. Nonetheless, to simple hedonists, all other pursuits may be estimated as nothing more than a waste of time. We should all "eat, drink, and be merry, for tomorrow we may die!" Then, there are those who devote themselves entirely to the pursuit of wealth. Again, such a life is not inherently bad, and in most cases accumulating money requires work and shrewd thinking (unless of course one inherits all their money!). But wealth alone hardly qualifies as the greatest good to which one can devote one's life, primarily because it is only a means to another end. However, for those individuals to whom wealth is the only goal worth pursuing, the rest of us – especially liberals whose goal it is to change the world, or deep thinkers devoted to the proverbial "big questions" – ought to relinquish our trivial and impractical pursuits and set our heads to more pragmatic affairs, like making money! As for those whose chief goal it is to earn honor in the eyes of others, without such esteem and validation, nothing else matters, including those lives that may be sacrificed for the greater good. And lastly, the philosophers, those devoted to the life of contemplation, perhaps are inclined to see themselves as being above all others, superior to those trivial, earthly pursuits that can never yield complete fulfillment.

Aristotle and Bacon's Idols of the Marketplace: How does Aristotle's sys- tem combat the confusion that can arise over miscommunication and the meanings of words? The fact that Aristotle created the first sophis- ticated system of logic demonstrates his concern with these sorts of problems just as much as it does his concern for idols of the tribe. But his additional contributions of the distinction between substances and accidents, as well as his doctrine of the four causes also seem specifically to address the sorts of errors that arise from idols of the marketplace. Aristotle's distinction between substances and accidents arose largely in response to the inadequacies he discovered in Plato's account of predication. Plato's theory of the forms supposedly accounts for the general meaning of terms. The reason that anyone can use a general term such as "dog," "cat," "human," etc., is because there is a universal form corresponding to each term, serving as the basis of its meaning. But Aristotle noticed that such a solution raises more questions than it answers. While I already noted some of these problems, the one under consideration here concerns a basic fact about language and its evolution: Terms can be used in many ways without any strict principle unifying their meaning. For example, consider the term "good." It is possible for a person to be described as a good friend, a good husband or wife, a good father or mother, or good at whatever happens to be one's choice of vocation. Moreover, a person's diet can be described as good insofar as it is healthy, just as a tool can be described as good insofar as it serves its intended function. But the most popular sense of the term "good" is its moral sense. Certainly, it is possible for an individual to be good at his job, but not be a good man, just as it is possible for a man to be a good father to his son, even though he happens not be in a very unhappy marriage, and thus cheats on his spouse. Such indiscretions certainly would not make such a man a good husband, even though he still provides for and offers tutelage to his son after his marriage dissolves. Thus, there just seems to be no general sense that unifies the various meanings of "good." Aristotle maintained that general terms such as "good" are used analogically, or comparatively based on the context of their usage. The substance/accident distinction is the basis for this account of predication because the distinction provides a more practical and natural account of the relationship between objects and their properties.

As for Aristotle's doctrine of the four causes, each was described at length above. But Aristotle made such distinctions to accentuate and encourage the development of complete and lucid explanations of natural phenomena. Such clarity may only be achieved if the various types of causes are not conflated with each other. Aristotle applies this distinction himself in the analysis of humanity.

Aristotle and Bacon's Idols of the Theater: Aristotle had a great sense of history and the thinkers who preceded him. Thus, his system shows a deep sensitivity to idols of the theater, since Aristotle did not merely subscribe to the ideas of the thinkers that preceded him, but rather built his own system through critical synthesis. Predominantly, Aristotle addresses these sorts of idols through his understanding and resolution of the problem of change and permanence in addition to his various criticisms of Plato. The problem of change and permanence can be stated in the following way: How can reality remain the same when it consists of so many different things? Plato's solution consisted in his theory of the forms. Physical reality changes, but they are grounded in the permanent, eternal, and reality of the forms. While Aristotle clearly had qualms with this theory, he also paid respect to the resolutions of the pre-Socratics, especially the argument of Parmenides on the impossibility of change. For Aristotle, change occurs, but always within a substance or subject. A substance remains permanent, its attributes, or accidents, can change.

Aristotle's sense of history also afforded him the material for his doctrine of the four causes. The earliest pre-Socratics and even the later ones, such as Democritus and Leucippus, all had a strong sense of material and efficient causes. The Pythagorean notion that numbers are the basis of reality emphasized the importance of formal cause. This idea inspired Plato, but Aristotle's mentor also hit upon the notion of final cause, especially in terms of his conception of the form of the good. Aristotle systematically and explicitly combines and applies them all.

Lastly, Aristotle, like many other thinkers to be addressed in this book, seemed profoundly to be inspired by the Heraclitean maxim that "war is the father of all things," especially in terms of his account of happiness.

Not only does one have to engage in a lifelong process of development through much trial and error in order to achieve virtue, but such a process will inevitably involve a struggle. And a journey that's difficult is much more rewarding than the quick and easy path. The road to eudaimonia is long and hard, achieved only if one is willing to augment one's abilities independently through experience. There is no simple and easy blue-print to be given for such a task.

Did Aristotle Succumb to any of Bacon's Idols? There will always be a measure of difficulty in assessing a thinker in terms of some of Bacon's idols, especially idols of cave, since to give an accurate estimation on such a topic demands knowledge of the preferences of the thinker in question. Nonetheless, despite his majesty in the canon of Western thought, many criticisms can be made of Aristotle. The way in which he seems to be most vulnerable to the idols of the tribe is in his epistemology. Aristotle assumes a basic form of naïve realism. That is, the world basically just is what we experience, and, thus, all knowledge arises from sense-experience. This idea marks a major departure from his predecessors, especially Plato, and seems to underestimate the potential for sensory illusions and their implications. Moreover, he acknowledges that there is, in fact, a difference between an object that is sensed and the sense-perception itself, which implies, at the very least, a soft distinction between mind and reality and the view that what we experience are predominantly representations of the real world.

With respect to idols of the cave, Aristotle came from a family firmly rooted in naturalism. And his system, unsurprisingly, places far greater emphasis on the natural world than did Plato's. Whether Aristotle maintained such a position purely out of bias is unlikely, but it is a somewhat dubious coincidence that such an analytical thinker like Aristotle would so strongly endorse a perspective on reality that most certainly was instilled within him at an early age. Furthermore, the fact that he fudges on this matter casts an even more dubious shadow on his commitment to naturalism, as I will discuss below.

As for idols of the marketplace, the primary point of vulnerability in Aristotle concerns his description of the human mind and its relation to the soul. Recall that Aristotle defines the soul as the "first *act* of a living body that has life *potentially*." The soul, thus, is part of the body insofar as it is the form of the body. But then, Aristotle distinguishes the mind apart from the soul, as though it were a faculty. Aristotle's term for the human mind is the *passive intellect*, which is fully spiritual for reasons discussed above. Aristotle later contrasts this intellect with *agent intellect*, or the *active intellect*, which can effectively create the reality it thinks. The chief difference between the two is that the active intellect has no distinction between actuality and potentiality, since whatever it thinks is real rather than merely possible. But if Aristotle is to remain consistent, the only possible mind that the active intellect could be is the mind of God, the Prime Mover, which illuminates the passive intellect as an efficient cause of understanding. Later thinkers, especially Islamic and Christian philosophers, identified the active intellect with God. Here's the problem: if the human mind is part of the soul, then it is mortal even though it is spiritual; but Aristotle maintains that *the final cause of humanity is pure contemplation, which can only be achieved by a fully spiritual being*. It is, thus, unclear, whether Aristotle believed that once a person achieves happiness, or eudaimonia, that individual becomes a God. Moreover, if the soul gives life to the body, and the mind is a part of the soul, an ability built into humanity, then how could it ever be separate from the body? It seems that either it cannot, or that Aristotle must commit to the possibility of immortality.

In connection with this last problem is Aristotle's potential vulnerability to the idols of the theater. Aristotle's conception of the active intelligence seems to indicate that he never fully escaped the doctrines of his mentor, as it is a heavily Platonic notion. Moreover, Aristotle's considerations of the different options of life are very similar to those found in Plato. The life of pleasure and wealth loosely corresponds to the artisan class, who manufacture the objects needed to meet basic needs and desires and whose lives are devoted to the accumulation of money. The life devoted to honor loosely corresponds to the life led by the guardian class, who devote their lives to protecting the citizens through service to the city. The life devoted to contemplation loosely corresponds to the life led by the ruling class, who must possess knowledge of what is understanding and the development of a grand unified theory of everything. But such an achievement sounds very similar to Plato's conception of noetic insight through the Form of the Good. Moreover, given his reflections on the active intellect, Aristotle was not totally immune to such an idea, although he endorsed a much different version of it.

In conclusion, the chapter opened with an implied question about which of the two greatest thinkers of the west should be followed, Plato or Aristotle? The answer to that question can be rephrased: Is physical life merely a "cave of illusions" to be transcended, or is it a world of real experiences to be discovered and more perfectly understood? With respect to human beings, a similar question can be posed: Are people spirits trapped within bodies, liberated by death, and then eternally reborn, or are they animals with rational abilities? Perhaps the two sets of questions diverge, since the thought of Plato and Aristotle may be more closely aligned than Herman's thesis implies, given Aristotle's remarks on the nature of human happiness and virtue, in addition to the implications of his prescription for human fulfillment as the life of contemplation. Both giants of thought seem to agree that humans are more than mere animals, and that the meaning of life requires transcendence beyond the mundane frivolities of everyday life. Nonetheless, the answer as to which of these two magnificent thinkers will ultimately win the "battle for the soul of western civilization" cannot be answered here, and it will be left to the readers to read more deeply and critically the writings of both and make an autonomous and informed decision.

Chapter 2 Worksheets

1. What do you think of Herman's thesis about Plato and Aristotle? Try finding some examples from your own life and from other courses of study that support this claim. Can you ascertain any evidence against Herman's thesis?

2. In addition to the points of comparison and points of contrast made by the author, are there any other ideas that Plato and Aristotle agreed about? Are there any other ideas they disagreed about?

3. Apply Aristotle's conception of the four causes to some of the items that you encounter in your daily life. Can this conception of causality be applied more abstractly, such as to groups, corporations, governments, countries, cultures, or perhaps to behaviors?

4. Find a movie or an episode of television that illustrates any of Aristotle's ideas. How does your chosen medium do so?

5. Find a person from your personal life, history, or a character from any fictional work and indicate whether your chosen figure meets Aristotle's criteria for virtue and for overall flourishing.

6. Are there any connections between Aristotle's concept of the Prime Mover and the concept of God as described in any of the world's three major monotheistic religions – Judaism, Christianity, or Islam? If so how? Does Aristotle's concept of the soul overlap with the concept of a person in any of these traditions?

7. Apply Aristotle's criteria for happiness to your own life. Are there any areas of your life in which Aristotle would want you to improve, and if so, how?

The Legacy of Plato and Aristotle— Hellenistic Philosophy, Christianity, Augustine, and Aquinas

People are often willing to destroy themselves and the world around them to improve the conditions of life, measures that are, ironically, unnecessary. Christianity, the single most influential religion the world has ever seen, begins with the shared tendency among people to make things worse but always with the intention to make them better. Along with the ideas of the most influential philosophers the western world produced, Christianity produced a rich heritage of scriptures and thinkers, two of which are the focus of this chapter – St. Augustine and St. Thomas Aquinas. Many centuries of thought, however, stand between these two pillars of what is called the Medieval Tradition and the thinkers of Greek antiquity. Hence, this chapter is organized into the following parts: (I) a brief discussion of the Hellenistic tradition of thought following the death of Aristotle; (II) a brief overview of the Bible and the basic principles of Christianity; and (III) an overview of the themes of the writings of Augustine and Aquinas purely through the lenses of Bacon's Idols.

(I) The Hellenistic Tradition

After Aristotle's death, Greece entered a period of political and cultural decline traditionally referred to as the Hellenistic period, which began roughly with the death of Alexander the Great in 323 B.C.E and ended in 31 B.C.E. Given that the Greeks were absorbed into the burgeoning Roman Empire, the major philosophies that emerged during this period were perpetuated mainly by the Romans. The three major schools of thought associated with the Hellenistic period are Epicureanism, Stoicism, and Skepticism.[1]

Epicureanism: Epicureanism is based largely on the teachings of Epicurus (341–270 B.C.E.). In today's world, this philosophy has become associated with gluttony and sensuality, and the mantra that we all ought to "eat, drink, and be merry, for tomorrow we die!" This idea, however, represents a perversion of the teachings of Epicurus. In fact, such a misrepresentation of Epicureanism is in some ways the exact opposite of the philosophy. While the ideas of Plato and Aristotle were built on solid, intricate metaphysical foundations, the thinkers of the Hellenistic period focused more on the practical question of how we should live. Epicurus, however, did have some metaphysical presuppositions, mostly based in the materialism of Democritus. Recall that Democritus maintained an early atomic theory, the idea that reality, at bottom, consists of tiny indivisible atoms constantly smashing into each other and forming bonds that give rise to the visible structures of reality, constantly undergoing change. Based on this outlook, good and evil may be defined purely in terms of pleasure and pain, in which the good is that which produces pleasure and the bad is that which produces pain. Hence, Epicurus believed that the goal of life is the pursuit of *physical pleasure* and the avoidance of *physical pain,* as determined by human desires.

Epicurus distinguished between two types of desire – natural and artificial. Natural desires consist of the desire for food, water, sleep, sex, and various other physiological drives. Artificial desires consist of the desire for lavish clothing, extravagant décor, and perhaps some expensive "toys." Natural desires further break down into necessary and unnecessary. For example, the desire for food, water, and sleep are

---

[1] There is a fourth school of thought in the Hellenistic tradition – Neo-Platonism. But I chose to reserve my discussion of this topic for the section devoted to St. Augustine.

natural and must be satisfied to ensure the survival of the person. The desire for sex, on the other hand, may be neglected without disrupting a person's basic survival. In short, Epicurus diagnoses the human condition as devoted to the pursuit of desires that are either totally artificial, or unnecessary. Such desires lead to pursuits that often result only in more pain for the individual. If one becomes romantically involved, one's partner may die. Or, one's romantic pursuits may be met only with rejection, leaving the feelings unrequited. The pursuit of fancy decorations and gadgets forces one constantly to compare oneself to others, addressing oneself to the possibility of judgment, and compelling the waste of resources that could be used more prudently. Hence, the goal of life is to train oneself to overcome the desire for both artificial and unnecessary desires, and in so doing, one can devote oneself to rest and repose. Note the similarity with the teachings of Buddha, specifically, the noble truths that (1) life is full of suffering, (2) attachment is the root of suffering, and (3) suffering can be overcome. While Epicurus did not prescribe the eightfold path to overcome suffering, his suggestion is, arguably, simpler and easier to follow.

In addition, Epicurus's contributions to the meaning of death is noteworthy. As a materialist, Epicurus maintained that there is no God and no afterlife. The only thing we can really be afraid of is physical pain, a sensory phenomenon that can only affect us while we are alive. Since death consists only of the cessation of physical senses, death cannot harm us. And since there is no need to fear that which cannot harm us, there is no need to fear death. Thus, not only does Epicurus provide a way to overcome the sufferings brought about by needless attachments, but he also provides a consolation on the universal fear of the inevitable death that we all will experience. The problems, however, are that his consolation says very little about the fear of the process of dying, which can be extremely painful. And whatever causes death certainly can be deemed harmful and worth fearing. But more importantly, Epicurus's teachings leave little room for the drives of ambition and the search for deeper meaning that motivate many of us.

Had his ideas been more influential, perhaps the world never would have seen the resources it has today. While the prospect of repose is enticing, it can easily manifest itself as an unbearable ennui that is far worse than death!

Stoicism: The founder of Stoicism was the Greek philosopher Zeno of Cyprus (334–262 B.C.E.). Additional famous thinkers associated with Stoicism were the Roman statesman, Seneca (4 B.C.E–65 C.E.), Epictetus, author of the *Enchiridion*, and the Roman Emperor Marcus Aurelius (121–180 C.E.). Like Epicureanism, Stoicism embraced a form of materialism comparable to the ideas of many pre-Socratic philosophers and concerned itself primarily with the practical question of how we should live. Unlike Epicureanism, the Stoics insisted that the goal of life is the pursuit of *virtue* rather than pleasure. Virtue, however, meant something quite different for the Stoics than it did for previous virtue ethicists, such as Plato and Aristotle. The Stoics insisted that much of what happens is beyond our control, and the attempt to impose our will on that which is entirely beyond our control results in misery. Ultimately, the Stoics insist that we ought to train ourselves so that we want only what the universe wants. If everyone were to train oneself in such a way, then everyone would always get what they want. The term for the state of mind achieved when one reaches this state is *ataraxia*, a kind of detached, emotional indifference. The term "stoic," in fact, has come to refer to an individual who shows very little emotion, as the Stoics insisted. Since even extreme events, be they very fortunate for us, or disastrous for us, are beyond our control, we should not display extreme happiness or sadness at anything that happens.

In addition, also like Epicurus, the Stoics provided a consolation on death that aligns with their unique principles. The Stoics insist that reality could not impose on us anything that we could not handle. Moreover, even if it did, then at a certain point, we would simply lapse into unconsciousness and feel no more pain. Hence, we should confront death with the same attitude of detached resignation as anything else in life. They do, however, leave open a provision for suicide. If an individual achieves ataraxia, but life imposes on that individual some incurable form of suffering that threatens it, then that individual would be justified in committing suicide. On the face of it, this addendum seems to be a contradiction, as if one achieves ataraxia, one would be indifferent to one's own suffering. However, if a condition really is terminal, and will result in death, then the act of suicide may, in that case, be considered acceptance and commitment to what is inevitable.

Overall, Stoicism can provide comfort in especially difficult times. But if one embraces its principles fully, one seems committed to the idea of a fatalistic universe. The problem raised by this idea is that the very act of conditioning oneself to want what the universe wants depends on some minimal amount of free will that can, in fact, stand apart from the events of life. If, in fact, one can train one's mind to be resigned to the ways of the universe, then not everything can be fated to happen, otherwise, one's very emotions would be fated to happen! Emotions, however, are at least in part under an individual's control, as they emerge from the ways in which one interprets a situation and expects it to unfold. One cannot become angry with a person unless there is the expectation that such a person ought to act in a way contrary to their actual behavior, just as one cannot be happy unless the trigger of one's happiness meets one's expectations. In short, Stoicism seems to imply fatalism, but the prescription to train one's emotions renders fatalism extremely dubious, if not false.

Skepticism: The last group of thinkers to be treated in this section, the Skeptics, are the most radical and, in some ways, the most influential on several modern ways of thinking that will be addressed in later chapters. Major figures associated with this school of thought are Pyrrho, the founder of Pyrrhonian Skepticism, Sextus Empiricus (roughly 250–327 C.E.), the best known of the skeptics, and Arcesilaus, the founder of Academic Skepticism. Basically, the skeptics cast doubt on virtually all claims to knowledge. Knowledge, in their view, would be limited primarily to principles of logic, mathematics, and in some cases, sensory experiences, although some denied even the veracity of the senses. Like the Stoics, the Skeptics maintained that we ought to strive to achieve a state of ataraxia, but by suspending all judgments and claims to knowledge. The main problem with Skepticism is that if it were taken seriously, it would be impossible to live life. One would doubt the very existence of the people one meets, the uniformity of the world one inhabits, whether one's life is real, or only an intricate dream concocted by an evil demon. The figure who is the subject of the next chapter, Rene Descartes, raises these very questions, but provides a more efficient resolution to them.

(II) The Bible and Christianity

The three major monotheistic religions of the world are Judaism, Islam, and the focus of this section, Christianity. In addition to being monotheistic, what they also have in common is that they trace back to Abraham, the putative father of the Israelites. Since they trace back to Abraham, all trace their origins, in some way, to the Judeo-Christian Bible, or the Bible, as it is more commonly known. The major sub-division of this seminal book is between the Old and New Testaments. The religion of Judaism is based predominantly on the writings of the Old Testament, which the Jews refer to as the Tanakh. The vast majority of Islam is based on a book called the Qu'ran, a series of revelations delivered piecemeal to Mohammed, believed by the Muslims to be the final messenger of God, known as "Allah" in Islam. However, Mohammed's bloodline traces back to Abraham's illegitimate son, Ishmael. Moreover, the Qu'ran acknowledges the majority of both the Old and New Testaments, although it reinterprets many stories and Biblical vignettes to accommodate the revelations supposedly delivered to Mohammed directly. While Christianity acknowledges both the entire Old and New Testaments as scripture, its practitioners also profess faith in Jesus Christ, who is believed to be the son of God and the savior of humanity. In the pages the follow,

I will provide a brief overview of the themes of the Bible and of the distinctive features of Christianity.

The Bible – A Very Brief Overview: The Bible, as it is understood today, technically, is not a single work crafted by one person, but rather an anthology, a collection of writings from many authors compiled over a period of roughly 1500 years. The Old Testament, or the Hebrew Bible, is believed to have been written 500 to1000 years before the compilation of the New Testament. The first five books of the Old Testament, the Torah, are believed to have been written by Moses. The first book of the Bible, Genesis, devotes its first 11 chapters to a story of universal human history, in which God creates the heavens and the earth, and all things within them, including humans. Adam and Eve are the first humans, living together in harmony in a paradise called the Garden of Eden. However, a serpent (traditionally believed to be Satan) tricks them into eating fruit from a forbidden tree, after which they are expelled from the Garden. They have two sons, Cain and Abel, the former of which murders the latter, and is subsequently exiled with a mark upon him as protection. Cain founds the first city, Canaan. Eventually, God becomes frustrated with humanity and destroys the entire world with a flood, saving only a righteous man named Noah, and his family, who then must repopulate the earth. There is also a fable about a tower, Babel, which people tried to build in order to reach into the heavens. God, however, confuses their language, so they cannot complete it.

Soon after, the narrative of Genesis switches to the history of the Israelites, beginning with an elderly couple, Abraham and Sarah. God comes to them in a dream telling them to leave their land, promising to them a son, progeny, and a powerful kingdom, of which Abraham will be the patriarch. As previously mentioned, Abraham has an illegitimate son, Ishmael, whom he disowns, and later has the child God promised, Isaac. Isaac has two sons, Jacob and Esau. While Esau is the firstborn, Jacob hoodwinks him out of his birthright and flees.

He then spends 21 years as an indentured servant, marrying the daughter of his host and bearing 12 children, later returning to his homeland. On the night of his return, he is confronted by and combats a stranger, revealed to be the angel of God. After the struggle, Jacob is renamed "Israel," meaning "he who struggled against the angel of God." He reconciles with his brother and raises his family. His favorite son, Joseph, is sold into slavery by his brothers out of jealousy. Joseph, however, eventually curries favor with the pharaoh of Egypt due to his ability to interpret dreams. He predicts a famine that will happen within 7 years and helps the pharaoh to take precautions against it. He is later reunited with his brothers and his father. At this point, the book of Genesis ends.

Most of the rest of the Old Testament is devoted to the history of the Israelites, the descendants of Joseph. Eventually, a new pharaoh emerged, who "knew not Joseph," and he enslaved the Israelites for 400 years. The books of Exodus, Leviticus, Numbers, and Deuteronomy detail the escape of the Israelites from captivity, led by the surrogate brother of the pharaoh, Moses, to whom God revealed Himself in the form of a burning bush, compelling Moses to lead the Israelites to their homeland promised to Abraham eons prior. Once escaping the Egyptians, the Israelites spend 40 years wandering through a desert, as punishment for their grievances against the God who delivered them. After the death of Moses, Joshua becomes the leader of the Israelites, and the book by the same name details the various escapades of the Israelites under his leadership. The Book of Judges details the steady downward spiral of Israel into moral depravity, also devoting attention to the various authorities among the Israelites who succeeded Joshua (the "Judges"). Of note are Othniel, Ehud, Deborah, Gideon, Jephthah, and, perhaps the most famous of all, Samson, whose strength derived from his hair.

The books of 1st Samuel through 2nd Chronicles essentially tell a continuous story of the development of the kingdom of Israel. Samuel, the last judge of Israel, nominates a king for the Israelites, as they expanded greatly and needed central leadership. He chooses Saul, who is anointed by God, and is an effective king. Saul, however, soon loses God's favor. He is replaced by David, chosen by God directly. David slays the Philistine champion, a giant named Goliath, using a sling shot. He becomes a great warrior and leader of Israel. Despite spiraling into moral depravity of his own, David repents of his sins. The books of 1st and 2nd Kings tell the tale of Solomon, David's son and successor to the throne of Israel. Solomon refurbishes the temple and Israel flourishes under his rule. The kingdom soon, however, becomes divided as a result of a schism instigated by one of Solomon's servants, Jeroboam. Solomon's son, Rehoboam, was in line to become King, but Jeroboam demanded lighter taxes, which Rehoboam refused. As a result, 10 of the tribes rejected Rehoboam and anointed Jeroboam as their king. These 10 tribes became the northern kingdom, and the 2 tribes remaining loyal to the legacy of David became known as Judah.

Given Israel's increasing divisiveness and moral depravity, God sent the prophets to warn Israel of her impending punishment. There are 16 books in the Bible devoted to the prophets, the four major prophets – Jeremiah, Daniel, Ezekiel, and Isaiah, and 12 minor prophets – Hosea, Joel, Amos, Obadiah, Jonah, Micah, Nahum, Habakkuk, Zephaniah, Haggai, Zechariah, and Malachi. Amos produced one of the strongest messages: "You of all the nations have I known, therefore, I will punish you," (Amos, 3: 2). The message not only is one of immanent punishments, but also disappointment. God delivered and protected the Israelites, making them a very powerful people. But the general moral failings of the Israelites demonstrated that they were unworthy of God's blessing. God gave so much to the Israelites that He demanded more of them. The form this punishment took was the destruction of the temple of the Israelites by the Babylonians and their subsequent captivity lasting from 586 B.C.E until 506 B.C.E.

When the Babylonians were overthrown by the Persian Empire, led by Cyrus the Great, Cyrus commissioned the rebuilding of the temple of Jerusalem and put Ezra in charge of gathering what remained of the Hebrew scriptures to synthesize what is now the Hebrew Bible. Our modern Bible is based on a Greek translation of the Hebrew Bible that began around 250 B.C.E., the *Septuagint*.

Other authors carried on the message of the prophet Amos, but also prophesized about a savior who would remove the curse of the Fall. Specifically, Isaiah conveys just such a message, suggesting that there will be a universal peace between humans and animals, and that the Kingdom of God will be inaugurated by the Messiah (65: 23–25). Christians believe that Jesus Christ was this savior, which brings us to the subject of the New Testament.

The New Testament is believed to have been written 50 to 75 years after the death of the Christ. It basically consists of three groups of writings. First, it contains supposedly first-person accounts of the life and ministry of Jesus Christ, the four gospels, Matthew, Mark, Luke, and John. Second, it contains writings on the Early Christian Church. These writings include the letters of Paul, the Acts of the Apostles, and general letters by various authors. Lastly, it contains a book of apocalyptic visions of the end times, the Book of Revelation (believed to be written by the same author as the Gospel of John, John of Patmos), which supposedly details what will happen at the very end of the world, when God will bring everyone to judgment, the living and the dead. The major themes of Christianity are the subject of the next section.

Christianity – An Overview of Themes: Even though the themes of the Old Testament's writings shift in tone, a pattern repeats itself, even from the very beginning. God offers paradise to humans, but humans reject this paradise in favor of something that they believe will be even better, but their actions subsequently only make matters worse. Typically, the humans are punished by God in some way, but it is no worse than the circumstances brought about by their own actions.

Nonetheless, God still cares intensely for humans and protects them. As a professor of theology once told me, the narrative of the Bible represents God trying to get humanity back *into* the Garden of Eden, the paradise that was intended before the original sin of Adam and Eve. But for humanity to be reconciled with God, original sin would have to be washed away. The New Testament seems to tell the story of the reversal of original sin and the ultimate salvation of humanity. In short, God became a man, Jesus Christ, and died for the sins of mankind. Three days later, Jesus Christ rose from the dead, not only establishing that life after death is possible, but making eternal life possible for any and all people who profess faith in Him. There are four distinctive doctrines of Christianity: incarnation, redemption, resurrection, and the trinity.

First, the doctrine of incarnation suggests that Jesus Christ is not merely the son of God, but He is literally God, that is, God in human form. Supposedly, Jesus Christ was born to a virgin, Mary, in an immaculate conception. As God in the flesh, as a human being, it may be inferred that Jesus represents the complete realization of humanity, the fulfillment of what God intended the original human beings to be.[2] The opening words of John's Gospel make clear Christ's divinity: "In the beginning was the Word, and the Word was with

---

[2] As previously mentioned, the life and ministry of Jesus Christ is addressed by the Gospels, the first four books of the New Testament. The first three, Matthew, Mark, and Luke are usually referred to as the Synoptic Gospels, since they primarily summarize the various teachings and events in the life of Christ, whereas John's Gospel focuses on Christ's divinity, and, hence, is the most philosophical of the Gospels. Each of the synoptics also focuses on a specific aspect of Christ's character and being. Matthew focuses on Christ as the true king of the Israelites, and goes out its way to show that Christ's teachings are consistent with the Old Testament, especially in passages such as the Sermon on the Mount and the Beatitudes. Mark emphasizes the human aspect of Jesus, portraying him at his most vulnerable, establishing that Jesus kept his identity secret from most people since he was misunderstood by many. Luke is the most universal of the Gospels, establishing that Christ's mission is to save all humanity, not only the Israelites, hence, the meaning of parables such as the Good Samaritan. For passages that address the early life of Jesus see the following: John 1: 1–18, "the Word made Flesh," often called "the Logos," Matthew 1, and Luke 1: 26–38, for Jesus's birth announcement, Matthew 2: 1–12 and Luke 2: 1–40, for Jesus's birth, Matthew 2: 13–23, for Joseph and Mary's journey out of Egypt, Luke 2: 39–40, for Jesus's life in Nazareth, Luke 2: 41–52, for the trip to Jerusalem, Luke 1: 5–23, and 39–80, for an account of John the Baptist, and Matthew 3, Mark 1, Luke 3, and John 1, for Jesus's Baptism.

God, and the Word was God...The Word became flesh and made His dwelling among us," (1: 1–14). In addition, the two most prominent ways in which Christ is manifested as humanity fully realized are through his various miracles detailed in the Gospels and by overcoming the temptations of the devil. I will focus on the latter.[3] The temptations of Christ occur in Matthew 4: 1–11. While fasting in the desert for 40 days, Christ is tempted by Satan three times. First, he is tempted to turn stones into bread and sate his hunger. Second, he is transported to the top of the temple of Jerusalem and told to jump off and count on the angels of God to intervene and protect him. Lastly, he is offered all the kingdoms of the world if he will worship Satan. In each case, Christ refuses. The significance is that in each temptation, Satan uses a passage from scripture that calls back to the Fall, and Christ counters with a different passage from the Old Testament. Ultimately, the scene establishes that Christ succeeds where Adam and Eve failed. Moreover, some authors interpret the temptations of the devil as representing three fundamental life options, courses of life chosen by different people. The first represents people who are totally enslaved by their bodily desires, and, thus, seek the comfort and security of provisions. The second represents people who wish to escape life by losing themselves in what they believe are exciting adventures, thrill-seeking activities. And the third represents the desire for pure, unadulterated power. In each of the temptations, the devil's goal is to remove the burden of independence and free will from the tempted, offering to do all the work for him, thereby stifling the realization of the person's potential.[4] Since Christ is a manifestation of the full realization of humanity, and he overcomes these

---

[3] For passages in the New Testament that focus on Christ's miracles, see the following: Mark 2: 1–12, in which he forgives and heals a man who cannot walk, Mark 5: 1–20, in which he casts out a legion of demons from a man who lives among the tombs, Mark 5: 21–43, in which he heals a hemorrhaging woman and resuscitates a dying girl, John 6: 1–71, in which he feeds the masses with only two fish and five loaves of bread, and John 11: 1–44, in which he raises Lazarus from the dead.

[4] See Clyde F. Crews, *Ultimate Questions: A Theological Primer* (Paulist Press, 1986), especially Chapter 9, "Christ: The Ultimate Questioner."

temptations, for humanity to become fully realized, they must expose themselves to rigorous tasks and face uncertainty and the possibility of failure. After all, what is the worth of power if one could not achieve it on one's own? Such power is, ironically, only a manifestation of one's powerlessness.

The second distinctive feature of Christianity is the idea of redemption. That is, Christ was executed by crucifixion, a horrifically mortifying form of hanging developed by the Phoenicians and perfected by the Romans. Through Christ's death, human beings are redeemed, or absolved, of original sin. By simply accepting Christ as both God and savior, a person is forgiven for any sin they ever committed. For instance, if you accept Jesus Christ as your Lord and savior, then anything you ever did, thought about doing, or will do, is forgiven. He died for that sin, and bears the burden of the sins of the world. Through the process of Christ's death, one could say that a path of communication opened between God and humanity. Through the sacrifice of Christ, it is now possible for humanity to have life after death.

That leads to the third distinctive feature of Christianity, Christ's resurrection. On the third day after his death, Christ presumably rose from the dead, in the flesh, revealing himself to his circle of followers, his Apostles, thereafter. Not only does this event supposedly establish the possibility that there is life after death but serves as an indication that we will all be resurrected, in bodily form, on the last day, to be brought to final judgment before God. In order to be worthy of eternal life, we all must undergo a metaphorical resurrection of sorts, a spiritual rebirth in which we must be "dead" to our former selves. In Paul's letter to the Romans (8: 1–12), he draws a distinction between being "born of the flesh" and being "born of the spirit," in reference to this spiritual rebirth, calling back not only to Christ's literal resurrection, but also to his overcoming of the temptations of the flesh at the behest of Satan. But what, exactly, does it mean to be "born of the flesh?" We are all humans. We have bodies, and, hence, bodily needs. We need to eat and sleep, and we have sex drives to satisfy. Moreover, we require other materialistic goods to meet these needs, such as money. Does Paul literally mean that we should not eat or sleep? Does he mean that we should not work to earn wages? I doubt that. More likely, a person "born of the flesh" is one whose desire for such earthly goods interferes with his relationship with God, usually to the point that one would be willing to mistreat others only for one's own selfish gain, or to the point that one would disconnect from life altogether and live in leisure in his own private world of darkness, no better than a prisoner in Plato's cave. As a pastor once told me, "Money is only bad when it interferes in our relationship with God, and it interferes in that relationship primarily when our desire for it causes us to mistreat others."

Lastly, a concept that is deeply associated with Christianity is that of the trinity, the idea that God somehow exists in three *persons* but as one *substance*. The three persons are God, the father, Jesus Christ, the son, and the Holy Spirit. One way of understanding this concept is to suggest that God can be manifested in three different ways, in sort of the same way that a piece of clay can be shaped in different forms. As Himself, He is a formless, all-powerful, all-knowing, purely spiritual being. As a human, He is Jesus Christ. As the Holy Spirit, He is basically the voice of conscience that we all hear from time to time. If you do something that you know is wrong, and you feel guilt after, that feeling is the Holy Spirit compelling you to confess. If you ever feel compelled to donate money or personal items to those less fortunate than you, that feeling comes from the Holy Spirit working within you. If you were to stop along the highway to help a stranded motorist, it was, perhaps, the Holy Spirit that compelled you to do so. Theologically, it is through Christ that our awareness of the Holy Spirit is possible. God loved humanity so perfectly that he became a literal person to die for our sins. Moreover, the relationship between God and his "son" is itself one of the perfect unions. Hence, this relationship materializes in the form of a "personal voice" that speaks to humanity. Undeniably, the trinity is one of the most controversial and confusing topics in religious studies and cannot be further explored here.[5]

(III) St. Augustine and St. Thomas Aquinas

For roughly 300 years after the death of Christ, Christianity spread, mostly through the Roman Empire. This newly emerging religion encountered great difficulty, often due to the violent measures of repression taken against it by the Romans. However, in 313 C.E., the Roman Emperor Constantine became a Christian and made Christianity the official religion of Rome. For roughly 200 years thereafter, proponents of Christianity and early church fathers turned to a tradition of thought now called *Neoplatonism* as a way of establishing a philosophical basis for their religion. Neo-Platonism is, basically, a mystical form of the ideas of Plato. Its chief proponent was Plotinus (204–270 C.E.). Just like Plato before him, Plotinus insisted that absolute truth and knowledge cannot be obtained in the world of sense. Unlike Plato, however, Plotinus proposed that absolute knowledge can only be achieved through mystical union with "the One," the Absolute, or God, in place of Plato's form of the Good. The ontology of Plotinus runs parallel to Plato's analogy of the divided line, but also takes on the form of Pantheism. For Plotinus, all of reality consists in a series of emanations from God. These ideas heavily inspired the fathers of the early church and Christian philosophers. The most important of these philosophers was St. Augustine of Hippo (354–450 C.E.).

During his youth, St. Augustine latched onto a school of thought called *Manichaeism*, a Persian religion that emerged during the third century, whose basic idea is that reality consists in an eternal struggle

---

[5] For a more in-depth treatment of the Bible, see Chapter 6 of Stevenson's *Twelve Theories of Human Nature*, "The Bible: Humanity in Relation to God," in addition to Pojman's *Who Are We? Theories of Human Nature*.

between the forces of good and evil. This duality presents itself as the world of our experience, and the soul is a representation of the force of good, whereas the body is representation of the force of evil. After becoming disillusioned with *Manichaeism*, St. Augustine soon turned to Neo-Platonism. Augustine's thought can best be described as a defense of the basic teachings of Christianity based on the central concepts of Neo-Platonism. I will explore these basic ideas directly through Bacon's Idols of the Mind.

Augustine on Idols of the Tribe: Idols of the Tribe are the capacities for error shared by all humans, universally, based entirely on human nature itself. Hence, an author's general theory of human nature, the "tribe," reflects the way that author addresses those very idols. Augustine addresses Bacon's Idols of the Tribe primarily through his conception of reality and humanity's place in it. Not only is Augustine one of the most famous philosophers from the Christian tradition, but also one of the most important Neo-Platonists. Augustine essentially identified the God of Christianity with the "One" of Plotinus' philosophy. Since God created everything, all reality is, in some way, an extension of God's being, a *great chain of being*. Since God is good, everything that exists is good insofar as it came from God. Hence, something is only "bad" or "evil" insofar as it lacks reality, or lacks *being*. In other words, *evil is an absence of the good*, just as darkness is an absence of light, just as coldness is an absence of heat. In terms of Bacon's Idols of the Tribe, one could say that the human capacity for error is due to the very same sort of lack to which Augustine attributes evil.

Augustine's conception of evil has various manifestations. Many violent criminals, specifically those classified as psychopaths, and especially serial murderers, usually differ most prominently from those who are not prone to violence against others, from those who are not prone to cold-blooded murder, in that they *lack empathy*, in that they are devoid of the ability to assume the emotional viewpoint of other people and fully understand how their actions will affect them. The fall of humanity as described in the third chapter of Genesis lends itself as an illustration of evil as an absence of the good. When the serpent tempted Eve to eat fruit from the tree of the knowledge of good and evil, he insisted that despite God's command not to eat from that tree, he really would want humans to do so, since they would *be like God* if they did. What Eve forgets is that she is already created in the image and likeness of God, hence, is already like God, but in physical form. Humanity's lack of foresight and lack of the knowledge of God's plan and the full reality of God Himself leads to their attempt to transcend themselves and become more than what they are. As a result, they become self-aware and ashamed of their nakedness, hide from each other. The result of their sin is *alienation* from each other and from their original blissful unity, disconnection. This same alienation leads to the first murder, in which Cain kills his brother, Abel, and subsequently becomes the founder of the first city. The same disconnection that characterizes many violent criminals traces back to the first sin of all humankind and their attempt to achieve something greater than God intended.

For Augustine, in some way, all evil is characterized by an absence of being and manifests itself as humanity's desire for lesser goods, the desire for the wrong things. Recall that for Aristotle, the pursuit of pleasure, wealth, or earthly honor can never bring about true happiness, as such things are fleeting, ephemeral, will eventually fade away and perish. For Augustine, people seek out sensual pleasures and wealth hoping to find complete and total satisfaction and consistently fail. The only thing that can truly fulfill us, the one thing that we truly desire, is *God*.

Like Plato, Augustine maintained that all human beings are born with some innate knowledge. It is through such knowledge that we are aware of God, and we are, thus, restless until we find him. We are all, in some away, aware of our own finitude, since we all are aware of things greater than ourselves. The sun, the moon, the stars, the ocean, many of the creatures around us are all much bigger and much more powerful than us. Our awareness of the finite leads us to the concept of the infinite, which is God, Himself. Since God created everything, God can be found in everything. In other words, there are "signs" everywhere that lead humanity to God. Just as the human eyes need light to see, the human intellect needs divine illumination in order to have complete understanding. Just as light is an external source of revelation, so God is an external source of revelation to the human mind. Humanity, thus, can come to know God through the mediation of and by analogy with the natural world, as well as through the revelations of the scriptures.

Augustine's reasoning from humanity's awareness of God lent itself as a source of inspiration for what is now known as the ontological argument for God's existence. St. Anselm of Canterbury is credited with being its founder. Basically, the argument takes the form of what is called a *reductio ad absurdum*, or "reduction to absurdity." This form of proof begins by assuming the opposite of its intended conclusion and establishes that such an assumption leads to a contradiction. On that basis, the opposite of the original assumption must have been true all along. Anselm's version of the argument can be reconstructed in the following way:

1. Let's assume that God, the greatest conceivable being, that than which nothing greater can be thought, exists only in the mind alone, but not in reality.

2. It is greater to exist in reality than it is to exist in the mind alone. Surely, if one is hungry, it is better to have real, edible food, as opposed to imaginary food!

3. Based on (1) and (2), if God, the supposedly greatest conceivable being, existed only in the mind, but not in reality, there would be something *greater* than the greatest conceivable being.

4. However, it is impossible for there to be something greater than the greatest conceivable being.

5. Therefore, God must exist in reality, otherwise God would not be the greatest conceivable being.[6]

If this argument is sound, then God, surely, exists. Of note is how heavily Platonic the argument is, as Palmer notes in his discussion of medieval philosophy. Not only is the argument totally rationalistic, not relying at all on the empirical data of sense-experience, but it assumes that the best possible thing is also the most real, an idea inherent in Plato, Neo-Platonism, and Augustine.[7] The basic point is that human beings seem to have an innate awareness of the greatest possible thing, and an awareness that such a thing must indeed be real, and this thing we call God.

A question remains, however: If humanity has an innate awareness of God, the greatest possible thing, why do they still choose lesser goods? Augustine's answer, in short, is free will, and that is the primary subject of the next section.

Augustine on Idols of the Cave: Idols of the Cave refer to errors that arise from prejudices, biases, and personal preferences. Since the previous section addressed humanity's capacity for loving lesser goods, the current section is in some ways an extension of it. Augustine addresses the idols primarily through his conception of free will. The problem of evil motivated Augustine's intellectual pursuits prior to his discovery of Neo-Platonism. Recall that he entertained the Manichean school of thought during his youth. Traditionally, evil in the world is cited as

---

[6] The literature responding to this argument is enormous. While it is not my purpose to analyze this argument in detail, I will make note of Thomas Aquinas' criticism to it in the section devoted to his thought.

[7] See Donald Palmer's *Looking At Philosophy: The Unbearable Heaviness of Philosophy Made Lighter*, New York: McGraw-Hill, 2013, p. 126.

evidence that there is no kind of God. The argument usually relies on a supposed incompatibility between the following statements:

1. There is a God who is omnipotent (all-powerful), omniscient (all-knowing), and omnibenevolent (perfectly good).

2. There is evil in the world.

Supposedly, if (1) were true, then the only way that (2) could be true is if God either (a) is not powerful enough to prevent evil, (b) does not have knowledge of all the evil in the world, or (c) does not care to stop all the evil in the world. If God lacks the power to stop evil, then he is not all-powerful, and thus, not truly God. If God does not have knowledge of all the evil of the world, then he is not all-knowing, and thus, not truly God. If God does not care to stop all the evil of the world, then he is not perfectly good, and thus, not truly God. But since there is in fact evil in the world, "God" as traditionally understood, must lack at least one divine attribute. Hence, there can be no God.[8]

Disappointed with the Manichean resolution to the problem of evil, Augustine formulated his own solution, based largely on his own conception of evil and reality. Recall that Augustine conceived of all reality as extending from God. Hence, *prima facie*, if there is evil in the world, God would have to be the source, since He created everything. But also recall that for Augustine, evil is an absence of the good. Moreover, evil entered the world through humanity's free choice of the will. But why would God allow human beings to make choices if their choices bring evil into the world? Evidently, free will is worth the risk of evil, or worth the risk of the error in choosing lesser goods over those God intended. It is better that people have a choice between good and evil, rather than merely being programmed to follow a plan.

---

[8] This version of the problem of evil is sometimes called the "logical problem" of evil, since it maintains that divine attributes are incompatible with the existence of evil in the world. A second version, sometimes called the "empirical problem of evil," is *probabilistic*. That is, it emphasizes not the mere existence of evil in the world, but the fact that there is so much evil in the world that it cannot possibly serve any part of God's divine plan. Hence, it is *unlikely* that God exists. Augustine's response to both problems would reflect a version of what I refer to as the freewill defense.

For example, suppose that you are seeking a romantic companion. Imagine that you ask your closest friend for advice about who and where to find such a companion. You and your friend discuss the qualities of a good romantic partner and you ultimately develop both a strategy for finding such a person in addition to a scheme that outlines what you want in this person. Much to your surprise, you find a suitable companion very quickly, a person who has all the qualities you find endearing. You and this person see each other for several months and the relationship seems ideal. You propose to your companion, who accepts, and the two of you get married. But then your very close friend, whose counsel you sought before meeting your partner, is diagnosed with a terminal illness. You visit your friend in the hospital, virtually on his death bed. And he confesses to you: He set the whole thing up! Your partner is, in fact, not even a human being, but an android, a perfect replica of a human being, designed by your friend and preprogrammed to be your companion for as long as you should live. Granted, people may react differently to this difficult piece of news. There are some who may not be so disturbed by the prospect of having an eternally loyal and devoted companion. But I also have no doubt that most people would be profoundly disappointed and even *disgusted*. Not only would most people feel somewhat betrayed by their friend, despite his intentions, but most people would suddenly be repulsed, to some degree, by their companion, not merely because the android is not even human, but *because the android had no choice about its relationship*. People want to be *wanted* by others. For Augustine, God's relationship with humanity is no different. God wants human beings to choose Him over lesser goods. But in order to make such a choice, people must have free will. And free will always runs the risk of error.

Furthermore, not only can people not truly be happy without friends and companions who choose to spend time with them, but people cannot truly be happy unless they can make their own choices. People must have not only free will in order to make choices, but must have options to choose between, and some of those options will be better than others. In other words, for people to truly be happy, they must be able to make a choice between good and evil, and free will provides the opportunity for evil to exist.

Idols of the Marketplace: As Idols of the Marketplace refer to errors that emerge from confusion over the meanings of words and language, Augustine's conception of language and the acquisition of ideas illustrates his concern with such a capacity. Like the other themes in his thought, Augustine's conception of language is heavily Platonic. Recall that Augustine, like Plato, insisted that people are born with innate ideas. Language, words, consist of signs that represent these ideas. Ultimately, people do not learn, or acquire ideas, through language alone, since no one could understand language unless they already had in mind the ideas to which the words refer. For example, suppose I say to you, "All sheep are kafoofafaffills." You likely would not understand me, since you would have no idea of what "kafoofa-faffill" means. Ultimately, no one ever learns anything from other people. The best that a teacher can do is act as a coach to students, just as Socrates would act with his interlocutors. Knowledge is really a gift from God, divine illumination.

Augustine on Idols of the Theater: Since Idols of the Theater refer to errors that arise from adherence to false worldviews or false learning, Augustine's rejection of Manichaeism and his unique resolution to the problem of evil establish his concern with these sorts of errors. However, the fact that his thought is primarily a synthesis of the central doctrines of both Christianity and Neo-Platonism leaves Augustine himself liable to the errors of both. Christians rely heavily on the doctrine of faith, specifically, faith in both God and Jesus Christ, God in human form and the savior of humanity. Acceptance of Christ as one's savior is based largely on the testimony of witnesses to his miracles, teachings, and resurrection, of which the gospels offer varying accounts. Hence, Christianity demands faith that these allegedly first-person accounts of the ministry of Christ are true, even though it is virtually impossible for anyone to substantiate them beyond a reasonable doubt. Augustine, nonetheless, seems to anticipate such an objection through his idea that faith is prior to understanding. For Augustine, in fact, faith is necessary for knowledge, and it is employed not only in matters of religion, but more generally. For instance, all people, from very early in their childhood, begin learning by first believing what others say before they can test what they are told for themselves. That is, we all begin by first trusting what others tell us before we move on to rational demonstration. When learning a theory in science, before a student can understand how to perform an experiment to test the theory, the theory must first be understood. Before one can test Boyle's theory of gases, one must at least know what the theory is, just as one must know what the concept of natural selection means before it can be tested. Augustine, thus, offers the prescription *credo ut intelligam*: believe so that you may understand. The problem with this prescription, however, is that it is always possible to separate belief from understanding. One can certainly understand a theory without accepting it.[9]

St. Thomas Aquinas (1224–1274): Between the death of St. Augustine and the birth of St. Thomas Aquinas are 794 years of history. There are only 745 years separating the death of St. Thomas Aquinas from our present year. Thus, there is more time between the birth of Thomas Aquinas and St. Augustine than there is between the death of Thomas Aquinas and our time. Nonetheless, Aquinas was heavily influenced by the writings of St. Augustine in addition to the contributions of Aristotle. The most important historical events that took place between the lives of Augustine and Aquinas were the Crusades, a series of

---

[9] For similar textbooks with chapters devoted exclusively to St. Augustine, see R.C. Sproul's *The Consequences of Ideas*, Louis Pojman's *Who Are We? Theories of Human Nature*, and Thomas Wall's *On Human Nature*. For primary sources, see Books II, VIII, and X of Augustine's *Confessions*, translated by Henry Chadwick, (New York: Oxford University Press, 2008). Also, see *On Free Choice of the Will*, translated by Thomas Williams (Cambridge: Hackett, 1993). Focus on Books I–III of *Free Choice*, selections from which are available in Wall's anthology.

holy wars fought between the Christians and the Muslims, which were eventually won by the Muslims. After these wars, Muslim philosophers gained access to the writings of not only the Christian philosophers, but also the ancient Greeks as well. A few of the most prominent of these thinkers were Ibn Sina (Avicenna) (980–1037), Al-Ghazali (1058–1111), and Ibn Rushd (Averroes) (1126–1198). Avicenna synthesized Aristotle's distinction between the active and passive intellect to develop a theory of prophecy in which he claimed that God speaks through the active intellect, whereas the passive intellect (the human mind), requires images to express the truths of religion. Al-Ghazali wrote a book called *The Incoherence of the Philosophers*, in which he criticized Islamic thinkers such as Avicenna for using the ideas of Greek thinkers to interpret the Qu'ran. He favored, instead, a return to religious orthodoxy. Averroes, in direct response to Al-Ghazali, wrote *The Incoherence of the Incoherence*, in which he insisted that it is impossible for Muslims to avoid the use of rational argumentation, since the Qu'ran demands some rational interpretation. However, his system implied that there are different realms of knowledge, and, hence, that there can be things true in religion that are false in science, and vice versa.

Aquinas became familiar with this intellectual tradition. He was rather precocious as a child. He joined the Abbey of Monte Cassino when he was only 5, and he enrolled in the University of Naples when he was only 14. His teacher was Albert the Great, the most respected theologian in the world at the time, arguably a teacher whose reputation rivaled that of a Plato or an Aristotle in ancient Greece. Although taciturn as a child, leading many of his students to nickname him the "dumb ox," the thought of Aquinas, a vast synthesis of the Bible, Aristotle, and various other philosophers, became the foundation of what is now called scholasticism. His best-known work is the *Summa Theologica*, often called the Summa for short. Moreover, his thought formed the basis for much of the catechism of the Catholic Church.

As with Augustine, I will provide an overview of Aquinas's thought in terms of Bacon's idols directly.

Aquinas on Idols of the Tribe: Like Aristotle, Aquinas embraced a form of realism, a commitment to the idea that the world of sense is in fact the real world, although in Christian terms, it is all part of God's revelation to humanity. And also like Aristotle, Aquinas rejected the claim that humans are born with any innate ideas, as all knowledge begins with and arises from experience. Furthermore, Aquinas adopted a version of the distinction between the active and passive intellect, also found in Aristotle. In Aquinas's version of this distinction, the mind forms generalizations that it stores in the passive intellect. It is the active intellect, however, that has the rational power to understand general ideas. For instance, we observe many dogs. By doing so, we form the general idea of what a dog is, based on the reflective capacity of the active intellect, which recognizes the form or patterns that all dogs share. Once these ideas are formed, they are stored in the passive intellect. Through the formation of concepts, people can understand the patterns of nature, which ultimately leads them to God.

Since knowledge is not innate, Augustine's conception of innate awareness of God, and especially, Anselm's ontological argument are erroneous. If everyone had an innate idea of God, everyone would believe in God. The same would be true if the existence of God were self-evident, as St. Anselm's argument seems to imply. In addition, even if there is an idea of God in the human mind, it would be an imperfect or an incomplete idea. For Aquinas, humanity's awareness of God is restricted to the limitations of the human intellect. Our knowledge of God, as humans, is transmitted, or mediated, through God's creation. The concept of mediation can be understood by analogy with television. Suppose that you are watching football game on television. You do not experience the game directly, rather it is transmitted to you through the *medium* of television. Looking at pictures of something conveys a similar concept. A picture of your best friend is a medium that allows you to experience that person indirectly. The world that we experience, as God's creation, provides a medium through which we can experience God, albeit indirectly. In fact, Aquinas provides five proofs of God's existence, the "five ways," each of which is based on the medium of God's creation.

Although Aquinas provides five ways to prove the existence of God, each of these proofs have the following in common. First, they are all based on sense-experience, God's primary medium. They are based primarily on items that can be readily observed. Second, they all turn on an impossibility of an infinite regress of causes. That is, for an effect to be accounted for, there must be a cause of that effect. Perhaps it is possible that this cause also has a cause. However, this chain cannot go on forever, but must stop somewhere, at a first cause that is the ground of itself. Imagine a long row of dominoes. If that first domino never falls, then neither will any of the others. It will merely remain stagnant. Third, once a first cause has been established, it is concluded that the only possible being that could be this first cause is God Himself. Lastly, each argument focuses on a specific Aristotelian concept of causality. The first three ways emphasize efficient causality. The fourth way emphasizes formal causality, the most Augustinian of the arguments. The fifth way emphasizes final causality, or teleology.

The first way is "from motion." Aquinas observes that there are items in the world that move. Since nothing moves unless it is moved by something else, everything that moves has a cause of its motion. But there cannot be an infinite regress of possible causes. If there were, then motion could never begin. Hence, there must be a first cause of all motion, a first mover. This mover is God. Notice that this argument does not say that all things move. It merely states that motion in the world is observable.

The second way is "from change." The primary difference between this proof and the first is that the second emphasizes the difference between a cause and an effect. An effect is something that requires or is dependent on a cause for its existence. In the world, there are both causes and effects. Since anything that is an effect requires a cause, and since, as established in the first way, there cannot be an infinite regress of possible causes, there must be a first cause that is, itself, not an effect, and hence requires no cause or explanation for its existence. This first cause is God. Notice that this argument does not say that *everything* has a cause. It implies that there are items that require no cause, hence, why God demands no explanation.

The third way is, in some sense, an extension of the first two, especially the second. It is sometimes called the way "from contingency," or "from possibility and necessity." It is the most complex of the five ways. In the world, there are beings that are contingent, or merely possible. If a being is contingent, then at one time, that thing did not exist, and at another time, it will not exist. That is, if something is merely possible, then it is possible for it *not* to be. Now, if everything that exists were merely contingent, merely possible, then at one time, there would have been nothing. But recall from Chapter 1 the Greek maxim that from nothing, nothing comes. Hence, if at one time, there existed nothing at all, nothing would exist now! But obviously, things exist now. Thus, not everything is contingent, or merely possible. That is, there must be at least one *necessary* being, something that has to exist, something that cannot *not* be, something that does not depend on anything else for its existence, something that always existed. Once again, since there cannot be an infinite regress of necessary beings, there must be one ultimate necessary being. This being is God.

The fourth way, "from gradation," emphasizes formal causality. It begins with the observation that in the world, some things are better than others. That is, there are "gradations" of being. Some people, for instance, are stronger than others. Some people are smarter than others. Some people are more talented than others. But wherever there is a better, there is a best. That is, in order to make judgments of value, there must be a standard for comparison. This best thing is called God. Notice that this argument appeals to conception of reality like Plato's and Augustine's.

The fifth and final way, "from the governance of the world," also called the argument from design, emphasizes final causality, the concept of purpose. It begins with the observation that in the world, there are non-intelligent beings that act in intelligent ways. That is, such beings act with purpose. Ants, for instance, are capable of building intricate colonies. Bees pollinate flowers and make honey. No insects, however, could behave in such ways unless they were guided by a being that is itself intelligent. The same can be said about inanimate organisms, such as plants and trees, which manifest a built-in order according to which they function. There must be an intelligent being that is the source of this order. There cannot be an infinite regress of such beings. Hence, there must be one supremely intelligent being that guides all things. This being is God.

Before proceeding to the next section, Aquinas's conception of the soul remains to be addressed. Recall that Aristotle denied the immortality of the soul. While Aquinas accepted Aristotle's conception of the soul as the formal cause of the body, he had to reconcile this conception of the soul with the doctrine of immortality. In short, since the human soul is rational, and since rationality does not demand the use of the body, it is possible for the soul to exist apart from the body. This argument ties into Aquinas's conception of the formation of universal ideas. Since the active intellect abstracts beyond material objects in order to discern the universal in them, it transcends matter and form. Just as the active intellect can separate form from matter, so the rational soul can be separated from the body. Moreover, the soul is a fully spiritual substance. Since spiritual substances have no parts, they cannot be broken down, and, thus, cannot be destroyed. Hence, the soul cannot be destroyed and will exist forever. However, in Aquinas' view, it is not *natural* for the soul to be separated from the body. For this reason, upon our natural death, our soul is temporarily separated from the body, and will be rejoined with it when our bodies are resurrected on the last day for final judgment.

Aquinas on Idols of the Cave: The most salient way in which Aquinas addresses Idols of the Cave is through his conception of free will. Basically, we have the capacity to make choices, especially since we are responsible for our own salvation. We must choose to follow God's commands and the teachings of Christ. Otherwise, we could not be judged for failing to do so. However, our choices are restricted to the options that are available to us. That is, our choices are restricted by external circumstances. Our choices are also restricted by internal forces, that is, the tendencies of our own human nature. For Aquinas, we are all inclined to choose those things that we believe will be good for us, those items that we think will lead to our happiness. On this matter, Aquinas would agree with Plato, for whom no one ever *knowingly* acts in a way that brings about their own unhappiness or bad consequences. However, because humans are finite, imperfect creatures, we are often mistaken about what will bring about our happiness. Often, people do the wrong thing thinking it to be right. On many occasions, however, people might knowingly commit an action that is wrong, but only because they believe that such an action is merely a *means* to a much better *end*, which, again, is perceived to be good. People can, unfortunately, develop the habit of frequently choosing the wrong thing, believing it to be good. Or, one might develop a habit so strong that even if one knows one's actions are wrong, they cannot stop themselves. Aristotle referred to this state of character as *akrasia*, or weakness of the will. St. Paul wrote of the very same inclination in Chapter 6 of his letter to the Romans.

Like Aristotle, Aquinas insisted that people must work to fashion their character in the right way, so that they will want to do only those things that will bring about true happiness. Freewill should be guided by reason, which God gave to humanity so that they will be able to discern the natural order and His plan for creation. This doctrine is called Natural Law Ethics. Recall Aquinas's fifth way to prove God's existence, the way from the governance of the world, or from design. The principle on which this argument is based is that everything in nature has a purpose built into it by God. Since God built into each thing its nature, it follows that what is natural is not merely *descriptive*, but *prescriptive*. That is, by observing nature, we can discern not merely the way that things are, but how they *ought to be*. Nature stipulates the standards set by God. Those standards determine a function that everything is designed to perform. If anything neglects the purpose of its design, then it can never be happy. For instance, a rabbit can never thrive if there are no plants available for it to eat, just as a lion can never thrive if it has no meat to eat. Reason guides human beings to make observations and discern what is best for them, what is best for human nature. What we observe are tendencies that all human beings have, instincts and urges that all humans share. All humans have the instinct to eat, drink, sleep, and have sex. The primary function of sexuality, for example, is procreation, the perpetuation of the human species. Hence, humans will be much happier if sexuality is reserved for marriage, and if it occurs between men and women. It is for this reason that many people believe that homosexuality is wrong, since it seems to be unnatural and cannot lead to the reproduction of offspring. Bodily health lends itself as a useful analogy. One will be very healthy if one consumes foods that are, themselves, wholly natural, or organic. Those with too many synthetic preservatives, consumed over the long term, can only damage one's health. If one is unhealthy, one is less happy. Unfortunately, if one devotes too much time to consuming foods that taste good, but are unhealthy, one becomes more inclined to continually consume such foods, perhaps even knowing that their health will only atrophy as a result. Morality and happiness share a similar connection, since it is very easy to habitually do things that will only contribute to one's unhappiness, even to the point that one knows what will happen as a result.

Aquinas on Idols of the Marketplace: The most prominent way in which Aquinas addresses himself to these idols is through his adoption of Aristotle's conception of analogical predication. Aquinas applies this concept to humanity's knowledge of God. Recall that Aquinas recognized that people can understand God only in a limited way. God's being is mediated to us through creation, and through our capacity to discern the patterns throughout nature that lead us to both God's existence and to what is necessary for our happiness. As a result, what we can know about God, we can know only analogically. An analogy is a comparison between two or more things, a statement about how two or more things are similar. Thus, what human beings know about God, they know by comparison with things that are more familiar to them. For instance, when a person asserts that God is powerful, that claim is made based on one's experience of powerful people, or powerful forces observable through nature. When a person asserts that God is good, or merciful, that claim is made based on one's experience of people who have done good deeds, or who have shown mercy.

Aquinas on Idols of the Theater: Aquinas addresses himself to Idols of the Theater primarily through his synthesis of his predecessors, including Aristotle, Augustine, the Islamic philosophers, and the Bible. He not only borrowed from various thinkers, but produced a profoundly original and influential system, building on all of them. More specifically, Aquinas addresses these idols through his conception of different kinds of truth. Recall that the contributions of the Islamic thinkers, especially Averroes, led to the idea that there are ideas that can be true in one area, but false in others. For instance, the existence of God might be true in religion, but false in science. For Aquinas, it is impossible for truth to contradict truth. Aquinas did not want to separate philosophy and religion, but instead wanted to demonstrate their unity. Hence, he worked out a different schema. Indeed, he distinguished between different kinds of truth, although he believed divine revelation to be the most primal form of truth.

In short, Aquinas distinguished between three spheres of truth. First, there is the sphere of grace, or theological truth, which can be known only by the special revelation of God. An example is God's specific plan of salvation for the humanity. One would have to read the Bible to know this plan, specifically, one would have to know and follow the teachings of Christ, affirming him as the savior of humanity. Second, there is the sphere of philosophical and scientific truths, which can be known only through reason and observations of God's general revelation. For instance, if one wishes to know how the human body works, one must investigate the human body and all its various organs and systems. One cannot gain such knowledge by reading the Bible. The third sphere consists of "mixed articles." This sphere consists of truths that can be known either through God's special revelation, or through reason. The most prominent example is the existence of God. To know that God exists, one can read the Bible, just as one can be informed of his existence by a religious authority, or one can observe the general order of nature and reason to God's existence through one or more of the five ways. It is ultimately through reason that people can navigate different schools of thought and separate truth from falsity in each.[10]

Even though both Augustine and Aquinas addressed themselves to the Idols of the Mind outlined by Bacon, the irony is that medieval thought, the scholasticism built on the thought of Aquinas, was Bacon's chief target when he first wrote of the four idols. His idols became points of focus for the majority of the thinkers in the modern tradition, the putative father of which is Rene Descartes, who is the subject of the very next chapter.

---

[10] For similar textbooks with chapters devoted exclusively to Thomas Aquinas, see R.C. Sproul's *The Consequences of Ideas*, Roger Trigg's *Ideas of Human Nature*, and Wall's *On Human Nature*. For an excellent and accessible introduction to the thought of Aquinas, see F.C. Copleston's *Aquinas*, (Bergenfield, NJ: Penguin Books, 1956). For primary source readings, see the following pages 173–188 of Wall's anthology. These selections cover Aquinas' proofs for God's existence, the active intellect, free will, the natural law, the nature of the soul. Peter Kreeft's *Summa of the Summa* (Ignatius Press, 2011), for a greater selection of primary source readings.

Chapter 3 Worksheet

1. Which of the three major Hellenistic Philosophies – Epicureanism, Stoicism, and Skepticism – is YOUR personal favorite and why? Explain at least three ways that your chosen philosophy applies to your personal life.

2. In what ways do the major Hellenistic schools of thought and Christianity address humanity's general attempt to make their lives and circumstances worse but usually with the intention of making them better?

3. Read "The Grand Inquisitor" from Dostoevsky's *The Brothers Karamazov*. How is this selection relevant to the temptations of Christ? What does it imply about modern conceptions of Christianity?

4. Find at least three examples from your daily life that illustrate Augustine's conception of evil as an "absence of good," or as an "absence of reality."

5. Consider Augustine's claim that we must first believe in order to understand. Explain one way that this idea applies both to your academic education and to your personal life.

6. St. Thomas Aquinas maintained that his five ways were sufficient to prove God's existence, but that they would change and become more complicated over time. Find at least one example of a more complex but contemporary version of one of Aquinas's five ways.

7. Explain how Plato's Allegory of the Cave applies to Christianity in general, as well as to the thought of Augustine and Aquinas.

8. Explain how the thought of any three thinkers or schools of thought in this chapter are illustrated in a movie, television show, novel, comic book, or any other work of fiction.

Descartes and the Birth of the Modern Mind

Imagine that you grew up in a small town, where all the residents know each other quite well, and where there is very little crime beyond minor traffic violations or occasional trivial squabbles between the citizens. Suppose that you take a month-long vacation and upon your return, your best friend recounts a riot that took place in the city hall of your hometown. He describes the issue that led to the town meeting, the events at the meeting that precipitated the outbreak, who "fired the first shot," so to speak, who became injured, and how it all eventually ended when the state police arrived to restore order. While you would likely be very intrigued and entertained by your friend's anecdote, his detailed account of the events is certainly a poor substitute for *experiencing* the events of this alleged riot for yourself. In fact, your friend's story seems so fantastical that maybe it never really happened. So, you attempt to verify the story by consulting reliable sources. You read the local newspaper and speak to others who are less familiar to you, those with whom you share less of a connection and, thus, expect to be more objective. You not only wish to verify this story, but to reconcile such an outlandish course of events with your perception of your hometown as a relatively small, docile community of amiable people.

This scenario highlights two features about people. First, as creatures gifted with rationality, people instinctively try to reconcile seemingly incompatible ideas. Any hint of contradiction or inconsistency produces genuine psychological pain,[1] and all organisms tend to seek pleasure and avoid pain, be it physical or mental. Second, it is always preferable to experience something for oneself, firsthand, rather than secondhand, via mere testimony. Most would agree that it is much more desirable to travel around the world oneself and take in all the world's wonders rather than to hear a description of such experiences from someone else. And even though a picture may be worth a thousand words, looking at a picture of something is far less preferable to seeing the thing itself.[2] These two distinctly human qualities give rise to the development of worldviews in general, but especially to the modern worldview. Just as all children must eventually assert their independence and face the challenges of life's quest on their own, the thinkers of the western world, in the pursuit of truth and wisdom, had to do the same.

For over 300 years, Aquinas's synthesis of philosophy and the doctrines of Christianity dominated the western intellectual tradition and served as the foundation for the principles of Catholicism. But the medieval tradition and scholasticism came to an end as the result of three historical movements: the Renaissance, the Reformation, and the rise of modern science. Each of these movements lent itself as a source of inspiration for the thinker who is the subject of this chapter, Rene Descartes. Just like the subject of the scenario described above, Descartes witnessed significant conflict between the ideas he was taught and accepted his whole life, and, thus, sought to reconcile them by adopting the position of skepticism and extreme doubt, attempting to establish a solid and coherent worldview autonomously and independently.

---

[1] Recall that in the introduction I referred to this phenomenon as cognitive dissonance, the term modern psychologists use to describe the mental disharmony caused by items of information that conflict with each other.

[2] The 20th century philosopher Bertrand Russell referred to the distinction between knowledge by *acquaintance* (experiencing something firsthand, directly for oneself), and knowledge by *description* (experiencing something only indirectly, in a secondary way). See Chapter 5 of Russell's *The Problems of Philosophy* (New York: Oxford University Press, 1959).

(I) The Reformation, the Renaissance, and the Birth of Modern Science

The developments that led to the modern worldview emerged due to challenges to the authority of the Catholic Church and the principles of scholasticism, in addition to the geo-centric model of the universe which maintained that the sun, stars, and all the other planets revolve around earth. The *Reformation* refers primarily to the work of Martin Luther, who in 1495 nailed 95 theses to a church in Wittenberg, whose aim was to reform the catechism the Catholic Church, to which his theses objected. For example, at every Catholic mass, the priest consecrates the eucharist, in which it supposedly becomes the literal body of Christ. The same is done to the wine, which supposedly becomes the literal blood of Christ. The reason that Catholics believe that such a transubstantiation occurs is that Christ refers to himself as the "bread of life" in the gospels. At the last supper, he refers to bread as his body, and to wine as his blood. However, there are also passages in which he referred to himself as a light, as a doorway, as a shepherd, and as a vine. Luther found it somewhat arbitrary that the authorities of the church focused only on the passages they chose, and in such a literal way. Luther attempted to reform the Church from within, but failed. Hence, he formed his own church, which eventually became the denomination of Protestantism. Whereas Catholicism is rooted in the idea that the church is a teaching authority whose job is to interpret the Bible for people, Luther and his followers insisted not only that non-ordained people can read and interpret the Bible independently, but that they must do so, rather than merely deferring to the authority of religious figures in mere perfunctory acts of ritual and worship. As a further blow to the authority of the Catholic Church, by 1531 King Henry VIII established the Church of England.

The *Renaissance* began with the fall of Constantinople to the Turks in 1453. At this point, Greek literature long preserved by the Eastern Empire became available to Christians in the west, leading to more scholars challenging scholasticism. Moreover, the discovery of classical languages, texts, and art galvanized the humanistic worldview entertained by the Greeks, emphasizing humanity's dignity and capacity to discover truth through reason alone. Works of art piqued interest in the details of human anatomy and physiology.

These developments coincided with the rise of modern science. The most prominent contribution during this time was the establishment of the model of the solar system that prevails to this day. Since Aristotle, western thinkers maintained that Earth was the center of the entire universe. Even though Nicholas Copernicus (1473–1543) was not the first to suggest that the Earth revolves around the sun (that was Aristarchus in ancient Greece), he is credited with being its first truly ardent supporter since Aristarchus, and, thus, the thesis is now called the "Copernican hypothesis." While the Medieval theologians insisted that the natural place of Earth is at the center of the universe, there are problems with this point of view. For example, the planets behave in a very peculiar manner. Mars, for instance, often seems to slow down, stop, and then move backward for several months before moving forward again. If one assumes a geocentric universe, Mars must travel backward at times. The model in which the sun is at the center of the solar system is much simpler, and one can more easily explain the motion of Mars, since Earth moves faster in its orbit around the Sun, in which case it looks as though Mars must move backward.

Copernicus's book, *On the Revolutions of the Heavenly Spheres*, was published on his deathbed, and it sold very few copies, primarily because it was unintelligible. Like many artists, however, Copernicus's contributions were more appreciated after his death, as astronomers and various thinkers began to embrace the message of his book roughly 50 years after his death. One such thinker was Johannes Kepler (1571–1630). While he agreed with Copernicus that Earth stood at the center of the solar system, he wanted to explain the orbits of the planets. His book, *Mysterium Cosmographicum*, marks an important departure from the Medieval worldview, since it postulated that a *force,* in the sense of an efficient cause as opposed to a final cause, radiating from the sun caused the planets to move as they did.

Because Kepler knew that more work had to be done, he turned to the mathematician and astronomer, Tycho Brahe (1546–1601). The Danish king gave Brahe an entire island in 1576, where Brahe built the Observatory Uraniburg and spent two decades making very precise astronomical observations. Brahe met Kepler near Prague in 1600, but he died suddenly only 18 months later. Kepler kept his data, and nine years later published his *Astronomica Nova*, in which he stated the first two laws of planetary motion. He would not discover the third until 1618, since he had to take time off to defend his mother in a witch trial. The most important of these laws was Kepler's discovery that planetary orbits are not perfectly circular, but *elliptical.*[3]

The astronomer who had the greatest influence on Descartes was Galileo Galilee (1564–1642). Galileo furnished empirical proof for the Copernican hypothesis. At first, he disagreed with Kepler, believing the motion of the planets to be circular. When Olaus Roemer invented the telescope in 1609, Galileo acquired one and modified it. Based on his observations, he published the *Sidereus Nuncius,* "Starry Messenger," in which he announced several discoveries, including the discovery that Jupiter has four moons. Prior to this publication, it was believed that Earth was the only planet with a moon. In 1610, Galileo also discovered the phases of Venus, which proved that it could not possibly orbit the Earth.

---

[3] The law that each planet moves in an elliptical orbit with its star (the Sun) at one focal point, is the first. The second law, "the law of equal areas," states that a planet in orbit will take the same amount of time to travel between two points, A and B, on one side of the ellipse, as it will to travel between two additional points, C and D, on the opposite side of the ellipse. The third law, "the law of harmonics," states that the square of a planet's orbital time is proportional to its average distance from the star (Sun) cubed.

In 1632, Galileo published his *Dialogue on the Two Chief World Systems,* a defense of the Copernican hypothesis, in which the geo-centric position was put into the mouth of a character unwisely named Simplicio. Brought to trial and found guilty on suspicion of heresy, he was forced to recant under the threat of being burned at the stake. He spent the rest of his life under house arrest. Galileo used his time under house arrest to write the *Dialogue on the Two New Sciences,* in which he reported the results of his experiments on motion from 25 years earlier. In *Two New Sciences,* Galileo soundly refuted the Aristotelian theory that heavier objects fall faster than lighter objects, showing that all objects fall at the same rate.[4] He also discovered what is now known as the Law of Inertia, the law that unless an object is acted on by a force, it travels in a straight line, or, if an object already is at rest, it stays at rest unless acted on by some external force, another blow to Aristotle's theory of motion.[5]

A final point of significance of Galileo's contributions is that his idea of motion without air resistance demanded a conception of the world as it not experienced. That is, he *imagined* observed motion to arise from sources that cannot be readily observed: a continuous unchanging motion and a frictional force hindering that motion. Aristotle's view was much closer to ordinary observations. Galileo imagined an ideal case with no frictional forces that would continue to move in the same state unless acted upon. Galileo's methodology not only continued the modern search for efficient causes rather than final causes, but also implied a distinction between properties that are independent of observation and those that depend on the observer. The first kind of properties are sometimes called *primary,* whereas the second

---

[4] It would not be until Isaac Newton's formulation of the law of gravity that the western world would understand why all objects fall at the same rate.

[5] For a more detailed, yet accessible account of the transition from the geo-centric to the heliocentric conception of the solar system, see Chapter 1 of Tony Rothman's *Instant Physics: From Aristotle to Einstein and Beyond* (New York: Ballantine Books, 1995).

are sometimes called *secondary*. This distinction figures heavily into Descartes' conception of reality and humanity's place in it.[6]

(II) The Cartesian Conception of Reality and Human Nature

In general, the developments that gave birth to the modern world-view followed three general trends, each of which profoundly influenced Descartes. The first trend constitutes a shift from idea that nature is teleological, or purposive, to the idea that nature operates according to forces, or efficient causes. Thinkers emphasized less the question of why things happen and instead emphasized how they happen. This trend tied inextricably into the second, the shift from a geo-centric conception of the universe, the idea that Earth is at the center of the universe, to a heliocentric conception of the solar system, the idea that Earth revolves around the sun. The third trend consisted of a shift from epistemic realism, the idea that the data of sense-experience corresponds to reality, to a form of skepticism, the idea that the senses cannot always be trusted. The emergence of technological instruments such as the telescope and the microscope lent credence to skepticism. The telescope revealed that items very far away look much different than they appear. Many stars, in fact, are so far away that they burn out before their light can reach human eyes. Hence, it is possible to see the residues of stars that no longer exist! And microscopes reveal that items look much different to the naked eye than they do when magnified. A flat surface, such as a table for instance, certainly does not appear to be flat under a microscope.

These challenges to the senses coincided with an increasing rejection of the authority of traditions that prevailed for several centuries,

---

[6] For a more detailed discussion of Galileo's contributions, see Ian G. Barbour's *Religion and Science: Historical and Contemporary Issues* (New York: HarperCollins, 1997), specifically pp. 9–16, under "Galileo's Two New Sciences."

motivating the search for a new unshakeable foundation of knowl-edge. Descartes embraced skepticism as methodology for discovering such a foundation. My examination of Descartes will focus on his best-known work, *Meditations on First Philosophy.* Descartes was both a rationalist and a mathematician. He is, in fact, the founder of analyt-ical geometry. Descartes hoped to achieve the same certainty in phys-ics and philosophy as reflected in mathematics and logic. The *Meditations*, thus, reads as an extended geometry proof, and includes the following themes: (a) Descartes' methodical doubt; (b) Descartes' foundational principle; (c) Descartes' proofs of God's existence; (d) Descartes' account of the possibility of error; and (e) Descartes' ver-sion of substance dualism.

The Method of Doubt – Meditation I: Imagine that you have a barrel of apples, and you know that some of them are contaminated. Thus, you will need to sort out the bad ones from the good ones. The most effi-cient way to sort out the bad apples would be to flip the barrel over and find the bad ones. Once you discard the bad apples, you can retrieve the good ones and replenish the barrel. This procedure mir-rors the process by which Descartes constructed his own worldview. He begins by subjecting all his beliefs to doubt. Some of them are likely to be false, and the false ones need to be sorted out from the true ones. Those that survive the "doubt test" employed by Descartes can be used later in the reconstruction of his worldview.

At the first stage of his methodical doubt, Descartes questions all his beliefs based on sense-perception. Our senses often deceive us. Recall the sensory illusions from the introductory chapter, or instances in which a straight stick appears bent when placed in water. But if our senses sometimes deceive us, they may always deceive us. Just as it is virtually impossible to trust an individual who lied to you in the past, it is also impossible to trust one's senses if they are often unreliable. However, it is usually possible to test one's senses to see if they match reality. For instance, if you believe that you hear a person in the next room, but you are not sure, you can always check the room, just as two lines that seem to be different sizes can be measured in order to verify their lengths. Moreover, we would have no conception of the difference between an erroneous perception and one that matches reality unless our senses were correct at some point and we had some standard or method by which to assess them.

At the second stage of doubt, Descartes recalls that often in the past, he had difficulty distinguishing his dreams from waking life. That is, often dreams seem so vividly real, that one might believe that one is awake, even though one is only dreaming. In short, our dreams often seem like reality. It is, therefore, possible that we are always dreaming. In fact, it is possible that my entire life has been one long dream from which I will awake someday. But, as with the first stage of doubt, perhaps we would not even know the difference between dreaming and being awake if we were not awake at some point in our lives. And, perhaps, as before, it is possible to perform a test to determine whether we are, in fact, awake. However, it is possible that any test we can perform to make such a distinction is itself only a dream. Nonetheless, there are two kinds of beliefs that we can affirm with absolute certainty, those of mathematics and logic.

However, at the third stage, a truly horrific possibility is considered: What if one's entire life is merely an illusion crafted by an omnipotent evil genius? What if such a malevolent figure deceives me not only about the reality of the world around me, but also about the principles of mathematics and logic that I hold so dear? Perhaps this demon deceives me about my own existence! But therein lies the solution to this dilemma. Even if this demon exists and placed me in a virtual reality whose intricacies rival those of *The Matrix*, at the very least, I must exist! If I am deceived, I must exist in order to be deceived. Here, Descartes discovers his foundational principle: *Cogito, ergo sum*, or, "I think, therefore I am."

The Foundational Principle: The "cogito," as Descartes' foundational principle is often called, serves as Descartes' Archimedean point. Archimedes was a Greek scientist and mathematician who claimed that with a long enough lever, he could move the world. The principle Descartes discovered may not literally be enough to move the world, but it lends itself as the foundation for which Descartes could construct a view of his world. The cogito seems to have three features that make it a credible foundation. First, it is indubitable. That is, it cannot be doubted without the fear of contradiction. If I were to assert that I do not exist, I must at least exist to make such an assertion! Second, it is a completely independent claim. It requires no prior assumptions for its justification. It is the one claim Descartes knew with absolute certainty even under conditions of the most extreme doubt. Even if an all-powerful, malicious entity imprisoned me in an inescapable virtual reality of his own design, I can still know, beyond a shadow of doubt, that I exist. Finally, this principle applies to something that, in fact, exists, the thinker himself. Because it applies to a real object, it is possible to use it as a basis to make judgments about other real objects.[7]

Concomitant with Descartes' discovery of his foundational principle was his discovery of the criteria for truth. Descartes' existence, even in the face of extreme doubt, was clear and distinct to him. Clarity and distinction, thus, are the standards by which any idea or belief must meet in order to be true. To be clear, an idea must be logically consistent or coherent. That is, it cannot be a self-contradiction. For instance, I know that there can be no such thing as a four-sided triangle, since, by definition, a triangle can have only three sides. To be distinct, the idea must not be confused with any other idea. For example, suppose an acquaintance told you that he had two imaginary friends, a purple dragon and a pink giraffe, with whom he frequently converses.

---

[7] Descartes, in fact, lays down these three criteria in his *Rules for the Direction of the Mind*. See also the chapter on Descartes in T.Z. Lavine's *From Socrates to Sartre: The Philosophic Quest* (New York: Bantam Books, 1984), pp. 94–95.

Perhaps your acquaintance can distinguish between his two "friends." You, however, may have more difficulty. Since these creatures are imaginary, you have no way of determining whether they are in fact two *distinct* creatures who are independent of each other. As another example, suppose that your same acquaintance told you that there is both an imaginary bald man in his bedroom as well as an imaginary obese man in his bedroom. Because these two figures are imaginary, you can form no distinct idea of them. That is, it is impossible to determine whether the bald man is the same as the obese man. You do, however, have clarity in each situation so long as you know what the words purple, pink, dragon, giraffe, bald, and obese mean.[8]

At this point in his *Meditations*, Descartes still cannot be sure that the ideas he experiences match up with reality. All he purports to know with certainty, at this point, is that he has experiences, even though the world beyond his experience may be quite different. He uses a honeycomb wax analogy as an example. While a honeycomb wax, at first, is a solid object, when it is heated it melts. Its shape, size, and consistency all change. The piece of wax, virtually everyone believes, remains the same piece of wax even though all its qualities as they appear to the senses change or disappear when it burns. Its real properties, those in virtue of which the piece of wax remains the same, remain within the wax. More generally, the real properties of anything remain constant, whereas non-essential properties are subject to change. In the case of wax, its only real properties are that it is extended in space and capable of change, which are true of any material body. These real properties are known by the mind, not the senses. Colors, tastes, sounds, and odors are not necessary for physical things to exist in the world, whereas spatial extension, size, and shape are. Moreover, we have a clear and distinct idea of spatial extension, but not of

---

[8] This distinction between the imaginary bald man and the imaginary fat man also applies to Descartes' ontological argument for the existence of God, which is addressed below. W.V. O. Quine's "On What There Is," in *From a Logical Point of View*, ed. W. V. O. Quine (Harvard University Press, 1961), pp. 1–19 makes this observation.

the color, sound, taste, odor, or texture of the wax as essential to it. Our sense organs are stimulated by a variety of objects in the external world, and their various processes and arrangement trigger sensations. This distinction evokes Galileo's discovery of the distinction between primary and secondary qualities.

There are several additional implications of this analogy. First, it implies that one can be more certain about what is in the mind than what is in the external world, primarily because it suggests that only the mind can ascertain essences, those properties about a thing that do not change, whereas the bodily senses only perceive that which is fleeting, in flux. Second, since science is limited to the bodily senses, the knowledge that can be obtained through science is inferior to that which can be obtained through mathematics and logic. Ultimately, science is limited to the study of shape, size, and motion. Third, this analogy implies that not all learning takes place through sensation alone. There must be a feature of learning that appeals to a faculty that is different from the bodily senses, otherwise, no one would believe that the wax remains the same piece of wax despite its changes. Moreover, the destruction of a physical object cannot destroy one's memory image of that object. And even people who are blind, or deaf, or both can still think and form ideas. Lastly, the analogy implies that there is a distinction between the mind and the body, hence, ties into Descartes' first argument for substance dualism.

Just as one can be more certain of what is in the mind than the physical world, one can also be more certain of the mind itself than of the body. That is, it is always possible to doubt the existence of one's body. However, it is impossible to doubt the existence of one's mind, since one must have a mind in order to doubt. Hence, the mind and the body must be different things. Admittedly, this argument does not work very well. A common objection to the argument refers to Lois Lane and her relationship with Superman and Clark Kent. Superman, a powerful and indestructible alien from the planet Krypton, masquerades as Clark Kent to keep his identity secret. Clark Kent works with Lois Lane for *The Daily Planet*. Suppose Lois Lane is accosted by a mugger. Clark Kent quickly transforms into Superman and saves Lois without her noticing the switch. In the aftermath, Lois Lane is certain that Superman saved her, but she certainly doubts that Clark Kent did. Hence, she would likely conclude that Superman and Clark Kent are not the same person. But, in fact, they are the same person! The problem with Descartes' initial argument seems to be that the ability to doubt one thing, x, but not another, y, does not indicate a distinctive property that the two items do not share. Descartes provides a stronger argument closer to the end of his *Meditations*, but that argument relies heavily on his proofs of God's existence.

Proofs of God's Existence – Meditations III and V: Descartes' next step is to assess his idea of God. He begins by distinguishing three classes of ideas – innate, adventitious, and invented. Innate ideas are totally a priori, as we are born with them. Examples of such ideas include the laws of logic, such as the law of contradiction, the law of excluded middle (that no statement can be both true and false), and the law of identity (that every statement implies itself). Adventitious ideas are those that derive from sense-experience. Examples of such ideas include claims such as, "Some apples are green," "Some trees are pine," and "Some dogs are Labradors." Invented ideas are those that are made up by the thinker. Examples of such ideas include the items of fantasy, such as griffins, unicorns, or mountains made completely of gold.

The question, thus, is in which category does the idea of God belong? Since God is a totally spiritual being, the idea of God cannot be adventitious, as totally spiritual beings cannot be sensed empirically. Thus, the idea of God is either invented or innate. Ultimately, Descartes determines that God belongs in the latter category, which lends itself as the basis for his first proof of God's existence, which is the most unique of his arguments. One of Descartes' principal assumptions is that our ideas must have a cause. But the idea of God is the idea of a totally perfect being. In fact, it is the idea of an infinite being. Human beings, however, are finite, imperfect beings. Hence, the being of humanity is inadequate to produce the idea of a supremely perfect, infinite being. This claim is supported by Descartes' second assumption, the causal adequacy principle, which states that there must be at least as much reality in the cause of an effect as there is in the effect itself. Just as 10 ounces of clay is not adequate to produce a statue that weighs 15 ounces, a limited being with only finite reality cannot produce an idea that is infinite. Thus, only God is adequate to cause our idea of God, which means that God must exist.

Descartes next asks how it is that he came to have this idea of God. His answer is that God imprints this idea on the mind when he creates us, as an artist would leave his or her signature on a painting. This claim ties into Descartes' second proof of God's existence, which is very similar to Aquinas's cosmological arguments. Descartes obviously cannot be the cause of his own existence, as that would be illogical. Moreover, even though Descartes came from his parents, the causal chain cannot stop there, since they were caused by Descartes' grandparents, who were caused by Descartes' great grandparents, and so on ad infinitum. Like Aquinas, Descartes recognized the impossibility of an infinite regress of causes. The buck must stop somewhere, and it stops with God, as the ultimate cause of everything.

These two proofs of God's existence occur in the third of Descartes' *Meditations,* while his final proof for God's existence occurs in the fifth. Before addressing the subject of Meditation IV, I will address Descartes' final proof of God's existence. On the surface, Descartes' third proof of God's existence is a paraphrase of St. Anselm's ontological argument, although he words it differently. It can be summarized in the following syllogism:

1. God has all perfections.
2. Existence is a perfection.

Therefore, God has existence.

If God "has existence," obviously he exists. Like Anselm, Descartes assumes that it is greater to exist independently in reality than it is to exist in the mind of the thinker alone. Since God is totally perfect, he must exist, otherwise he would not be perfect. Thus, the fact that God exists is true by definition, just as it is true by definition that a triangle is a three-sided figure.[9]

On the assumptions that these proofs are sound, and that Descartes has, in fact, established that God exists, he now needs to determine whether God would deceive him. That is, he must determine whether God is the evil genius he imagined in Meditation I. Moreover, if God would not deceive, then what makes error possible? These questions are the subject of Meditation IV.

Deception, Error, and Free Will – Meditation IV: Descartes' proofs of God's existence rest on the assumption that God is a completely perfect being. God's perfection provides the solution to the question of whether God is a malicious, deceptive evil demon. Because God is perfect, he would never deceive. Deception, maliciousness, and even evil itself, are marks of imperfection, privation, a lack of some kind. Like Augustine, Descartes conceived of evil as an absence of the good, or an absence of reality. In fact, deception is only employed as an instrument in the pursuit of one's goals when one lacks the power to achieve such a goal by more judicious means. People become malicious when they fail to satisfy needs vital to their well-being. Moreover, as the chapter on Plato indicated, injustice of any kind, including deception is harmful to the perpetrator. Surely, an all-powerful, omnipotent being would be aware of the deleterious effects of acts of deception, and would not need to take such measures anyway.

---

[9] There are many criticisms to these proofs, but I prefer to postpone my discussion of those criticisms until the section in which I assess the extent to which Descartes avoids the Idols of the Mind.

However, the question remains: If God would not deceive us, then why are people so often mistaken in their judgments? Descartes' response is twofold. On the one hand, he draws a distinction between the intellect and the will. Whenever the intellect has a clear and distinct perception of an idea about which to make a judgment, it cannot be wrong, since clarity and distinction entail truth. However, if an individual decides to make a judgment about a perception before the intellect has a clear and distinct perception of it, then it is possible to be mistaken. In short, for one to "leap before one looks" is for one to invite error. Suppose that you briefly glance at a painting at an art museum, only for a few seconds, and you then determine that it is a painting of a volcano erupting. But the acquaintance who accompanied asked what you thought of the painting of the face above the valley. Puzzled, you go back and look more closely at the painting, and you discover that, indeed, it is a face that only looks like a volcano erupting! For another common example read the following sentence out loud:

Bridgeport in the the winter.

Did you read it correctly? If you think you did, go back and look more closely. I'm willing to wager that you overlooked the second "the" in the sentence.

On the other hand, one might still ask why, if God is perfect, would he allow people to be wrong in their judgments so frequently? Why would he allow people to make mistakes, not only about trivial matters such as in the previous example, but about much more significant matters, such those that drastically affect the course of one's life? Why would God allow people to make decisions that inevitably result in unhappiness? Once again, Descartes takes inspiration from his medieval predecessor, St. Augustine, insisting that God gave people free will, and that people are ultimately much better off if they can make their own choices even if those choices result in drastic mistakes than they would be if they were merely programmed to make whatever decisions God wills. Just as free will is worth the risk of evil, it is worth the risk of error. Now that Descartes established both that God exists and that God would not deceive, he is prepared to offer his final argument for dualism, which occurs in Meditation VI.

The Real Distinction Between the Body and the Mind – Meditation VI: Recall that Descartes' initial argument for substance dualism did not work very well. His proofs for God's existence and his examination of the perfect nature of God, however, lend support to a stronger argument for the distinction between the mind and the body. His argument can be reconstructed in the following way:

1. I have a clear and distinct perception of my mind as separate from my body.
2. God exists and he would not deceive me.
3. God can create whatever I clearly and distinctly perceive.
4. From (2) and (3), it follows that whatever I clearly and distinctly perceive is true.
5. Therefore, my mind is distinct from my body.

What justifies premise (1)? Descartes furnishes the example of a chiliagon to help establish it. Remember the difference between clarity and distinction, where an idea is clear so long as it is logically coherent, and distinct if it is not confused with any other idea. Suppose I told you that a chiliagon is a closed geometrical shape with 1,000 sides. So long as you understand what a "closed geometic shape" is, and so long as you understand what it means for this figure to have 1,000 sides, you have a clear idea of a chiliagon. However, try to picture such a figure. That is, try to form a mental image of what this figure would look like. It likely is not as easy to picture such a shape as it is to picture a simple triangle or a square. What you imagine probably resembles something like a circle with edges. Thus, while you have a *clear* conception of a chiliagon, you do not necessarily have a *distinct* conception of such a shape. This illustration ties into Descartes' argument for substance dualism because clarity, understanding, is inclined toward the intellect, whereas imagination is inclined toward the bodily senses. Hence, there is a distinction between the mind and the body.

Two additional considerations also help to elucidate Descartes' argument. The first is that matter is infinitely divisible. That is, any material object can, at least conceivably, be cut into pieces ad infinitum. The mind, however, is a perfect unity, perfectly complete. Whereas the parts of a piece of wood can be cut up and rearranged and reshaped, a complete thought, such as "Gold is a yellow metal," would lack meaning if the parts of the sentence were separated. Second, since the physical world is constantly changing, constantly in flux, just like the physical properties of the wax from the analogy in Meditation II. Since the physical world is constantly changing, we constantly learn more about the matter that comprises it. That is why scientific theories frequently change and are expanded upon, while the mind ascertains essences that are universal and do not change.

At the end of his *Meditations*, Descartes believes that he proved both that God exists and would not deceive, and that there is, in fact, a distinction between the mind and the body. Moreover, Descartes insists that the two substances interact with each other. That is, the body can affect the mind, and the mind can affect the body. Bodily hunger, for instance, can distract one's attention, just as pain or the symptoms of physiological illness can make it difficult to concentrate. On the other hand, beliefs, thoughts, and desires influence one's behavior and materialize as physical actions. People are often willing to fight and die for their religious beliefs. In a more mundane, pragmatic context, most people's everyday activities are the result of their beliefs. An action as simple as purchasing one's morning coffee emanates from the belief that the establishment that provides such a service – be it a Starbucks, a Dunkin Donuts, or some other such restaurant – is open for business and functional. Often, when an item is misplaced, it cannot be readily acquired in part because of the belief that it can be found in its usual place. The traditional label for Descartes' conception of the human person, thus, is *interactive dualism*.

Lastly, recall that Descartes insists that no one has any direct access to the external world. All that can be accessed directly are the contents of the mind, which contain only representations of the external world. However, since God creates world and humans, and since God would not deceive us, we can trust that the contents of our subjectivity correspond accurately to the external world. As God is wholly perfect and beneficent, he created the universe and set it to function like clockwork. The physical world, thus, can only be truly understood through mechanical, efficient causes, rather than through purposes or final causes. Hence, Descartes seems, once and for all, to lay the prospect of an evil demon to rest, along with the radical skepticism he initially endorsed.

(III) Descartes' and Bacon's Idols of the Mind

It is impossible to overestimate Descartes' influence on modern thought and developments in both mathematics and science. However, he is often the target of much criticism, mostly because of his methodological skepticism in the initial stages of his *Meditations*. Even though there appears to be no direct connection between Descartes and Bacon, Descartes seemed to address the same sorts of problems that arise from Bacon's Idols of the Mind. Nonetheless, it remains to be determined whether he avoided these idols himself.

Descartes and the Idols of the Tribe: Descartes seems to address himself to the idols of the tribe in the following ways: (1) through his methodological skepticism and (2) through his acknowledgment of humanity's imperfection. Since idols of the tribe concern errors that arise from the very nature of humanity, and the most glaring examples of such errors are mistakes in judgments about sensation and perception, the stages of doubt through which Descartes proceeds clearly establish his attunement to the idols of the tribe. Descartes recognizes not only the fact that human perception is often faulty and erroneous, but also the tendency of human beings to accept what they see or hear all too hastily and usually without question, a proclivity that arises from the desire for security and comfort, and the need for a familiar and recognizable routine to preserve them. Human beings are creatures of habit, and habits can be beneficial in that they can enable the mind to focus on multiple tasks. Often, victims who survive traumatic experiences can hasten their recovery and re-acclimate themselves to their lives by adhering to a simple schedule that distracts them from the memory of the experience. But every benefit comes with a price, and the price of habits is they can dull the mind by forcing its activity into perpetual remission. Change is difficult, because it forces us to breach our comfort zones. One of the most dreadful difficulties of all is the possibility that the lives we lead and the interactions that give our lives meaning and value are not real, or, at the very least, not what they seem. Equally dreadful is acting on this possibility and determining just what lies beyond the veil of experience. Perhaps the mind has its own law of inertia, whereby it remains at rest unless acted on by a force, but if the mind is indeed different from the body, the forces that compel the mind to act must be different as well, especially since they can so often be ignored.

It would not be possible to ignore a call to action were it not for free will. It is in virtue of our freedom that error is possible, when judgments are made too quickly and with little deliberation. The mistakes that arise from the misuse of free will and hasty judgment are inherent in the "tribe" of humanity, since we are all finite and imperfect creatures. Subsequently, none of us can know all the possible outcomes of our actions and judgments must often be made quickly, and usually such judgments defer to personal preferences that arise from the "cave" of the individual.

Descartes and the Idols of the Cave: Unfortunately, there is not too much to say about Descartes' estimate of Idols of the Cave, as his method of doubt addresses these very sorts of errors as well. However, while Descartes' methodological skepticism lent itself as a sorting agent to filter out false beliefs, such a method also allows a thinker to adopt a position bereft of any preconceived notions, at least as much as it is possible to do so. It is often said that one cannot be a true theist, a true believer in God, unless one was first an atheist. Descartes attempted to adopt the position that one cannot understand truth unless one first doubts everything that is possible to doubt. Hence, Descartes' method of doubt constitutes his attempt to adopt what Nagel calls the "view from nowhere," whereby a thinker stands outside of his own worldview to adopt a position that is as objective as possible. In this way, Descartes' *Meditations* may be read as a Socratic dialogue in which the "meditator" acts as his own interlocutor. Just as Socrates had to lead his interlocutors to recognize their own ignorance before they could genuinely pursue truth, so Descartes had to accept the possibility that all his alleged knowledge was merely an illusion before he could fully embrace reality.

Descartes and the Idols of the Marketplace: Since idols of the marketplace refer to errors that arise from confusion over the meanings of words, Descartes' insistence on clarity and distinction as his criteria of truth serves as the primary way in which he addresses himself to these idols. Clarity as mere logical coherence is usually easier to establish than is distinction, which requires the thinker to know that the idea under consideration is not confused with any other idea. Words represent ideas, and, thus, understanding an idea clearly and distinctly includes understanding the term that represents it in addition to the item to which it corresponds. In part, the correct application of these criteria is strengthened by Descartes' recognition of a difference between the processes of the intellect and those of bodily sensations, since the latter are typically less certain and less clear than those ideas grasped fully by the intellect.

Descartes and the Idols of the Theater: Just as Descartes made a conscious effort to divest himself of personal preferences and prejudices, he attempts to find a foundational principle on which to construct his own unique worldview without merely adhering to any one prior school of thought. In keeping with the tenor of his time, Descartes' chief targets were the principles of scholasticism. Specifically, Descartes rejected the heliocentric worldview, the Christian conception of dualism, in which the soul and body are incomplete without each other, and the teleological conception of reality. Descartes rejected the idea that the body survives death, insisting that only the soul is immortal. Moreover, his conception of the physical world as a system of efficient rather than final causes marks a sharp break with the Aristotelian conception of nature favored by the medieval theologians. In *Meditation IV*, in fact, Descartes remarks that he believes the search for final causes to be "totally useless in physics." Nonetheless, many ideas of his predecessors are built into Descartes' system, even the foundational principle that supposedly had no prior assumptions, and it is the question of the extent to which Descartes avoided the Idols of the Mind to which I turn next.

An Assessment of Descartes in Terms of the Idols of the Mind: In terms of the idols of the tribe, Descartes acknowledges fully that he is an imperfect being and is liable to the mistakes in judgment concomitant with his finitude. Given his emphasis on logic and mathematics, however, it is difficult to find any ways in which he succumbed to idols of the tribe. However, there are at least two possible examples of such errors that occur in his *Meditations*. First, just as the method of doubt established that Descartes wished to address the idols of the tribe, it can also be viewed as an indiscriminate form of intellectual paranoia whose result is that far too high a standard for knowledge has been set. It is virtually impossible to conduct any inquiry without some presuppositions, some given assumptions. While Descartes acknowledges that one's existence cannot be doubted without contradiction, the reason for such an acknowledgment rests on an additional assumption – the idea that thought requires a thinker. Such a presupposition seems to accept the Aristotelian-scholastic distinction between substance and accident, which Descartes never really subjected to doubt. Thinkers such as Pierre Gassendi, one of Descartes' contemporaries, as well as the 18th century German philosopher Georg Lichtenberg, and the 20th century philosopher Bertrand Russell,[10] maintained that the thinker cannot deduce his own existence from thinking, but only that there is thinking happening. Moreover, perhaps the existence of an external world consisting of physical objects cannot be doubted either. Why would human beings have sensations if they corresponded to nothing, or, at least, if they did not correspond to some item that mostly resembles them? Descartes, in fact, never *proves* that we cannot know directly what is in the external world, rather, it is loosely deduced from the fact that the properties of physical objects undergo change even though the mind recognizes the unity of the object itself. But such a recognition is perfectly natural, especially if one witnesses the changes that take place within an object.

The second way in which Descartes seems to fall victim to an idol of the tribe is through a famous problem often referred as the "Cartesian circle." Recall the second argument for dualism Descartes provides at the end of the *Meditations*. The primary difference between this argument and his first is that, by the end of his inquiry, he has proven that God exists and will not deceive. Thus, Descartes can trust all his clear and distinct perceptions. However, his initial proof of God's existence was predicated on a clear and distinct perception of the idea of God, a wholly perfect and benevolent being, after he established clarity and distinction as the criteria for truth. The "circle" can be stated in the following way:

1. I know that God exists because I have a clear and distinct idea of him.

2. I can trust my clear and distinct perceptions because God exists and would not deceive.

---

[10] See Russell's *History of Western Philosophy* (Allen & Unwin, 1961).

So, which is it? If Descartes can trust his clear and distinct perceptions only because of the existence of God, then how does he prove
God's existence? God's existence becomes an assumption rather than
a demonstrated fact. But if he knows that God exists because of his
clear and distinct perceptions, why does he need God in order to
establish the duality of body and mind, as well as the truth of the
external world? Clarity and distinction should be sufficient to establish these two principles of Descartes' system. In his book on the history of modern philosophy, Garret Thomson makes a somewhat
plausible suggestion. Basically, Descartes realizes at the end of the
meditations that, since he proved God's existence and total benefi-
cence, his radical doubt in the first meditation was never justified in
the first place.[11] Moreover, Descartes' argument for God's existence
was more complicated than a simple appeal to clarity and distinction.
Clarity and distinction were merely the starting points for the idea of
God. However, the proof itself is based on an idea that may not be
clear and distinct. If humans really are finite, then how can they have
a clear and distinct idea of perfection, or of anything infinite, for that
matter? It seems that Descartes simply *wanted* God to exist.

Affirming an idea because of one's desire is a prejudice, a bias. Thus,
Descartes' first proof of God's existence constitutes one way in which
he seems to fall victim to Idols of the Cave. While he intended to construct a worldview without making any assumptions, taking no belief
for granted, Descartes certainly seems to have the God of Christianity
and Judaism in mind. Not all cultures believe in this God, however.
Since the belief is not universal, the idea of God is probably not innate,
but only something that Descartes acquired from his culture and
wanted to justify.

In addition, Descartes' commitment to rationalism and the superiority of mathematics are indubitably true, they are empty without the

---

[11] See Garrett Thomson, *Bacon to Kant: An Introduction to Modern Philosophy* (Long Grove, IL: Waveland Press,
2012), pp. 34– 35.

data of experience. Granted, Descartes held that a foundational principle must apply to an object that exists so that it is possible to derive from it claims about other existent objects. However, the existence of anything can always be doubted, since it is always possible to imagine without contradiction that something does not exist. Hence, there seems to be an inconsistency between the criterion that a foundational principle must be impossible to doubt and that it must apply to an object that exists. A similar problem applies to Descartes' version of the ontological argument, which supposedly establishes that the very idea of God, by definition, entails his existence. That is, it should be impossible to deny the existence of God without contradiction. But it certainly seems possible that there could be no God. And even if it is impossible to deny the existence of a God, this God may not be the one Descartes has in mind.

Descartes' version of the ontological argument also marks an instance of an idol of the marketplace. This sort of error plagues not only Descartes' version of the argument, but most versions, including St. Anselm's. Basically, the argument attempts to *define* God into existence. But to treat existence as a property that may be added to an idea is, at worst, totally incoherent, and at best, dubious. The process seems to be illogical because in order to have any properties at all, a thing must first exist. Both Descartes and St. Anselm might respond that this criticism applies only to finite objects. It does not apply to God because God is the greatest possible being, and the greatest possible being necessarily exists. So, basically, the argument only works if God is the object to be proven. But if one marshals such a response, one might as well just assume God's existence from the outset without furnishing proof.[12]

---

[12] Not only did Gassendi also anticipate this criticism in the fifth set of Objections to Descartes' *Meditations*, but the most famous statement of this criticism was made by Immanuel Kant, who insisted that existence is not a predicate. That is, existence cannot be added to a concept to extend its meaning.

An idol of the marketplace also seems to apply to Descartes' initial argument for God's existence, based on both the idea of God and the causal adequacy principle. The "causal adequacy argument" turns on a distinction between *formal* and *objective* reality. According to Descartes, the formal reality of the idea is merely the idea as part of the mind's subjective content. The objective reality of an idea refers to its *content*. For example, imagine an item that has the shape of an apple, but nothing underneath. Such an object has the formal reality of an apple, but it is not objectively an apple. Since the idea of God is the idea of an infinite being, it has more reality than any other idea. Thus, God is "more real" than anything else. However, just what exactly does it mean to say that one thing is more real than some other thing? A thing either exists, or it does not. It seems that he uses the formal/objective reality distinction to, once again, justify a belief that he wants to be true.

Descartes' proofs for God's existence are not the only areas of the *Meditations* in which he seems to commit idols of the marketplace. Descartes' method of doubt, as previously noted, is not all inclusive, as there were several implicit assumptions that made Descartes' conclusions possible. One such assumption was that Descartes never seems to subject language to doubt. Certainly, it is possible for an evil genius to deceive a thinker about the meanings of the words by which he thinks. Moreover, Descartes, whose native language was French, originally wrote his *Meditations* in Latin because he wanted to go over the heads of the authorities at his university, *La Fleicsh*, since Latin was the predominant language of the scholastics. Hence, he attempted to use language as a vehicle to make his system seem more intellectually prodigious.

It may be argued that Descartes' entire system relies on the theatrics of a skeptical and rationally objective investigation into the questions it purports to answer. But the author of this system borrows heavily from others. One such assumption is the Aristotelian distinction between substance and accident, which seems to underly Descartes' alleged foundational principle. His arguments for God's existence also seem merely to paraphrase those given by Aquinas and Anselm. Augustine, however, is the author to whom Descartes seems most indebted. First, the very style in which Descartes wrote his *Meditations* echoes that of Augustine's *Confessions*, a sort of interior dialogue that the author has with himself. Even Descartes' foundational principle, "Cogito, ergo sum," paraphrases Augustine's "Si fallor sum," which means, "If I am deceived, then I must exist." Moreover, Descartes' distinction between degrees of reality reflects the neo-Platonic conception of reality endorsed by St. Augustine. Perhaps the most prominent Augustinian theme in Descartes' *Meditations* is his explanation of why God would not deceive and its subsequent implications for free will. Just as Augustine maintained that evil is an absence of being, Descartes insisted that God would not deceive, since deception is a mark of imperfection, a lack of reality, a void of being. And not only is it human free will that makes error possible, but Descartes insists that free will is worth the risk of error.

The parallels between Descartes and Augustine illuminate a more general connection between Descartes' system and those of the medieval theologians: teleology. Teleology seems to be built into Descartes' system despite his attempt to distance himself from the notion. First, Descartes' version of the freewill defense suggests that free will and the possibility of error serves the greater good of God. That is, it assumes that God has a plan and that both humanity and nature are part of that plan. In addition, Descartes' distinction between degrees of reality, while not entirely clear, suggests a hierarchical conception of reality, a distinction between greater and lesser beings. Such a distinction implies a natural order and natural goals, purposes that are implanted by God. Moreover, Descartes' distinction between the body and the mind, his distinction between physical and mental substances, implies a distinction between mechanism and purpose.

That is, matter operates according to efficient causes, but non-physical substances operate according to final causes, purposes. Furthermore, Descartes' search for a system of reality is motivated by an intrinsic human need to find answers to ultimate questions. As rational creatures, human beings have rational instincts to answer or at least improve their understanding of abstract questions that resist easy solution. And unless people contend with such questions, they can never be truly happy. Ultimately, thus, Descartes' *Meditations* represents the lifestyle that he believes will lead to ultimate happiness, a rationalistic life of the mind in which one attempts to put oneself in the place of a child with no preconceived notions and using the basic instruments of one's being to solve the riddles of human existence.

Of course, there is one problem with the lifestyle that Descartes would want his audience to engage in, and it comes back to the very beginning of his *Meditations* – the method of doubt. While Descartes may believe that he is a role-model for the philosophical lifestyle, his method of doubt does not seem to apply to practical matters of everyday life. It seems only to be an academic exercise. That is, suppose that you attempt to engage in a series of "meditations" as did Descartes, in which you subject as many of your beliefs as possible to doubt. Eventually, you will become hungry. At this point, you will likely dispense with the philosophical games and raid your refrigerator for a snack, or perhaps go to the nearest restaurant to refuel. You will probably not suspect that some evil genius is deceiving you into thinking that your hunger is merely an illusion and that you may go without eating. The same assumption can be made if you developed a headache from all your deep thought, or if you grow tired and have an urge to take a cat nap. You will most likely not assume that your pain is an illusion, or that you do not need sleep.[13]

---

[13] For primary source readings, see *Meditations, Objections, and Replies*, edited and translated by Roger Ariew and Donald Cress (Indianapolis, IN: Hackett Publishing Company, Inc., 2006). For an accessible introduction to Descartes' thought, see John Cottingham's *Descartes* (Wiley-Blackwell, 1991).

Descartes borrowed from the theatrics of his predecessors and constructed his own, even though his chief intentions were to divest himself of illusions and live his ideal lifestyle. Many thinkers followed in his footsteps, but others questioned whether rationality is the principal guiding force of humanity, a true subversion of one of the pillars of the theater of the western intellectual tradition. In the coming chapters, we will examine thinkers from both sides.

Chapter 4 Worksheets

1. Imagine that you have no education in astronomy, physics, chemistry, biology, or religion. Briefly describe what you believe your view of reality would be. Do you think that you would believe that earth is at the center of the universe? Do you think that you would believe in God? Do you think that you would believe in one, underlying substance, like most of the pre-Socratics did? Explain. Your response should be at least five sentences.

2. Consider the following quote from Machiavelli's *The Prince*: "A question arises: Whether it is better [for a prince] to be loved than feared or feared than loved? One should wish to be both, but, because it is difficult to unite them [being loved and being feared] in one person, it is much safer to be feared than loved, when, of the two, one must be dispensed with. Because this is to be asserted in general of men, that they are ungrateful, fickle, false, cowards, covetous.... and that prince who, relying entirely on their promises, has neglected other precautions, is ruined, because friendships that are obtained by payments may indeed be earned but they are not secured, and in time of need cannot be relied upon. Men have less scruple in offending one who is beloved than one who is feared, for love is preserved by the link of obligation which, owing to the baseness of men, is broken at every opportunity for their advantage; but fear preserves you by a dread of punishment which never fails." How does this

quote relate to the tenor of the modern times, particularly to (a) the rejection of the Catholic church as both a religious and political authority, and (b) to the trend toward skepticism?

3. Explain in as much detail as you can, a time when you were dreaming but thought you were awake. Did you have to wake up to know that you were dreaming? If not, how did you determine that you were in a dream? If so, what do you think you could have done differently to figure out that your dream was only a dream?

4. Watch the *Twilight Zone* episode "Perchance to Dream," and explain how it is relevant to all three of Descartes' stages of doubt. There is a clue to how the episode will end. What is it?

5. Whose proofs of God's existence do you think are stronger – those of Descartes or those of Aquinas? Explain.

6. The author explained the various ways that Descartes borrowed from Augustine. Explain at least three ways that Descartes borrowed from the thought of Plato.

7. Whose conception of the relation between the body and the soul do you find more plausible – Descartes' or Aristotle's (which profoundly influenced Aquinas)? Explain.

CHAPTER 5

Hume—The Newton of the Mind?

Aesop's fable of the scorpion and the frog goes as follows. A scorpion and a frog meet near a riverbank. The scorpion asks the frog to take him across the river. The frog asks for some reassurance that the scorpion will not sting him, to which the scorpion replies, "If I do, I will die, too." Content with this response, the frog takes the scorpion on his back and begins swimming across the river. However, once the two creatures are midstream, the scorpion stings the frog. When paralysis sets in, the frog begins to sink, and demands an explanation from the scorpion for his actions, to which the scorpion replies, "Because it's my nature." The scorpion might just as well have answered, "Because I'm a scorpion."[1] Across the animal kingdom, creatures do things seemingly for no other reason than because it is in their nature to do them. Dogs chase squirrels because they are dogs. In virtue of being cats, cats chase mice. Suppose that you leave one of your pets outside unattended and a neighbor's escaped pet python happens to find itself in your very yard. The odds are that the python will at least attempt to feast on your pet, if it is hungry. Of course, these animals cannot be blamed for their actions, as it is purely and simply "their nature" to do what they do. But human beings are supposed to be *rational animals*. It is supposed to be within human nature to act in a rational way, yet, like the scorpion in Aesop's fable, people often act contrary to reason. How is this possible?

---

[1] One variation of this fable features a scorpion and a turtle, in which the events unfold in the same manner.

Perhaps such an incongruity rests on a misconception about people. There is no doubt that human beings are creatures endowed with rationality, as evidenced by logic, mathematics, literature, poetry, mythology, the existence of colleges and universities, and various other media. And perhaps rationality is the most distinctive feature of human beings. But does rationality act as the true guiding faculty of humanity? Human beings have passions and desires as well and, thus, are feeling beings just as much as they are thinking beings. Love, hate, pride, fear, ambition, envy, anger, and the drive for self-preservation are not only intrinsically human but frequently override rationality. Virtually everyone walking Earth has or will at some time betray logic for the object of one's affection, since "Love is blind" and all people instinctively desire such a connection with others. Most people will have experiences in which they "see red," and betray all rational decision making, acting from rage alone. Usually, the decisions one makes are based on non-rational criteria, such as what one likes or dislikes. Often, an individual likes a song not because he or she analyzed the structure and composition of the song in detail and assessed it in terms of objective musical criteria, but because the sound of it is simply pleasant to their ears. The same can be said about various media of entertainment, be they novels, stories, or films, as can be said about attraction. In other words, perhaps reason "is and ought to be the slave of the passions," as the thinker about whom this chapter is written once said. Perhaps the dictates of human nature flow not from reason, but from passion.

In many ways, Hume's thought can be understood as the culmination of two trends in the modern era: (1) the fallout from Descartes' contributions, which gave rise to a variety of different conceptions of the human person and the world, and (2) Newton's discovery of gravity and the laws of the motion. First, each of these trends will be examined. Then, the themes of Hume's thought will be examined. Finally, Hume's thought will be assessed in terms of Bacon's Idols of the Mind.

(I) Rationalism, Empiricism, and Newton

From a 21st century perspective, the most prominent thinkers of the 16th to 18th centuries can be subdivided into two groups: rationalists (the label that best suits Descartes) and empiricists (the label that best seems to suit Hume). Despite the differences between the individual rationalists, they all subscribe to at least two principles. First, at least some knowledge is innate, or, all people are born with some knowledge. For instance, Descartes maintained that all people are born with ideas such as the law of non-contradiction, the difference between substance and accident, and God. Second, reason alone can extend human knowledge in important ways. That is, simply by thinking alone, it is possible to achieve new knowledge. Descartes attempted to demonstrate this possibility in his *Meditations*. The two most basic principles of empiricism can be understood as the denial of the two principles of rationalism. For instance, empiricists believe that none of our knowledge is innate, but that all knowledge in some way traces back to experience. Second, empiricists maintain that only experience can extend our knowledge in important ways. Principles such as the law of contradiction and the law of identity are practically empty if there is no concrete data to which they can be applied.

In addition to Descartes, other thinkers who may be grouped under the rationalist label are Baruch Spinoza, Gottfried Leibniz, and Nicolas Malebranche. The two most prominent empiricists prior to Hume were John Locke and George Berkeley. Their contributions are integral both for an understanding of the context of Hume's thought and the thinkers that followed.

Recall that Descartes maintained not only that there is a distinction between the mind and body, but that the two interact. Hence, his position may be called *interactive dualism*. There are, however, two obvious problems with this position. First, if the mind and the body are different substances, then *how* can they interact? How can something that is non-physical influence something that is physical, concrete? Secondly, where exactly does interaction occur? Descartes believed that the soul was contained by a gland in the brain, the pineal gland. But if so, then it seems as if interactive dualism is doomed from the start, since the soul would in fact be part of the body. Descartes' successors attempted to resolve these problems with theories of their own, each reflective of the presuppositions of the school to which they subscribed.

Spinoza—Neutral Monism: Like Descartes, Spinoza privileged the geometric method. His magnum opus, *Ethics,* in fact, reads more like an extended geometric proof and is even more systematic than Descartes' *Meditations.* As a rationalist, Spinoza also subscribed to what is called the *principle of sufficient reason,* the idea that everything has a complete explanation. While there are different variations of this principle, the rationalist model of explanation is logical deduction, in which reason alone can discover the complete explanation of anything. For the sake of brevity, I shall have to do great injustice to many of the thinkers in between Descartes and Hume by compressing their most salient arguments, and Spinoza is no exception.

In short, for Spinoza, there cannot be two substances, but only one. For Spinoza, a substance is something that (a) can exist in and of itself, and (b) must be conceived in and of itself. That is, a substance must be totally independent. Certainly, it is possible for two things to exist independently, but if there are, indeed, two such things, then neither can be conceived in and of itself. In order to define the one, it would be necessary always to compare and differentiate it from the other, in which case both would be limited by the other. But a substance, if it is to exist in and of itself, must be infinite, since no finite thing can be the ground of its own being. Hence, the only true substance is God. It follows, moreover, that everything that exists is a manifestation of God, or a *mode* of the one universal substance. There are, furthermore, two principal *attributes* of the one universal substance—thought, or mind, and extension, or matter. Each mode, therefore, can be understood either as a mind or a body. Basically, the mind is the idea of the body. Mind and body are, thus, different aspects of the same substance, just as every coin has two sides. So, all of us human beings, ultimately, are modes of the one universal substance that can be conceived as physical bodies, or as non-physical minds. Spinoza's conception of God and reality constitutes a form of *pantheism*, the idea that God is everything, imminent in all things. And since there exists only one thing, which can be conceived in different ways, his position may also be called *neutral monism*.

One significant consequence of Spinoza's conception of God and humanity is *determinism*, the idea that there is no free will. Since God is the one universal substance and God could not choose differently than he does, it follows that no one can act contrary to what happens. Spinoza's ideas colored him in a controversial light, especially within the Jewish community, from which he was excommunicated.[2]

Parallelism—Leibniz and Malebranche: Like Spinoza, the German philosopher Leibniz was both a rationalist and a mathematician. He not only invented a rudimentary calculator, but also discovered calculus at the same time as Newton, which led to a debate between the two about which thinker plagiarized the other! And like Spinoza, Leibniz subscribed to a version of the principle of sufficient reason. But unlike Spinoza, Leibniz was not privy to any form of pantheism, Spinoza's conception of an imminent God. He favored, instead, a return to a system more like that of Descartes, with a transcendent God and concrete individuals.

A logical principle of which Leibniz makes use is the law of identity, the law that every statement implies itself, or that every statement is

---

[2] For primary source readings on Spinoza, see Parts I and II of *The Ethics*. The text *Modern Philosophy: An Anthology of Primary Sources* (Indianapolis, IN: Hackett Publishing, 2009), edited by Richard Ariew and Erick Watkins is an excellent compilation of readings from the early modern period, including selections from Descartes through Kant. The relevant passages on Spinoza can be found on pp. 144–196.

identical to itself. Leibniz maintains that every statement is essentially a form of the law of identity. Why? Because God created everything, and anything that God wills must happen necessarily. Hence, all truths must be both necessary and knowable a priori, through thinking alone. But how do we know that God created everything? Again, because of the principle of sufficient reason, from which it follows that there must be a complete explanation for the existence of the world and the universe. For Leibniz, the only plausible explanation for the existence of a universe is that it must have been created by an omniscient, omnipotent, and omnibenevolent being, God. Moreover, since God is an omnibenevolent being, he would create the best possible universe.

So, what are people in this best possible world? Recall that Leibniz wanted to return to a system with independently existing individual persons and entities. These things he called *monads*, the term he uses to designate substances (derived from the Greek term, "monas," meaning unity). Monads, like minds, are not spatially extended. Moreover, given the law of identity, all monads are fully equipped with attributes that unfold over the course of their lifetimes. In addition, again, per the law of identity, all monads are necessarily connected with each other, each with a completely unique perspective on reality. No two monads can be exactly alike. Lastly, no monad has any direct access to anything outside of itself. Each monad, that is, has a window through which it views reality.

Since everything is completely synchronized, Leibniz maintained that there is a *pre-established harmony* between all things. More specifically, there is a pre-established harmony between efficient and final causes. Everything that happens is determined to happen, but for a reason, as part of God's unfolding plan. For example, imagine an arctic fox. Such a fox has brown fur in the spring, but white fur in the winter. The change in the pigmentation of its fur can be accounted for either mechanically, in virtue of the biology of the fox itself, or teleologically, by an appeal to the idea that through seasonal changes in the color of its fur, the fox can more easily hide from predators. In Leibniz's view, both are true. That is, God arranged the biology of the fox for the purpose that it can hide from predators. Hence, everything that happens is meant to happen.[3]

The same principle applies to the relationship between the mind and the body. That is, the mind and the body do not interact with each other, but they exist parallel to each other in pre-established harmony. The mind experiences whatever befalls the body according to God's plan. Supposedly, this resolution fixes the problem of interaction in Descartes' system. An alternative form of parallelism is called *occasionalism*, championed by Descartes' contemporary, Nicolas Malebranche. On this view, God implants a sensation into the mind of the person whenever a parallel event happens to the body.

Spinoza, Leibniz, and Malebranche are often referred to as the *continental* rationalists, since they lived and operated on the continent of Europe. The thinkers who are grouped under the label of empiricism lived and operated in the United Kingdom, Locke in England, Berkeley in Ireland, and Hume in Scotland. Hence, they are sometimes called the *British* empiricists.

Locke—Cartesian Empiricism? Even though Locke is best classified as an empiricist, many of his ideas resemble those of Descartes, including his belief in God and the fact that he maintained a version of both substance dualism and representationalism. Nonetheless, as an empiricist, he maintained that the primary source of knowledge is experience rather than reason. The mind, at birth, Locke famously claimed is like a "blank slate," or an empty tablet, upon which our experiences write. First and foremost, if people had innate ideas, innate knowledge, then there would be much less disagreement

---

[3] For primary source passages from Leibniz, see *The Monadology.* The complete text can be found in the Ariew and Watkins anthology, pp. 275–284.

between them, especially between people of different cultures. Recall that one of the ideas Descartes classified as innate was the idea of God. But while Descartes seemed, specifically, to have in mind the God of Christianity, not all cultures believe in such a God. Truly, the people of most cultures believe in *some* transcendent reality, but the earliest forms of religion and those of many indigenous people tend to be polytheistic and rooted mostly in their observations of the world around them, that is, in their experience, in which animistic and anthropomorphic constructions typically prevail.

While the previous argument is negative, Locke constructs a positive account of the way in which the mind acquires ideas. For Locke, all knowledge arises from experience, but in two ways: through sensation and through introspection or reflection. Through the former, we receive ideas of external objects, and through the latter, we develop psychological ideas. Locke defines reflection as our "perception of the operations of our own minds within us."[4] For example, I received my idea about what an apple is by looking at apples, through sensation. But through the process of reflection, I come to understand what it means to think, observe, and make decisions.

As for the types of ideas we acquire through experience, Locke distinguishes between simple and complex. Simple ideas are the basis for all other ideas, and complex ideas emerge based on the operations of the mind alone. Simple ideas, for Locke, are received completely passively, whereas complex ideas are formed through the activity of the mind. In addition, Locke distinguishes between ideas and *qualities*. Whereas ideas constitute the immediate objects of perception and thought, qualities are powers within the objects to produce similar effects in the mind. Locke distinguishes between two types of qualities, primary and secondary. Primary qualities consist of shape, size, and solidity, and represent intrinsic properties of the object itself.

---

[4] *Essay Concerning Human Understanding*, II.I.4, cited in Thomson's *Bacon to Kant*, p. 151.

Secondary qualities consist of properties perceived by the mind alone, including colors, sounds, tastes, smells, textures, heat, cold, pain, and pleasure. For example, the roundness and the size of an apple match up with the apple itself. However, the redness (or greenness) of the apple, its taste, how it feels when you hold it, and the scent of the apple are all in the mind of the perceiver alone. Consider the old question, "If a tree falls in a forest, will it make a sound?" The answer to the riddle, of course, is that there is a sound only if there is a person nearby who can perceive the sound. Hence, the answer to this riddle encompasses Locke's conception of secondary qualities.

Locke's distinction between these two qualities is sometimes called his *resemblance thesis*. That is, primary qualities resemble the objects that are sensed, whereas secondary qualities do not. Locke provides many arguments for this distinction, but his two strongest are the following. First, consider pain and nausea. Imagine that your friend quickly jabs you with a pin. You would likely feel a sudden sensation of pain. But there is nothing resembling "pain" in the pin. A similar argument can be made with respect to pleasure. Recall the example of the apple. Just as the taste is not in the apple, but in your mind, the pleasure evoked by the taste resembles nothing in the apple itself. The same can be said about the viruses that cause illness. Second, try to observe a supposedly colored object in the dark. Once the light is turned off, the color disappears, but the shape and size of the object remain the same. It is reasonable to conclude that the shapes of different surfaces reflect light differently, thus, causing the idea of color in the mind.

Two salient conclusions may be drawn from Locke's contributions to epistemology. First, what most people accept as reality is constructed by the mind, and does not in fact resemble the objective, external world. The features of such a world none of us can directly observe. Second, in connection with the first point, the mind is not merely passive, but active. Most of the ideas we possess are complex, and, hence, were not obtained from sensation alone. That is, none of us get our ideas merely by looking at external objects, but through the mental processes that accompany sensation. Locke, thus, changes the Cartesian project by shifting priority to experience over reason alone and by broadening experience to include the processes of the mind.[5]

Berkeley—Subjective Idealism: Like Locke, Irish Bishop, George Berkeley subscribed to the presuppositions of empiricism. However, he denied that there existed any mind-independent entities. For Berkeley, *esse est percipi*, or "to be is to be perceived." Hence, everything is mind dependent. The existence of anything depends on its being perceived. Since everything that exists is entirely mind dependent, it follows that physical matter does not exist! So, there is no physical world, only an external world consisting of minds and the ideas within them.

Berkeley accepts this idea primarily because of the failure of Locke's resemblance thesis, which he rejects for two reasons. First, shape, size, and speed of motion, which Locke lists as examples of primary qualities that are intrinsic to objects, can vary with perception and point of view just as secondary qualities can. A perfectly round object, for instance, might look like an oval from the right angle. From a distance, the size of an object can change. Observe any car, truck, or bus from the top story of a building, and it will appear as though you can fit it between your fingers!

A 20th century contribution to arguments such as Berkeley's derive from Einstein's work on the special theory of relativity, in which he established that speed of motion can vary from different perspectives. One of his thought experiments consisted of a train moving east with a passenger standing directly in the middle of one of the cars and an observer watching from the outside. Suppose that two lights flash on at both ends of the car. From the perspective of the passenger, both

---

[5] Locke's *Essay Concerning Human Understanding* is his most relevant work on epistemology, of which Parts I and II address the material covered here. Selections from Locke's *Essay* can be found in Ariew and Watkins, pp. 316–422.

lights flash on simultaneously. But from the observer's point of view, it will appear as though one light flashes on before the other, the light closer to the direction in which the train is moving. A related example consists of two passengers in a car of the same train who are tossing a frisbee back and forth. Imagine also that once again there is an observer outside the train. From this bystander's perspective, it will appear as though the frisbee moves at two different speeds. When tossed toward the east by the first passenger, it will appear to move at the same speed as the train. But when tossed toward the west by the second passenger, it will appear to move more slowly. Hence, speed of motion seems to vary based on perspective.

An additional point of support for Berkeley's argument comes from quantum physics, specifically, from the work of German theoretical physicist, Werner Heisenberg, the *uncertainty principle*. This principle is a mathematical law that governs the behavior of sub-atomic particles, such as photons (light particles). In short, the principle suggests that the more one knows about a particle's position, the less that one knows about the particle's momentum, or force. In connection with the uncertainty principle is the "observer effect." Basically, if an experiment is set up to study light as a particle, a single-slit experiment, then light will behave as a particle. If an experiment is set up to study light as a wave, a double-slit experiment, then light will behave as a wave. Thus, the behavior of light, and more generally, the behavior of sub-atomic particles, which supposedly constitute the basis of matter, varies with the activity of the observer. An observer, therefore, is never merely a passive bystander, but a part of the world process.

Berkeley's second point of contention with Locke's resemblance thesis is the claim that ideas cannot resemble anything but other ideas. In other words, no idea can resemble an independently existing object. To illustrate Berkeley's point, imagine your favorite food. Simply imagining this food does not fill your stomach and sate your hunger. Your idea of this food is virtually identical to all your other ideas. It is no different than your idea of Santa Claus, Charlie Brown, Puff the Magic Dragon, or unicorns.

So, physical matter does not exist. How, then, do we get our ideas? Since Berkeley is an empiricist, he maintains that our ideas come from experience. But they cannot come from physical matter if there is no such thing. Moreover, no individual's ideas can come from that individual. If they did, every individual would craft a much different and more pleasant life experience for himself or herself, a life without sickness, suffering, irritation, or pain. And since ideas can only resemble other ideas, our ideas cannot come from other ideas. Moreover, there is great uniformity to our experiences, which means that there must be some being to sustain perceptions even when no human receives them. Such a being must be both very powerful and very benevolent. The only place from which our ideas can come, thus, is directly from God, who, himself, stands in need of no observer.

Since Berkeley maintains that only minds and the ideas within them exist, and that all anyone experiences directly are those items that exist within the sphere of one's subjectivity, his position is best classified as *subjective idealism*. Before moving on, there is an obvious problem with Berkeley's arguments denying physical matter. Basically, they fail to *prove* that there is no such thing as physical matter. Even if his arguments are sound, at best, all they establish is a form of representationalism, the idea that the items of our experience differ from the external world. It seems, thus, that the existence of physical matter should be retained, along with some principles about how such matter operates.[6]

Newton and the Invention of Mechanics: Given that Isaac Newton was generally unpleasant and secretive, it is difficult to pinpoint exactly

---

[6] The two most relevant of Berkeley's writings to the arguments discussed here are his *Principles of Human Knowledge* and *Three Dialogues between Hylas and Philonous*. Selections from *Principles of Human Knowledge* and the entirety of *Three Dialogues* can be found in the Ariew and Watkins anthology, pp. 438–454, and 454–504, respectively.

when he arrived at many of his conclusions. We do know, however, that in 1655, while a student at Trinity College, Cambridge, the closure of the university due to an outbreak of the Black Plague forced Newton into a sabbatical, during which he supposedly began his research into optics and mechanics.

Basically, Newton picked up where his predecessors, specifically Galileo, left off, making several crucial discoveries. Recall that modern thinkers tended toward explanations in terms of efficient causes, forces. More specifically, thinkers such as Kepler and Galileo took interest in the question about the force that keeps the planets in motion, revolving around the sun. One of Newton's monumental contributions was his precise definition of a force. Generally, a force refers to a push or a pull, but in precise physical terms, a force refers to the mass of an object multiplied by its acceleration or its change in velocity. In other words, force refers to how big something is multiplied by the extent to which it speeds up in motion. The second of Newton's monumental discoveries begins with the legendary apple that fell on his head. This event left Newton with the insight that the same force that pulled the apple to his head also keeps the planets in motion. This force we now know as *gravity*. Galileo discovered that all objects, regardless of their weight, fall at the same rate. Newton discovered the mathematical law that explains why.[7]

---

[7] As it is not crucial to the text, I included the formula and explanation of the law of gravity here. Basically, the universal law of gravitation states that the gravitational force between two objects is proportional to the product of their masses and inversely proportional to the square of the distance between them. It is symbolized in the following way: $F = Gm_1m_2/r^2$. The symbol "G" refers to the gravitational constant. When the m's are in kilograms and the r is in meters, $G = 6.67 \times 10^{-11}$. According to his formula, suppose that m(1) is the mass of the Earth, r is the radius of Earth, and m(2) is you. Then, we call F your *weight*. Weight is a force. Newton's second law—$F = ma$—is always true, where (a) and (m) refer to the same object—in this case your weight. Imagine setting your weight equal to Newton's second law. Your mass would cancel out from both sides of the equation and your acceleration is just the Gravitational constant multiplied by the mass of the earth divided by the square of the Earth's radius, illustrated by the following formula: $g = Gm_{Earth}/r^2_{Earth} = 9.8 \text{ m/s}^2$, where "g" represents the acceleration of gravity on Earth. Since acceleration does not depend on the weight of a falling object, all objects fall to the Earth at the same rate, just as Galileo observed.

Newton published his discovery of the law of gravity in addition to his three laws of motion in *Principia Mathematica* (1687). The first law of motion Galileo discovered, the law of inertia, which states that an object travels at a constant speed unless it is acted upon by an outside force. The second law is basically Newton's definition of a force, denoted by the equation $F = MA$, described above. The third law states that every action has an equal but opposite reaction, best illustrated by an athlete bouncing a basketball. Before proceeding to the work of Hume, two observations about Newton's laws deserve to be noted. First, these laws share with other laws of physics what scientists refer to as the *Axiomatic Property*. That is, they cannot be *proven*, but only postulated and tested by experiments. Like all scientific theories, Newton developed his laws based on the interaction between observation and rational deduction. Second, and more importantly, these laws imply *universal causal determinism*. Basically, if one knows the initial position and velocity of any object, in addition to the forces acting on it, the behavior of that object at any time can be predicted. Theoretically, it would be possible to predict the future of the entire universe! The deterministic implication of Newton's laws supported the denial of free will and led to changing conceptions of God and his relationship to the world. While Newton himself believed in God, now it seemed that God was only necessary to create the universe, setting everything in motion, after which all its processes basically operate independently. This position is called *Deism*, according to which God has no special relationship with the world or with humanity.

(II) Hume—Radical Empiricism and Naturalism

Even though David Hume had a highly respectable reputation as a scholar, and the author of a very famous history of England, he could not procure a teaching position in his lifetime. Nonetheless, he is one of the most prolific thinkers the United Kingdom ever produced. Hume's work can be understood as the culmination of three movements in the history of modern thought. First, the growing trend toward skepticism exemplified by the early stages of Descartes' *Meditations* in conjunction with the general rejection of the authority of the medieval schoolmen and various religious institutions, in many ways epitomizes Hume's analysis of the origins of beliefs, including those that are common and allegedly indisputable. Second, the contributions of modern empiricists, especially those of Locke, and the idea that the world of experience is constructed from human experience are integral to Hume's conception of the human mind. Third, the principles of modern science and especially the work of Newton and his successors influenced Hume in two ways. On the one hand, Newton's discovery of the laws that govern the physical world led Hume to believe that the mind operates according to laws as well, and, thus, he made it his mission to become the "Newton of the human mind," discovering its principles just as Newton discovered those of the universe. On the other hand, the implications of Newton's laws for the conception of God led many thinkers to abandon spiritualism in favor of materialism, naturalism, and atheism. Pierre Laplace, for instance, once remarked to Napoleon that he "had no need for [the God] hypothesis" in his system, which he carried beyond Newton's. Hume not only perpetuated the trend toward naturalism through his various critiques of religion and intelligent design, but by proposing a prototypical theory of evolution, and a unique conception of human faculties.

The most prominent themes in Hume's thought are the following: (a) the distinction between matters of fact and relations of ideas; (b) his epistemology; (c) his critique of causality and induction; (d) his conception of naturalistic justification; and (e) his critique of religion and intelligent design. Each of these themes will be addressed in turn.[8]

---

[8] In the pages that follow, I will draw primarily from three primary sources: Hume's *A Treatise of Human Nature*, in Norton & Norton (Eds.) (New York: Oxford University Press, 2002), *An Enquiry Concerning Human Understanding*, in Beauchamp (Ed.) (New York: Oxford University Press, 1999), and *Dialogues Concerning Natural Religion*, in Kemp-Smith (Ed.) (New York: MacMillan, 1987). The second of these works is largely a recast of Part I of Hume's *Treatise*, often referred to as the *First Enquiry*.

Hume's Fork—Matters of Fact and Relations of Ideas: The rationalists generally agreed that reality manifests a logical order and can be understood *a priori*, in which causes can be discovered in virtually the same way that a geometric proof can be completed. Moreover, as the label rationalism implies, the thinkers of this tradition gave priority to reason, more specifically, to the truths that can be known through reason alone rather than ideas or beliefs that derive from sense-experience. As an empiricist, Hume gave priority not to reason, but to sense-experience. Nonetheless, he maintained that there are purely formal truths, such as principles of logic and mathematics. These types of propositions he called *relations of ideas*. An example would be a statement such as "All triangles are three-sided figures." Such a statement basically states the definition of a triangle. To deny it would result in contradiction. The second type of proposition he called *matters of fact*, which basically consist of our perceptions and sense-experiences.

The importance of this distinction is its implications for the claims that Hume believes are demonstrable, or provable. According to Hume, a statement can only be proven, or demonstrated beyond a shadow of doubt, if its denial results in a contradiction. It seems to follow, thus, that only relations of ideas are demonstrable. A matter of fact can always be denied without contradiction, since the opposite of any matter of fact is always possible. If I happen to see a blue jay land on the railing of my porch, for instance, it is entirely possible that I made a mistake in judgment, and that the bird is really a pigeon. It is also possible that there is no bird on my porch at all and that I imagined the whole incident. Hume's critique of demonstrability has wide-reaching implications. For instance, since all scientific theories depend on observation, no scientific law can ever be proven, as established in the section devoted to Newton, and, thus, we can never be certain that they are true. In addition, the existence of anything can never be proven, since it is always possible to imagine the non-existence of anything. This implication applies to Descartes' foundational principle, the Cogito. One of Descartes' criteria for a foundational principle is that such a principle must apply to an object that exists. But in that case, such a principle is never totally indubitable. Whereas most of the thinkers after Descartes devoted themselves to fixing his system and making scientific progress, Hume seems to tear down not only the Cartesian system, but also the very possibility of progress in the natural sciences.

Hume's Conception of the Mind—Perceptions and the Law of Association: Hume's epistemology parallels that of Locke in many ways, but it is far more radical. For Hume, everything in the mind is a *perception*, of which he distinguishes two kinds, *impressions* and *ideas*. Impressions include immediate sense-experiences, emotions, and passions. Ideas are basically copies of impressions. Hume describes the difference between ideas and impressions by suggesting that impressions are always more vivid and lively, whereas ideas are only the images we have of impressions, which are later employed in thinking and reasoning. Hume maintains that both impressions and ideas may be simple or complex. Simple perceptions cannot be broken down into further components, whereas complex perceptions can. For example, an impression of a banana is complex, because it may be divided into separate colors, tastes, and odors, each of which are simple. Whereas all complex perceptions are built from simple perceptions, all simple ideas trace back to simple impressions.[9] This idea is sometimes called Hume's *copy principle.* That is, unless an "idea" that one claims to have traces back to a simple impression of which it is a copy, then there is no idea. According to Hume, people believe that they have ideas of objects of which they have no original simple impression. His distinction between ideas and impressions, and his copy principle, thus, forms the basis for many of his later arguments. A second

---

[9] See Thomson's *Bacon to Kant*, pp. 231–232.

principle Hume invokes is sometimes called the *separability principle*, the idea that every perception can exist independently of all others.[10]

Since Hume describes the passions as types of impressions, reflective impressions to be exact, it is best to address them here. For Hume, all passions derive the simple impressions of pleasure and pain. He subdivides the passions into three categories: direct, basic indirect, and derivative or compound. The direct passions emerge instantaneously from simple impressions of pleasure and pain, and there are four pairs: desire and aversion, joy and grief, hope and fear, and despair and security. For example, desire and aversion develop when one thinks about possible future pleasure and pain. Joy and grief arise when one believes that possible future pleasures and pains are unavoidable. One feels either fear or hope when one is uncertain about whether the future holds pleasure or pain.[11]

The indirect passions emerge from a combination of the simple impressions of pleasure and pain with other ideas, and there are two pairs: pride and humility, and love and hate. These four basic indirect passions derive from either thinking about oneself in a positive way (pride) or in negative way (humility), or from considering others in such ways, where thinking of others in a positive way gives rise to love and thinking of others in a negative way gives rise to hatred. These four basic passions give rise to derivative indirect passions, including envy, pity, malice, generosity, ambition, and vanity.[12]

In addition to the brute fact that the mind copies impressions to form ideas, and can build complex perceptions from more simple impressions, including the development of the passions, the primary law by which the mind operates is the *law of association*. This law can loosely be defined as a regulative principle by which the mind establishes

---

[10] See Hume's *Treatise* 1.1.1, in Norton, pp. 7–11.

[11] See Hume's Treatise, 2.1.1–4, in Norton, pp. 181–187. Also see Thomson's Bacon to Kant, p. 260.

[12] Thomson, *Bacon to Kant*, p. 260.

connections between objects or events that resemble each other or are close together in time. If you meet a person who reminds of your brother, your mind will associate the two. When you see one, you will most likely think of the other. If you have a friend that usually wears a red t-shirt, any red item, especially red articles of clothing, will likely remind you of your friend, per the law of association. If you begin to feel the effects of a seasonal virus on the same day that a fire drill takes place at your workplace or university, then, per the law of association, since the two events happened so close together in time, fire alarms will likely evoke memories of your illness.[13]

The law of association no doubt influenced the pioneers of behavioral psychology, a school of thought that emerged in the late 19th century. A famous example of this principle consists of Pavlov's experiments with his dogs. Pavlov would ring a bell while feeding his dogs. Eventually, simply the ringing of the bell alone would evoke salivation from the dogs, per the law of association. This process is now referred to as *classical conditioning.* According to Hume, our alleged ideas of causal relationships emerge from the law of association as well. Since scientific laws are laws that purport to explain how the universe works, the laws of the universe are largely a product of the laws of the human mind.

Hume's Critique of Causality, Induction, and Personal Identity: According to Hume, many of our ordinary beliefs about matters of fact are not as indubitable as most of us think. One such belief is the universal affirmation of the law of cause and effect and all the instances of it. Hume's critique of causality is primarily a critique of efficient causes, the so-called forces making up the laws that govern the universe. For one item or event, A, to be the cause of another item or event, B, three conditions must obtain. First, A and B must be temporally contiguous, or close together in time. Obviously, for A to be the cause of B, A must

---

[13] See T.Z. Lavine, *From Socrates to Sartre*, pp. 163–165.

precede B, but B must happen soon after A. For instance, if I were to drop my pen on the floor, and then 2 hours later, one of my housemates drops a pile of dishes on the kitchen floor, the two events are so far removed from each other in time that the first almost certainly has no causal connection with the second. But if a friend and I go to a restaurant and my associate begins wheezing and turning blue within seconds after eating an appetizer laced with peanut oil, the appetizer most likely is the cause of my friend's ailment. However, closeness together in time is insufficient for establishing a causal connection between two or more events. If I were to scratch my head and then seconds later there occurs an earthquake in California, it would be absurd to assume that my actions caused the natural disaster, since it fails to meet the second criterion for a causal connection, *constant conjunction*. That is, the two events, A and B, must always occur together. Whenever A happens, soon after, B happens. However, two items may be constantly conjoined, but share no causal connection. Suppose that my grocery shopping schedule coincides with one of my housemate's exercise routine such that whenever I go shopping, she goes to her recreational facility of choice. These two events may always happen together, and perhaps when I initiate my shopping errands my housemate exercises soon after, but there is no *necessary connection* between the two, the third criterion.[14]

Two questions concerned Hume. First, he wondered why people believe in cause and effect in the first place. Second, he wondered why people believe in necessary connections. But the answer to both seems to be *merely because of the psychological propensity to associate ideas*. According to Hume, no one has any idea of any necessary connection between events or objects. Recall that any idea must trace back to a simple impression. But whenever a judgment is made about a causal connection between two or more events, the judgment is based on multiple impressions. Consider the seemingly simple

---

[14] For Hume's critique of causality, see his *Treatise*, 1.1.4–5, and 1.3.2–15, in Norton, pp. 12–16, and pp. 52–118.

scenario of one billiard ball striking a second. At the very least, one has the impression of the first billiard ball striking the second, the second billiard ball moving, the motion of both billiard balls, the shape of each ball, and the colored patterns and numbers on each ball. But what one has no impression of is the *cause* itself. It could very well be that there is an invisible Leprechaun behind the second billiard ball causing it to move. While this possibility is not very probable, it certainly is conceivable, which leads to a second problem. Even if one did have an impression of the cause, it would be a matter of fact, a sensible event. But per "Hume's fork," no matter of fact is necessary, since the opposite of any matter of fact is always at least conceivable. Even for the allegedly most infallible of "causal laws," it is at least conceivable that at some point, they may fail to obtain. One example concerns the law of gravity. It is always conceivable that when I release a pen from my grip, it will remain suspended in the air, just as it is imaginable that I might suddenly be able to leap from Earth to the surface of the moon in a single bound.

On what basis, then, do we believe in the necessity and universality of causal laws? Hume insists that it is mostly out of custom or habit, in keeping with the law of association. Since the judgment that "A causes B" requires a constant conjunction of A and B, when the two events accompany each other enough times, the mind conceives of the relation between the two as necessary. Furthermore, often we feel exertion on ourselves when engaged in difficult physical tasks, such as exercise or manual labor. We then project that same exertion onto the external world, in which the causes that we believe exist are forces.[15]

Hume's critique of induction is similar. Basically, inductive claims are claims about what is likely to happen, or what is probable, which include claims about the future. An example of an inductive claim is that "The sun will rise tomorrow." Such a claim is not justified by

---

[15] See Hume's *Enquiry Concerning Human Understanding*, in Beauchamp, p. 136.

logic or reason alone, since it is at least conceivable that the sun will not rise tomorrow. Hence, claims about the future are not relations of ideas. Moreover, claims about the future, in this case, whether the sun will rise, are not matters of fact that we can observe. Since the events of the future did not yet happen, we can have no impression of them. Hence, we believe that the sun will rise tomorrow simply because it always has. The principle of induction, thus, can be formulated as the idea that the events of the future will resemble those of the past. However, the justification for this principle is doomed to be circular, since if one asked why the principle of induction should be accepted, the answer would most likely be because it always has been reliable in the past! And the critique of the judgment about the sun applies to virtually all other inductive claims, such as those concerning which foods will nourish us, and which activities will benefit us. Why should we continue eating apples? Because they were always healthy in the past. Why should we exercise? Because it has always helped us to sustain our health in the past.[16]

In short, no one can ever discover any indubitable truths about reality. Logic and mathematics are purely formal and, thus, can only help us to draw conclusions about matters of fact. And since science deals predominantly with observations, matters of fact, the so-called "laws of nature" are only regularities, patterns that seem to repeat themselves so frequently that people just feel that they are true. In addition to the once seemingly inviolable laws of nature, many other ordinary beliefs are subject to the same limitations of the mind, including our beliefs about personal identity. Most of us believe that we go through life as the same person. That is, I am at 36 years old, the same person I was at 30, the same person I was at 25, the same person I was at 15, the same person I was at 10, the same person I was at 5, and so on. But per Hume's principles, I can have no idea that does not trace back to a simple impression. Moreover, every one of my sense-impressions

---

[16] Ibid, pp. 116–117, and p. 121.

and each idea copied from each impression is capable of existing separately and independently from all others. Thus, I literally have no idea of *myself*. And since Hume's principles apply to the minds of all people, no one has any idea of a self. The self is nothing more than what Hume calls a "bundle of perceptions."[17]

Hume's principles may be extended to other beliefs. None of us has any proof that objects continue to exist when they are not within our immediate experience. Coupled with modern scientific principles, such as those in the field of quantum physics, Hume's principles seem particularly troubling. Even though idealists such as Berkeley failed to prove that physical matter does not exist, Hume's principles suggest that we cannot prove that there is no independent material world apart from our experience, and that such a world is constructed from our perceptions, just as the observer effect implies.

It seems that Hume's principles leave us in the despairing throes of irreversible skepticism. We need most of our beliefs in order to live. If I am not the same person today that I was yesterday, how can I be held accountable for my actions? If the university where I am employed ceases to exist when I leave, then why should I make the effort to travel there each day? Why should I believe anything at all? Hume's answer seems to invoke that of the scorpion in Aesop's fable: because it is our nature.

Naturalistic Justification, Free will, and Morality: Bear the following two points in mind: First, Hume never thought that he *disproved* the existence of causal laws, personal identity, or the existence of an independent material world. Second, Hume would not necessarily want any of us to stop believing in such things. His purpose was to uncover how they emerge and what they really mean. He believed that he showed that such ideas do derive neither from sense-experience nor from reason alone. How then do we get such beliefs? For Hume, it is

---

[17] Hume's critique of personal identity in occurs in the *Treatise*, 1.4.6, in Norton, pp. 164–171.

because *by nature*, we are inclined to develop beliefs that we simply feel are true. Humans are inclined to make judgments about causal relationships, the continued existence of objects, personal identity, and an independently existing material world because doing so is necessary for their survival and continued existence. The principal caveat with which Hume leaves us is that such beliefs are not certain and indubitable, and, thus, cannot be proven.

Such beliefs are grounded in a "gross earthy mixture," our natural inclinations regulated by the law of association in conjunction with sufficiently repeated experiences and observations. By contrast, Hume wishes to depart with the "fiery particles" that constituted the thought of prior, classical thinkers, especially the rationalism of Plato, Aristotle, and Descartes, and the idealism of Berkeley.[18] Just as a bird requires wind resistance to fly, and just as boats often require anchors, our beliefs must remain tethered to our experience, and we must be aware of the limitations set by our nature. It is for this reason that Hume insists that "reason is and ought to be the slave of the passions."[19] While human beings are possessed of rationality, rationality is purely formal and empty without the passions, which are self-regulating.

Eminent scholar, Gaskin lists the following as criteria for a Humean natural belief. First, the belief must be ordinary, one that emerges in common, everyday life. Second, the belief derives neither from reason nor from experience alone. Third, the belief is necessary, in that we cannot function without it. Fourth, and finally, the belief must be universal, one that all people generally share.[20] Personal identity fits these criteria. People just naturally and instinctively believe that they

---

[18] Hume's *Treatise*, 1.4.7, in Norton, pp. 176–177.

[19] Hume's *Treatise*, 2.3.3.4, in Norton, p. 266.

[20] See J.C.A. Gaskin, *Hume's Philosophy of Religion* (London: MacMillan, 1988). This list of criteria can also be found in Andrew Pyle's *Hume's Dialogues on Natural Religion: A Reader's Guide* (New York: Continuum International Publishing, 2006), pp. 115–116.

remain the same across time. They need not meditate, nor engage in deep, theoretical, abstract thought to arrive at such a conclusion. As Hume establishes, such a belief is not merely logical, since a person's identity is a matter of fact, and no one sense-impression gives rise to a self. Moreover, people in fact do change over time. Children age, grow taller, and mature. Personal interests and appetites change. Happily married couples grow apart. Why? Because human nature is a tumultuous river of various experiences. Each impression a person has constitutes a change in that person. And if the observer effect applies to introspection, one's awareness of one's own existence influences the determinations of one's identity. That is, how one chooses to see oneself influences, to a significant extent, what and who one is. The idea of personal identity is universal. Any stable, rational individual subscribes to such a belief, regardless of culture, attitude, or persuasion. And lastly, without personal identity, without the belief that one is the same person throughout time, one could not live one's life. One would not seek employment, live in the same home, associate with the same people, or regularly engage in one's hobbies. Without such a belief, one could not recognize oneself or one's possessions, and one could not be blamed or praised for one's actions. One could not be held responsible for anything.

Morality, thus, is made possible by the idea of personal identity. Moral beliefs, too, are natural, justified by the evaluative nature of humanity rather than by reason. For Hume, moral evaluation basically explains which actions and underlying character traits people approve of and why. Our nature, our instincts, give rise to specific feelings and desires, and from these feelings and desires emerge general moral principles and rules. The two most basic feelings that give rise to moral principles Hume refers to as *approbation* and *disapprobation*, or approval and disapproval. Imagine that you are casually walking down the street one day. Suppose that during your stroll, you see woman pushing a baby carriage, and she is accosted by a man who then rips the baby out of the carriage and chucks it into traffic. According to Hume, the vast majority of people would feel revulsion and disgust by such a scenario. They would disapprove. Why? Because such behavior is not useful to humanity. If we all attempted to kill each other, soon there would be no human race at all. The feeling of disgust and revulsion that leads us to disapprove of actions such as the murder of innocent children gives rise to the general moral principle that no one should needlessly harm others. On the other hand, if you were to see this same man carry this woman's groceries to her car for her, a concomitant feeling of pleasure and warmth would likely wash over you. You would approve of such behavior since it is conducive to the continued success of humanity. This feeling of approval culminates in the general moral rule that you should always help those in need.[21]

As it is our nature that determines moral principles, only passions can motivate moral action. In the first place, we are apt to confuse calm passions with reason. Merely because one feels a sense of tranquility or serenity does not necessarily mean that one is engaged in deep thought, rather one associates such a feeling with an activity or character trait of which one approves. Reason is merely the process of deriving conclusions from premises or evidence. There are two kinds of these processes–deductive (which reveals the logical relations between ideas) and inductive (which concerns probabilities about matters of fact). Without a relevant passion or desire, we are entirely indifferent to what is true or likely to be true. Reason only draws attention to facts that are relevant to our passions. For instance, reason can remind us of the painful consequences of an action, but in that case, what motivates us is the aversion to pain rather than reason itself. Moreover, while reason can determine the relevant means to some end, only our passions and desires can determine what ends we have.

---

[21] Hume does not advance a normative moral theory in the way that many other philosophers do, such as Immanuel Kant, Jeremy Bentham, or John Stuart Mill, although, he is interpreted as proposing an early version of utilitarianism. That is, he seems to establish a connection between approval and utility, since he insists that we approve of those actions that are useful to us but disapprove of those actions that are not.

Reason consists of propositions which merely represent what is true and false, unlike the passions. It is possible to like or dislike things that are totally imaginary. Furthermore, unless one already has a vested interest in something, no rational argument can motivate a person to take an interest in the subject in question. In the sphere of romance, if a person just simply is not attracted to another, then no logical proof or argument can induce a feeling of attraction in that person. In addition, if a person happens not to be a fan of a sport, be it football, basketball, baseball, or any other athletic competition, then one will likely have no interest in the outcome of a game in any of these sports. Perhaps if one's home team is playing, one might be invested. But that investment is rooted in a sentimental feeling of solidarity, rather than rationality.[22]

In addition, it seems to follow from his remarks about reason being motivationally impotent that moral claims cannot be rationally justified. Moreover, the terms reasonable and unreasonable can be applied only to beliefs, since beliefs alone can be true or false. Passions and desires are merely felt or performed. They do not represent states of affairs. Hence, they cannot be true or false. As such, they cannot be judged as complying with reason. In connection with this argument is Hume's "fork." Moral claims are not based on reason alone because they cannot be demonstrated through deductive a priori reasoning and they are not based on inductive reasoning regarding matters of fact. That is, our moral claims are neither relations of ideas, nor are they based on inductive inferences from our observations. In addition, Hume notes that we can never give a rational justification for our human ends in terms of rational principles. For instance, I can justify my daily exercise in terms of my desire for health, and my desire for health in terms of my aversion for pain, but I can't justify my aversion to pain. It is ultimate. All reasoning concerns only means, which in

---

[22] See Hume's *Treatise*, 2.3.3.4, in Norton, pp. 266–267. See also Thomson, *Bacon to Kant*, pp. 262–263.

turn can be justified in terms of ends, but ends are simply what agree with our feeling or what we desire. To make the point more clearly, Hume once claimed that it is "not contrary to reason to prefer the destruction of the whole world to the scratching of my finger." This quotation recalls Hume's definition of passions as real existences. As such, they are unlike beliefs, which purport to represent the world truly, whereas preferences and choices are neither reasonable nor unreasonable. Lastly, one cannot derive logically a sentence about what one ought to do from any combination of sentences about what is. His idea is that reason can only produce true or false sentences about how things are, and that no claim about what ought to be done can be deduced from such sentences. In contemporary language, Hume seems to be asserting that no evaluative "ought" can be deduced from a set of true descriptions or that there is a logical gap between moral evaluations and factual descriptions.[23]

Since morality demands the possibility of human free will, Hume's position on the matter deserves attention. If people have no control over their actions, then they cannot be held responsible for them. But remember that Hume subverts reason to the passions. It seems to follow that personal actions are merely the result of their passions, over which people have little or no control. But it would be a leap too far to suggest that because people are primarily passionate animals, they lack free will. Hume's position on free will is best described as *compatibilism*. That is, he believed that free will is consistent with *determinism*, the idea that all events have an antecedent cause. The latter position maintains that since everything has a cause, there is no free will. A third position is called *libertarianism*, which denies the thesis of determinism. Libertarians insist that not everything has a cause, and at least some human actions are among those things. Thus, human beings have free will.

---

[23] Most of these arguments can be found in the *Treatise*, 3.1.2, in Norton, pp. 302–307, in addition to 2.3.3, pp. 263–268. See also Thomson, pp. 263–265, for his summary of these arguments.

Even though Hume denied that the idea of universal causality does not derive from either experience or reason, he would insist that such a principle is justified as a *natural belief*. Ultimately, he maintained that the idea that actions have no cause whatsoever leads to a double-problem. On the one hand, this idea conflicts with the way in which people are inclined to assess the reality of the physical world. Since the belief in causality is universal, and since people are a part of nature, they must, to be consistent, believe that this principle applies to their actions. In fact, even our estimation of other people presupposes an implicit acceptance of causality. Hume uses the example of a prisoner who would rather dig through the cement of his cell than attempt to convince a guard to set him free. Such a person believes that the best indicator of future behavior is past behavior. People never assume that an individual's actions are totally chaotic and random. On the other hand, if one's actions had no cause, then it seems to follow that people would have no control over their actions. That is, a person may be the cause of his or her actions. Thus, even if an action is dictated by a passion, so long as that passion is not contrary to the nature of the person, then the actions that result from such a passion are under the control of a person. The only sense in which a person lacks free will, for Hume and for most compatibilists, is through coercion, if a person is forced against their will to commit an action that they otherwise would not commit, such as situations in which individuals are compelled at gun point to act against their will.[24]

Hume's Critique of Religion — the Dialogues: Recall that deism became popular during the Enlightenment. Despite the modern departure from the classical teleological conception of reality, most forms of deism recognized that the universe was the product of design, except that once God designed the world, he had no further relations with

---

[24] For Hume's account of free will, see his *Treatise*, 2.3.1–2, in Norton, pp. 257–265. See also *An Enquiry Concerning Human Understanding*, in Beauchamp, Section 8, pp. 148–165.

humanity. Hence, popular versions of the design argument during Hume's time became the focus, but not the only objects of his attack. Hume produced three major attacks on traditional religion, one of which was an essay, "The Natural History of Religion," which in many ways anticipates critiques from the likes of Feuerbach, Nietzsche, and Freud. In addition, Section 1.2.4 of his *Enquiry Concerning Human Understanding*, "Of Miracles," critiques the rationality of religious beliefs based on alleged miracles. An epilogue to the same work provides a brief critique of arguments from design. Hume's most famous attack on religion he delivered in the form of a much more detailed, posthumous publication, *Dialogues Concerning Natural Religion*, on which this section will focus.

Before fully immersing ourselves into Hume's *Dialogues*, it will be beneficial to summarize two provisional points of Hume's critique of religion. First, recall the rules of Hume's empiricism, according to which the mind holds no ideas that do not trace back to simple impressions. Since no one has any impression of a being called "God," no one can have any idea of God. If this argument is sound, it follows that systems whose authors purport to demonstrate God's existence based on the idea of God are completely erroneous, as are all versions of the ontological argument. Moreover, the existence of anything, including God, is a matter of fact, and no matter of fact can be proven. What's more, even if God's existence can be demonstrated, the non-existence of anything is always conceivable. But if it is conceivable that God does not exist, God would be merely contingent, rather than a necessary being.

Second, Hume's argument on miracles ties in with the connection between causes and natural laws. Typically, when someone suggests that a miracle happened, they mean to suggest that an event occurred that violated a natural law, a causal law. For example, when Christ changed water into wine, fed thousands of people using only five loaves of bread and two fish, gave sight to the blind, walked on the sea of Galilee, raised Lazarus from the dead, and returned from the dead himself, these feats may be called miracles in that they violated the laws of nature. However, the laws of nature emerge from our experience of the constant conjunction of events. The impressions that give rise to these laws constitute evidence that far outweighs any single claim to the violation of such a regularity. As with the libertarian denial of the thesis of determinism, consistency demands that we reject the testimony of miracles. In cases in which a miracle is reported, it is more likely that the witness suffered a delusion, or a mistake in judgment.

While Hume certainly did not subscribe to the design argument, he respected it more than he did both the ontological argument and the testimony of miracles. Hume's *Dialogues* consists of conversations about religion between three principal characters: Demea, who represents traditional religious orthodoxy, Cleanthes, who represents the moderate position of natural theology, or "accurate philosophy," and Philo, the most skeptical of the three. While each of these characters, in some way, represents Hume's thought, the consensus is that Philo represents the bulk of Hume's position. Primarily, the *Dialogues* represents the conflict between the worldviews of Philo and Cleanthes, with Demea entering the conversation only to bolster the intellectual prowess of Cleanthes when he seems sufficiently refuted by Philo.

Most of the discussion between these characters concerns the design argument, first presented by Cleanthes in Part II:

> Look around the world: Contemplate the whole and every part of it: You will find it to be nothing but one great machine, sub-divided into an infinite number of lesser machines, which again admit of sub-divisions, to a degree beyond what human senses and faculties can explain. All these various machines, and even their most minute parts, are adjusted to each other with an accuracy, which ravishes into admiration all men, who have ever contemplated them. The curious adapting of means to ends, throughout all nature, resembles exactly, though it much exceeds, the productions of human contrivance; of human design, thought, wisdom, and intelligence.

> Since, therefore, the effects resemble each other, we are led to infer, by all the rules of analogy, that the causes also resemble; and that the author of nature is somewhat similar to the mind of man; though possessed of much larger faculties, proportioned to the grandeur of the work, which he has executed. By this argument a posteriori, and by this argument alone, we do prove at once the existence of a deity, and his similarity to the human mind and intelligence.[25]

It can be summarized in the following way:

1. The universe is like a huge, man-made machine made up of many lesser machines, except that the universe is much more complex than any man-made machine.
2. Like effects have like causes.
3. Machines and human artifacts have intelligent creators.
4. Therefore, probably, the world has an intelligent creator.
5. This creator is God.[26]

Two notable features of this argument are, first, that it concerns causal relationships (the relationship between an artifact and its creator), and second, it is *analogical*. An analogy basically consists in a comparison between two or more things, a statement of the ways in which they are similar. An argument by analogy is a form of inductive reasoning in which a conclusion is drawn based on an analogy. For instance, suppose that you know two people, Adam and Jack. Suppose that Adam and Jack have the following properties in common: they are both fans of the New England Patriots, the Boston Red Sox, the Chicago Bulls, and Connor McGregor. Suppose also that Adam has an additional property, he is a fan of the Marvel Cinematic Universe (MCU). You do not know for sure that Jack is a fan of the MCU. But based on the properties he has in common with Adam, you

---

[25] Hume, *Dialogues Concerning Natural Religion*, in Kemp-Smith (Ed.) (New York: MacMillan, 1987), p. 143.

[26] This reconstruction of Cleanthes' version of the argument is provided in Cornman, Lehrer, and Pappas's text, *Philosophical Problems and Arguments* (Indianapolis, IN: Hackett, 1992), p. 242.

conclude that, probably, Jack is fan of the MCU as well. Notice that the version of the design argument presented by Cleanthes differs from Aquinas's "fifth way," which is a deductive argument. The strength of an analogical argument depends on the strength of the comparison drawn between the items being compared, which is based on experience.

Philo presents many criticisms to this argument. The most prominent may be summarized as follows. First, the argument seems to commit both the fallacies of hasty generalization and composition. With respect to hasty generalization, the conclusion is drawn far too quickly. Since the world in which we live is the only one of which we have any experience, there are not enough representative samples from which to infer intelligent design. Moreover, the argument itself rests on an ambiguity. It suggests that the whole world resembles a giant human artifact because it contains several instances of intelligent design, plants, animals, oceans, mountain valleys, etc. all seem to be the work of an intelligent being. But from such observations, it does not follow that the whole world is the product of design. Merely because the porch outside your house is constructed of oak does not mean that your entire house is made of oak.

In addition, an intriguing criticism is that the argument seems to mis-apply the *anthropic principle.* That is, it assumes that because the world is so suitable for and conducive to human life, the world must be designed specifically for humans by an intelligent being. Hence, the order manifested by the world may be nothing more than humanity's projection of their own attributes onto the external world, not all that different from the projection of forces onto the external world in the development of ideas of natural laws and causes.

Furthermore, a very damning criticism is that the analogy on which the argument is based is quite weak. The argument compares the order manifested by the natural organisms of the world with that of the synthetic artifacts and machines created by human beings. But these are two different types of order. The order of organisms is internal to the item that possesses it. Plants and animals develop from genetic codes inherited from their parents. Machines have an external order, imposed on them from without. The world, thus, resembles more a giant plant or an animal than it does any human invention. If so, it is more likely that the world just "grew" into being.

Moreover, Cleanthes' argument relies heavily on experience, observations. But the world which we inhabit is the only one with intelligent life of which we have any knowledge. None of us has access to any worlds that we know to have intelligent creators. If we did, it would provide a basis for comparison with our own world and, perhaps, would strengthen the argument. Obviously, if these worlds were vastly different than ours, it would weaken the argument Cleanthes presented. Certainly, we can observe individual acts of creation, be they synthetic or natural, and we can observe the visible world, but no one ever observed the creation of an entire world or universe. There exist aspects of the universe that exceed modern technology. That is, we cannot even observe our universe in its entirety. Since no one has any impression of such events, per the principles of Hume's empiricism, no one has any idea of the creation of any world.

Furthermore, since the argument in question invokes intelligent design, it implies that there is some purpose to the world. Usually, an item is created for a reason, to serve some function. But what exactly is the purpose of the world itself? As with many philosophical questions, the major problem with this last one is not that there are no answers, but that there are far too many, and any attempt at an answer is bound to be speculative. One might hazard that the world exists to serve the will of God, but that alone does not establish the existence of God.

A final problem with this argument concerns its second premise, "Like effects have like causes." In other words, since the world and machines are similar, the things that created them must be similar, too. In the first place, previous objections established that the natural world and synthetic machines are not as similar as they appear to be. However, if they are, then if the second premise of this argument is true, it would force us to attribute some very ungodlike qualities to God. If God is like human beings, then God would share similar flaws and frailties. Moreover, if God indeed created the world, an unintended consequence would be that God is responsible for the banes of earthly existence, including disease, natural disasters, famine, war, and general acts of cruelty.

Cleanthes may be down after listening to Philo's criticisms, but he certainly is not out! In Part III of the *Dialogues*, he presents an example of intricate design, the human eye. His presentation of this analogy emphasizes the "feeling" that "immediately flows upon [one] with a force like that of a sensation" when one observes an eye. The same could be said about many other natural items, especially now that microscopes allow for the magnification of items that elude raw, unassisted observation. Bacterial flagella, for instance, the tails on bacterial cells that allow them to move, resemble outward boat motors, machines that we know are designed. His point is that *the idea of design arises from such observations in practically the same manner that an idea arises from a simple impression.* Cleanthes regards this appeal as natural and convincing, as it would take more effort to justify disagreement.

Cleanthes uses two additional analogies to support his claim. First, he asks Philo to imagine a voice speaking from the clouds, intelligible across all languages. Suppose that any of us can hear this voice. If we did, we would not only assume that it is a voice, but that it is the voice of an intelligent being. Such a conclusion would be instinctive, immediate, and natural. Disagreement would provoke accusations of mental instability! Second, he asks Philo to imagine a library of books that grew naturally. Since this second analogy is somewhat obscure, I chose to replace it with a similar one. Imagine that you are driving down a highway, and you notice a pattern of greenery that reads "WELCOME!" Automatically, you would assume that this sign did not happen by random accident, but that an intelligent being purposefully crafted it. Cleanthes' second argument, sometimes called the "irregular design argument," is simply that our experience of these two scenarios, the voice in the clouds and the natural library, are analogous to our experience of design in nature. Since in each of these scenarios, we instinctively and universally conclude that there is an intelligent being behind the voice and the library, we may conclude that, probably, there is an intelligent being that designed the world.

His initial argument did not convince Philo, but the skeptical interlocutor never truly marshals a reply to this appeal, indicating that even Hume himself had sympathies with the idea of design as natural, universal, and necessary to function. As the irregular design argument suggests, the belief that the natural wonders of the world are the product of design is an ordinary belief of everyday life that occurs virtually to everyone and anyone, rather than an idea developed over long periods of introspection and abstract thought that is endorsed only by a select few. As such, such a belief derives neither from reason, nor from any one single, simple impression. Even though it takes effort to justify disagreement, there certainly is no contradiction in denying design. Finally, the belief that the world and the items within it are the product of design make such things much easier to navigate. If one is lost on a highway, one could not find one's way without the assumption that it was built by an intelligent being according to a plan that specifically anticipated the possibility that people may get lost and would need to find their way. The same assumption enables people to makes sense of natural phenomena such as the tides, the motion of lakes, rivers, and streams, the positioning of the stars, the changing of the seasons, and the mating habits of animals.

(III) Hume and Bacon's Idols of the Mind

Hume's goal to become the "Newton of the mind" established his own intent to avoid Bacon's idols as well as his awareness of the extent to which his predecessors fell victim to them. But despite Hume's penchant for skepticism and systematicity, did he succeed?

Hume and Bacon's Idols of the Tribe: The very title of Hume's first major publication, *A Treatise of Human Nature*, indicates that his entire philosophy constitutes an attempt to construct a system that accounts for the idols of the tribe, since such idols arise from human nature itself. Hume's empiricism, conception of the origin of ideas, critique of causality, induction, and personal identity, the origin and function of the passions, the origin of morality and moral evaluation, and critique of religion and intelligent design all illustrate his deep attunement to the idols of the tribe and his own commitment to avoiding them in addition to his mission to showing his audience how to avoid them.

Hume addresses himself to the idols of the tribe in two general ways. First, he establishes that many of our beliefs have their basis not only in the way the mind forms ideas through the copy principle and the law of association, but also in the fact that humans are constituted in such a way to make judgments and evaluations. The way that the idols of the tribe may be avoided is through an awareness of the inherent capacity to project elements of our own being and experience onto the external world, and to recognize that the laws that we discover may be subject to change based on our experiences. Second, he subverts the traditional model of human faculties by placing the passions at the helm, over reason. The passions determine our ends, and as such, influence the belief-systems we construct and the ways in which we interpret the world. The ends we have, furthermore, distract us from matters in which we have no interest.

Hume and Bacon's Idols of the Cave: Hume's discussion of the passions also illustrates his awareness of the idols of the cave. That is, people will believe not only what they *feel* to be true, but also that which pleases them. In addition to his account of the origin and nature of human passions, the primary way in which Hume addresses himself to the idols of the cave is through his appeal to custom as the basis for most of our beliefs. We believe that patterns of events will repeat themselves primarily because we have the habit of experiencing them in a specific way. This tendency applies not only to causal and scientific laws, but to our judgments about the future in general. People instinctively believe that events will continue to unfold in the future as they did in the past. Such events include the effects of the behavior of people, both individually and collectively. The belief that one remains the same person over time, itself, too, illustrates this very expectation. In short, people expect and, in fact, crave what Nietzsche will call an "eternal return of the same." Normalcy provides security, safety, and, in the minds of many, happiness.

Hume's principles also imply that idols of the cave are made possible by the fact that people can directly perceive only their own ideas. And since the world that we "know" we construct largely from our own mind, such a world is, essentially, a cave of our own construction. Hume's model of the mind he intended as a map of this cave. None of us can ever betray the "gross earthy mixture" of our nature by liberating ourselves entirely from our own private cave, but we can understand that cave nonetheless. We may not be completely free, but so long as we have understanding, we are not slaves either.

Hume and Bacon's Idols of the Marketplace: The major way in which Hume addresses himself to the idols of the marketplace is, once again, through the principles of his empiricism. Words, in short, represent ideas. Or, at the very least, the only significant words will stand for impressions. Hume insists that most of our "ideas" are not really ideas, since they trace back to no impression. And if a belief has its source in an "idea" with an unclear source, then that belief is probably false. While Locke and Hume shared similar conceptions of language, Hume aimed to elucidate the origins of the impressions and ideas that are the sources of the most basic components of language. Language, after all, is the process by which the contents of one's mind are made available to others. Moreover, since the laws that govern the world originate within the mind, it is crucial to understand the symbols that represent those laws.

In addition, Hume's distinction between matters and fact and relations of ideas, the two principal types of propositions, also reflect his awareness of the idols of the marketplace. Since matters of fact refer to the objects of experience and perception, they are, for Hume, more meaningful, even though they are not provable. Given that the rationalists gave priority to relations of ideas, they were arguably less cautious of the idols of the marketplace than was Hume.

Hume and Bacon's Idols of the Theater: The radical nature of Hume's empiricism illustrates his departure not only from traditional rationalistic schools of thought, but from other empiricists as well. Locke and Berkeley had more appealing accounts of personal identity, for instance. Locke believed that memory accounted for personal identity, whereas Berkeley, ultimately, would maintain that we all depend on God for our continued existence. Moreover, Locke subscribed to a form of dualism, whereas Berkeley was an idealist.

However, the most general way in which Hume avoids idols of the theater is through his insistence that experience serves as the basis of belief rather than reason alone or testimony. While reason has its place among the human faculties, it is both motivationally inert and cannot extend our knowledge in important ways. Hence, Hume departs from the traditional model of the faculties held by the classical thinkers such as Plato, Aristotle, and Aquinas, in addition to his more immediate predecessors such as Descartes, Spinoza, and Leibniz. All that reason can do, really, is help people to calculate probabilities and determine the most feasible way to achieve our goals. In other words, reason can only help us to "figure things out." Reason is like a dictionary. It can tell us what the words mean, but it cannot, in and of itself, tell us how to write an essay or a book!

More importantly, Hume's critique of causality, induction, and religion casts a dubious shadow not only on traditional religious ideas, the institutions of which began losing their authority centuries before Hume's birth, but also on popular conceptions of the world edified by the science of Hume's day. Hume's principles imply that any discipline, in fact–whether it be science, philosophy, or theology — have as their subject the *human mind*, rather than the external, physical world. One of Hume's goals, thus, was to expose most previous philosophies as predominantly exercises in theatrics. But what about the theatre created by Hume himself?

Does Hume Avoid Bacon's Idols of the Mind? As with previous authors, Hume's susceptibility to both the idols of the tribe and cave seem to run together. With respect to the idols of the tribe, Hume would have to realize that his own mind is subject to the same proclivities as all others. Thus, any of his beliefs that do not have as their source a simple impression are, at best, questionable, and at worst, false. In addition, the fact that humans have what may be called rational instincts calls into question Hume's claims about the impotence of reason. Recall that people suffer mental disharmony between conflicting or contradictory ideas, and instinctually try to resolve such a conflict. Hume might respond that such an instinct is rooted in the passions, as unless one were emotionally invested in the ideas that conflict with each other, one would not be motivated to resolve them.

Hume seems to commit a more serious error, though. This problem is elucidated if one imagined a tribe of persons whose mental capacities include only Hume's principles of association.[27] Surely, persons in this condition could make generalizations such as "If I put my hand into the fire, it will hurt." They might even be able to make a broader generalization such as "Fire is hot." But were a traveler to come upon

---

[27] Susan Neiman employs the same thought experiment in *The Unity of Reason: Rereading Kant* (New York: Oxford University Press, 1994) p. 69. The example is also used by John Rawls in "Kantian Constructivism and Moral Theory," in *The Journal of Philosophy*, 77, pp. 515–572.

them and ask them who they believed created the world, they would not know how to respond, primarily because they would be unable to conceive of the non-existence of the world. They would not even understand such a question. In order to be able to answer such a question, one must have the capacity to imagine that, at one time, the world as it is did not exist. Not only could such persons not imagine this particular state of affairs, but they would probably lack even the capacity to imagine any state of affairs being different than their acquaintance with it. Such persons would lack natural science as we know it, apart from a limited technology, and they would also lack any sophisticated form of religion and philosophy. Such people simply would *lack that which makes curiosity possible,* and, thus, would lack that which enables inquiry. It also seems to follow that such a tribe of people would be unable to generate a more complex idea of systematic unity between the particulars of their experience. That is, they would not even have a notion of "world," let alone its absence. And since nothing within their mental framework could activate inquiry, they would not be compelled to seek such unity.[28]

Another way to conceptualize this problem for Hume and for empiricism more generally, is to consider what human beings would be like if all human knowledge depended on sense-experience. Were this the case, then human beings would not be capable of forming images or concepts of those items of consciousness that do not exactly correspond to the external, physical world. Consider a cube, for instance. Imagine that four of its sides are painted purple, that one of its sides is painted red, and that the last of its sides is painted yellow. Were an individual to see only a purple side of the cube, that same individual would undoubtedly be able to form a mental image of the whole cube, *with each of its sides painted purple.* Yet, the actual cube is multicolored. If all of human knowledge depended only on *sense-experience,* then it would not be possible to form such an image after seeing only one side

---

[28] See Neiman, p. 69.

of the cube. That persons are quite capable of forming not only images of things which they have never experienced, but also concepts of much larger and more complex things that transcend sense-experience testify to the flaws of radical empiricism.

What this problem essentially means for Hume is that the principles of association in themselves are not enough to explain the kinds of generalizations human beings can make. While I have not attempted to show that Hume's critique of causality fails to establish that sense-experience alone is not enough either to justify or provide a necessary connection between events, I have shown that Hume *presupposes* that there is nothing within a person's *rational* framework to motivate the search for unity in nature and the design of the world.

Moreover, if reason truly is the slave of the passions, then Hume's work would largely be the product of his own passions, interests, and *cave*. Hume's commitment to empiricism seems largely to derive from a personal preference, just as much as its radical nature seems to be an exaggeration. Moreover, how can one purport to explain how all minds work if we are all limited to the experience of our own perceptions? Hume's answer seems to be because we are determined by nature to make such judgments. But if that's true, then why do we so often get things wrong? Should we not be determined to judge the world more accurately? Moreover, Hume seems to imply that many of our beliefs we accept are based on their alleged instrumental value. Why, then, is there a need for theory construction at all? Humanity is determined to seek the meaning behind their actions beyond mere survival and preservation. If people were not so determined, then it would be impossible to ask "Why?" beyond a certain point. Once Newton discovered the laws of mechanics, Hume's *Treatise* and his subsequent *Enquiries* would not have been necessary.

With respect to idols of the marketplace, even though Hume seemed to design his system with the intention of clarifying the connection between words, ideas, and experiences, he decides himself what the terms "perception," "idea," "impression," and "passion," among other terms, mean in his system. To an extent, even his insistence about the motivational impotence of reason seems to be based on presuppositions that are never really proven. Moreover, he never considers whether there is any other sense in which "reason" can be understood other than in the theoretical sense in which he employs it. For all its insights, Hume's system becomes mere theater of illusions based on these considerations.

That brings us to the idols of the theater. While Hume attempts to avoid defaulting to any preconceived positions, he no doubt subscribes to the school of empiricism, and never seems to question whether the contingent nature of experience provides a substantial enough foundation on which to build a philosophical system. Moreover, if there is such universality to the laws according to which the mind works, then perhaps they are more than merely habits, unless of course Hume wishes to write off his principles as only psychological propensities. Despite his shortcomings, however, Hume truly was a remarkable thinker, not only in terms of his own contributions, but also in terms of the work that he inspired.

Chapter 5 Worksheet

1. Identify the ways in which Spinoza and Leibniz address Bacon's Idols of the Mind. How well do they avoid these idols?

2. Identify the ways in which Locke and Berkeley address Bacon's Idols of the Mind. How well do they avoid these idols?

3. Do you prefer rationalism, empiricism, or neither? Explain.

4. Give at least three examples of ordinary, everyday beliefs that are rendered dubious by Hume's principles. Are they justifiable based on Gaskin's four criteria for a natural belief? Explain.

5. Does Hume adhere to his own principles? That is, does he put forth any arguments that presuppose ideas that cannot originate in experience?

6. Give an example of a subject that you are passionate about and, then, a subject that you are not passionate about. Is there anything that could convince you to become interested in the second topic? Is there anything that could cause you to lose interest in the first? Explain.

7. Which of the three positions on free will do you favor: libertarianism, determinism, or compatibilism? Explain.

8. What is your impression on the design argument? Are there any strong responses to Philo's criticisms? Explain.

Rousseau—The Natural Goodness of Humanity

The critically acclaimed television series, *The Walking Dead*, depicts what is left of the world following the outbreak of a virus that turns the dead into flesh-eating zombies (frequently referred to as "Walkers" on the show). The fourth episode of season 6, paradoxically titled "Here's Not Here," provides some much-needed backstory for the character, Morgan, conspicuous by his absence for several seasons after saving the show's main protagonist, Rick Grimes, in the show's pilot episode. "Here's Not Here" initially displays Morgan as a shell of his former self, irreparably traumatized by the death of his son, but nonetheless resilient enough to dedicate the rest of his life to a single-minded mission: "clear" the world of all Walkers and anyone who gets in his way. Morgan demonstrates his ruthlessness early in the episode when he savagely kills a father and son for intruding on his territory, where he marked a stone with the titular "Here's Not Here." These words cleverly encapsulate the state of the world after the zombie outbreak, in which the derelict and tattered remnants of civilization are little more than relics to a time that humanity may never recover by reducing people to life in a "state of nature." The houses in which people grew up are no longer their homes, but only provide flimsy and temporary refuge from the horrors of the new world. The wide open, grassy meadows in which families had picnics and children played are veritable warzones. The luxuries people so often take for granted – grocery stores, shopping malls, restaurants, gas stations, etc. – now serve as desperate and pitiful means to survival.

Even though "Here's Not Here" in the world of the zombie apocalypse, the question remains as to whether humans are still *human*. Equally compelling is the question of just who exactly the real monsters are: the flesh-eating Walkers or the hostile, aggressive, and occasionally sadistic humans? In times of crisis, people often reveal their true selves, stripped of all the personae designed to perpetuate the masquerade of social conventions. But the world of *The Walking Dead* finds humanity trapped in a perpetual crisis and struggle for survival, which would likely reveal human nature in its purest form. The collapse of regulative administrations such as governments and institutions leave what's left of the human race to congregate into various small groups of vagabonds constantly at war with each other over Earth's rapidly diminishing resources. Thus, the zombie apocalypse seems to reveal that people are intrinsically bad, voracious, violent, and asocial, joining forces only if it is necessary to do so. If people were basically good, then would they not more readily join with each other and collaborate in finding a cure for the "zombie virus" and reconstruct the world, reclaiming their place at the pinnacle of the animal kingdom? Certainly, if the once courageous, benevolent, and loving father that was Morgan can be reduced to a paranoid, heartless killer, then the virtues so cherished by civilization are nothing more than masks, thin veneers that can disappear at any time. Even the very best of us can, at any time, be too far gone to save.

"Here's Not Here," however, remains one of the most optimistic of *The Walking Dead's* episodes, as the scenes depicting a ruthlessly violent Morgan occur entirely in flashbacks narrated by a now-reformed Morgan who took a vow never to kill again. The end of the episode reveals that Morgan is speaking to the leader of "the Wolves," who survived a previous encounter with Morgan and returned with his pack of vandals to pillage the Alexandria safe zone. It becomes clear that Morgan wishes to reform the Alpha Wolf just as he reformed. Somewhere along the way, Morgan recovered his humanity, and his transformation began when he met the reclusive Eastman, who subsisted in a remote cabin with his loyal goat, Tabitha. In their initial encounter, Eastman disarms and subdues Morgan using a bo staff. After trapping Morgan in a homemade cage, Eastman reveals that before the outbreak, he was forensic psychiatrist, and that "the state [of Atlanta] employed [him] to determine if certain people who did very bad things would do them again if they were released from prison." Musing on the reason for Morgan's state of mind, Eastman says,

> I saw a wedding ring. You had someone you loved, didn't you? Children? You loved them. You loved them a lot if you're like this. You saw it happen. That's how this started, right? It's all happening right in front of your eyes over and over? Your body's here, but your mind is still there. There's a door, and you want to go through it to get away from it, so you do, and it leads you right back to that moment. And, you see that door again, and you know it won't work, but, hell, maybe it'll work, so you step through that door and you're right back in that horrible moment every time. You still feel it every time. So, you just want to stop opening that door. So, you just sit in it. But I assure you, one of those doors leads to help, my friend.

Morgan retorts that he has no friends and that he fully intends to kill Eastman, who scoffs, replying,

> We're not built to kill. We don't have claws or fangs or armor. Vets. They came back with PTSD. That didn't happen because we're comfortable with killing. We're not. We can't be. We feel. We're connected. You know, I've interviewed over 825 people who did terrible things. I've only met one evil person. Some of them were born with bad brains. Some of them got sick along the way. The rest were just damaged people who traumatized themselves like you, but they could heal, some more, some less, but they can. We all can. I know it. It's all a circle and everything gets a return.

He then reveals that the door to Morgan's cell is, and always was, unlocked.

This exchange between Morgan and Eastman presents two positions on human inclinations. The first, represented by Morgan, is that people are basically selfish, deceitful, and dangerous. Thus, it is necessary to take pre-emptive action by "clearing" the world of all who may oppose you and your interest. Morgan never even tries to open the door to his cell. Instead, he fashions a makeshift tool that he uses to attempt to dig the bars out of the window sill so that he may escape. The second, represented by Eastman, is that people are basically good, in which the "we" in his monologue refers to all humans. In his view, most people would do terrible things only for one of two reasons. First, people might be naturally defective, such as those who were "born with bad brains." Or, something goes wrong in the course of person's development. The astute reader will also note that Eastman reiterates the Socratic maxim that injustice harms the perpetrator more than his victim, as proven by the fact that military veterans often suffer from post-traumatic stress disorder (PTSD). In either case, violence and cruelty are not intrinsic to humanity. Moreover, Eastman notes that the extent of Morgan's trauma would not be so severe were it not possible for his mind to heal. Anyone inherently bad would not be negatively affected by the state of the world but would more likely prefer it to the old one.

Nonetheless, there are two questions about Eastman that beg to be answered. First, who is this truly evil person that he once met? Eastman acknowledges that such people are rare, even among the most hardened of criminals. Second, why does Eastman have a cage in his cabin? The answer to both questions reveals to the audience that Eastman speaks from experience when he recounts his relationship with a prison inmate he interviewed, Crighton Dallas Wilton. In short, Eastman claims that Wilton was very charming, affable, and liked by most people, but that he "saw right through him," believing Wilton to be a pure psychopath. Eastman, thus, had every intention of keeping him incarcerated for life. In one of their exchanges, however, Wilton intuited Eastman's intentions and attacked him, but having learned aikido, Eastman defended himself and survived. Nonetheless, Wilton subsequently escaped prison and killed Eastman's entire family, after which he surrendered himself. In retaliation, Eastman built the cage in his cabin, kidnapped Wilton, locked him inside, and starved him to death, which, according to Eastman, took 47 days. He later says, "What I did to him, it didn't give me any peace. I found my peace when I decided to never kill again, to never kill anything again." Eastman's experience coupled with the rarity of people like Crighton Dallas Wilton testify to the natural goodness of most people, as does the fact that severely traumatized people can not only heal, but become stronger despite their trauma.

The general storyline of *The Walking Dead* is relevant to the study of the French thinker, Jean-Jacques Rousseau not only because, like Rousseau, it imagines humanity existing in a state of nature, but primarily because it forces the audience to contemplate the question of whether human beings are basically good or basically evil. While Rousseau did not elaborate a rigorous system of his thought in any one work, he once remarked that the single unifying theme of his work is that human beings are basically good, and it is through social institutions alone that they become bad. Despite its relevance to Rousseau's thought, however, *The Walking Dead* portrays a state of nature envisioned by a thinker who seemed to endorse the exact opposite sentiment, more specifically, that of Thomas Hobbes. In the pages that follow, I will first present an overview of the doctrine that opposes Rousseau's fundamental principle, focusing on the version offered by Hobbes. Next, I will give an account of Rousseau's conception of natural goodness, which will be followed by an assessment of Rousseau's thought in terms of Bacon's idols.

(I) Human Nature is Basically Evil—Hobbes and *The Lord of the Flies*

Melzer[1] maintains that in formulating his principle of natural goodness, Rousseau intended to deny three historical doctrines. First, he rejected the Christian concept of original sin, according to which all

---

[1] Arthur Melzer, *The Natural Goodness of Man: On the System of Rousseau's Thought* (Chicago, IL: University of Chicago Press, 1990).

people are born selfish and prideful, as all people inherit the sin of Adam and Eve. The only way to overcome sin is through salvation, by the grace of God. Second, he rejected the "classical dualism" of thinkers such as Plato, Aristotle, and Aquinas, which insisted that the human faculties are naturally in conflict with each other. That is, reason, passion, and desire naturally oppose each other. Third, he rejected the Hobbesian idea that all people are natural enemies of each other. Since Hobbes's vision of the state of nature and his portrayal of humanity are the most directly opposed to the position of Rousseau, and since the two other topics were addressed in previous chapters, this section will focus on developing Hobbes's view.

Golding's *The Lord of the Flies* lends itself as one of the most powerful indictments of the claim that human beings are naturally good by presenting a popular version of Hobbes's state of nature. The novel takes place on an uninhabited Pacific island on which a group of preadolescent boys from a British military academy are stranded after a plane crash. Total chaos is prevented for a while. For example, a white conch found on the beach becomes a symbol of authority. That is, only the individual who holds the conch during an assembly may speak. Furthermore, a leader of the group is chosen democratically and invested with limited powers. And responsibilities are delegated among the members of the group.

However, after some initial euphoria, the children begin to encounter the typical banes of social life: competition for power and status; neglect of social responsibility; the failure of public policy; and escalating violence. Originally "elected" to be the group leader, Ralph, eventually must struggle to maintain his role against Jack, a former choir boy. Their rivalry generates the formation of two factions: Jack's "choir boy" hunters and Ralph's faction, whose responsibility is the construction and maintenance of shelters. Soon, freeloading becomes common, as most of the children would rather play on the beach than perform their chores. Ultimately, dereliction of duty leads to a fire being extinguished, resulting in the failure of the boys to be rescued by a plane which passes overhead. The only tasks which are undertaken with any seriousness are the pig hunts in which Jack's faction engages.

In addition to Ralph and Jack, the character Simon figures largely in the novel. Simon is often interpreted as the symbol of religious consciousness, in connection with Simon Peter, the first of Christ's disciples. After a pig hunt, Jack and his cohorts sever the head of their prey, mounting it on a stick before a cave as a "sacrifice" to a "beast" they believe dwells therein. In a crucial scene, Simon "converses" with the severed head, and is tempted to embrace the ways of most of the other children on the island, a temptation to "be like ordinary men." Ignoring the admonition of the pig's head, Simon discovers that the "beast" dwelling within the cave is their wounded pilot. Hence, Simon discovers that "the beast is just us." When he returns to deliver the "good news" to the rest of the boys, they slaughter him in an orgiastic frenzy. Passive observers to the slaughter of Simon are Ralph and "Piggy" (Percival Madison), the fourth of the central characters. Whereas Simon symbolizes religious consciousness, Piggy is often interpreted as the representative of "philosophy," of the embodiment of reason and common-sense. Not only does "Piggy" show the boys how to build a sun dial when they arrive on the island, but his glasses are needed to ignite fire, hence come to represent *technology*.

As these events indicate, Golding suggests that *human beings are natural enemies of each other and perverse in fundamental ways.* The very title of the novel "The Lord of the Flies" is a translation of the Greek word "Beelzebub," the same term which, in the Bible, often refers to the devil. Golding suggests, metaphorically, that human beings need no external devil to bring about evil, but that the devil is "just us." "Beelzebub's" ascendancy proceeds through fear, hysteria, violence, and death. Originally, the boys hunted pigs for food, which is not intrinsically bad, but necessary for their survival. However, they begin enjoying the kills, and drown out their shame by covering themselves with mud painted red, supposedly signifying their full liberation from their "social selves." That is, by disguising themselves, they create sanctuaries in which they can hide from their own compunction.

Piggy eventually suffers the same fate as Simon, dying at the hands of Jack's faction. The deaths of the symbols of religion and philosophy signify to Ralph the depths of evil in humanity. Piggy's spectacles, the sole example of modern technology present in the novel are ultimately used by Jack to ignite a forest fire intended to smoke out Ralph, although it also destroys nearly everything on the island. Jack's use of the spectacles in this way suggests not only that human beings have a capacity to misuse technology, but that human beings will almost always choose to do evil rather than good.[2]

While *The Lord of the Flies* has many dimensions, in this context, the most important and relevant is that of Hobbes's vision of the state of nature, and what it reveals about human nature. According to Hobbes, "In the nature of man, we find three principal causes of quarrel. . . First, *competition*; secondly, *diffidence*; thirdly, *glory*."[3] Understanding how such capacities cause quarrel can be understood only if one first understands Hobbes's assessment of man "as nature made him":

> Nature hath made men so equal, in the faculties of body and mind; as that though there be found one man sometimes manifestly stronger in body, or of quicker mind than another; yet, when all is reckoned together, the difference between man, and man, is not so considerable, as that one man can thereupon claim to himself any benefit, to which another may not pretend as well as he. For as to the strength of body, the weakest has strength enough to kill the strongest, either by secret machination, or by confederacy with others, that we are in the same danger with himself.[4]

---

[2] Pojman's *Who Are We? Theories of Human Nature* provides a similar summary of the *Lord of the Flies* in connection with Hobbes' account of the State of Nature. Pojman's chapter also devotes a section to Rousseau as a contrast to Hobbes, though not with the intention of developing a reply to Hobbes on Rousseau's behalf.

[3] *Leviathan*, I.13, p. 76.

[4] *Leviathan*, p. 75.

Thus, nature has made human beings basically equal in physical and mental abilities. Even though someone may be physically stronger and/or smarter than another, each can harm or kill any other, either alone or with the help of others. From this "equality of abilities"

> . . .ariseth an equality of hope in attaining our ends. And therefore if any two men desire the same thing, which nevertheless they cannot both enjoy, they become enemies; and in the way to their end, (which is principally their own conservation and sometimes their delectation only) endeavor to destroy, or subdue one another. And from hence it comes to pass, that where an invader hath no more to fear, than another man's single power; if one plant, sow, build, or possess a convenient sea, others may probably be expected to come prepared with forces united, to dispossess, and deprive him, not only of the fruit of his labor, but also of life or liberty.[5]

Because we all equally want to attain our goals, which include having sufficient food, shelter, security, power, wealth, glory, and other resources, the "state of nature" is characterized by *competition* for resources and *fear* (or *diffidence*) of all those in the state of nature who could potentially deprive one of not only the "fruits of one's labor" but also of one's very life. Underlying Hobbes's reflections on competition and diffidence is his view that there is a natural scarcity of things necessary for human survival in the state of nature. In addition, since Hobbes believes that people need certain items to survive, he believes that human beings are motivated primarily by a desire for self-preservation. Only those who can achieve what is available in the state of nature will preserve themselves. From competition and diffidence proceeds warfare, as Hobbes explains in the following passage:

> And from this diffidence there is no way for any man to secure himself, so reasonable, as anticipation; that is, by force, or by wiles, to master the person of all men he can, so long till he sees no other power great enough to endanger him: and this is no more than his own conservation requireth and is generally allowed.[6]

---

[5] Ibid, p. 76.

[6] Ibid.

Accordingly, *fear* motivates one to launch pre-emptive strikes against those who might threaten one's self-preservation. The key word in the passage cited above is "anticipation," as, for Hobbes, natural man wants to assure forever that he has a way to satisfy his future desires. Thus, Hobbes characterizes anticipation not only as a concern for the future, but as a ceaseless desire for power after power that ends only in death.

"Glory" is best described as a kind of *pride*, or *vanity*. It is the only one of Hobbes's causes of quarrel in the state of nature that does not directly emanate from man's desire for self-preservation. He describes this motivation in the following passages:

> Also because there be some, that taking pleasure in contemplating their own power in the acts of conquest, which they pursue farther than their security requires. . .For every man looketh that his companion should value him, at the same rate he sets upon himself; and upon all signs of contempt, or undervaluing, naturally endeavors as far as he dares. . .to exact a greater value from his condemners, by dommage, and from others by exemplar.[7]

Hence, in "natural man," there is both a desire for self-preservation and, it seems, a desire to be viewed by others as competent in battle, an attribute that develops over time. When one's competence is somehow insulted or challenged, it leads to violence. And since this attribute is related to war, it is also related to self-preservation, even though it is not directly motivated by it. Hobbes summarizes the three motivations of "quarrel" in the state of nature in the following passage:

> The first maketh men invade for gain; the second, for safety; and the third, for reputation. The first use violence to make themselves masters of other men's persons, wives, children, and cattle; the second, to defend them; the third for trifles, as a word, a smile, a different opinion, and any other sign of undervalue.[8]

---

[7] Ibid

[8] Ibid

Ultimately, Hobbes maintained that the following conditions will always be manifested outside of a civil state with no external authority:

> Hereby it is manifest, that during the time men live without a common power to keep them all in awe, they are in that condition which is called war; and such a war, as is of every man, against every man. For war, consisteth not in battle only, or the act of fighting; but in a tract of time, where in the will to contend by battle is sufficiently known. . .so the nature of war, consisteth not in actual fighting; but in the known disposition thereto, during all the time there is no assurance to the contrary.

> Whatsoever therefore is consequent to a time of war, where every man is enemy to every man. . .[in such a condition] there is continual fear and danger of a violent death; and the life of man, solitary, poor, nasty, brutish, and short.[9]

Thus, Hobbes's state of nature, as described thus far, is a state of instability, scarcity, and insecurity. In a state of nature, people fear each other, especially since they all want and need the same things for the sake of their own self-preservation and possess an equal ability to harm each other.

Ultimately, Hobbes insists that escape from the state of nature requires that people formulate a set of agreements and principles, the most important being that they will not harm each other. Abiding by this rule requires that everybody exercise some self-control for the greater good. In addition, there must be a way to guarantee that people abide by this social contract. Hence, an individual with absolute power must enforce it, a sovereign, or a king. Hobbes compares this individual to the image of the Leviathan in his book by the same name. The Leviathan is a monstrous sea creature referenced in the Hebrew Bible. Prior to the discoveries of modern science, many people feared travel by sea due to the possibility that such a creature may be lurking.

---

[9] Ibid, p. 77.

Hobbes would insist that the sovereign who makes possible the social contract must be cloaked in the same mystique as this mythological creature, in which people are far too afraid that the Leviathan will know if they violate the contract and dispense retribution. Allegedly, people believed in the existence of such a creature because from the shore, the activity of dolphins, diving in and out of the water, appeared to be a giant serpent, or dragon. Just as dolphins are far less threatening than the Leviathan, familiarity with the sovereign diminishes his power by diminishing the extent to which people fear him, which, in turn, diminishes his capacity to enforce the contract. And if the contract breaks, humanity descends in the perpetual state of war that characterizes the state of nature.

Hobbesian presuppositions about human motivation parallel those of Machiavelli, who famously asserted that it is safer for a ruler, a prince, to be feared rather than loved. Both thinkers agree, thus, that given the human capacities for selfishness and deception, people must be coerced if they are to behave. People, generally, will not help others or act for the greater good unless they stand to gain something. For Hobbes, what people stand to gain by agreeing to a social contract is protection from the state of nature and the continued enjoyment of a civil society that promises security and the fulfillment of basic needs. Moreover, Both Hobbes and Machiavelli would agree that people naturally view each other as obstacles to power, and, hence, we are natural enemies. Hobbes conceived of reality as nothing more than physical matter in motion, and, thus, of humanity as merely collections of matter. We are reactive. The drive for self-preservation is primarily negative, an instinctive mechanism of defense against the external world. Like the sophist, Thrasymachus, Hobbes conceived of reality as a manifestation of power, and it is, therefore, sheer, brute power that makes civilization possible.

Conversely, it is power that can break down such a civilization, and therein lies the flaw of Hobbes's contract. What if someone clever enough can violate the contract without getting caught? If so, then the sovereign literally has no power to punish the perpetrator. In that case, it seems to follow that the culprit did nothing wrong, since the contract is enforceable only if the sovereign has the power to punish the individual. Equally problematic is that power is relative. If this clever culprit also will risk rebelling against the sovereign, it will potentially usher in a new regime. Hence, Hobbesian principles can yield no absolute contract. The power of the sovereign depends largely on perception, and whether his subjects believe him to be truly insuperable.

Additional problems emerge from the idea of the "state of nature," which may be interpreted in more than way, of which Hobbes seems to have two in mind. First, it may be interpreted as the original condition of human beings prior to any existing social arrangement. In other words, a "state of nature" may refer to the living conditions of human beings in the early stages of their evolution. Second, it may be interpreted as any state of affairs in which human beings live without a central governing authority to enforce rules, laws, and regulations, including the conditions that would prevail upon the collapse of a prevailing government, regime, or community. These two conceptions of the state of nature raise a double problem. On the one hand, any description of the primordial living conditions of early humans is bound to be speculative to *some* extent, despite the evidence that contemporary evolutionary biology affords us. On the other hand, the ideals of a society into which people were enculturated will inevitably emerge, at least to some degree, even after the collapse of that society, in which case, the behavior of people in the state of nature that follows may be the result of nurture, rather than nature. Perhaps, then, Hobbes, Golding, and *The Walking Dead* depict people only as they would be after living in modern society. Maybe humanity would be much better off if civilization never existed.

(II) Rousseau on Education, the State of Nature, and Natural Goodness

In fairness to both Hobbes and Rousseau, one should note that they would agree on many points. In the present context, the following are most relevant. First, both Hobbes and Rousseau provided conceptions of the "state of nature." Second, both seem to maintain that people are *naturally equal* in many capacities, that there is no provision *in nature* that entitles any one person to rule over another. Third, they each agree that human beings are not *naturally social*, from which it follows that society and morality are conventional, or, in their case, contractual. Fourth, they would agree that the events depicted in works of fiction such as Golding's *The Lord of the Flies* and *The Walking Dead* are *possible* in the absence of social constraints. Fifth, and finally, they would both agree that any attempt to return to the state of nature, or the emergence of any conditions that would constitute a "state of nature" would not necessarily be in anyone's interest.

Both Hobbes and Rousseau made use of introspection in the development of their conceptions of the state of nature. Whereas Hobbes conceived of life in the state of nature as "solitary, poor, nasty, brutish, and short," Rousseau maintained that such conditions reflect artificial human tendencies, capacities that they would develop only after spending significant time in society. Thus, any attempt to return to humanity's primal state of existence is doomed to failure. For humanity to attempt to resume life in a state of nature would result only in a corrupted state of nature, given the corrosion of human nature by society.

Rousseau outlines his conception of the state of nature in his *Discourse on the Origins of Inequality* (also called the *Second Discourse*). Part I of this work describes natural human beings in a state of nature, an account which is in every way the opposite of that described by

Hobbes. Part II of the *Second Discourse* describes the process by which people became corrupted through society. Rousseau distinguishes between two forms of inequality. First, *natural inequalities* are purely physical, and depend on age, health, bodily strength, and qualities of the mind, or soul. Second, *social*, or *economic inequalities* refer to different privileges that people enjoy, albeit at the expense of others. Rousseau's central thesis is that social inequalities are artificial and the source of human misery.

Prior to Part I of the *Second Discourse*, Rousseau makes clear that he has no intention of describing the factual, historical conditions of early humans, but that much of what he says is conjectural:

> Let us therefore begin by putting aside all the facts, for they have no bearing on the question. The investigation that may be undertaken concerning this subject should not be taken for historical truths, but only for hypothetical and conditional reasonings, better suited to shedding light on the nature of things than on pointing out their true origin.[10]

While it is not my intention to summarize the *Second Discourse*, I draw from it to reconstruct Rousseau's conception of natural goodness, since he believed that we must have some idea of what such a state would have or could have been like to judge accurately our present condition.

In the pages that follow, I will focus on two themes in Rousseau's thought. First, I will discuss his remarks about education by drawing from his treatise on the subject, *Emile*, in addition to the central thesis of his *Discourse on the Arts and Sciences* (also called the *First Discourse*) and his conception of the general will in *The Social Contract*. Second, I will provide a reconstruction of what Melzer calls Rousseau's argument for natural goodness, which draws from several of Rousseau's writings.

---

[10] *Second Discourse*, in Cress, p. 17.

Rousseau on Education: According to Rousseau, there are three kinds of education. First, *education from nature* refers to the internal development of human faculties and organs. This kind of education illustrates the natural creativity of human beings. Creativity does not necessarily refer to originality, but autonomy in thought and action. Two people may develop the exact same invention, but so long as they did so independently, both are creative. The first creative activity of humans is learning how to walk, since doing so forces humans to break free of habitual patterns and figure out how to do something new on their own. For Rousseau, this kind of education is the most primal, and demonstrates humanity's natural spontaneity.

Second, *education from other people* consists in the use we learn to make of our faculties once they develop. This kind of education is the most conventional and consists mostly in the processes of socialization into a specific society or culture. Conventional education does not necessarily extend a person's intelligence or improve their understanding but prepares people to observe and safeguard the values of a community, which are usually determined by those with the power and authority to do so.[11]

Problems emerge when education from others goes against an individual's natural development and genuine desire for truth and understanding. Rousseau makes note of this problem in his first major publication, his *Discourse on the Arts and Sciences,* written as a response to a question posed by the Academy at Dijon: "Has the restoration of the arts and sciences had a purifying effect on morals?" Rousseau's answer was a resounding, "NO!" Rousseau's essay is divided into two parts. In Part I, Rousseau enumerates several examples of cultures that became far more depraved despite achieving sophistication, including the Greeks and the Chinese, but the most prominent example is that of the Roman Empire. Emperors such as Nero, a

---

[11] There is more to be said about this point, but it will be explored in further detail in the chapter on Marx.

murderer and a necrophiliac, as well as Caligula, who bestowed consulship on his horse merely to make a point about his authority, testify to the claim that sophistication in the arts and sciences does not alone make people morally reputable. In Part II, though, Rousseau explains why sophistication in the arts and sciences cultivates moral deterioration. In short, academia in Rousseau's time emphasized the achievement of esteem, reward, and glory, rather than virtue and truth. Once a position, such as a professorship, is valued within a society, one might seek such a position merely for material reward, thereby disrupting personal integrity. Moreover, a coveted position may be achieved only by an elite few. Those in such positions may, to reinforce their own sense of superiority, oppress and shame others. In turn, those who cannot achieve these positions feel resentment and envy toward those who do. Institutional education, thus, constitutes an education in name only and really impedes both education and happiness.

Third, *education from things* consists of what comes to our experience from the things that affect us. While this kind of education may include our social and cultural experiences, Rousseau seemed to have in mind an individual's unique, personal experiences, the lessons one learns from one's own interactions with the natural world, and through the failures that result from one's own experimentation. A child who injures himself climbing a tree, or who falls ill eating plants not intended for the human stomach constitutes instances of an education from things. This kind of education, thus, parallels an education from nature.

Since Rousseau's image of a "corrupted state of nature" closely parallels the "state of nature" as described by Hobbes and Golding, he would not suggest that if children of the kind described in *The Lord of the Flies* were left to their own devices on an uninhabited island, they would live peaceful, cooperative, and idyllic lives.

The following passage that opens Book I of *Emile*, in fact, suggests just the opposite:

> Everything is good as it leaves the hands of the Author of things; everything degenerates in the hands of man. He forces one soil to nourish the products of another, one tree to bear the fruit of another. He mixes and confuses the climates, the elements, the seasons. He mutilates his dog, his horse, his slave. He turns everything upside down; he disfigures everything; he loves deformity, monsters. He wants nothing as nature made it, not even man; for him, man must be trained like a school horse; man must be fashioned in keeping with his fancy like a tree in his garden.
>
> Were he not to do this, however, everything would go even worse, and our species do not admit of being formed halfway. In the present state of things, a man abandoned to himself in the midst of other men from birth would be the most disfigured of all. Prejudices, authority, necessity, example, all the social institutions in which we find ourselves submerged would stifle nature in him and put nothing in its place. Nature there would be like a shrub that chance had caused to be born in the middle of a path and that the passers-by soon cause to perish by bumping into it from all sides and bending it in every direction.[12]

The first sentence of this passage is comparable to the opening line of *The Social Contract*: "Man is born free, but everywhere he is in chains." Rousseau's views on education and child rearing are not as simple as many of his critics might suppose. Rousseau insisted that simply leaving children alone completely would bring about much worse consequences than even subjecting children to a leading paradigm of civil education. Other passages in Book I of *Emile* also illuminate Rousseau's views that children will need a guide in order to be raised properly: "To be led well, the child should follow only a single guide." Such rearing will include not merely "preserving" the life of the child, but "teaching one how to preserve oneself."[13] Essentially, the system of education Rousseau describes in *Emile* depends on the total control of the pupil by

---

[12] In Bloom, p. 37.

[13] Ibid, BK I, p. 42.

a tutor. Even though the pupil should only "do what he wants," Rousseau maintained that *he should only want to do what the tutor wants*.

Rousseau's theory of education has many parallels with the theory of political freedom he proposes in *The Social Contract*. For Rousseau, freedom is identical with the overcoming and elimination of all arbitrariness, replacing such things with a categorical and strict law that the individual erects over himself and to which he submits. Free consent to such a law characterizes Rousseau's view of political freedom, a character that is realized by Rousseau's "general will." Even though the state will, ultimately, "claim" the individual completely, it does not do so coercively, but puts the individual under an obligation, the necessity of which he recognizes. Thus, for Rousseau, the central problem of politics is a question of the *kind* of community that will protect every individual within the political organization. However, to achieve these conditions, the social order must be radically transformed, and individuals must be educated to recognize what Cassirer refers to as "the inner necessity of law."[14]

In terms of the coincidence of Rousseau's theory of political freedom with his theory of education as revealed in *Emile*, even though the tutor possesses control over the pupil, one fundamental idea of Rousseau's education is that no physical obstacles are to be removed from the path of the pupil if he is to be educated to independence of will. He can be "spared no suffering, no effort, no privation." However, *he is to be protected only from violent coercion from an outside will, the necessity of which he does not understand.* This claim characterizes Rousseau's education as "negative" or "protective." The question that remains, however, is just what is to be protected?

---

[14] See Ernst Cassirer, *The Question of Jean-Jacque Rousseau* (Tr. Peter Gay), (Indiana University Press, 1975) pp. 55–60, for a more developed discussion of Rousseau's Social Contract and its relation to Emile. Cassirer devotes much attention to "Rousseauian Ethics" and its unquestionable influence on Kant. For primary passages from *The Social Contract* relating to the issues discussed in this paragraph, see Book I.6, 8, and Book II.4. For an exhaustive commentary on *The Social Contract*, see Gildin Hilail's *Rousseau's Social Contract: The Design of the Argument*, Chicago: University of Chicago Press, 1983.

Rousseau's Conception of the Natural Goodness of Humanity: The obscurity of Rousseau's principle makes its systematic reconstruction just as difficult as it is valuable, particularly because Rousseau elaborates his principle in no one place. However, it is beneficial to begin by explaining what Rousseau's principle *does not* mean. First, it does not mean that people are *naturally inclined* to act benevolently toward each other. And second, it does not mean that human *passions* are restrained by *reason*. In Rousseau's view, the qualities of *solitude* and *ignorance* characterize human beings in their natural condition:

> We could say that savages are not evil precisely because they do not know what it is to be good; for it is neither enlightenment nor the restraint imposed by the law, but the calm of the passions and the ignorance of vice which prevents them from doing evil. *So much more profitable to these is the ignorance of vice than the knowledge of virtue is to [civilized men].*[15]

Thus, the deeds of natural human beings are simple. As they do not know of anything that exceeds their capacities, they seem to be incapable of desiring such things. Any desires that go beyond physical needs are relative, arising only from a concern with the opinions and actions of other people. But since natural humans have no social relations, they have no relative desires. Thus, the natural condition of humanity entails self-unity and natural freedom, since in this state, human desires do not exceed human needs.[16]

Ultimately, Rousseau believes that the extent of human corruption makes it impossible to ever reclaim the primordial unity enjoyed by natural humans. In his various works, he suggests several ways to approximate original goodness, however. First, people may attempt to become good citizens, a process Rousseau describes in *The Social Contract*. Second, people may attempt to recover their natural spontaneity, which Rousseau describes in *Emile*. Third, people may attempt to live a genuinely

---

[15] *Second Discourse*, in Cress, p. 36.

[16] See Marc Plattner's *Rousseau's State of Nature: An Interpretation of Rousseau's Discourse on Inequality* (Dekalb, IL: Northern Illinois University Press, 1979), Chapter 4 for further details on "ignorance" and "solitude."

philosophical and solitary life, which Rousseau attempted himself, and of which *The Reveries of the Solitary Walker* provides an account.

Even though Rousseau would not call all people "good" in the same sense that the citizens of *The Social Contract* or his pupil, Emile, are good, just as it is impossible to fully reclaim natural goodness, it is equally impossible for humanity to fully divest itself of goodness. Melzer's reconstruction of Rousseau's argument for the natural goodness of humanity consists of two broad parts: a positive part and a negative part. The positive part *consists* of Rousseau's acknowledgement of intrinsic qualities that make people good, while the negative part consists of Rousseau's attempt to establish that people would not be bad if not for external forces. The positive part of Rousseau's argument may be subdivided into both an introspective and psychological part. The negative part of Rousseau's argument may be subdivided into aspects that address humanity's disharmony and penchant for injustice, human malleability, the events of history that corrupted humanity, and the contradictions inherent within human society.[17]

Rousseau's Positive Argument: In developing his thesis, Rousseau made use of introspection. But in Rousseau's view, the proper introspective procedure requires solitude, since human nature has been disfigured by society. Only a fully detached individual would be relatively free of its corrupting influence.[18] Under such conditions, however, introspection reveals that barring rewards and considered only in itself, harming others naturally repulses us, while benevolence seems naturally to content us.[19] This thesis is not completely novel, since many thinkers, including Hobbes, would agree that no one takes pleasure in

---

[17] Melzer appeals to Book II of *Emile* (p. 92 in Bloom's translation) as evidence that Rousseau was aware of these two aspects of his principle. Unfortunately, I am forced to go great injustice to the work of both Melzer and Rousseau, since I will have to compress this argument.

[18] See *The Second Discourse*, in Cress, pp. 10–11, 18–19, *The Reveries of the Solitary Walker* VI, in Butterworth, pp. 81–82, and Melzer, p. 31.

[19] See *Emile* IV, in Bloom, p. 287, *The Second Discourse*, in Cress, pp. 18–19, and *Reveries* II, in Butterworth, p. 13, V, p. 69, and VI, pp. 74–75, and Melzer, pp. 31–34.

cruelty for its own sake and that no one can procure true inner peace through fighting. But insisting that such tranquility can be discovered as easily as Rousseau suggests is more problematic than he makes it seem. Some, particularly Hobbes, deny that it can be found at all while others, perhaps Plato, claim that only a minimal form of it is accessible to human beings.[20] However, Rousseau's obvious reply would be that the proponents of these views have forgotten the "sweet sentiment of existence, independent of any other sensation."[21] Rousseau does not deny that human beings in their current form are wrought with vice and iniquity, but he consistently maintains that society engenders and develops such attributes, that they are distortions of something more fundamental which he believes he rediscovered. For Rousseau, men can be inclined to a positive goodness or benevolence under the right circumstances: "If I had remained free, obscure, and isolated as I was made to be, I would have done only good; for I do not have the seed of any harmful passion in my heart."[22] On this basis, simple feelings of warmth and contentment reveal to us the truth about our nature: Goodness fulfills us, and iniquity both horrifies us and causes harm to those who do it.

By itself, Rousseau's introspective argument cannot sustain the conclusion that society alone corrupts human beings. However, the method uncovers humanity's two primary passions: pity and self-love (*amour de soi*). Pity is best described as the ability to identify with others, which enables human beings to experience rudimentary feelings of compassion. Self-love Rousseau describes as, "The source of our passions, the origin and the principle of all the others, the only one born with man and which never leaves him so long as he lives. . . a primitive, innate passion . . . of which all others are in a sense only modifications."[23]

---

[20] For a more detailed analysis of the differences between Plato, Hobbes, and Rousseau on the sentiments accessible through introspection, see Melzer, pp. 32–34.

[21] See *Reveries* V, in Butterworth, p. 69.

[22] See *Reveries* VI, in Butterworth, pp. 81–82.

[23] See *Emile* IV, in Bloom, pp. 212–213.

According to Rousseau, it is "always in conformity with order," but "becomes good or bad toward others only by the applications made of it." For Rousseau, observation seems to show that *we seek to preserve our lives not merely reflexively, out of fear of death or love of pleasure, but out of affection for ourselves.*[24] Rousseau's conception of self-love, thus, differs starkly from the Hobbesian conception of self-preservation, in which one seeks to preserve one's being defensively, against outside forces. In Rousseau's view, the negative conception of self-love seems to be true of humanity only after they are corrupted. For instance, peasants, savages, and even non-human animals seem to derive much pleasure from *idleness*, which certainly could not be the case if one only sought to preserve oneself when opposing an external force. Hence, there is at least some evidence that the root of life is a positive affection for oneself. The goals most people develop in their lives strengthen Rousseau's appeals. Very few people desire a totally passive life. People wish to pursue their interests and develop their talents, be they in art, music, literature, entertainment, or business. People who work long hours during the year eagerly anticipate their vacations, not merely as opportunities for rest and relaxation, but out of a persistent and positive affection for the sights, sounds, and pleasures afforded by the experience. How many people would opt to live their entire natural lives in a climate-controlled cage without any possibility of seeing the light of day? Such an existence would likely be free of risk, disease, harm, and even work, but also devoid of meaning.

Based on his conception of self-love, Rousseau insists that people are basically (1) *good for themselves,* and (2) *good or neutral toward others.* The life or existence that is the object of human love is positive and absolute.[25] However, self-love exists in a corrupted form described by the term *amour-propre*, which may be translated as egocentricity, or

---

[24] See Melzer, pp. 35–37; He also comments on Rousseau's awareness of earlier views on self-love, making specific references to Cicero's *De Finibus*. Marcus Cato, an interlocutor in the dialogue, claims that self-preservation is not merely negative but positive.

[25] See Melzer, pp. 40–41.

vanity. While natural humans are basically neutral with respect to other beings around them, amour-propre develops when human beings develop the ability to make comparisons between themselves and others:

> In proportion as ideas and sentiments succeed one another and as the mind and heart are trained, the human race continues to be tamed, relationships spread and bonds tightened. People grew accustomed to gather in front of their huts or around a large tree; song and dance, true children of love and leisure, became amusement or rather the occupation of idle men and women who had flocked together. *Each one began to look at the others and to want to be looked at himself, and public esteem had value.*[26]

Of importance in this passage is the connection between the congregation of people with the development of *vanity* and *envy*. In *Emile*, Rousseau discusses amour-propre as both a passion that prevents one from being able to esteem oneself unless others esteem one first, and as a passion that makes difficult the recognition of the necessity in certain events and the acceptance of those things over which one has no control, such as death, the fear of which Rousseau insisted is artificial.[27] This discussion points to an additional point of agreement between Hobbes and Rousseau: that human beings seem to believe that everything is an extension of oneself. However, Hobbes held that such a view is *natural*, whereas Rousseau believes that he is providing evidence that such a state of mind is engendered by a faulty education. To elaborate, because adults "serve" children, *children learn that control over other people is more useful than adaptation to things,* thus, seek control over others. This is, in part, how anger develops in children. Through amour-propre, the child sees intention to do wrong in anything that opposes him, even in those things that lack will or volition. Rousseau insisted that *human beings are always more troubled by the intentional infliction of harm done to them than they are by events*

---

[26] *Second Discourse*, in Cress, p. 49.

[27] See BK I, in Bloom, p. 68.

that happen at random. Thus, a child must be educated so as not to find "will" or "intention" in everything that opposes it.[28]

In Rousseau's view, *amour-propre* ruptures the self-unity signified by *amour de soi*. The anger one experiences when one believes that some independent "will" conspires against it is in part an illustration of how *the desires of civilized humans come to exceed their abilities*. In terms of Rousseau's theory of education and proposal for political freedom, amour-propre reflects the disunity between the necessity one can recognize in one's own will but is unable to recognize in the will of another. To the degree that natural humans are devoid of amour-propre, he is *resigned to the necessity of all random events, even his own death*.[29]

Nonetheless, Rousseau's theory of self-love and his introspective discovery of the sentiment of existence face serious problem: *the viciousness and malevolence of human beings in their current condition*. Given such rampant depravity, no *positive theory* can establish Rousseau's fundamental principle. However, Rousseau was well aware of such a problem, hence his "negative argument" for natural goodness.

Rousseau's Negative Argument: How is it that all human beings are born good but become bad? In their current condition, Rousseau insists that human beings are corrupted in two ways. First, all people manifest a disunity of soul, as indicated in the discussion of amour-propre. Second, people manifest injustice, both against themselves and others. Since Rousseau produced his writings primarily in the 18th century, he never witnessed the horrific tragedies of the 20th century, such as the Jewish Holocaust of the 1930s and 40s, the dropping of the atomic bomb in Hiroshima and Nagasaki to end World War II, and Stalin's implementation of Gulags during the peak of the Soviet Union. Ironically, the more civilization grew, the

---

[28] See *Reveries*, in Butterworth, VIII, p. 114.

[29] See Bloom, "Introduction to *Emile*," where he provides a useful discussion of amour-propre and fear of death and how they relate to Rousseau's "theory" of education.

less *civilized* humanity became. Had Rousseau lived to see these events, would he be inclined to change his mind about the natural goodness of humanity? Probably not. In fact, Rousseau would more likely insist that the severity of such injustices and the extent of human misery are far too great to be natural. That is, in their current form, human beings are so bad that they cannot possibly be that bad through nature alone. One might draw a parallel between this last claim and the elaboration of a bad liar, which often clues one into the fact that such a person simply must be lying. Social psychologists also developed the concept of "group polarization" to explain why people who hold similar beliefs and prejudices become much more *extreme* in those beliefs when they congregate in large groups.

People, thus, are *malleable,* capable of being influenced and changed by their surroundings. Rousseau maintains that the two qualities that make human beings malleable are also the same two qualities that distinguish humans from other animals: *freewill* and *perfectibility* (the capacity for self-perfection). Rousseau considers freewill in a positive way, not merely as the absence of constraint, but as autonomy, the capacity to determine goals and aims for oneself, unlike non-human animals which are almost entirely mechanical. Perfectibility consists in the capacity of humans to make comparisons between themselves and other animals, thereby enhancing their chances of survival:

> "[T]here is another very specific quality that distinguishes [man and animal] and about which there can be no dispute: the faculty of self-perfection, a faculty which, with the aid of circumstances, successively develops all the others, and resides among us as much in the species as in the individual . . . It would be sad for us to be forced to agree that this distinctive and almost unlimited faculty is the source of all man's misfortunes; that it is this faculty which, by dint of time, draws him out of that original condition in which he would pass tranquil and innocent days; that it is this faculty which, bringing flower over the centuries his enlightenment and his errors, his vices and his virtues, in the long run makes him the tyrant of himself and of nature."[30]

---

[30] See the *Second Discourse*, in Cress, pp. 25–26.

Like humanity, the capacity of self-perfection is good-in-itself, since it enables individuals to survive. Moreover, it is neutral to others, as one need not harm others for any reason other than self-defense. However, because perfectibility is infused with good intentions, it is poised to become bad. But how, exactly, did it become bad?

Rousseau insists that there must be some historical event in the evolution of humanity that changed humankind for the worse. Original human goodness is characterized by the limited development of human faculties, limits which are, in turn, connected with the natural solitude of human beings. Thus, the event, or events, which changed people must be linked to the moments in which they abandoned their solitude and formed large organized societies with agriculture, division of labor, private property, and coercive government. Departing from his introspective approach, Rousseau invoked *empirical* evidence for his claim that historical events must have changed human beings. Such evidence was based largely on his travels throughout Europe and through all his experience of 'social classes.' Rousseau preferred to seek the natural in the primitive and the infantile, in the study of men who have remained in the savage state, in the company of children rather than adults. In fact, he remarks in the Preface to *Emile* that "the wisest of thinkers always try to find the man in the child without thinking of what he is before being a man." The closer a nation is to "nature," the better it is. Conversely, the more men come together, the more they are corrupted.[31] Rousseau estimates that the trend toward human corruption began the first time one person needed the help of another, the first time in which one person could not complete a task on one's own. In that instance, human beings began to develop needs that exceeded their own capacities, which led to the emergence of larger groups of people living and collaborating, giving rise to more complex living conditions and the typical banes concomitant with them, such as vanity, jealousy, envy, and greed.

---

[31] See Melzer, pp. 69–70.

Thus, the initial condition that gave rise to "evil" as it began in the state of nature is "personal dependence," the dependence of one human being on another. Personal dependence is a "self-contradiction," and disharmony arises from that contradiction. If one needs the aid of another human being to obtain something, then one does not have the power within oneself to obtain it. Ultimately, *society unites human beings through the contradiction of personal dependence.* Rousseau elaborates on the connection between personal dependence and wickedness in more than one work. In Book I of *Emile*, he suggested that, "All wickedness comes from weakness. The child is wicked only because he is weak. Make him strong; he will be good. He who could do everything would never do harm."[32] In the following passage from *The Reveries of the Solitary Walker*, he draws a connection with the Ring of Gyges from Plato's *Republic*:

> If I had remained free, obscure, and isolated as I was made to be, I would have done only good; for I do not have the seed of any harmful passion in my heart. If I had been invisible and all-powerful like God, I would have been beneficent and good like Him. It is strength and freedom which make excellent men. Weakness and slavery have never made anything but wicked ones. If I had been the possessor of the ring of Gyges, it would have freed me from dependence on men and made them dependent on me.[33]

Not only is this passage consonant with Rousseau's remarks in *Emile*, but it further develops the relationship between *weakness* (in this case, dependence) and *wickedness*. His remarks suggest that *invisibility* correlates with *power* in the sense of self-sufficiency.

Human dependence is only worsened by the human use of *means* in the pursuit of ends, increasing their weakness. Non-human animals, by comparison, have needs, but pursue them *directly*. If a lion cannot catch its prey, for instance, it will soon give up completely. The same is true of virtually all other non-human animals. Thus, they are *resigned to necessity*. However, men turn their attention to the pursuit of means that enable

---

[32] In Bloom, p. 67.

[33] In Butterworth, pp. 81–82.

them to more easily survive as soon as their minds develop. Once established, they become dependent on those means. Not only does their dependence on means weaken human beings, but it generates *alienation* as well, apparently, alienation from a previous state of self-unity.

The emergence of pride, amour-propre, is connected not only with the development of the human mind and increase of humanity, but also with the *human pursuit of refined and more sophisticated means of survival*, means that implicitly develop from the natural human being's capacity to *compare himself* to other animals. Man's pursuit of the means to his survival by the creation of new instruments to that end is *indirect*. Thus, it alienates human beings from themselves, a decisive stage in the process of disunity. By turning to external means, we turn away from our natural inclinations, but then become dependent on our artificial creations. The power needed to acquire, protect, and use means ultimately outweighs the good obtained from them. Thus, once one obtains certain means, one must acquire more power. And once one begins to acquire power, one cannot stop. One is simply drawn into a self-perpetuating quest for more power. While one might conclude that such an argument merely confirms part of Hobbes' vision of the state of nature, Rousseau's crucial new insight is that *society alone is responsible for human misery*, rather than a resolution to it. One must be careful, however, not to confuse the *quest for power* with the *absolute power* possessed by an omnipotent being. The power obtained from the use of means is always *unstable*, because it perpetuates an endless need for more power. In this sense, it is truly a sign of *weakness* in contrast to the absolute power of God.[34]

A related theme prominently emerges in *The Social Contract*: *one who believes himself to be a master of others is a greater slave than they*. To illustrate, even though a tyrant seems to be free and seems to have power over others, he must do things he does not want to do in order to keep

---

[34] Melzer, pp. 71–73.

his power. Thus, he is enslaved by his power. Such an individual's quest for power only enhances his feeling of dependence, and with the growth of dependence is the growth of vice and wickedness. In the entire human race, the growth of vice and wickedness is exponentially greater than in only a single individual. Only by engaging in relations with each other could people experience such dependence, thereby enhance the degree of disharmony they display in civil life. Thus, *contradiction is the foundation of society*.

In addition, in Book II of *Emile*, Rousseau calls attention to the distinction between abiding by one's own will and abiding by the will of another. For Rousseau, true power consists in the freedom one experiences by obeying the laws one gives oneself. And if one has true power, one must be able to obtain what one needs. But if one's needs do not extend beyond one's capacities, one will obtain all of one's needs independently. However, the influences of external circumstances, first, generate "needs" that extend beyond human capacities, and then "trap" human beings between their selfish desires and internalized need to serve others, those on whom they come to depend based on their artificial needs. This form of disunity represents a split between the inner and the outer. That is, *people must seem to be what they are not.* They must pass through life claiming to feel as they do not feel, claiming to believe what they do not really believe, and claiming to care about what they do not really care about. As soon as one man needs another's help, he looks upon him as a useful object, thus breaking the bond of identification: "Dependence on men engenders all the vices, and by it, master and slave are mutually corrupted."[35] What Rousseau meant by the

---

[35] *Emile*, BK II, in Bloom, p. 85. Melzer also discusses this "split" between the "inner" and the "outer." He goes so far as to claim that through the "exploitative relation" that "needing others" becomes, love actually "disappears." The problem raised by such a claim, however, is that it conflicts with an implication of Rousseau's theory of self-love, that there are certain passions central to human beings that cannot be damaged even by the corrupting influences of society. Perhaps my reading of Melzer is inaccurate. If may be, however, that if "love" between two individuals disappears, that "self-love" need not disappear. Furthermore, a split between the "inner" and the "outer" may not reflect irreparable damage to the "inner" by external corrupting influences, even though the "split" itself may be too severe for full repair.

"contradiction of society" can be summarized as follows: *the very essence of civilized societies is to unite men through the contradiction of personal dependence*. It is, thus, the social bond that generates injustice and disunity.[36]

Rousseau's argument for natural human goodness, thus, can be summarized as follows: Through introspection, Rousseau discovered that generosity naturally pleases human beings, while iniquity naturally repulses them. Furthermore, by identifying the primary human passion as amour de soi, Rousseau established that the basis of human motivation is a positive affection for life. These two discoveries constitute the positive aspect of Rousseau's principle of natural goodness. But, because human beings in their current form are unjust and lack the inner harmony that his theory of self-love entails, the positive content of his principle of natural goodness cannot show that society alone is responsible for making human beings bad. However, the extent of human injustice and disunity is so severe that they must be artificial. Human beings are susceptible to the influences of their environment, although they cannot be changed in fundamental ways. Empirical evidence reveals that the closer human beings are to nature, the better they are, whereas the more they come together, the worse they are. Thus, some historical series of events must have changed human beings for the worse, and these events are connected with the moments in which human beings abandoned their solitude to seek the help of others. Once social relations increased, human beings became dependent on each other, hence developed needs that exceeded their capacities. To the extent that people are disunified, they oppress and use others as mere means to their selfish ends. Thus, society alone is responsible for human vice.

---

[36] See pp. 77–78 of Melzer for more details on what he calls Rousseau's "social argument."

(III) Rousseau and Bacon's Idols of the Mind

Frequently overlooked in discussions of modern philosophy, Rousseau's thought, nonetheless, reflects a keen awareness of the sorts of problems addressed by Bacon's idols. Rousseau even names Bacon as an exemplar of genuine intellectual inquiry in a footnote to his *First Discourse.* However, like his predecessors, Rousseau was not totally immune to them.

Rousseau and the Idols of the Tribe: Rousseau addresses the Idols of the Tribe primarily through his account of natural human beings and his proposals for the ways that natural goodness can be recovered. Recall that Rousseau prescribed a "negative education" to safeguard people from the dangers lurking in the potential proliferation of artificial needs and desires. Humanity is best served learning only what is necessary and when it is necessary, especially since people, much like the prisoners in Plato's cave, tend to resist the imposition of an external will, regardless of that will's intentions. The ascent out of the cave of artificial fire and puppetry into the natural light of the sun must first be desired by the prisoner, or any attempt at education will reinforce his preference for the comfort and security of slavery, hence, why true freedom consists in the adherence to laws that one legislates for oneself, the essence of the general will.

In addition, Rousseau acknowledges in his account of perfectibility that such a faculty serves as the source and root of human misery and suffering, a condition for the possibility of artificial desires. By the very nature of humanity's adaptability and creative imagination, necessary for survival, they inevitably develop the chains of dependence wrought by technology and civilization that transforms the positive impetus to extend one's being into an egocentric vanity, in which one loves oneself only to the extent that one is loved by others. Nonetheless, the fact that natural human beings must be conceived with some degree of foresight and comparative abilities only reflects the extent of their corruption, the fact that a purely unified and happy natural human is only an idea filtered by the determinations of a corrupted mind.

Rousseau and the Idols of the Cave: The same corruption extends to human preferences. Rousseau addresses the idols of the cave through his distinction between natural and artificial needs. That is, the objects of one's desire in the modern world are mostly artificial. Those things that one believes one needs are not only items that what one can live without, but items that one should want to live without, as they are far more likely to enhance one's misery and suffering by perpetuating one's dependence. Founded on the contradiction of dependence, out of society grows a paradox of desire, such that what people believe they want is not at all what they truly want or need. The coffee that seems to be a luxury afforded by our world becomes a necessity without which no one can function. The automobiles that we use to transport ourselves to our destinations more efficiently not only demand many of our resources – such as time and money – for their maintenance but can leave us hopelessly stranded if they cease to function. Much like our very own creations, our possessions, come to own us, our desires cultivate only the illusion of freedom. While technology, in many ways, makes life easier, it succeeds by making its creators weaker.

Rousseau and the Idols of the Marketplace: One way that Rousseau addresses the idols of the marketplace is by specifying the meaning of natural goodness, discussed at length above. Recall that Rousseau did not intend to suggest that people are born possessed of all the virtues possessed by Aristotle's 'Magnanimous Man' or with the moral integrity of a Socrates, but that people are naturally ignorant of the needs and desires that can lead to vice. Moreover, if people are not naturally benevolent and altruistic, they are, at the very least, docile and have much more moderate appetites than thinkers like Hobbes insisted.

More importantly, Rousseau's account of language seems specifically designed to address the idols of the marketplace. Like Aristotle, Rousseau recognized an inextricable link between sociability and the capacity to communicate through speech. But language becomes more complex as society develops. In turn, the more complex language becomes, the more it contributes to human corruption. Complex language involves the use of vague or abstract terms that have no correspondent object. Thus, complex language contributes to the distortion of our conception of human nature. The fact that language can distort our conceptions of human nature indicates a connection between language and thought. Rousseau's attentiveness to this connection establishes that he intended to develop a conception of human beings that avoided the idols of the marketplace, one that coincides both with his notion of a negative education and his conception of natural human beings as good in the sense that they are ignorant of unnecessary desires and the words that signify them.

Rousseau and the Idols of the Theater: Rousseau addresses the idols of the theater through his denial of the traditional conceptions of humanity as evil, his conception of the primal unity of human faculties, his claim that human beings are naturally asocial rather than social, and his insistence that human beings are primarily passional creatures, rather than rational creatures. Previous sections addressed Rousseau's denial of the doctrine of original sin and the Hobbesian claim that human beings are natural enemies of each other. Rousseau's conception of the primal unity of the faculties may be interpreted as his rejection of the bifurcation of the human soul that traces back to Plato. Recall that Plato's conception of the human soul pitted reason in conflict with both the faculties of appetite and spirit. Conflict, in fact, revealed that the human soul has multiple faculties. For Rousseau, conflict within the soul can emerge only after people are introduced to artificial desires that exceed their genuine needs. Hence, the Platonic conception of the soul and all similar models of the soul developed by Plato's successors, including Aristotle and Aquinas, describe humans only after they are corrupted.

In addition, most thinkers prior to Rousseau insisted that people are naturally social creatures. Plato's ideal city had as one of its foundational principles, human sociality, the fact that all people depend on others to some degree. Aristotle insisted that human beings differ from all other creatures not only in virtue of their rationality, but because they are naturally suited for politics, especially because they have speech. Once again, however, for Rousseau, human sociality is not only incidental to humanity, but the source of their corruption.

Finally, like Hume, Rousseau conceives of humanity as governed principally not by reason but by passion. And like Hume, Rousseau understood natural human beings as governed by passions that are self-regulating, at least prior to their corruption. But unlike Hume, Rousseau recognizes the power of reason in its power to corrupt, its power to stimulate the imagination and cultivate needs that require others and, thus, perpetuate the contradiction of mutual dependence.

Does Rousseau Avoid the Idols of the Mind? While Rousseau certainly seemed to be aware of the idols of the mind, his system is not totally immune to a Baconian critique. With respect to idols of the tribe, Rousseau's primary error consists in his inability to describe a perfectly pure, natural human being, devoid of any anticipation or foresight. Perfectibility, the condition for the possibility of making comparisons between oneself and others, by default, makes possible human corruption. While perfectibility is not in itself bad, the fact that it is a distinguishing feature of human beings means that people are poised to become bad, and that they can be so easily corrupted as to render any goodness they possess trivial.

With respect to the idols of the cave, one can surmise that Rousseau's conception of natural human goodness is little more than a projection of what he wanted humanity to be, and that his so called "system" consists merely of loosely connected aphoristic passages that amount only to an elegant form of wishful thinking. Nonetheless, Rousseau acknowledges that his conception of human beings in their natural condition can only be vaguely approximated by a mind corrupted by modern society. But such an acknowledgement did not stop him from trying to live out his idea of a genuinely philosophical life, as portrayed in the *Reveries*, and it certainly did not compel him to impose any strict rules or discipline on his own children.

Rousseau seemed to understand that any language he employed in his descriptions of natural human beings would inevitably suffer the pitfalls of vagueness and metaphysical speculation. However, a precise reading of Rousseau's conception of natural goodness, thread throughout his versatile corpus, must be laboriously dug out, as it was by authors such as Melzer and Velkley.[37] Rousseau himself did not seem concerned with making his terms clear.

Lastly, while Rousseau's conception of humanity represents a departure from traditional ideas of human nature, he employs a method popular in his time by appealing to a "state of nature." Not only did Hobbes appeal to this image, but Hobbes's successor, Locke, did as well. While Rousseau's description of the state of nature differs greatly from those found in his two predecessors, it is worth wondering whether he would have employed such an image at all if not for their work. Moreover, his description of the state of nature conveys the image of something quite familiar: a veritable Garden of Eden, albeit devoid of any theological determinations.

Ultimately, Rousseau is one of the most profound yet underappreciated thinkers in the history of philosophy. While Hume sets out to be the "Newton of the Mind," the thinker to be addressed in the next chapter recognized Rousseau as deserving of that very title.

---

[37] More specifically, see Richard Velkley's *Freedom and the End of Reason: On the Moral Foundations of Kant's Critical Philosophy*, (Chicago: Chicago University Press, 1989), and *Being After Rousseau: Philosophy and Culture in Question*, (Chicago: Chicago University Press, 2002).

Chapter 6 Worksheet

1. Which author has the more plausible conception of the state of nature: Hobbes or Rousseau? Is there a better option than either offered by these two thinkers? Defend your view!

2. Does Golding's *Lord of the Flies* accurately depict a Hobbesian state of nature? Do you think Golding's primary intention was to portray such a state of nature? Why or why not?

3. Based on the passages selected from Hobbes's *Leviathan*, how does Hobbes address Bacon's Idols of the Mind? Does he avoid them successfully? Explain.

4. Do you think that Rousseau's negative education would be more effective than the modern American educational system? Why or why not?

5. Does Rousseau's conception of "perfectibility" conflict with his thesis about natural human goodness in any way? Why or why not?

6. Do you believe that human beings are naturally solitary creatures, or that they are more socially inclined, as Plato and Aristotle maintained?

Kant—The Best of Both Worlds

Speculation about lofty, abstract matters – such as the ultimate nature of reality, the existence of God, and whether people have free will and control over their actions – have a practical basis. Usually, such questions emerge naturally from reflections about how people ought to live, whether life has any meaning, and how to cope with tragedy, loss, and suffering. The widespread belief in a transcendent reality, such as an all-powerful and totally spiritual God, for instance, accounts for why people ought to live justly and respect the well-being of others and for the ultimate meaning of life. If people lead wicked lives and harm others, they will be punished by God in the afterlife. Even though it seems that the good suffer while the wicked prosper, good will ultimately prevail over evil, as cosmic justice reigns supreme. Those who live moral lives do not do so in vain. Not only will the virtues of humility and generosity be met with reward, but resilience through the frustration and turmoil of suffering and failure sweetens the flavor of ultimate triumph.

Perhaps none of the thinkers addressed thus far succeeded in proving that God exists, that the human soul survives death, or that the just life is inherently better than a life devoted solely to fulfilling one's selfish desires at the expense of others. But maybe that is only because such matters cannot be resolved merely through logic or theoretical speculation. Perhaps they have a *practical* resolution, as was the position of the thinker about whom this chapter is written, the 18th century German thinker, Immanuel Kant.

Historians of thought frequently refer to Kant's contributions as "critical philosophy," owing mostly to the titles Kant chose for his three major works: *Critique of Pure Reason, Critique of Practical Reason,* and *Critique of Judgment.* Generally, Kant had three sources of inspiration. First, Kant possessed a natural affinity for rationalism, especially that of Leibniz, in addition to contemporaries such as Christian Wolff. Second, Kant's reading of Hume famously "woke him from his dogmatic slumber." In this case, Kant's "dogmatic slumber" can be understood as his adherence to rationalist principles. Third, and perhaps most importantly, Kant recognized Rousseau as being the true "Newton of the Mind." In fact, it is rumored that when Kant became engrossed in Rousseau's *Social Contract,* he missed his walk through the Lindell trees, part of his daily routine by which people could presumably set their proverbial watches!

Leibniz, Hume, and Rousseau comprise quite a motley trio. Just how do they run together in Kant's thought? Since Leibniz was a rationalist and Hume a radical empiricist, there is an extent to which Kant's thought may be understood as a synthesis of both schools of thought. Moreover, Kant's optimism about the future of humanity and the pursuit of cultural progress reflects Rousseau most basic and integral principle of human goodness. Unlike Rousseau, however, Kant's thought not only has the rigor of a true system, but is heavily architectonic, just as difficult as it is significant. The highlights of his thought can be understood as answers to three basic questions. First, *what can I know?* This question concerns metaphysics and epistemology. Second, *what ought I to do?* This question concerns morality and ethics. Third, *what may I hope?* This question concerns the meaning of history and the ultimate resolution to ultimate questions through *practical* rather than *theoretical* reason. Kant's answers to each of these questions will be examined respectively.

(I) What Can I Know?

Hume's critique of causality based on his radical empiricist presuppositions seemed to make it impossible to achieve scientific knowledge. At the very least, Hume's principles make the development of such knowledge excruciatingly difficult. Enticed by the prospects of modern science and the Enlightenment, Kant sought to establish a foundation for such knowledge, and his resolution to the problems raised by Hume breaks down into three categories. First, he distinguishes between three types of judgments: analytic a priori, synthetic a posteriori, and synthetic a priori. Second, he distinguishes between three faculties, each of which contributes a different component to knowledge: sensibility, which contributes the sensory component, understanding, which contributes the conceptual component, and reason, which contributes a regulative component. Third, Kant distinguishes between phenomena and noumena, the former of which consists in the way in which the human mind represents things, the latter of which consists of things-in-themselves, stripped of all the determinations of human consciousness.

Three Kinds of Judgments: Each of Kant's three types of judgments includes two distinctions. The first is the analytic/synthetic distinction, which is semantic, concerning the meaning of terms. A sentence is analytic just in case its predicate adds nothing to the subject. In other words, the predicate of an analytic sentence merely states the definition of the subject. A sentence is synthetic just in case its predicate adds to the concept of the subject. Synthetic sentences, thus, do not merely state definitions. For example, "A bachelor is an adult unmarried male," may be labeled analytic, since the predicate merely states the definition of the subject. However, the sentence, "Josh Lott is a bachelor," may be labeled synthetic, since the predicate adds to the concept of the subject. That is, there is nothing in the definition of "Josh Lott" that entails the definition of bachelor. The second distinction in each kind of judgment is the a priori/a posteriori distinction, which is epistemic, concerning knowledge. A judgment is a priori just in case it does not depend on any experience. For instance, laws of logic such as "Nothing can both be and not be," or "Everything is identical to itself" require no observation if they are to be known and understood. However, statements such as "John's house is painted blue," require a direct observation to be made of John's house in order to be known.

Recall Hume's distinction between matters of fact and relations of ideas. Hume's relations of ideas resemble Kant's *analytic a priori* judgments. Such judgments depend on no experience or observations and consist of sentences in which the predicate adds nothing to the concept of the subject. For Kant, examples include not only laws of logic, but statements such as "A triangle is a three-sided figure." Like Hume's relations of ideas, to deny an analytic a priori judgment results in contradiction. Hume's matters of fact resemble Kant's *synthetic a posteriori* judgments, which result from direct observations and experiences and the predicate adds to the concept of the subject. The statement, "Some apples are green," constitutes an example. The concept of "apple" does not include the concept of "greenness." Moreover, knowing that some apples are green demands that some apples at least be observed. Other examples include "The sun is 93 million miles from Earth," and "Water freezes at 32 degrees Fahrenheit." The concept of the sun does not include the concept "93 million miles," and one must measure the distance between the two objects to establish such a judgment. Moreover, the concept of water includes neither the concept of "freezing," nor the concept of "32 degrees Fahrenheit," and one must observe the conditions under which water freezes.

Kant's conception of *synthetic a priori* judgments marks one of his most unique contributions, in addition to one of his key points of divergence from Hume. For Hume, mathematical judgments – such as $2 + 2 = 4$ – qualify as relations of ideas. For Kant, however, such judgments do not qualify as analytic a priori. Certainly, such a judgment is a priori, as it constitutes a law of arithmetic. But it is not *analytic*, for the concept of "4" does not include the concept of "2." The same may be said of any arithmetical judgment, such as $7 + 5 = 12$, since the concept of "12" includes the concept of neither "5" nor "7." It may also be said of the principle of Euclidean geometry that the shortest distance between two points is a straight line. The concept of "shortness" does not include the concept of "straightness." Nonetheless, when doing arithmetic or geometry, must not contradict oneself. Such judgments, thus, belong to a third category, in which *knowledge does not depend on experience, but the predicate adds to the concept of the subject*, extending knowledge in some way.

In addition to judgments of arithmetic, judgments in metaphysics, science, and morality, Kant maintained, consist of synthetic a priori judgments. One example includes the claim that, "Every event has a cause." Such a claim is not merely a statement of definition, but it cannot be known merely by making observations, since one cannot observe ALL the events that take place in the world. How then can anyone possess such knowledge? The answer, as will be shown is that while all knowledge, indeed, *begins* with experience, not all knowledge *arises* from experience. That is, the minds of all people are constituted in such a way as to allow for knowledge, but experience must first awaken the mind. The mind imposes order on that experience.

The Faculties: Kant suggests that the human mind consists of three faculties, each of which makes an important contribution to knowledge – sensibility, understanding, and reason. Sensibility provides the two conditions for the possibility of sense-experience – space and time. Basically, the mind is equipped to detect sensory data occurring in places at specific times. No one could have sense-experiences unless they occurred in space and time. These conditions also make both arithmetic and geometry possible. To perform arithmetical operations requires counting, which implies time. Moreover, doing geometry requires drawing figures in space. Try to imagine any item completely divorced from space or time. It is impossible. Even a dark, blank void still is conceived by the mind as a space, and certainly you would log this experience as happening at a specific moment in time.

The understanding provides the equipment to organize sense-experience. Kant claimed that this faculty consists of a priori concepts or categories that actively impose themselves on the data of experience. Since such categories are a priori, they logically precede experience. While raw sensations would indeed be possible without them, they would have no coherently discernible order or pattern. Experience would be nothing more than a purely chaotic flux of events. Furthermore, such categories are independent of experience. That is, they are not built from experience in the Lockean sense that simple ideas construct more complex ideas. Rather, they are conditions for the possibility of experience itself, and, thus, they are necessary. Finally, such concepts are universal across all human minds.[1]

Kant lists 12 of these a priori concepts. They include the concepts of cause and effect and substance and accident. For instance, all people, universally, maintain that a thing's properties depend for their existence on the host, the substance. A ball is a substance, while its shape, color, and texture are all accidents, properties. However, the idea of a substance cannot derive from one's observation of the ball, or of any one thing. When one domino knocks over a second, anyone, universally, will judge that the first domino caused the second to fall. However, the idea of causality does not derive from such an experience. Hence, the mind must be equipped with them prior to any experience. Without a concept of substance and accident, no one would be able to distinguish an item from its properties, and no one would be able to identify that first domino as the cause of the row falling. Imagine that the mind has a filtration system of various "shapes" resembling a

---

[1] See Lavine, *From Socrates to Sartre*, p. 194.

cookie-cutter template. Everything that comes into the mind would conform to the various shapes. Each shape is a specific concept that gives form to the material from experience.

Like Hume, Kant insisted that ideas such as "substance" and "causality" cannot derive from sense-experience. However, unlike Hume, Kant insisted not only that we have such ideas, but that without such ideas, experience itself would not be possible. But what about the self? Recall that Hume denied that anyone has any idea of a self that remains identical across time, since no one has any single impression of a self. But if that were true, then where do any of our experiences occur? Kant maintained that there are two "selves." The first he called the *empirical ego*, the physical self as it is experienced. You experience yourself as going through various changes throughout life. Nonetheless, you remain the same person. Thus, there is unity in your experiences. Such unity, however, is elusive, as no one sensation can pinpoint it. Kant called this second self the *transcendental ego*. The fact that we can postulate such an idea justifies the concepts of the understanding, since it is through the a priori concepts of the understanding that such unity is possible.

Reason is the third faculty. Unlike the concepts of the understanding, which determine our experiences to conform with a priori conditions, reason is *regulative*. That is, reason functions as a guide to inquiry about the knowledge gained through the concepts of the understanding. The key feature of reason, for Kant, is autonomy, freedom. Einstein famously asserted that "Imagination is more important than knowledge." That is, understanding the system of reality requires one to think beyond mere experience, beyond what is merely given. The concepts of the understanding can establish only very specific items of knowledge, such as "A causes B," or "X is a substance with properties y and z." Understanding, however, cannot synthesize causal laws into a *system*. Through the cognition of the understanding alone, no one would ever ask, "Why does A cause B?" No one could ever ask,

"What purpose does substance X try to fulfill?" The concepts of the understanding allow us to make very specific associations between our experiences, such as "If I touch the fire, it will burn my hand," or "If I jump into the water, I will get wet." But through the concepts of the understanding, I would never be able to ask deeper, more reflective questions, such as "Why does the world exist?" or "What is the meaning of life?" Also, I would not be able to construct a theory about how reality operates. I could never construct a system of laws that explains nature and the relations between everything in it. Why? Because to create such a system, and to answer such questions about the meaning of life and the existence of the world, I must first be able to consider the possibility that such things do not exist, or at the very least, that they could have been very different.

Like Rousseau, thus, Kant maintained that freedom, specifically, the freedom of reason, distinguishes human beings from all other animals and reason seeks ways to improves one's surroundings. Hence, not only is reason practical, but it makes possible the motivation of inquiry. It is far from instrumental and impotent, as Hume suggested. The system that reason seeks naturally culminates in a teleological system of purposes, of which Kant's conception will be further explored below.

The Phenomena/Noumena Distinction: In short, Kant insists that knowledge develops in the following way. Sensibility provides the "stage" for sensations to occur, in space and time. Just as a literal stage makes it possible for actors to perform a play, space and time make sensations possible. The concepts of the understanding give shape or form to those sensations. Finally, the regulative principles of reason allow us to ask why such sensations occur in the first place and then organize theories to answer those questions. Thus, the mind actively organizes the world around it. But that raises a problem: Our cognitive framework can falsely represent the world. Kant was aware of this problem, hence, his phenomena/noumena distinction. The phenomenal realm refers primarily to the way in which we represent things in terms of the concepts of the understanding. The noumenal realm refers to things-in-themselves, of which no one can have any direct knowledge. This distinction becomes a major concern for the faculty of reason, since it has a speculative dimension.

For Kant, reason can easily become involved in antinomies, or contradictions. For example, one can easily provide a proof that God exists (and we examined several in previous chapters). But in terms of the concepts of the understanding, no such being can be observed. On that basis, one can easily provide a proof that God does not exist. The same may be said about free will. Since the concepts of the understanding impose the law of causality on all experiences, it seems as though everything is determined. But one could easily provide a proof that not everything is determined, since the faculty of reason itself implies freedom. Kant's resolution to both antinomies makes use of his phenomena/noumena distinction. That is, in the phenomenal realm, God does not exist and everything is determined. However, in the noumenal realm, God exists and there is free will.[2] But how can we have knowledge of any such things-in-themselves? The answer lies in the remaining sections.

(II) What Ought I To Do?

Kant's moral philosophy consists of the following themes: (a) the goodwill, (b) the motive of duty, (c) the rationality of morality, (d) the categorical imperatives, specifically, the universal law and end-in-itself formulas, and (e) the distinction between perfect and imperfect duties.

---

[2] For any brave souls who wish to try reading Kant himself, his *Prolegomena to Any Future Metaphysics* is more student friendly than his much longer and more difficult *Critique of Pure Reason*. The former is, basically, a more concise version of the latter, but students interested in pursuing Kant further should consult this text. The Cambridge edition is the most accessible to students. A.C. Ewing's *A Short Commentary on Kant's Critique of Pure Reason* (Chicago: University of Chicago Press, 1996) is also very reputable. Sebastian Gardner's *Kant and the Critique of Pure Reason* (New York: Routledge, 1999) is extremely helpful and provides a broad context for the general study of Kant.

The Goodwill: It is necessary to hold people responsible for their actions. But what is the basis for right and wrong? What makes morality possible? The possibility of morality demands that there be something *good without qualification*. That is, there must be something such that if it were added to any situation, it would not make that situation morally worse. This condition differs from an item being merely *intrinsically good*, or inherently good. Pleasure, for instance, is inherently good. People seek pleasure for its own sake. However, pleasure can be obtained through reprehensible actions. Moreover, Kant would agree with Aristotle that pleasure alone cannot satisfy humanity. Intelligence poses similar problems, since it can be used for either good or evil.

The Motive of Duty: Ultimately, Kant maintains that only the *goodwill* is good without qualification. A goodwill is an individual who does his or her duty *because* it is his or her duty, and for no other reason. In other words, a goodwill is a person who acts purely *from the motive of duty*. For Kant, only actions done from the motive of duty have *moral worth*. Consider the following scenario. Suppose that during your morning routine, you notice a woman's wallet fall from her purse. So, you return the wallet, but only because you hope that she will reward you in some way. In this scenario, you did the right thing, but you acted *merely in accordance with duty*. Since your motive in returning the wallet was the reward only, your action lacks moral worth. However, had you returned the wallet simply because it is the right thing to do, your action would be *from* duty, and would have moral worth.

The following scenario carries the same message but strikes many as counterintuitive. Imagine that there are two parents. The first parent loves her daughter. Thus, she devotes her life to raising her child with generosity, patience, and compassion. She ensures that her daughter has everything in life that a parent can possibly provide. The second parent, on the other hand, never wanted children. To an extent, she resents her daughter, feeling cheated of her own youth by her unplanned parenthood. Nonetheless, she is moved by her duty as a parent to provide for her child, just as much as the first parent. Intuitively, most people are inclined to believe that the first parent is better than the second. To an extent, even Kant would maintain that such people's actions should be praised and encouraged. However, only the second parent acts from the motive of duty, and, thus, only her actions have true moral worth.

The difference between each parent highlights Kant's insistence that morality derives from reason, from the rational nature of humanity. If given the choice, most people would probably prefer the first mother over the second. But suppose that the first mother suddenly lost her passion for her daughter. What would happen? More than likely, she will stop providing for her child. On the other hand, the second mother provides for her child despite what her passion dictates. Thus, she acts with *autonomy*, free will.

The Rationality of Morality: For Kant, it is free will that makes morality possible. It is often said that *"ought* implies *can,"* which means that if a person, S, ought to perform some action, x, then S must at least be able to perform x. But people must be held responsible for their actions. Hence, people must have free will. Free will, moreover, must come from reason. Without reason, people would not be able to act contrary to the dictates of their passions and emotions. Recall that reason is the faculty that enables people to think beyond the automatic cognitive determinations of the categories. Morality is different in that the moral law must be discovered through a rational will. Were people always and only "slaves to their passions," as Hume insisted, then morality would be impossible, since rules and laws would change as frequently as an individual's state of mind. Morality must be absolute, but the only way that morality can be absolute is if morality derives not from the passions, but from reason. Consider a person who behaves irrationally. A person who meets such a description fails to deliberate on alternative courses of action and make sound decisions. Such a person's behavior is triggered merely by responses to feelings and desires that may be self-destructive. The cycle of addiction constitutes a prime example. Irrational behavior, thus, is not *free*. Rationality implies that one has control over one's actions, and that one acts from and with consciousness of the laws of one's conduct. In short, free will is a condition for the possibility of morality, reason makes free will possible.

The Categorical Imperative – Universal Law: Despite the rationality of morality, it is not entirely clear just how exactly human beings can discern the moral law. How can anyone know the difference between right and wrong? How can anyone do their duty if duties cannot be known? For Kant, morality consists of *categorical imperatives*, or universal, exceptionless commands. Such commands contrast with *hypothetical imperatives*, which are conditional, such as "If you want to be happy, you must live a moral life." A categorical imperative merely states, "Live a moral life!" In Kantian terms, a categorical imperative would mandate, "Do your duty!" Remember, morality is absolute, not conditional.

While Kant insists that there is truly only one categorical imperative, he gives several formulations of it. The two most popular are the *Universal Law Formula*, and the *Formula of the End-in-Itself.* The universal law formula states, "Act only on that maxim that you could will to be a universal law." In other words, according to this formulation, we always ought to act only in a way that everybody could act. Prima facie, this formula seems to be a more complex version of the golden rule, "Do unto others as you would have them do unto you." However, Kant's formulation addresses the main flaw in the golden rule. The golden rule seems to permit people to treat others in morally reprehensible ways, so long as the perpetrator would not object to the same treatment. For instance, since a sadomasochist enjoys being tortured, the golden rule would permit a sadomasochist to torture people. Kant's universal law formula is far more restrictive, as it allows people to act only in a way that everyone could act *universally*. For instance, since most people do not enjoy being tortured, a sadomasochist cannot use Kant's universal law formula to justify his or her behavior. Basically, according to Kant's universal law formula of the categorical imperative, if one is considering a course of action – for example, driving through a red light without stopping – one should first ask oneself, "Could I live in a world where everyone ran through a red light?" If everyone behaved in such a way, there would be far more automobile accidents, and concomitantly far more deaths and injuries. Hence, everyone ought to stop at a red light, as to do the opposite is not universalizable.

The Categorical Imperative – End-in-Itself: The formula of the end-in-itself states, "Act only in such a way that you always treat humanity, either in your own person or in that of another, as an end-in-itself and never as a means merely." For Kant, rationality includes awareness of a principle that can be recognized as universally valid. But rational agents act with a goal in mind as well. That is, rational agents have an end. As this second formulation implies, Kant insists that the only "end-in-itself" is humanity, not only the humanity of others, but the humanity of oneself as well. That is, not only can another person not be used as a means merely, but one cannot use oneself as a mere means either. The final two words of this second formulation are crucial. A person may be used as a *means*, but not as a *mere means*. As social creatures, there is an extent to which we all depend on each other, and, thus, we all will need to use each other as means to an end some of the time. A trip to the grocery store to buy food usually involves requesting help from one of the clerks or cashiers. Dining out requires that one accepts the service of cooks and waiting staff. If one becomes sick, one will need the services of a physician. However, in each of these cases, the freedom and well-being of the people whose help we seek is not severely compromised. But suppose that you are locked out of your car. To get inside, you grab the nearest person and use his head to smash through your window! In this instance, the poor soul whose head you used to get into your car became a *mere means* to your end.

Why did Kant insist that humanity is an end-in-itself? He seemed to hold this view for two reasons. First, human beings are a source of value. That is, they can give value to objects that otherwise lack value. For example, without a person to use it, a pen has no value. It cannot write on its own. It only has value if there is an agent who can use it for the purpose of writing. The same can be said of virtually any tool or instrument. Keep in mind, though, tools and instruments, be whether they are pens, markers, knives, axes, saws, or more complex machines such as automobiles, planes, and computers, all came from humans, inventions of the power of reason and imagination. Second, human beings can choose their own goals, their own *ends*. People appropriate the necessary instruments to meet their goals. In short, people are ends-in-themselves in virtue of their freedom, which is both the key feature of reason and is necessary to make morality possible.

Perfect and Imperfect Duties: According to Kant, these two formulations of the categorical imperative are equivalent, since he insisted that the same duties can be derived from them. Each formulation of the categorical imperative constitutes a very general guide to action. But Kant specifies many individual duties that can be derived from them, many maxims, or rules of intent, on which we may act. There are two general types of duties, *perfect* and *imperfect*. To do the opposite of an imperfect duty is not even in principle universalizable and would result in an outright contradiction. Two examples of perfect duties are honesty and to refrain from suicide. For example, imagine that you are trying to will the maxim, "I will tell a lie whenever it benefits me." The very attempt to will such a maxim requires honesty, since one must be willing to adhere to the maxim. That is, one must will a world where everyone is honest but also dishonest, which is a contradiction. A similar problem occurs if one attempts to will the maxim, "Whenever I need money, I will make a lying promise to repay a loan."

In principle, one would be willing a world in which banks exist to make loans, but also a world in which banks do not exist, as a necessary consequence of nobody repaying their loans. Moreover, were one to will the maxim, "I will commit suicide whenever I am unhappy," one wills a world with suicidal people, but, consequently, a world where no one exists, since everyone would be dead!

Imperfect duties, indeed, are absolute and exceptionless, as are perfect duties. Unlike perfect duties, willing the opposite is logically possible, but no one would want to live in a world where such maxims prevailed. Two imperfect duties Kant derives from the categorical imperative are the duty always to help those in dire need and the duty to develop one's talents. Suppose a person tried to will the maxim, "I will never help anyone who needs my help." It is conceivable that such a world would exist, in which no one ever helped anyone else, or gave to charity. But such a world is undesirable, especially since most people desire friendships and romantic relationships. Such relationships demand reciprocity, equal contributions from each side. If you have a friend, occasionally, that friend will want your help, be it advice, or help moving, or a financial loan. If you constantly deny your friend's request, then your friendship will not last. Moreover, the day may come when YOU are the person who desperately needs help. With respect to the duty to develop one's talents, imagine living in a world where no one became a physician, where no one with a talent for engineering pursued a career in technology, where no one with musical talent became a musician, where no one with artistic ability became an artist. Such a world, again, is *logically* possible, but still undesirable. No one would really want to live in a world without medical and health care practitioners, technology, music, or art.

These scenarios illustrate additional differences between perfect and imperfect duties. Typically, perfect duties are owed to a specific person, can only be done either once or in a very specific way, and once they are completed, carry no additional demand. For example, if I have a duty to repay a loan, then I owe that loan to a specific person or agency, owe a very specific amount, and once that amount is paid, I do not have to pay it a second time. Imperfect duties, however, are typically owed to no one in particular, can be done in more than one way, and can be done more than once. For example, if I have a duty to give to charity, then I do not have to give to any one specific charity. I am at liberty to choose to whom I will donate money and how much money I will donate. Moreover, I can help a charity in more than way. Instead of giving money, I might choose to donate my time, perhaps by working at a shelter. Furthermore, if I donate money to a charity on Monday, that one act does not absolve me from helping a stranded motorist on Tuesday. I am still under an obligation to help despite my prior monetary donations. With respect to the duty to develop one's talents, every person can choose which talent to develop. For instance, if a person has a talent for both medicine and music, he need not develop both. He may choose. In addition, if the same person decides to become a physician, that same person may later decide to develop an additional talent. The development of his talent is not owed to any one person, but anybody who may benefit from it.[3]

Note that Kant's conception of the categorical imperative and the duties that derive from it coincide with his notion of synthetic a priori judgments. Moral judgments are necessary, and so do not derive from experience. But at the same time, such judgments are not merely analytical, not merely "relations of ideas." For instance, the concept of "talent" does not include the concept of "duty," and neither do the concepts of "charity," "honesty," or "self-preservation." Moreover, since we come to know the moral law through reason,

---

[3] For primary sources on Kant's moral philosophy, I am partial to Paton's translation of Kant's *Groundwork for the Metaphysics of Morals*, as Paton provides an interpretative essay to accompany the text. Kant's much longer and more difficult *Critique of Practical Reason* is recommended for more enthusiastic and advanced students. Lewis White Beck's *Commentary on Kant's Critique of Practical Reason* (Chicago: University of Chicago Press, 1960) is a very helpful guide to Kant's second critique.

and free will comes from reason, reason is not merely theoretical, but *practical*. As illustrated above, practical reason is the basis for science, from which it follows that science has the same basis as morality and religion.

(III) What May I Hope?

Recall that in Kant's system, the only actions that have moral worth are those that are done from the motive of duty, and that the person who acts from such a motive is a goodwill. The problem, however, as Kant acknowledges, is that *we cannot be certain that anyone ever has acted from the motive of duty*. Human motivation is very complicated and moral decisions are never made in a vacuum. Not only is it difficult to understand fully the motives of another person, but we can rarely understand *our own* motives. When you returned that purse, did you really do it just because it was the right thing to do? Maybe you returned it not for a reward, but perhaps only to make yourself feel better, as you would feel guilty if you allowed a woman to lose her valuables. When you give to charity, do you really do so for the well-being of others, or, once again, because it makes you feel good to do so? And if you only help others to help yourself, is there not a sense in which you use such people as mere means, since you likely will never meet such people and cannot care for them in the same way you care for those closest to you. Even more problematic is that Kant seems not to be concerned with happiness. We all must live so that our free will conforms to an abstract moral law even if doing so does not make us happy.

The Viability of Morality in the Realm of Nature: As mentioned, Kant acknowledges these concerns. In the first place, Kant maintains that morality must allow some reasonable concern for happiness. However, he insists that morality does not consist in an individual pursuing one's own happiness. Contributing to the happiness and well-being of others is more important than pursuing one's own ends. Nonetheless,

Kant holds that if everyone devoted themselves to trying to conform their free will to the moral law, then a Kingdom of Ends would be the result, a world in which everyone treated everyone else as an end-in-itself. Ultimately, such a kingdom will lead to happiness. But the question remains: Are acts of goodwill even possible?

In short, Kant insists that we must believe that they are, for if morality is impossible, then so is happiness. Even though happiness is not the motive of morality, it cannot be achieved without it. In the *Metaphysics of Morals*, Kant asks us to imagine a man who is presented with the option of giving his own life to save someone else. Most people, when presented with this option, would at least hesitate and consider the possibility carefully. At the very least, this scenario establishes that a pure act of goodwill is possible. If an individual sacrifices his or her life to save another, said individual gains no benefit from the act whatsoever.

Not only must we believe in the possibility of morality, but we must believe that the Kingdom of Ends is possible as well. That is, Kant maintained that humanity must understand itself as engaged in a process of continual progress. But once again, he recognized humanity's "asocial sociability" as a problem. Human beings seem to be basically selfish, which is why it is so difficult to believe in the possibility of morality. Hence, the establishment of what Kant called a "completely just civic constitution" seems inconsistent with human nature. So, if humanity is to believe that progress is possible, it is necessary to posit *teleology* in nature. More specifically, it is necessary to understand reason as operating within human nature from humanity's very origins. Kant disagreed with Rousseau on this matter. For the latter, reason developed in humanity only accidentally and operated much to the detriment of humanity. For Kant, in order to conceive of the perfection of morality as the goal of humanity, reason cannot merely intervene accidentally in human development.

Nature's Contributions to Human Development: Kant suggests, thus, that nature must be viewed not only as purposive, but as aiding the development of human reason. In his view, it does so in three ways. First, nature *challenges* human beings. The natural world confronts human beings with storms, harsh climate conditions such as extreme heat and cold, predatory animals much larger and stronger than human beings, and limited resources. Thus, nature forces human beings to develop the skills necessary for their survival. Second, nature *cultivates* human taste. Coarse appetites become much more sophisticated as humanity develops. The drive to satisfy hunger eventually develops into luxurious culinary arts. The need for shelter from the elements leads not only to elaborate living conditions, but to architecture and technology. The sex drive develops into poetry, art, and deep, reflective appreciation for beauty. Third, and finally, nature forces humanity to recognize their *freedom.* Since we must conceive of nature as purposive in order to understand it, we are led to seek out an ultimate, final goal of nature, a purpose of nature itself. But the only viable end of nature is humanity as a moral agent, in a kingdom of ends. Since morality requires freedom, our conception of nature leads to the discovery of our freedom. Moreover, the very idea of purposiveness itself is a reflective principle that demands the use of reason and imagination, thus, thinking beyond mere sensory data and the conceptual framework of human cognition.

Transcendental Ideas – God and Immortality: Not only must nature be viewed as purposive, but two additional presuppositions must be made. The first postulate is the *existence of God.* Kant notoriously criticized traditional arguments for God's existence. He insisted that the ontological argument, for instance, failed because it treats existence as a property. Moreover, cosmological arguments depend on the ontological argument, since they include the concept of a necessary being. Since the ontological argument is invalid, so are cosmological arguments. Then, there is the design argument. Both Kant and Hume had great respect for design arguments, but both severely criticized these arguments. While Kant insisted that the design argument cannot prove that God exists, his requirement that we posit teleology seems to support some form of the design argument, a moral design argument. That is, we must posit the existence of God as a guarantor of the possibility of achieving the highest good in nature, humanity as a Kingdom of Ends. God ensures that our moral actions are not in vain by ensuring that the good will be rewarded and the evil will be punished.

The second postulate is the *immortality of the soul*. The end of humanity, the final goal of life, is perfect virtue, the achievement of the Kingdom of Ends. But the conditions of life are inconsistent with perfect virtue. Remember, we cannot be sure that anyone has ever committed a single act of goodwill. Moreover, the achievement of perfect virtue cannot be achieved in any one lifetime. Thus, we must posit that there is an immortal soul, by which one can achieve perfect virtue.

From within the limits of practical reason, thus, there are three noumena, things in themselves, that we can know exist. The first is free will, which must exist as a condition for the possibility of morality. The second is the immortal soul, which must exist as a condition for the possibility of perfect virtue. Finally, God must exist to guarantee the possibility of achieving the final goal of nature, the Kingdom of Ends. Hence, not only does Kant improve upon Hume and Rousseau by providing a superior account of reason, but by providing more for which we can hope despite the processes of history.[4] But how much of Kant's system is true, and how much of it may be dubbed mere wishful thinking?

---

[4] For primary sources on Kant's essays on history, see the collection *Toward Perpetual Peace and Other Essays* (Ted Humphrey (Ed.), Indianapolis, IN: Hackett Publishing Co., 1992). Specifically, the essays "Idea for a Universal History with a Cosmopolitan Intent," and "Speculative Beginning of Human History." Yirmiyahu Yovel's *Kant and the Philosophy of History* (Princeton: Princeton University Press, 1982), and Richard Velkley's *Freedom and the End of Reason: On the Moral Foundations of Kant's Critical Philosophy* (Chicago: Chicago University Press, 1989) both provide detailed interpretations of Kant's writings on history but are intended for more advanced students. Susan Neiman's *The Unity of Reason: Rereading Kant* (New York: Oxford University Press, 1994) is a very respectable account of Kant's conception of practical reason, but should only be approached after reading Kant's primary sources.

(IV) Kant and Bacon's Idols of the Mind

Kant's position is often called *transcendental idealism.* As an idealist, he maintained that the world of our experience is predominantly mental, that the order of the world is imposed by the determinations of the mind. But what is meant by "transcendental"? The term must be distinguished from "transcendent," which implies the existence of an other-worldly object. *Transcendental*, in contrast, implies the necessary pre-supposition of ideas that cannot be established through empirical evidence. The transcendental ideas Kant claims demand our affirmation are God, freedom, and immortality, for the sake of achieving the highest goal of humanity, the Kingdom of Ends. But to what extent does Kant avoid Bacon's idols of the mind in his tireless labors to establish this claim? Like Bacon, Kant acknowledged that human beings often project their own attributes into the world of experience. However, Kant also recognized the impossibility of divesting oneself completely of such a capacity.

Kant and Bacon's Idols of the Tribe: Kant addresses himself to the idols of the tribe in at least three ways. First, he provides an extensively detailed account of the human faculties and their operations, establishing not only that what we experience is shaped by the determinations of the mind, but is in fact made possible by the structures of the mind, specifically by the forms of intuition – space and time – furnished by sensibility, and the concepts of the understanding. Kant's description of the faculties leads naturally into his phenomena/noumena distinction, in which he separates the world of experience from the realm of things-in-themselves. Kant, thus, goes far beyond Bacon, not only recognizing such a distinction but by elaborating on the conditions for its possibility.

In addition, Kant's conception of reason allows for the recognition of regulative principles that guide experience and various modes of inquiry, but that may not literally represent the world. Recall that the primary feature of reason is autonomy, freedom. Moreover, people are naturally inclined to view nature as purposive, since it is the only way that we can make sense of it. Realizing that such principles arise from human rationality function as a safeguard against projecting our own attributes into the world of experience. In short, Kant's system encourages epistemic humility in our estimation of the world.

Finally, Kant's moral philosophy recognizes a conflict built into humanity. Human beings have selfish instincts and coarse appetites. But at the same time, people must be held responsible for their actions, which demands the recognition of universal moral absolutes, which can only be possible if people act from the motive of duty. Kant not only acknowledges the difficulty in acting purely from the motive of duty, but the more troubling possibility that no single act of goodwill has ever been done! Kant's reasons for optimism and his suggestion that we must believe in both the possibility that every individual can act from such a motive and that all humanity can achieve conditions where all act from similar motives lend themselves as more than reasonable guardians against acting from rules that serve merely selfish motives. His procedure afforded by the universal law and end-in-itself formulas of the categorical imperative are invaluable in these respects.

Kant and Bacon's Idols of the Cave: Kant's efforts to address idols of the tribe coincide with the ways in which he addresses idols of the cave. Since the latter forms of error reflect personal biases and prejudices in judgment, Kant would insist that awareness of how human sensibility, cognition, and reason operate lends itself as a preservative against the nearly universal human tendency to jump to conclusions based on ideas that people simply want to be true. Many people who believe in God hold such a belief because they want it to be true, either out of fear of annihilation at the time of death, the possibility of punishment by a higher power, or hope for a reward from that same authority. In his later writings, Kant cautioned the use of what he deemed the "teleological principle," the heuristic idea that nature is the product of design, only as a guide to inquiry to which we may appeal when no better principle is available. Only when all other options that could explain some phenomenon are exhausted may we invoke an intelligent agent such as God as the cause.

The same may be said about the various justifications for our actions. Kant demands that we respect the humanity of all. Nonetheless, Kant still leaves reasonable "wiggle room" in the form of imperfect duties, whereby an individual is at liberty to choose which talents to develop and how to help others. Presumably in all cases, an agent would choose a course of action to which he or she is best suited, not necessarily a course of action that emanates solely from one's passions or desires, but one that represents an individual's true talent and purpose in life. If one is inclined toward the medical field, choosing to help others by providing health care certainly differs from the desire to provide health care only for the status and potential wealth it affords. Furthermore, the development of one's talents and commitment to charity are, indeed, for the benefit of everyone, since no rational person would will a world in which such things did not exist.

Kant and Bacon's Idols of the Marketplace: The most salient way in which Kant addresses himself to the idols of the marketplace is through his phenomena/noumena distinction. The cognitive machinery furnished by the concepts of the understanding seem to make free will impossible, since in the world of experience everything has a determined cause. But a world without free will is a world without morality. The same conceptual principles leave out God and immortality, each of which must be affirmed so as not to undermine the goals toward which we strive. Hence, Kant makes the distinction between the world of sense and the world of things in themselves. Kant's distinction offers the best of both worlds with an efficient compromise, providing a vocabulary for meaningful talk about freedom, immortality, God, and teleology despite the restrictions of the concepts that apply to phenomena. Kant's phenomena/noumena distinction is linked inextricably with Kant's clarification of the different roles played by the faculties, the principles they supply, and the judgments they license.

Kant's moral theory also highlights his attention to idols of the marketplace, since he distinguishes between acting merely in accordance with duty and acting from duty. This distinction elucidates the difference between an act that is morally right from an act that has genuine moral worth, and thereby allows people to estimate more accurately. the integrity of their own character and that of others. Moreover, Kant's conception of the goodwill as the only thing good without qualification adds a further point of clarification to the language of morality, as many items are intrinsically good, but may be used for evil. Nonetheless, Kantian ethics unifies virtue with moral duty with the exhortation that all people should habituate their character orientation to the point that they *want* to do their duty.

Kant and Bacon's Idols of the Theater: Kant addresses himself to idols of the theater in two general ways. First, Kant's penchant for critical synthesis marked a unique contribution to Western thought by integrating the best of both sides of many intellectual problems that resist easy solution. Rather than adhering to the principles of either modern rationalism or empiricism, he unified the two, recognizing that without experience, rationalism is empty, and that without reason, empiricism is blind, to paraphrase his famous expression. Instead of merely repeating Plato's distinction between the visible realm and the realm of the Forms, Kant innovates a phenomena/noumena distinction. Recognizing the validity of Aristotle's categories, Kant's unique interpretation implants them within the human mind. Despite his sympathies with religious beliefs, Kant did not latch on to any single proof for God's existence, but rather found a way to show that such belief is necessary to ground the highest aspirations of humanity. His understanding that happiness is not only conditional, but exceptionally rarer and inconsistent with the various manifestations of nature led Kant to insist that morality cannot be grounded in the pursuit of happiness in the autonomous conformity of the rational will the moral law, regardless of the consequences. Second, and more importantly, Kant recognized the *primacy of practical reason*, insisting that even natural science has the same basis as morality and religion, arising from humanity's search for meaning in life, and, hence, that theoretical problems have a practical resolution.

Does Kant Avoid Bacon's Idols? It is difficult to imagine how Kant could be vulnerable to any of Bacon's idols, given the intense labor and scrutiny he devoted to his work. But Kant was only human, after all. With respect to Bacon's Idols of the Tribe, Kant maintains that no one has any access to things in themselves, except for practical reason permitting the postulates of God, freedom, and immortality. However, Kant describes the human faculties and the concepts of the understanding. Are such items not things in themselves? If they are not, then what is the good of Kant's enterprise? Is his life's work nothing more than idle speculation? Kant intended to identify the conditions that make experience possible, which affords him some leeway, but he believed that he established the conditions for *objective* experience, since every individual mind supposedly possesses the same forms of intuition, concepts, and principles. But to derive objectivity from the sum of many subjectivities is, at best flimsy, and at worst a fallacy of composition.

Moreover, many of Kant's claims about morality and religion seem to amount to little more than wishful contrivances, designed to look as though they are disciplined by logical rigor. Hence, with respect to the idols of the cave, Kant seems most vulnerable. Kant had sympathies with rationalism, evidenced by his conclusions about a priori judgments and what he deems to be the necessity of the concepts of cognition. Kant's phenomena/noumena distinction, furthermore, seems to be a desperately ad hoc modification that intends to make room for the existence of God and the possibility of free will and immortality even though human cognition leaves no room for either.

These three transcendental ideas are especially dubious in the context of Kant's moral philosophy. Recall that Kant distinguished between actions performed from the motive of duty and actions performed merely in accordance with duty, but from a selfish motive. In his view, only the former carry moral worth. Nonetheless, Kant insists that morality is only possible if there is a God who can guarantee that our actions are not in vain, who will reward virtue and punish vice. But if morality is only possible if there is an ultimate judge who will reward the righteous and punish the wicked, does that not undercut the possibility of moral worth?

Again, Kant has some leeway for at least two connected reasons. First, if there were a disproof of the possibility of the Kingdom of Ends, that would be far more devastating to morality than the postulate of a being who ensures that good ultimately will prevail over evil and that cosmic justice reigns supreme in the universe. Hence, we all must posit the existence of God so that ultimate happiness is not impossible. Second, upon further consideration of this problem, often called "the impurity objection," one must also distinguish between the *motive* and the *end* of an action. Whereas the *motive* of an action constitutes the reason for which the action is done, the *end* of an action is best described as its purpose. Consider the Kantian notion of determining whether a maxim should be adopted. This process abstracts from the purpose of it and considers only its form. If the maxim has the form of a law, then it is accepted as universalizable. But *the end of a maxim does not determine its moral worth*. Hence, if the highest good is the *end* or *object* of moral action, it does not follow that it is the *motivation* for the action.[5] For example, imagine that you are considering whether you will donate $20 to pediatric cancer research. Suppose that you decide

---

[5] For more discussion on this topic see John Zammit's *The Genesis of Kant's Third Critique* (Chicago: University of Chicago Press, 1992), pp. 323–325; Mary-Barbara Zeldin provides a more detailed argument for this claim in "The *Summum Bonum*, the Moral Law, and the Existence of God," in *Kant-Studien* 62, 1971, pp. 43–54; Allen Wood, in *Kant's Moral Religion* (Ithaca, NY: Cornell University Press, 1970), and Thomas Auxter, in *Kant's Moral Teleology* (Macon, GA: Mercer University Press, 1982), also provide similar arguments.

to do so by adhering to the procedure Kant describes. You ask yourself whether you could live in a world where no one gave to charity, a world in which no one helped others. You also consider the humanity of the individuals who will benefit from your donation, in this case, sick children. Ultimately, you decide to donate the money. For Kant, you acted from duty, purely out of respect for the moral law. That is the *motive* of your action. The *end* of your action, however, is the ultimate creation of the Kingdom of Ends, the highest good, a world where everybody operates according to the moral law. However, a problem remains. You chose to donate the money because you would not *want* to live in a world devoid of charity.

Similar criticisms can be made with respect to the vocabulary that appears throughout Kant's corpus. That is, Kant's susceptibility to the idols of the cave may translate into similar vulnerabilities with respect to the idols of the marketplace. If many uniquely Kantian innovations such as synthetic a priori judgments, the concepts of the understanding, the transcendental ego, the phenomena/noumena distinction, acting from the motive of duty, and the distinction between the motive of an action and its ultimate end are merely instances of wishful thinking, then the words by which these ideas are identified reflect similar transgressions. Moreover, the notorious difficulty associated with Kant's work may be simply a way to countenance its arbitrariness with a more systematic appearance. It is sometimes said that when Kant wrote he forgot that he had an audience! Perhaps he simply intended to mislead that audience with esoteric neologisms and a complex architectonic.

Lastly, there is not much to say with respect to the idols of the theater. Kant certainly does not seem to imitate any one school of thought. While his work highlights many religious and rationalistic prejudices, Kant presents his take on them in a profoundly creative and unique way. However, his phenomena/noumena distinction seems to be little more than a modern re-imagining of Plato's distinction between the realm of the forms and the sensible realm, except that Kant treats this distinction as more epistemological than metaphysical. That is, in Kant's view, there really are not two realms, but one reality that humans can ascertain only through the determinations of their faculties. More problematic is that Kant believed in the goals of the Enlightenment and was a strong advocate of Newtonian science. In fact, one of his primary aims was to justify the possibility of Newtonian science against Hume's critique of causality. If Kant succeeded, then he did so only by reinforcing a new theater that would require modification by the 20th century.

Kant's legacy in European philosophy gave birth to two very relevant trends: Hegel's *absolute idealism* and Schopenhauer's *pessimistic idealism*. The former's philosophy dominated Germany in the 19th century, whereas the latter, like many artists, was far more appreciated posthumously. Like Kant, Hegel spawned several trends in Western thought, but none more influential than that of Marx and Marxism, the subject of the next chapter. Darwinism and Freud's psychoanalysis, on the other hand, owe a great debt to the insights of Schopenhauer, and they will be the subject of the chapter following Marx. Whereas Marx and various Marxists were followers of Hegel, the school of thought now known as *existentialism* characterizes a notable revolt against Hegelian principles and the entire history of thought. Existentialism is the subject of the final chapter.

Chapter 7 Worksheets

1. Why would experience be impossible without space and time? Explain using concrete examples.

2. Besides the law of cause and effect, find an example of an idea that does not trace back to any specific experience, but that is necessary to order experience.

3. Compare and contrast Kant's account of personal identity with both Descartes' "cogito" and Hume's critique of personal identity.

4. Develop your own examples of at least one perfect duty and one imperfect duty that are universalizable.

5. Kant was notoriously critical of consequentialism, the idea that an action is right or wrong based on its consequences. But does Kant's moral philosophy reduce to a form of consequentialism, specifically, in terms of his conception of universalizability?

6. Kant claims that we must believe in both God and immortality for the sake of morality. Do you believe that this mandate undermines Kant's conception of moral worth? Why or why not?

7. Do you believe that Kant's moral arguments for God's existence and immortality are justified, or are they only instances of wishful thinking? Explain.

8. Watch the movie *Hero* (1992), directed by Stephen Frears and starring Dustin Hoffman, Andy Garcia, and Geena Davis. Then, explain whether you believe that either Bernard Laplant (Hoffman) or John Bubber (Garcia) at any time act from the motive duty and whether their actions have moral worth.

Marx and Marxism—Finding Ourselves In Others

Many thinkers set out to change the world, but few ever do. The author about whom this chapter is written is an exception. Born in the year 1818 in Trier, Germany, Karl Marx received his education mostly from Catholic schools and was a devout Christian during his youth. However, he became an atheist by the time he finished high school. He eventually attended the University of Berlin, where he discovered the philosophy of Hegel, which upended his original plan to become a lawyer, steering him toward a career in political activism. In 1845, Marx moved to Paris, given that he edited a journal later suppressed by the Prussian government. In Paris, he met Friedrich Engels, with whom he collaborated on virtually every work and founded what is now known as communism. The most famous piece of writing the pair produced is *The Communist Manifesto*, in which Marx wrote, "Hitherto, the various philosophies have only interpreted the world in various ways; the point is to change it." The *Manifesto* embodies this thesis, combining an historical and socio-economic analysis of class struggle with a plan of action for overthrowing existing oppressive conditions. Upon the *Manifesto's* publication in 1848, several abortive revolutions erupted throughout Europe, but were summarily defeated, subsequently forcing Marx into exile in London. He lived in poverty, but subsisted on comparative journalism and gifts from Engels, whose family, ironically, owned a textile mill. Marx died while working at his desk in 1883.

This chapter begins with a brief exposition of the philosophical systems that influenced Marx and precipitated the construction of his system. Then, the thought of Marx himself will be addressed, followed by a brief discussion of the historical developments proceeding from the thought of Marx and an assessment of Marx's thought through Bacon's Idols of the Mind.

(I) Hegel, Feuerbach, and German Idealism

After Kant's death in 1804, the thought of Georg Wilhelm Friedrich von Hegel dominated 19th century Germany. Although the difficulty and complexity of Hegel's system rivals that of Kant, it is illuminating to view the Hegelian system as deriving from Kant's in three simple steps. First, recall that Kant drew a distinction between the realm of experience (phenomena) and the realm of things-in-themselves (noumena). Hegel insisted that if we cannot know anything about things-in-themselves, then we must simply eliminate all talk about them altogether. Second, Kant insisted that even though an absolute, permanent self can be derived neither from reason, nor experience, such a self must be postulated as a condition for the possibility of the unity of experience. This "self," Kant referred to as the *transcendental ego*, also known as the unity of apperception, or the "I think." Hegel reifies the transcendental ego. No longer is this item a postulate of the individual, but it is the mind of the entire world process. Hence, there are not individual transcendental egos, but one single world ego, one *absolute spirit*. Third, Kant insisted on the universal and objective validity of his categories, the concepts of the faculty of understanding that give structure to our experience. For Hegel, such concepts have no ahistorical validity. That is, their meaning and application changes over the course of history and, thus, have no necessity. History, moreover, is the driving force behind the processes of reality and is basically progressive.

Each of these transformations of Kant's transcendental idealism forms the basis for Hegel's *absolute idealism*. Reality, for Hegel, has the features of a mind, but that mind does not merely structure reality, rather it creates reality. The mind of reality can be conceived as the mind of God, which is divine and absolute. Moreover, the events and processes of history reflect the evolution of the world mind, whose content changes with each period of history. Hegel's version of idealism, therefore, is *dialectal*, affirming that reality is not static, but constantly undergoes change.

Hegel, however, had to address a familiar question: Why would God create anything in the first place? The answer seems to be that God, like all conscious beings, must experience himself in terms of "the Other," that is, in terms of an external being different than himself. Hegel's description of the logical beginnings of creation is complicated but can be summarized in the following way. At the beginning of creation, God attempted to think Himself. God, however, is pure Being. Pure Being, however, is an impossible thought, since the experience of oneself requires the experience of "the Other." Hence, God's attempt to think Himself implied the opposite, Nothingness. Nothingness, too, is an impossible thought. As addressed in the section on Parmenides, the attempt to conceive of nothingness results in the conception of *something*. Even the thought of a blank, empty, black space is still something insofar as it is a thought, an object of consciousness. Moreover, any conception of oneself implies a distinction between the self and the object about which the self thinks. For instance, try to conceive of yourself. The image that you conjure up, while a reflection of you, is still an object *other* than you. Self-awareness, thus, implies awareness of something else, something that is *not* you. Since God is pure Being, His awareness of himself implies the exact opposite, pure Nothingness.[1]

God's attempt to think Himself, thus, results in alienation, estrangement from his own Being. Hegel insisted that the religious image of Satan's fall from heaven may be interpreted as an allegory of the logical

---

[1] See Jonathan Wolff's *Why Read Marx Today?* (New York: Oxford University Press, 2002), p. 15.

process of creation, in which God divorces Himself from his own essence. Since human beings are merely manifestations of the mind of God, moreover, they experience the same sort of identity crisis. They, too, must experience themselves in terms of others. We all realize at an early age that we are neither self-created nor self-sufficient. Each of us came from somewhere, implying the existence of others. Furthermore, each of us relies heavily on others for the fulfillment of our needs. Confrontation with the other produces conflict. The processes of history, which involve progression through conflict, represent the processes of the divine mind. The mind of God split at the beginning of creation. Ever since, its goal is to retrieve its original unity, self-awareness. When this goal is achieved, history will come to an end.[2]

This process can be summarized by the famous Hegelian dialectical triad. There are two limitations of thinking and reality: Pure Being and Nothingness. What occurs in between these two poles is called *Becoming*. Pure Being may be called a *thesis*, Nothingness an *antithesis*, and Becoming a *synthesis*. The process of synthesis achieves three things. First, it cancels the conflict between the thesis and antithesis. Second, it preserves or retains the element of truth in both components. Third, and finally, it *rises above both*, sublimating the conflict into a higher truth. The processes of history reflect the cycle of this dialectical triad. Many examples abound, many of which may be found in the theoretical debates of the ancient Greeks, especially the pre-Socratics. Heraclitus' conception of reality as a process constantly in flux not only parallels closely Hegel's dialectical model of reality but may be viewed as a *thesis*. Parmenides's conception of Being as absolute, permanent, and unchanging may be viewed as an *antithesis* to the Heraclitean position. Plato's model of reality, on the other hand, may be viewed as a *synthesis* of the two. On Plato's theory, these two positions no longer represent a dichotomy, in which one must be true and the other false,

---

[2] See Donald Palmer's *Looking at Philosophy*, pp. 238–240.

hence, cancelling the conflict between them. In addition, since Plato's model of reality acknowledges that one part of reality changes while another does not, it preserves the elements of truth in both. Finally, Plato's stratification of reality into a divided line in which the Forms are the basis of reality sublimates the conflict into a higher truth.[3]

The conflict between rationalism and empiricism that emerged during the 16th through 18th centuries affords an additional example of the Hegelian dialectical triad. Recall that for the rationalists, at least some human knowledge is innate and superior knowledge derives from reason alone. This position may be called a *thesis*. The position of empiricism, on the other hand, according to which no human knowledge is innate, and that superior knowledge derives from sense-experience, may be called an *antithesis*. Kant's formulation of transcendental idealism, however, may be viewed as a *synthesis* of the two positions.

Hegel took specific interest in the Graeco-Roman period, in which the thesis of Democracy gave rise to the antithesis of Slavery, which in turn effected the synthesis of Medieval Feudalism. In Hegel's view, the master—slave dialectic consists in a relation of mutual dependence. Obviously, the slave depends on the master to be a slave. Without a master, there can be no slaves. But the master depends on the slave as well, in at least two ways. First, for the master to be truly a "master," he must be recognized as such by someone other than himself. That is, the master depends on the slave to recognize him as a master. Moreover, the master depends on the labor of the slave, without which the master would not be able to meet his basic needs. In addition, through his labor, the slave will discover himself and ultimately achieve his true freedom. The relationship benefits the slave not only in this respect, but also in the fact that the slave has an independent master as his mirror, whereas the master understands himself only in terms of a subservient slave.[4]

---

[3] See T.Z. Lavine's *From Socrates to Sartre*, p. 211.

[4] Ibid, p. 222.

History as whole, thus, represents the eternal process of the dialectical triad, in which theses give rise to corresponding and conflicting antitheses, the conflict of which is eventually eliminated and sublimated by syntheses. Hegel's view of history, though, is very optimistic, since not only does he conceive of history as essentially progressive, but as a manifestation of the *cunning of reason*. As the master—slave dialectic reveals, even regression conceals the progressive drive of history, since it is through slavery that the slave discovers his true self and independence.

Ultimately, Hegel's conception of religion had important implications for the State. Hegel conceived of Christianity as the highest form of religion. Moreover, since he maintained that the State basically represents God on Earth, the Prussian government perpetuated his philosophy. But like all theses, an antithesis emerged. On the one hand, the conservative, or right Hegelians maintained that the processes of history already led to the highest achievement on Earth in the form of the contemporary Prussian government. On the other hand, the liberal, or left Hegelians, also known as the "young Hegelians," insisted that the highest form of human freedom had yet to be realized, and it was up to the people to usher in the new order.

Among the young Hegelians were thinkers such as Ludwig Feuerbach and Marx himself. Feuerbach, like the rest of the young Hegelians, rejected Hegel's claims about Christianity. His critique of religion, specifically his 1841 publication *The Essence of Christianity*, basically dealt a death blow to the Hegelian view. On Feuerbach's view, Christianity represents humanity's idealization of itself, and God humanity's invention. Basically, people created the idea of an all-powerful God and instilled in this being all their noblest qualities and aspirations. God is not merely powerful, but perfectly good, perfectly just, merciful, forgiving, and all-knowing. However, throughout history, people forgot that they created God in their own image. In their collective amnesia, people began to believe that God created them in His image. Moreover, the ideals that humanity ascribed to God become standards and values which are impossible to satisfy. Subsequently, people feel estranged from the world, from other people, and even from themselves. We are unable to live lives that fully satisfy us because we try to achieve impossible ideals. Relationships fail to maintain the standard of perfect union of Adam and Eve before their fall and exile from paradise. People fail to exemplify perfect courage, moderation, and justice. Moreover, we are each estranged from the world, since our awareness of the vast cosmos accentuates the limitations of our finitude. Estrangement from the world parallels our estrangement from our very selves, since our awareness of our own existence implies an inevitable confrontation with "the Other."

Ultimately, the mythologies and doctrines of the world's religions are nothing more than idealized fantasies that undermine our actual existence. To find meaning in life, we first must recognize that God is humanity's invention, and then attempt to find the qualities of the divine within ourselves. But what exactly did Marx, also a young Hegelian, make of both Feuerbach and Hegel?

(II) The Thought of Marx

Like Feuerbach, Marx believed that humanity invented the idea of God, but Marx devoted more attention to why people would create such an idea in the first place. In short, Marx's answer is that religion is the "opium of the masses." Marx's use of the term "opium" suggests that religious beliefs afford humanity mechanisms of escape, not unlike recreational drugs. That is, the belief in an all-powerful God who will punish the wicked and reward the righteous in an afterlife diverts attention from the pain and suffering endured in this lifetime. But it also diverts attention from the problems that instigated the very invention of such beliefs, in which case the initial problem not only persists, but grows. Why would humanity need an opium? For Marx, religion is an instrument used by the upper class to exploit people into bleak resignation and complacency. If God is just, then the horrific injustices doled out to the working class in this lifetime will be redressed in the next. Moreover, to suffer the trespasses of others builds favor in the eyes of God. Long indulgence in such fantasies not only familiarizes them to the point of masking their outlandishness but makes them the collective addiction of those targeted by it, leaving them more vulnerable to continued oppression and exploitation.[5]

Replacing religion with a secular, humanistic naturalism based on camaraderie between people became one of Marx's primary goals. In order to achieve this goal, he knew that he could not merely interpret the world but that he had to motivate people to change it. In his view, in their attempt to do the opposite, all previous philosophers committed a grave error. I will address Marx's attempt to achieve his goal by examining the following themes in his thought: (a) Dialectical Materialism, (b) the Materialist Conception of History, (c) Exploitation and Alienation, and (d) the central argument of *The Communist Manifesto.*

Dialectical Materialism: Like Hegel, Marx maintained that reality consists of processes constantly in flux and that the human mind does not have a universal character that remains the same across history. But unlike Hegel, Marx was a materialist and an atheist. Hence, Marx's system may be categorized as *dialectical materialism.*

The materialistic aspect of Marx's thought indicates his belief that the natural world and physical matter are all that exist. While Marx propounded a dialectical conception of reality, he maintained that Hegel was far too abstract. Nonetheless, three laws of dialectic apply to his system. First is the *law of quantity and quality.* This law maintains that the more of something there is changes the kind of thing that it is, or that the quantity of a thing transforms its quality.

---

[5] See Wolf's *Why Read Marx Today?* p. 20 for his analysis of the meaning of the analogy between an opium and religious beliefs.

For example, individual human beings living together in a large group become a community. When this community expands it becomes necessary to establish rules and laws that regulate how people live together and treat each other, which in turn demands the creation of a legislative body to make and enforce those laws. As the community continues to expand, it becomes more than merely a community, something more like a city, of multiple communities, which demands the expansion of the laws to cover all citizens. Multiple citizens living under the same laws become a nation, which will require a complex governing body with a figurehead. Each individual citizen, moreover, is no longer just an individual, but a citizen of a nation. That is, each person is defined by the group of which he or she is a part. If one's home country is Germany, then one is German; whereas if one's home country is America, one is an American, and so forth. Furthermore, even the leaders of nations are defined in terms of their roles within a specific organization. Even the most powerful person in the world, supposedly the President of the United States, is defined in terms of the country he leads. It is the same for everybody, even at a very rudimentary level. Each of us is determined by the social group of which we are a part. More specifically, as far as Marx is concerned, each of us is shaped by the *economy* of which we are a part.

The second law of dialectic is that *change happens between contraries*. This law echoes the sentiments of both Heraclitus and Hegel. Marx would agree with both of his predecessors that "war is the father of all things." The "war" that causes change may be interpreted in at least two ways. First, it may refer to a *conflict* between different individuals or factions of a group, organization, state, or nation. This interpretation is applicable to Marx's conception of how one historical epoch typically transitions to another, especially to his account of how Medieval Feudalism transitioned to capitalism and his prediction about how capitalism will transition to communism. Second, it may refer to a *struggle* in a more general sense. If humanity transforms nature into culture, then the way in which they produce this transformation is through work, or through labor, productive activity. Labor is the activity that defines humanity, and it is essentially practical. That is, when people engage in any form of labor, they do so to fulfill specific needs. To hunt food, spears and arrows are necessary, as are bows to shoot the arrows. To cultivate the land and raise crops, tools are necessary. Usually, such instruments and the activities for which they are intended cannot be pursued without the help of others. Hence, the struggle to survive leads to labor, which in turn leads to interaction with people. As a group expands, it leads to the development of new needs, calling for the use of instruments to meet those needs, which requires more labor.

The third, and final, law of dialectic is that *each thing contains within itself the potential for a new system that will become its contrary.* This law can be seen throughout nature. Plants contain seeds to produce new plants that will replace the old. Many animals lay eggs that give rise to offspring who will replace their parents, just as humans contain within themselves the genetic material to reproduce offspring who will replace their parents. The same is true of nations. Each nation contains within itself the potential for conflict that will bring about change.[6]

The Materialist Conception of History: In the *Economic and Philosophic Manuscripts of 1844*, Marx wrote,

> It is above all necessary to avoid restoring society as a fixed abstraction opposed to the individual. The individual is the social being. Therefore, even when the manifestation of his life does not take the form of a communal manifestation performed in the company of other men, it is still a manifestation and confirmation of social life.[7]

---

[6] The laws of dialectic as I formulated them here reflect the systematization of Marxism with natural science achieved by Friedrich Engels, specifically in his work *Dialectics of Nature.* For a more detailed discussion of these laws, see Leszek Kolakowski's *Main Currents of Marxism* (New York: W. W. Norton & Company, 2005), pp. 317–321. Kolakowski's classic three-volume study provides a comprehensive account of the origins of and main themes of Marx's thought, in addition to subsequent historical and intellectual developments.

[7] In David McLellan, *Introduction to the Thought of Karl Marx* (New York: Harper & Row, 1971), p. 126.

In a later passage, he wrote, "Industry is the real historical relationship of nature, and therefore, of natural science, to man. If then it is conceived of as the open revelation of human faculties, then the human essence of nature, or the natural essence of man will also be understood."[8]

The previous section's discussion of the laws of dialectic serve to reaffirm the gist of these passages and Marx's assessment of humanity as a group of social beings whose most essential activity is that of labor. The theory of historical materialism, basically, is the theory of how human beings have shaped history through their labor and how they have been shaped by it. There are three components of Marx's materialist conception of history: the economic foundation, a superstructure, and an ideology.

The economic foundation, itself, includes three things: relations of production, material powers of production, and modes of production. The material powers of production refer to a combination of natural resources and the abilities of the people, including the instruments, tools, and labor by which goods are produced. Since the resources used to produce goods come from the natural world, the goods that any people can produce are limited by nature, as is the economy that arises from those goods. The modes of production refer to the ways in which items are produced. Relations of production refer to the relations between the workers and the owners of the natural resources and the instruments necessary to produce goods. For instance, suppose that you live in a part of your country that produces lumber. The material powers of production consist of the forests from which the lumber is obtained, the lumberjacks, the tools they will use to produce the lumber, and the vehicles they will use for transportation. The mode of production refers to the processes by which they produce the lumber and the chain of command on the job, basically, how the lumberjacks

---

[8] Ibid.

work together. For instance, there would likely be a foreman for each job, who oversees the work, in addition to a division of labor. There would be workers responsible for cutting down the trees, sawing trees into smaller limbs, loading them onto a truck, feeding them into a chipper, driving the trucks, etc. The relations of production refer to the division between the workers and the owner of the company for which they work as well as the owners of the land. Relations of production implies that the economy is divided into different classes, most basically, workers and owners.

Marx maintained that the forces of production give rise to the economic structure of a society. In the above example, the availability of lumber and the workers determine that there will be a "lumber economy." If one lives in Maine, the availability of lobsters and its location near the sea gives rise to a "seafood economy." Many states in the Midwestern United States are known for corn farming. Florida is associated with the distribution of oranges. Many countries in Africa are notorious for diamond mining. The resources that are available within a given environment dictate the means of subsistence for the people within that environment. Moreover, the instruments used in labor depend on the available natural resources as well. In addition, people tend to define themselves in terms of the economy in which they live and the role they play in it. One defines oneself both in terms of the products one creates and the work one does. A tool, after all, is primarily an extension of the human body that facilitates one's means of survival. Tools are not only extensions of the self, but living, potent symbols of one's value and power, as is the economy under which one toils. An individual raised in Maine will have a much different outlook on life than that of a wealthy socialite from Beverly Hills, California. A person who spent his entire life in Alaska certainly would not approach life in the same way as a person of the same age from Florida. Moreover, if one possesses knowledge of an individual's origins, it leads one to believe that one has privileged knowledge about the person in question. If James happens to be from Idaho, then he must be a "Potato Guy!" If Sam comes from Dallas, Texas, then he must be a "cowboy." People not only tend to identify with their economies but are also identified *by* them.

Since new needs are bound to develop, the forces of production will also become more complex over time. The instruments used in production become more intricate and require more people to ensure that they function properly. Hunting animals for food began with the use of manual weapons such as spears. Then, more complex instruments such as a bow and arrow were created. Eventually, guns were invented, and they became increasingly complex. Bolt action rifles gave rise to pump action rifles. Eventually, semi and fully automatic rifles emerged. Handguns evolved from six-shot revolvers into semi-automatic pistols. Inevitably, weapons expanded beyond mere hand-held firearms into weapons of mass destruction. Farming followed a similar course, as it originally involved the use of manual tools, and later involved the use of animals to drive plows, until finally tractors driven by humans were invented. Of course, the continued evolution and progress of tools requires people to manufacture such tools, which also requires the use of available resources and the permission of those individuals who own the resources. The use of animals to cultivate land requires knowledge of animals, how to capture, train, and tend to them.

Thus, the more complex the forces of production become, the more people will be necessary, and the more complex the economy will become overall, giving rise to the *superstructure*, the system of laws and government agencies that regulate people. Since there is a division of classes, principally between those who own resources and those who make use of those resources to make products, there must exist a system of laws to clearly stipulate the terms of ownership and employment. Laws must ensure people do not steal items that do not belong to them, just as they must ensure that dangerous instruments – such as pitchforks, tractors, knives, axes, and guns – are not used to harm others. The penalties for violating laws must also be stipulated, and there must be people capable of enforcing those stipulations.

But as the laws of dialectic imply, the existence of different classes is bound to cause conflict. There would not be a need for laws to protect people if there were not the potential for conflict in the first place. Conflict produces change, specifically, the kinds of change that can threaten the privileges of the dominant class of an economy. Hence, to protect their own interests, the dominant class creates an *ideology*, a system of ideas promoting those interests. Historically, religion succeeded as an important component of ideology, for reasons already indicated, to oppress and sedate the working class, keeping them happy with their lot and resigned to the status quo. Other aspects of ideology include arts and entertainment, mediums of distraction that protect the interests of the privileged. Theater plays that celebrate the virtues of the working class and portray the upper class as wise mentors that curry favor with the working class and nipping the possibility of civil unrest in the proverbial bud. In our own time, mediums such as *Netflix* and reality television provide such distractions. Why be bothered by the latest controversy surrounding the escapades of President Trump when one has a new series to binge-watch? Why fret over a government shutdown when *American Idol* has a new season to air?

But per the laws of dialectic, nothing lasts forever! People are mortal, and ideology along with the economies that they protect are created by people. But why and how will change come about?

Alienation: Marx insisted that people are generally and thoroughly unhappy, miserable even. The so-called "religious solution" to the problem of human misery failed. One of the reasons for its failure is that it keeps people passive and sedated, complacent with the prevailing social and economic conditions. But people are not merely passive subjects. Rather they are active participants in the processes of history, since it is in human nature to actively change the world though labor and the use of natural resources. However, along the way, people became estranged, or *alienated* in several ways.

Ironically, Marx developed his conception of alienation based in part on his reading of Adam Smith, a pioneer of capitalism. In his *Wealth of Nations,* Smith argued that when human beings are left free to pursue their own self-interests, they will without intending it, produce the greatest good for all, as if guided by an "invisible hand." Smith's argument rests on the assumption that human beings are naturally acquisitive creatures who have a propensity for trading. After his reading of Smith, Marx concluded that the conditions of capitalism are not only degrading and punishing, but that through such a system the lives of workers become subject to *alien forces.*[9]

Capitalism is a mode of production in which only a few people own and control the means of production as their private property and they employ workers who have nothing to sell but their labor. Ultimately, the value of the labor of the worker is equal to the amount of labor necessary to produce the product, but the owner of the means of production is at liberty to pay the worker less than his labor is truly worth, especially in times of surplus. Thus, the owner can very easily *exploit* the worker in order to turn a profit. Moreover, the ways in which products are produced involve the use of assembly lines, in which each worker produces only one part of the object. Hence, capitalism encourages a division of labor that does not demand a high level of skill from workers. Such circumstances leave people alienated in at least four ways.

First, people are alienated from the *product* they create. Every day, we use items such as computers, refrigerators, cars, and various other devices. But very few of us possess detailed knowledge of how these devices really function. If any of them were to break down, most of us would have to hire an expert to fix the item in question. A device such

---

[9] See Wolff's *Why Read Marx Today?* pp. 29–30.

as a computer, purchased from a local retail outlet, is not an item that many of us would personally create as an extension of our being, an active effort to engage with the resources of the world. It is merely an instrument that can remind us how little of the world we really understand.

Second, we are alienated from our *creative activity*. Since most of the items produced through capitalism are created on an assembly line, piecemeal, and such modes of production become a means of subsistence through which one earns wages. This process dulls the mind and distracts the individual from actively producing anything. Even when an item such as a piece of furniture is assembled by a consumer, the assembly is completed with the use of an instruction manual, accentuating the disconnection between person and product and relieving the person of the burden of figuring out how to assemble the item through critical reflection. The capitalist mode of production, therefore, discourages a way of life in which people must break free of habitual patterns and function with autonomous ingenuity.

Third, we are alienated from our *species being*. Since the primary way in which people interact with the world and effect change is through labor, to engage in a way of life that discourages creative labor leaves us estranged from our human essence. In other words, there is a sense in which human beings become *less human* and come to resemble conscious automata. Alienation from the self leaves most people feeling devoid of purpose, and, thus, desperate to fill that void. But the lack of creative development afforded by capitalism forces people to use items that only perpetuate the cycle of estrangement and misery. People merely distract themselves from the pain of alienation until boredom creeps in and they must find a new cheap thrill.

Fourth, and finally, we are alienated from *others*. On the one hand, capitalism forces people into competition with each other, in which case everyone becomes an obstacle to the fulfillment of an individual's needs. On the other hand, since labor is primarily a social activity through which we interact with others, a system that discourages the creative activity of labor encourages isolation. People no longer must collaborate in building shelters or hunting food. People can purchase their own domiciles and go shopping alone. Moreover, recreational items that are available intensify the level of isolation that prevails between people. People fond of their smart phones will instinctively abandon conversations and interactions with concrete people to engage in a seemingly more intimate interaction with an electronic device.[10]

Ultimately, a total paradigm shift is necessary. Mere civil liberties and political freedom under a capitalistic system will not be enough, since the rights and protections enjoyed under such a system only encourage further alienation. People may be free to do as they wish, but only if they do not harm anyone. While civil society demands that people refrain from harming each other, the mentality that it perpetuates is one of individualism, in which everyone must keep their own affairs and not meddle in those of others. The equality promised under capitalism applies to *individuals.* Security protects mostly private property. Moreover, the sorts of property modern technology afford us only further enhances alienation by drawing people away from others. Many social interactions take place remotely, removing the need for communication between concrete individuals. Thus, while people are naturally communal beings, they cannot properly engage in a community only because they have political freedom.[11]

The Communist Manifesto: Marx's best-known and most popular work details his analysis of the process through which capitalism became the world's dominant mode of production and his prediction of its inevitable dissolution into communism. Marx believed that the history of the world consisted of five epochs: Primitive Communism,

---

[10] For Wolff's account of Marx's conception of alienation, see pp. 31–37 of *Why Read Marx Today?*

[11] For Wolff's discussion of the themes of liberalism and emancipation, see pp. 40–46 of *Why Read Marx Today?*

Asiatic Despotism, Graeco-Roman Democracy, Medieval Feudalism, and Capitalism. Marx emphasized the transition from Medieval Feudalism to Capitalism, saying very little about the others.

To summarize Marx's argument, the Bourgeoise (upper class) arose with the discovery of the America's, the route around the cape, the Far East, and new colonies, which expanded trade. Such expansion revolutionized production and eventually brought the guild system of Medieval Feudalism to an end. During the feudal period, guilds were associations of craftsmen that sold their products to the lords of manors. The Bourgeoise revolution in production, however, brought in newly found natural resources from different parts of the world in addition to the sharing of ideas between different cultures. It became more feasible for lords to purchase goods from the "big businesses" created through the expansion of trade. Along with the dissolution of the guild system came the dissolution of the ideology of the feudal structure.

As a result, capitalism emerged, in which people could freely create their own businesses and compete against others that produced similar items. People who previously ran their own businesses had to work for the people who effectively destroyed their livelihood, inevitably making less money than they are truly worth. Along with the destruction of the feudal economic structure, professions are stripped of their honor, since mass production removes the personal and creative elements from the process of labor. One's work no longer reflects one's being but is merely a way to earn wages. Families are stripped of their sentimental value, since the value of individual people is equated with the amount of money they make. Finance becomes the dominant concern of families and individual workers become mere commodities.

But as the laws of dialectic dictate, capitalism has the potential for its own negation built into it. Capitalism produces two hostile camps: the Bourgeoise capitalists and the Proletariat workers. Since capitalists compete against each other, many businesses produce similar products, which inevitably leads to surplus. Surplus leads to the need to reduce the workforce, leaving many workers unemployed and without the skills to find employment elsewhere. Under these conditions, the proletariat will have no choice but to band together and revolt. Since there are so many more in the Proletariat class than in the Bourgeoise class, the proletariats will eventually win, overthrowing capitalism.

Crucial in this process is that the workers *themselves* be a part of the revolution that causes this paradigm shift, as Jonathan Wolff expresses: "[Revolution] on a mass scale is necessary. . . not only because the ruling class cannot be overthrown in any other way, but also because the class overthrowing it can only in a revolution rid itself of all the muck of ages and become fitted to found society anew."[12] The new order will be valued and appreciated much more by those who fought and bled for it, just as personal items are cherished much more by the people who made them. Moreover, human beings naturally find themselves through their labor. The labor of revolution will bring about humanity's true destiny in communism.

Subsequently, two stages will follow. Stage one will consist of a temporary period of dictatorship by the proletariat. During this stage, private property will be seized and made property of the state. Eventually, however, this period must come to an end, given that it is far too crude and simplistic to last. The conditions are far worse than those produced by capitalism. Stage two will consist of the formation of ultimate communism, through which everyone overcomes alienation from the products of their labor and come to see work as part of their species being.

Even before the *Manifesto's* official publication, a revolution overthrew the King of France in 1848. Other revolutions followed soon after in Switzerland, Hungary, Italy, and Germany, but were summarily defeated. As a result, on March 3rd, 1848, Marx received written notice

---

[12] Ibid, p. 46.

from the King of Belgium ordering him to leave the country within 24 hours. Marx eventually settled in London, where he lived until his death in 1883.

(III) Marxism After Marx and Bacon's Idols of the Mind

Marx's work gave rise to three major groups of followers: The Second International, Soviet Marxism, and Western Marxism[13]. The Second International obviously followed the First International, also known as *The International Working Men's Association*, established in London in September, 1864. It had a General Council of 34 members, a president, George Codger, and Marx himself was elected to the Council as the corresponding secretary for Germany. The Second International was established in 1889 as an association of mainly European socialist parties.

The thought of Engels contributed to the development of the Second International. After Marx's death, he sought to unify various socialist organizations under a single philosophy and natural science. Karl Kautsky became the dominant thinker of the Second International. Together with Russian intellectual, Georgi Plekhanov, he finished the process begun by Engels. The school of thought came to be called *Orthodox Marxism*. He embraced Engels' scientific version of Marxism, insisted that Marxism is the only system valid for the analysis of social phenomena, and predicted that capitalism would fail because it does not allow for an efficient use of humanity's evolved technology. Another contributor, Eduard Bernstein, sought to correct the philosophical foundations of dialectical materialism. The work of Bernstein

---

[13] The schools of Western Marxism include the Frankfurt School, Existential Marxism, Structuralism, and Post-Modernism. Since I cannot address the contributions of these schools of thought and the various thinkers associated with them in this chapter, I refer readers to David McLellan's *Marxism After Marx* (New York: Palgrave Macmillan, 2007). For his discussion of the Frankfurt School, see Chapter 19, pp. 295–324. For Existential Marxism, see Chapter 20, pp. 325–343. For Structuralism, see Chapter 22, pp. 348–357. For Post-Modernism, see Chapter 25, pp. 405–418.

and his followers came to be called *Revisionist Marxism*. The doctrine aimed to remove the Hegelian "blemishes" in Marxism, denied Marx's labor theory of value, and insisted that Marx's predictions about capitalism were erroneous, since revolution would be unlikely, superfluous, and undesirable. Ultimately, most Marxists leaned toward the work of Bernstein and Engels. Lenin eventually put some finishing touches on the doctrine, and it came to be called "Marxism-Leninism."

Soviet Marxism began to emerge in 1914, when the workers of different countries took arms against each other. These revolutions led to the complete dissolution of the Second International by 1917, culminating with the October revolutions and the Bolshevik seizure of power with Lenin taking over as its leader. After Lenin's death in 1921, Stalin took over as leader. The dictatorship itself lasted until 1991, but the Soviet contributions to the Marxist intellectual tradition were miniscule and designed only to perpetuate the existence of the Soviet Union. Other famous examples of dictatorships inspired by Marx's writings include Mao Tse Tung's regime in China and Fidel Castrol's regime in Cuba.

While the thinkers who contributed to Marxism certainly displayed original thought, many made it their purpose to twist Marx's thought to suit their own intentions. Marxism, thus, became a "theater" in its own right. But how well did Marx address himself to Bacon's Idols?

Marx and the Idols of the Tribe: Marx recognizes that human beings are both naturally social and naturally creative. Not only does our true destiny lie in communal relations with others, but in the exercise of our creative ability by changing the world through labor. However, the communal nature of humanity leaves people vulnerable to oppression. We rely on others so much that even relationships in which one must exist under the ministrations of a tyrant is preferable to being alone. Our susceptibility to oppression and tyranny forces us to search for fulfillment elsewhere, in an afterlife and a God who will punish the wicked and reward the righteous. Whatever comfort the illusions of religion provide, they only perpetuate the miserable conditions that compelled people to conjure them up in the first place. Even more terrifying is the prospect of becoming tyrannical and oppressive oneself. The Bolshevik revolution that overthrew the exploitative conditions that prevailed in the early 20th century led to the creation of the Soviet Union, whose atrocities far outweigh those of its predecessors. Marx's recognition that the goal of philosophy is to change the world, and his proposal for bringing about that change testifies to his understanding of basic human needs and how to fulfill them. Change comes about through conflict and people must themselves bring about such change by instigating conflict. Inevitably, this power struggle will lead to bloodshed and lost lives, but such losses will only sweeten the taste of ultimate victory. Not only can there be no progress without struggle, but life can have no meaning if one does not have to fight for it. In the end, people flourish in a community where everybody does what they are able and as a result obtains what they need.

Marx and Idols of the Cave: His account of ideology and the socio-cultural determinants of personality reflect the most obvious ways that Marx addresses the Idols of the Cave. Most of what people believe is a product of the ideology of the culture into which they are indoctrinated. That ideology, in turn, exists only to sustain the interests of the dominant class. The existence of multiple classes inevitably contains the potential for destruction of the prevailing ideology and its replacement with a new one. Ultimately, the only truth to be found within any ideology is that eventually they all change. Hence, an individual's unique preferences and biases reflect one's cultural ideology, which in turn reflects the ideas of the most powerful class of people of that culture, which in turn lends itself as the "cave" for everyone living in it.

Marx and Idols of the Marketplace: Marx's assessment of ideology simultaneously addresses both Idols of the Cave and marketplace, since the language of any ideology reflects the determinations of the dominant class and the goals its members wish to achieve. Moreover, Marx provides his own unique vocabulary, especially in the development of his mature theory, strictly defining such terms as capitalism and surplus, in addition to outlining his labor theory of value. Specifically, the terms of Democracy, under modern capitalism, perpetuate the idea that people are free when they are not. People are told that they can do as they wish, so long as they are not harming anyone, but what people can do is limited by their economic conditions, which often force people to work jobs that are incredibly unsatisfying and leave little time for the pursuit of other interests. And as previously mentioned, the liberty, security, and property afforded under a Democracy only reinforce alienation.

An additional and interesting way in which Marx addresses these idols consists in his account of money and credit. Marx seemed to share Shakespeare's assessment of money, as he cites *Timon of Athens*, of which the following lines seem the most relevant: "Gold? Yellow, glittering, precious gold? No, Gods, I am no idle votarist!...Thus, much of this will make black white, foul fair, wrong right, base noble, old young, coward valiant."[14] Much can be said about why Marx chose to include this passage in his early writings. Like Shakespeare, Marx believed that money not only had the potential to invert the natural order of things but also had a corruptive effect on everything that it touched. Money makes "foul fair" and "wrong right," because if a person accumulates enough wealth, then such a person may not only begin to believe that he is above the law, but so might law enforcement agents, who will absolve him of anything for the right price. Money makes the "base noble," since a criminal who steals enough money to be considered wealthy suddenly appears to have all the qualities associated with nobility. Money makes the "old young," in that a person with enough money has the resources to restore his or her youth as

---

[14] In Robert Tucker (Ed.), *The Marx-Engels Reader* (New York: W. W. Norton & Company, 1978), pp. 102–3.

much as is humanly possible. Lastly, money makes a "coward valiant," since a person with enough money can requisition others to fight his battles for him and, thus, need not fear anyone. Instead of acting from a sense of one's moral duty, people do the right thing hoping only to achieve a monetary reward or benefit. Money corrupts family values and parenting. Not only will many marriages disintegrate because of financial problems, but many people marry into money. Marriage, thus, becomes a business transaction. Even parenthood becomes a process of paying others to look after one's children.

In the same way, money has a corrosive effect on *language*. A person described as "rich" or "wealthy" may be assumed to possess the qualities such terms connote—power, influence, nobility, and good taste. Those who are described as poor have the opposite qualities. Many people are respected only because they are wealthy, whereas others are despised only because they are poor. Moreover, as Wolff notes, money can infect the *language of need*. Since money lends itself only as a mean to other ends, many of which – food, water, and shelter – are essential for survival, any need may be described as a need for money. Furthermore, those who lack money must often sacrifice their integrity and beg for what they need. The credit system exponentially exacerbates the cycle of infectious alienation introduced by money. Credit serves as a more abstract form of money, a form of money without a physical basis that forces the individual to become the primary unit of currency. To obtain credit, people often must lie, which in turn demands the need for investigators to authenticate the background of credit applicants.[15] Money and credit, thus, reinforce and perpetuate alienation by corrupting the primary means of communication between people.

Marx and Idols of the Theater: One way that Marx addresses himself to Idols of the Theater blends in to his awareness of Idols of the Cave, since any form of ideology would constitute a theater in the Baconian

---

[15] See Wolff's *Why Read Marx Today?* pp. 37–40.

sense of term, particularly those that become obsolete. In addition, Marx's use and modification of the philosophical systems popular in his own time reflect his sensitivity both to their utility and flaws. Marx agreed with Hegel that reality is dialectical, although he rejected Hegel's idealism, modifying Hegel's spiritualism and replacing it with a more concrete basis for economics and the eventuality of ultimate communism. Furthermore, Marx agreed with Feuerbach that religion is an illusion, but devoted more attention to the causes that gave rise to the illusion, thereby allowing for the possibility of its elimination and replacement with a superior resolution to the banes of existence.

Does Marx Avoid Bacon's Idols? With respect to Bacon's Idols of the Tribe, the primary question would be whether Marx avoids errors in his assessment of human nature in addition to any common logical errors or fallacies. The primary flaws in Marx's reasoning lie in his assumptions about the inevitability of communism. First, Marx maintains a dialectical conception of reality, according to which there is no universal human nature except for the very general transformational imperative shared by humans to change the world through their labor. But Marx also implies that the ideal communist state is humanity's true destiny, which raises a paradox. If reality constantly changes, then how can humanity have a true destiny? Moreover, why would a communist state fulfill such a destiny? Because Marx's claims about communism are largely forward-looking, it is impossible to know with any degree of certainty what exact conditions a communistic state would produce. But given the laws of dialectic, eventually would not such a state contain within itself the conditions for its own eventual dissolution? Furthermore, the revolutions Marx predicted never materialized in western industrial nations. Many attempted revolutions were aborted early on and communism proved to be an abysmal failure in Russia and Eastern Europe. Marxists may contend that communism simply has not been implemented correctly. Once it is, it will

prove to establish ideal conditions for all. But Marx believed his predictions to be based in science, specifically in the laws of history and
economics. If his theory truly is scientific, it must be *falsifiable*. For
Marxists to use the rejoinder that Marxism has not been properly
implemented assumes that the historical evidence of the failure of
communism should not be counted against it. Finally, Marx's predictions seemed indirectly to benefit capitalistic countries, since they
could take preventive measures against possible revolutions.

In addition, while Marx certainly addresses Idols of the Cave, he did
not seem to believe that the potential for such errors applied to his
own theory. If an individual's beliefs are products of their ideology
and socio-cultural conditioning, then would not Marx's predictions
merely be a product of the ideology under which he lived? The fact
that Marx insists that such a revolution is inevitable makes his writings even more dubious. Why fight for an inevitable revolution?

Marx's critique of religion, moreover, is seriously flawed. Truly, religion can and has been used to oppress people. Many people, furthermore, claim to be religious but only seem to mouth their prayers like
platitudes and go through the proverbial motions of religious rituals
as part of their perfunctory daily routines. Religion, for most, indeed,
is an opiate. But only because religious ideas can be misused does not
mean that all religious doctrines are false and it certainly does not
mean that religion cannot improve the conditions of life. Maybe Marx
did not want religion to be true.

Perhaps the same can be said about the universal communist revolution Marx predicted. That is, maybe he instigated workers to fight for
it because he believed that his writings would make such a revolution
inevitable. The fact that Marx's more famous works had the intention
of provoking a revolution reveal his vulnerability to idols of the marketplace. Marx intended to change the world, rather than merely to
explain it or to convey information. Hence, he had to choose words
and write in a style that evoke the emotional response necessary to

bring about significant social change. Questions may also be raised about whether Marx sufficiently understood the sources he adopted for his own purposes, such as Hegel, Feuerbach, and Smith.

Finally, the primary school of thought to which Marx subscribes is dialectical materialism. But the fact that he describes a true destiny of humanity seems to imply that such a worldview, if not entirely false, is seriously flawed. If everything changes, then so can human nature. If everything contains the basis for its own negation, then ultimately even communism would negate itself. And even if Marx completely avoided the idols of the theater, he did not avoid creating a theater of his own that would be used and abused for over a century after his death.[16]

Darwins Central Argu. Orgin of species
idea of evolution & stp
1) Variation of traits exist among indiv. given
2) Traits of parents are passed on to offspring
3) Popula. of species increase quockly
4) An envioment. forces. can't support
   such increases
Animal Behaviors.
Physiological, Developmental, Functional.
   Evolutionary.
Basic Premise: Evolved Psych. Mechanisms dictate
   Univeral Human Nature
2) These Adaptation selet ancestra k.)
3) Mind contains a number of
   These adaptu

---

[16] For a defense of Marx against common criticisms, see Terry Eagleton's *Why Marx Was Right* (New Haven, CT: Yale University Press, 2011).

Chapter 8 Worksheets

1. Find at least three examples of terms or ideas that may be understood in terms of their opposites.

2. Find at least three examples from history, different from those mentioned in this chapter, which reflect the process of the Hegelian dialectical triad.

3. Find at least three examples from your own observations that reflect the three laws of dialectical materialism.

4. Do you believe that human beings made up the idea of God? Even if this idea is a grand illusion, is there any reason for still believing it?

5. In addition to religion, find at least one other example of an "opiate" in daily life.

6. Indicate at least three ways that your culture and socialization influence your worldview. Then, explain how the worldviews of people from at least three different parts of the world will differ based on their social and economic conditions.

7. Explain whether you have experienced at least 2 of the 4 forms of alienation as conceived by Marx. Be as specific as possible.

8. Do you think that it is possible for Marx's ideal communist state to materialize? Why or why not?

9. Watch the first season of U.S.A's *Mr. Robot* and indicate how the ideas of both Marx and Feuerbach are relevant to the events of the series, especially the revelation in episode 9.

10. Find a movie, television show, novel, or current event to which Marx's thought is relevant and explain how.

Freud—You Don't Really Know Me, But Neither Do I!

Implied in many previous chapters is the idea that people frequently fail to understand the goals of their actions in addition to the motivations behind those goals. Subsequently, people often fail to realize their own capabilities. It is as though such aspects of human psychology operate below the surface of awareness, in an unconscious region. The fact that we have dreams not only testifies to the existence of such a dimension but may hold the key to understanding ourselves. The idea that most of an individual's personality is dictated by processes of which one is unaware and, thus, over which one has little control, is so familiar as to be a staple of modern psychology, but it was quite a revolutionary idea during the time of Sigmund Freud, especially since he proposed his version of psychoanalysis as a scientific theory.

Born in Moravia in 1856, Freud was a very precocious child who spent most of his life in Vienna. After receiving his medical degree from the University of Vienna in 1881, he began to specialize in the treatment of nervous disorders. Soon after, an Austrian colleague revealed the efficacy of a method of therapy that allowed for catharsis through the ventilation of feelings. In the 1890s, Freud began to analyze himself, more specifically, the analysis of his own dreams, which led to the publication of *The Interpretation of Dreams* in 1900. A gifted and prolific writer, Freud produced a series of brilliant publications for the rest of his life. Even though his theory initially faced opposition, its popularity soon began to spread not only throughout Europe and America, culminating in the school of thought now known as

Psychoanalysis. In 1936, the Nazis took over Austria and Freud fled to London where he lived until his death in 1939.

Like the other thinkers addressed in previous chapters, Freud's thought did not develop in a vacuum, rather it represents the culmination of a long intellectual tradition. Whereas Marx followed in the footsteps of Hegel, Freud followed in the footsteps of Kant's less appreciated intellectual heir, Schopenhauer, whose influence extends also to the evolutionary theory of Darwin. Both will be addressed before examining the thought of Freud himself.

(I) Schopenhauer, Darwin, and Modern Physics

While the influences on the development of Freud's thought are numerous, the two most significant developments that contributed to Freud's theory were Schopenhauer's version of idealism and 19th century science, specifically Darwin's theory of evolution and the formulation of the principles of the conservation of energy.

Schopenhauer's Pessimistic Idealism: Arthur Schopenhauer (1788–1860) is best characterized as a *pessimistic idealist.* Schopenhauer formulated his philosophy in Germany during the time that Hegel's popularity reached its zenith. Schopenhauer despised Hegel and aimed to revise Kant's philosophy properly. However, unwisely, he often scheduled himself to lecture at the same time as Hegel and found himself alone in the lecture hall. His work, thus, never received the recognition it deserved during its lifetime. But the fact that so many thinkers cited Schopenhauer as a source of inspiration testifies to his importance.

Like Kant, Schopenhauer distinguished two different realms. First, is the *World as Representation.* Representation is a translation from the German term "vorstellung," which may also be translated as "set in front of" or "placed before." Basically, the world as representation refers to the world as we experience it, as containing individual objects and organisms. Such things, however, are mere appearances, manifestations of the driving force behind reality that Schopenhauer called the *World as Will*. Ultimately, the World as Will constitutes the elusive realm of things-in-themselves which Kant claimed we cannot experience. Schopenhauer, on the other hand, maintained that we all, indeed, have experience of things-in-themselves, since *we all can experience our own willing*. Hence, we are all simultaneously knowing subjects and part of what is to be known.

Schopenhauer held that our bodies and, in fact, the bodies of all organisms are objectifications of the will. But the will itself has an inner principle driving it, a striving called the *will to live*. All nature, basically, moves in response to the will to live. Everything is motivated to act in a way that will preserve its being. Living things must eat and drink in order to survive. Organisms reproduce as a way of sustaining their being. Animals engage in sexual congress as a method of such reproduction. Even the human intellect is a manifestation of the will to live, since it developed as a mechanism of survival. For instance, the invention of hunting tools or farming equipment illustrate the activation of the intellect, but such tools are invented only to facilitate the acquisition of food. The same applies to the development of houses and complex shelters. Such items require the use of the intellect, but exist only to facilitate survival, protection from the elements. The fact that items such as tools and shelters become more lavish and complex over time evidences the insatiable striving of the will to live, unsatisfied despite achieving its apparent goal. Even when we sleep, our bodies continue to function, maintaining the endless driving of the will to live. Furthermore, the survival of one will usually requires the destruction of another. For one organism to eat, another organism must be consumed, plant or animal. Shelters enable people to survive, but the construction of such shelters requires the use of wood and various other resources. Not only must the lives of the resources be disrupted, but the habitats of other creatures become absorbed into others.

Now, it is apparent why Schopenhauer may be categorized as pessimistic. The will to live entails, ironically, that there quite simply is not much to live for, except perhaps the ephemeral pleasure obtained from the satisfaction of the hunger or sex drive. But the satisfaction of one desire usually only leads to its inevitable magnification that ceases only in death. Schopenhauer, thus, would agree with the Buddha that life is suffering and that attachment, indeed, perpetuates that suffering.

However, there is some room for hope, ways that the aggressive force of the will may be stifled, albeit momentarily. Schopenhauer suggested that aesthetics afford one avenue of escape from the will to live. Schopenhauer emphasizes listening to music as a mode of shifting focus away from the objects that stimulate hostile will to live and toward the universal in everything. Literature, drama, and art afford similar mechanisms of release. In addition, Schopenhauer maintained altruism – acting solely for the good of others – represents the highest ethics that humanity can achieve. If everything, including our own bodies, is a manifestation of the will, then at a fundamental level everything is connected. In other words, we are all connected with each other. Hence, to act for the good of others deflects our attention away from the selfish striving of the will to live and toward the universal, enabling the recognition that we are all ultimately the same being.

Schopenhauer articulated several doctrines that Freud adopted as the basis for his psychoanalysis. His concept of the will contains elements of Freud's concepts of the unconscious, the id, repression, sublimation, and free association. Most importantly, he articulates parts of what became a Freudian theory of sexuality, anticipating Freud's emphasis on it as our strongest drive, such as in the following excerpt from Volume 2 of *The World as Will and Representation* where he writes about sexuality:

> The sexual impulse is the most vehement of all craving, the desire of desires, the concentration of all our willing. This…is the piquant element and the jest of the world, that the chief concern of all men is pursued

secretly and ostensibly ignored as much as possible. But, in fact, at every moment we see it seat itself as the real and hereditary lord of the world, out of the fullness of its own strength, on the ancestral throne, and looking down from thence with scornful glances, laugh at the preparations which have been made to subdue it, to imprison it, or at least to limit it and if possible to keep it concealed, or indeed so to master it that it shall only appear as a subordinate, secondary concern for life.[1]

Darwin's Theory of Evolution and 19th Century Science: Charles Darwin was not the first thinker to propose an evolutionary theory of human origins, but he made the most famous contribution to evolutionary biology and is credited with discovering the mechanism by which evolution happened – natural selection – in addition to the evidence that the process occurred.

Prior to Darwin, many thinkers entertained the idea that living organisms, including humans, evolved from previous species that subsequently went extinct. Different versions of this idea were held by many thinkers during the Enlightenment. George Buffon (1707–1788), for instance, suggested that the fossil record indicated species that no longer existed. In addition, Jean-Baptiste Pierre Lamarck (1744–1829) proposed a now defunct version of evolutionary theory based on the "inheritance of acquired characteristics," according to which offspring are born with the traits of their parents that become increasingly complex over history. For example, the giraffe's long neck developed as the result of previous generations stretching out to reach the leaves on trees. While this theory which came to be called "Lamarckism" had several supporters, it ultimately fell out of favor and posed no real threat to Darwin's theory.

Influences on Darwin's theory can be found outside the scope of science. Schopenhauer's conception of the will to live certainly influenced Darwin's conception of natural selection, as did the writings of

---

[1] Cited in Pojman's *Who Are We? Theories of Human Nature*, p. 149.

Adam Smith. Recall from the previous chapter that Smith believed people left to pursue their own interests would be guided by an "invisible hand" to produce the greatest good for all. However, Smith also implied that economic success is ultimately a matter of "survival of the fittest." In addition, in 1838, Darwin read a famous essay by Reverend Roger Thomas Malthus, *Essay on the Principles of Population*. Malthus argued that population increase was always *geometric*, but that the natural resources populations need to survive multiply only at an *arithmetic* rate. Hence, not only is there a struggle for survival, but weaker life forms ultimately will likely go extinct in that struggle. This essay, in conjunction with the ideas of Schopenhauer and Smith, introduced Darwin to the mechanism by which evolution worked.

Darwin attended Cambridge initially to study medicine and theology, but he quickly took interest in biology. Thus, he accepted a position as a naturalist on the H.M.S. Beagle between the years of 1831 and 1836, during which the ship traveled around the world. Darwin found bones of gigantic but now extinct animals, the fossils of sea animals, and witnessed an earthquake in Chile that noticeably raised the earth. He also observed the traits of many birds and other animals, the most interesting of which were those on the Galapagos Islands, which displayed slightly different characteristics than those on the mainland. For instance, the sizes and structures of the beaks of the finches differed from one island to the next. Seemingly, each beak size developed to help the birds get food, hence were uniquely adapted to meet the specific needs of each creature.

When Darwin returned to England, he had the idea of natural selection, but did not publish his findings until roughly 23 years later, since he knew his theory was controversial. Between the years of 1836 and 1844, he developed his theory based on the evidence he collected. By 1858, Alfred Wallace, an associate of Darwin, sent him an essay in which he discovered virtually the same idea. Darwin, thus, finally published his work so he could get the credit for its discovery, hence,

On the Origin of the Species in 1859. Darwin would not publish his *Descent of Man* until 1871, in which he explicitly argued that humans evolved from apes, but Thomas Huxley proposed this idea by 1863.

Darwin's argument in *On the Origin of Species* may be summarized in the following way. There are many small variations in the individuals of a given species, many of which can be inherited by offspring. Whereas some variations are helpful to organisms, others are harmful. Given that there are limited resources for which all species have an equal need, there is a struggle for existence. Individuals with helpful variations are likely to survive longer, produce more offspring, and, thus, pass on those traits conducive to survival. In contrast, individuals with harmful variations are less likely to survive. Moreover, they will have fewer offspring, and pass on traits that are not conducive to survival. Thus, groups of individuals with substantially harmful traits will likely go extinct. Nonetheless, a group's characteristics can change gradually with increasing variations useful in an environment. Over very long periods of time, a group can evolve into a new species that can no longer interbreed with its original group. **Natural selection** is the process by which groups with favorable traits survive while others die out, and through which new species are created.

Natural selection basically combined three ideas. First, there is a *random variation of traits* within species. There is no way to predict with complete certainty which traits offspring will inherit from their parents. Second, there is a *struggle for survival,* given the limited natural resources and the equal need for them. Some variations will confer an advantage, whereas others are harmful. Think back to the small finches on the Galapagos Islands, for example. Suppose that finches with very short, fat beaks are trying to obtain food from within a long shell. Most likely, the birds will not be able to survive, unlike those with longer beaks. Or, as another example, if a crow preys on a specific mouse and one group of that species of mouse has white fur that makes its members stand out, that group is more likely to be eaten by the crow. However, if another group of that species has brown fur, which makes it easier for the mice in that group to conceal themselves, they are more likely to survive and pass on their traits. Third, as Darwin learned from his reading of Smith, the *fittest species will survive.*

In addition to natural selection, Darwin also maintained that all living beings originated from a *common ancestor* and that once originated, life becomes increasingly complex. Furthermore, Darwin had an interest in geology. By the early 19th century, geologists began to observe that rock strata formed by processes of eruption and sedimentation, erosion, and earth movement acting over vast periods of time, rather than only a few thousand years, as a literal reading of the Bible would suggest. Charles Lyell propounded this view in his *Principles of Geology.* Darwin's studies led him to concur.[2]

The publication and popularization of Darwinism profoundly influenced Freud and his predilection for biology. Other 19th century developments that significantly influenced Freud emanated from the work of Gustav Fechner (1801–1887) and Hermann von Helmholtz (1821–1894). Fechner published his *Elements of Psychophysics* in 1860, just one year removed from the publication of Darwin's magnum opus. Fechner attempted to provide evidence that the mind could be studied both empirically and quantitatively. His work represents the culmination of Newtonian physics combined with evolutionary biology. Darwin's theory effectively dealt a deathblow to the idea that human beings occupy a special place in creation. Human beings are merely animals, *highly evolved animals*, but still natural creatures that exist on a continuum with the rest of creation. And the rest of creation is subject to the same causal laws as the rest of the observable universe. Thus, the human mind is not only quantifiable, but its processes are determined and predictable. In addition, around the same time as the publications of both Fechner and Darwin, von Helmholtz formulated

---

[2] For a more detailed account of Darwin's theory of evolution and its subsequent developments, see Chapter 12 of Stevenson's *Twelve Theories of Human Nature*, pp. 245–278.

the principles of the conservation of energy, stating that energy is a quantity just as mass, that it can neither be created nor destroyed and that when it disappears from one place, it appears in another.

Darwin's theory of evolution not only lent itself to Freud as proof that human beings are purely natural creatures, but also furnished support for Freud's later writings in which he traces religious beliefs to the repression of primordial trauma in early human history in works such as *Totem and Taboo* and *The Future of an Illusion* in addition to his critique of culture in *Civilization and Its Discontents*. The work of Fechner and von Helmholtz provided a scientific basis for Freud's concepts of mental determinism, repression, and sublimation.

(II) Freud's Psychoanalytic Conception of Human Nature

Like the work of most great minds, Freud's work developed gradually. Initially, Freud wanted to become a physician, but from 1885 to 1895 he discovered an interest in psychology and a cathartic method for treating nervous disorders, sparked by his visit to Jean-Martin Charcot in 1885, under whom he studied in Paris. Charcot was a neurologist who became famous for using hypnotism and mental suggestion to treat nervous conditions. He performed striking demonstrations of the influence of hypnotism and mental suggestion on behavior. While impressive to Freud, Charcot's methods seemed only to provide a "temporary cure" for the problems they intended to treat. Freud's subsequent collaboration with Josef Breuer, with whom he co-authored *Studies in Hysteria*, narrowed the focus of his search for a new method. Breuer based his approach on the hypothesis that hysterical symptoms trace back to a traumatic experience apparently forgotten by the patient. His treatment induced the recall of that experience and discharged the corresponding emotion. From 1900 to 1920, Freud developed his unique theory of personality that developed into psychoanalysis – dream analysis, the unconscious basis of motivation, and the various forms of neurosis. From 1920 to 1939,

Freud revised his theory and applied it to religious, cultural, and social criticism.

The following themes in Freud's thought will be addressed: (a) the unconscious and mental determinism; (b) the instincts; (c) the Id, the Ego, and the Super-Ego; (d) the stages of development; (e) repression and defense mechanisms; (f) the critique of religion; and (g) the critique of civilization.[3]

The Unconscious and Mental Determinism: The most useful analogy in describing Freud's conception of the mind is that of an iceberg, 90 percent of which exists below the surface of the water. By comparison, most of an individual's personality is dictated by unconscious desires and instincts. Thus, people lack substantial free will in two senses. First, everything a person does, says, or thinks traces back to an underlying emotionally charged cause. Second, since such causes are unconscious, the ignorance most people have of them prevents them from changing their behavior. The virtual impossibility of assuming an objective point of view with respect to one's behavior compounds this second difficulty, dooming people to an eternity of their oft-repeated and frequently destructive patterns.

Freud's "iceberg model" of the mind contains three levels. First, the *conscious* level contains an individual's immediate thoughts, sensations, and perceptions. Second, the *preconscious* level contains mental states of which one is not immediately aware but may call to mind. Such items include recent or vivid memories and stored knowledge that one may need at any specific moment. For instance, right now I am consciously aware of four students in my classroom completing their midterm exam. However, if one of my current students resembles

---

[3] For an overview of Freud's ideas, see *An Outline of Psychoanalysis* and *The Ego and the Id*, both available from W. W. Norton & Company's Standard Editions of the Complete Psychological Works of Sigmund Freud series, edited by James Strachey. For an accessible secondary introduction to Freud's theory, see also B.A. Farrell's "A Reconstruction of Freud's Mature Theory," in Stevenson (Ed.), *The Study of Human Nature* (New York: Oxford University Press, 2000), pp. 170–184.

a previous student, I recall the memory of that previous student, stored in my preconscious, but admitted into my conscious. Finally, the *unconscious* level consists of mental states that are not admitted into consciousness under normal circumstances. To be recalled, such states require the intervention of a therapist or a hypnotist. They include items such as violent motives, immoral urges, fears, socially unacceptable sexual desires, irrational wishes, selfish needs, and shameful experiences. Additional items may include horrifically traumatic experiences such as instances of physical, sexual, or emotional abuse from which the unconscious shields an individual.

A startling implication of the existence of an unconscious level of the mind is that there is a sense in which no one ever forgets anything. Truly, it is possible to lose conscious awareness of some event, but the unconscious level keeps a detailed record of everything that we ever experience. Certainly, I might be able to recall the Pythagorean theorem, the quadratic formula, the procedure for calculating standard deviation, and the laws of Mendelian genetics. Such items are stored in my preconscious. However, I cannot recall verbatim the algebra problems I completed while in high school, or the experiments I completed as part my biology courses in order to better understand genetics. I certainly cannot recall, verbatim, any of the essays I submitted as a student. Nonetheless, under the right circumstances, such items of knowledge can resurface. That some of these items are harmful and exert an influence over us long after the passing of the ordeals that triggered them leaves humanity cursed with knowledge even after forgetting.

The Instincts: Freud maintains that there are two basic, primal instincts. The instincts are not merely innate impulses, but *drives,* motivating forces behind an individual's behavior. First, *Eros,* or the life instinct, serves as the basis for hunger, self-preservation, and sexual libido. If you feel your stomach growling around lunch time, the force of *Eros* compels you to seek food. If an attractive member of your species catches your attention and conjures up intimate fantasies, the force of *Eros* compels you to approach this person and attempt to establish a romantic connection. Perhaps the force of *Eros* will manifest itself in a different way, compelling you to ingratiate yourself to this person by sending flowers or writing a love poem. Self-preservation reinforces the drive to engage in sexual congress, which carries the evolutionary function of reproducing offspring to survive us when we die. Marriage, too, promises the stability of subsistence and a convenient way to meet one's sexual needs in addition to building a legacy that lives long after the husband and wife die. Eros can also represent the creative instinct in human beings, indicating a parallel between Marx and Freud, where humanity's natural tendency to transform the world by labor also represents an expression of the life instinct, since the tools people create always carry the intention of extending life and one's being.

Second, *Thanatos*, or the death instinct, serves as the basis for aggression, self-destruction, and violence. Imagine that while you walk down a path, there is a person in front of you walking more slowly. Instead of simply adjusting to the pace of this individual, you instinctively and aggressively move more quickly to pass the person. The drive to move faster than this individual is motivated by Thanatos. The jealousy and rage you feel when a potential lover fancies someone other than you arise from the death instinct, as does the ill will you intend toward those he or she fancies. Competition in virtually any form, be it over basic resources necessary for survival or privileges esteemed by one's culture or social group, has its source in the death instinct. Like the manifestations associated with Eros, those emanating from Thanatos transform into more socially acceptable forms. The violence one wishes to dole out to one's rivals receives cathartic release by participation in contact sports, such as football, boxing, or mixed martial arts. If one is less active, one may simply opt to become a spectator of such mediums of entertainment. One might also pursue catharsis through violent films or television shows. Perhaps one might find a fictional character with whom one can identify and live vicariously through that figure's imaginary success. Also originating with the death instinct is the innate and paradoxical fascination most people have with death and violence. People are instinctively repulsed by corpses and violence, but most are also simultaneously mesmerized by them. The popularity of violent sports, films, and television shows testifies to this fascination as much as it does to the human need for outlets of aggression. Try driving by a highway accident without taking at least a quick glance at the aftermath. In addition, despite their disreputable notoriety, convicted serial killers, rapists, and terrorists remain a permanent focus of journalistic and psychological inquiry not only to professionals but to the general public. Such figures live on our collective memories with much greater poignancy than do their victims. Every so often, the judicial system sanctions the execution of one of these violent criminals. But the dates on which such sentences are carried out rarely are met with solemn quietude. More typically, hundreds of civilians with no discernible history of violence congregate outside the walls of death row celebrating the most recent implementation of the oft-debated death penalty. The universal fascination with death lends itself as a reminder that the potential for extreme violence lies within us all.

Each instinct parallels aspects of Schopenhauer's will to live, which not only drives an individual to preserve one's being, but always does so at the expense of something else. Like Schopenhauer, Freud maintained that existence demands an exorbitant amount of energy. Our psychic instincts breed attachments and those attachments are the root of our suffering, to once again paraphrase the first two noble truths of the Buddha. The death instinct, thus, is the stronger of the two. The instinct to destroy overwhelms the instinct to create. Creativity and the processes of life proceed from the instincts, fueled by endless striving, thus, demand extravagant energy. It is always easier to destroy someone else's work than it is to create one's own, just as it is easier to imitate and conform to the behavior and ideas of others than it is to think and act with true autonomy. Like the Epicureans, Freud not only assumed a purely naturalistic worldview devoid of any God but concluded that rest and repose constitute the ultimate goals of all living things. What everyone really wants to do is return to a completely inorganic state. That is, everybody unconsciously wishes to die. Many forms of self-destructive behavior are overt, such as suicide and self-mutilation. Suicide usually presents itself as a convenient resolution to the stress and frustration of life, motivated by the belief that living is not worth the energy it takes. Self-mutilative behaviors, such as self-inflicted cutting or tearing out one's own hair, usually have as their sources tension brought about by an external trigger. Perhaps an individual becomes incensed by an associate's demeaning comment. A subject must deal with the emotionally charged energy attached to this experience in some way. But it certainly is not socially acceptable to take it out on another person. Hence, the energy turns against the self in search of release as a coping mechanism. The behavior of drug addicts present similar cases. The initial use of a recreational drug allows for momentary escape from reality. But the continued use of such substances not only have the opposite of the user's intended effect but hasten the march toward the inevitable grave awaiting us all. Perhaps even ordinary common-place activities have the same unconscious goal. Most people enjoy eating foods and drinking beverages that consumed over long periods of time result in severe health problems and eventual death. The irony of such behavior is not merely that such things are thoroughly appealing to the senses but that the danger involved in such self-destructive behavior is usually well established and understood by those participating in it.

The Tripartite Personality – The Id, Ego, and Super-Ego: Like Plato, Freud conceived of the human personality as having a three-part structure. The most basic, primal part of the personality is the *Id*, which is totally hereditary and instinctive. The Id consists of all the instinctual drives we inherit from our ancestors and it is the body's primary source of psychic energy. It operates on the *pleasure principle*, which aims to eliminate tension. Whenever you desire something, the Id seeks immediate gratification of that desire. Tension builds when desires are suppressed. The more one's drives are inhibited, the stronger they become and the more voracious they are upon their inevitable release. If you enjoy the taste of pizza, but ignore your craving of it for too long, when you finally decide to consume the food, you will likely gorge yourself with it. The same may be said about many other desires, such as the desire for sex, sleep, or recreational beverages. Everyone is born totally at the behest of the Id. Infants basically live in a completely undifferentiated state of consciousness. That is, they view the world as an extension of themselves, as does the Id itself.

The second aspect of personality, the *Ego* comprises one's conscious mental states. Many often use the term "self" to refer to the Ego. Recall from the previous chapter the dialectical principle that everyone must conceive of oneself in terms of "the Other." An individual's self-awareness emerges when one can distinguish oneself from other objects. Awareness of myself, for instance, simultaneously implies awareness of everything that is not me. The Ego develops in much the same way, based on the interface between the Id and the external world. An infant child eventually learns to differentiate itself from the world through its interaction with its parents. The development of a new aspect of personality implies a dynamic of interaction between the two. Whereas the Id operates on the pleasure principle, the Ego operates on the *reality principle*. Whereas the Id seeks immediate gratification and the elimination of tension, the Ego aims to balance the demands of the Id with those of the external world. The discovery of oneself as an object distinct from the rest of the world coincides with the discovery of the principle that one must learn to compromise one's immediate desires and tolerate at least some reasonable degree of tension. Becoming a true self, thus, means realizing that one cannot have anything and everything one wants at any given time.

Finally, the *Super-Ego* develops as the product of continual socialization by parents, authority figures, social institutions, and culture. The internalized principles of one's socialization represent ideal patterns of behavior individuals strive to emulate. How a person feels, regardless of one's success in living up to such patterns, may be described as the individual's *conscience,* which functions as a subsidiary of the Super-Ego. The child's parents serve as the most immediate source of the ideals of the Super-Ego. Hence, a child's values often reflect the parents' values. Suppose a child is raised in a very strict Christian home. The ideal values of the child would likely reflect those of the denomination of Christianity under which that child was raised. The feeling of guilt the child experiences if he or she behaves in a way that falls out of alignment with Christian principles emanates from the child's conscience.

Not only must the Ego contend with the demands of the Id and the external world, but it must balance the lofty and virtually impossible demands of the Super-Ego as well. The individual, as a conscious subject, is, therefore, under constant torment. Two problems may emerge. First, the *Id may overwhelm the Ego.* A person may be unable to balance successfully the demands of the Id with those of the external world. Possibly, individuals of this type did not have the proper rearing as children. On the other hand, such people perhaps tried too hard to suppress their desires until they grew to become far too powerful to control. People who are overly aggressive, violent, or too easily drawn into conflict represent those with an Id that disproportionately outweighs the Ego and the Super-Ego. Typically, criminals will manifest this sort of personality. To commit a crime, especially a violent crime, the process usually involves the objectification of the victim. Serial killers and rapists view their victims as mere instruments to be used to gratify basic needs, rather than individuals with goals, values, and wills of their own. The crime of theft fails to respect someone else's property. In each instance, the perpetrator displays an undifferentiated mentality developed not much further beyond that of a precognitive child. Such people wish to absorb into themselves the whole world at large. Second, *the Super-Ego may overwhelm the Ego*, in which case a person tries too hard to live up to standards that are impossible to satisfy. A Christian man may come to view himself as a sinner who will inevitably be damned to an eternity of punishment because he failed to divest himself of "impure thoughts." In the New Testament, Matthew 5: 28 explicitly says that anyone who so much as thinks about having sex with another has already done so. The very next verse, in fact, implies that if one cannot overcome such temptations, then one should castrate oneself! What if a person with a disproportionately large Super-Ego reads such a passage and takes it literally? To take another example, an overachieving student may become suicidal at the prospect of failing to achieve the perfect grades demanded by one's parents. The Super-Ego, thus, while emerging with the apparent intention of maintaining the order and structure of civilization can drive one to self-destructive behavior. Whereas the Id compels individuals to absorb the world, an unchecked Super-Ego leaves the individual to be absorbed by the ideals of others.

The Stages of Development: Freud insisted that everyone, universally, goes through five stages of psychosexual development. First is the *oral stage,* which comprises the first two years of life. At this stage, sucking at the mother's breast dominates the erotic focus of the child. Next is the *anal stage,* which occurs from 2 to 3 years of age. At this stage, the erotic focus of the child shifts from the mouth to the anus, particularly potty training. Whereas the oral stage emphasizes what goes into one's mouth, the anal stage emphasizes expulsion. Third is the *phallic stage* which occurs from 3 to 5 years of age. At this stage, each sex becomes fascinated with genitalia. Boys become fascinated with their penises, but according to Freud, girls wish they had one, hence, the notion of "penis envy" that continues to draw the ire of feminists to this day! Fourth, the *latent stage* occurs between 6 and 12 years of age. At this point, socialization becomes the primary focus, while sexuality fades into the background. Finally, the *genital stage* lasts from puberty until death.

The first 6 years of life basically form the foundation of one's personality. Supposedly, so long as an individual successfully completed each stage of psychosexual development, then there will be no problems in adulthood. Often, however, people may become fixated at a specific stage. For instance, an individual who is fixated at the oral stage may develop a fetish for placing objects in one's mouth. Individuals with severely strict parents often are referred to as "anal retentive," fixated at the anal stage. Such people may become extremely fastidious later in life, obsessed with order and neatness. On the other hand, people with permissive parents may develop the exact opposite personality, indulging a life of chaos and disorder.

One of Freud's interesting contributions is his conception of the *Oedipus Complex*, which boys go through during the phallic stage. The complex is named after Oedipus Rex in Sophocles' tragedy, who was destined to kill his father and marry his mother. Freud maintains that boys become amorously infatuated with their mothers. Wishing to marry their mothers, they subconsciously wish that their fathers were dead. However, fearing castration at the hands of the father, they are forced to repress their sexuality. Later, during puberty, sexuality resurfaces. According to Freud, females go through a similar process with their fathers, which he called the Electra Complex. While this complex need not be interpreted literally, it is reasonable to conclude that a child's relationship with his or her parents plants the seeds that grow into a healthy sexuality.

Repression and Defense Mechanisms:[4] In Freud's view, individuals are engaged in a constant struggle to balance the desires of the Id with the ideals of the Super-Ego and the demands of the external world. Pain, frustration, and various forms of psychic tension inevitably develop. Repression is the primary instinctive and reflexive defense mechanism to relieve such tension and avoid inner conflict. This process occurs at the subconscious level and the most decisive repressions trace back to early childhood, the first 5 years of life. Freud insists that this process is necessary but inevitably will fail, since repressed energy never simply dissipates. Eventually, it must be released. Why is the process necessary? Some events are far too overwhelming for the mind to handle, especially during childhood. When a loved one dies, the process of grief usually does not surface until after the services for the departed. One must remain functional in one's daily activities and see to the funeral arrangements before one can properly grieve. The energy connected with the loss is, thus, repressed.

Repression is the primary defense mechanism and it gives rise to several others. While Freud mentions many defense mechanisms in his own writings, for the sake of brevity, I will focus on sublimation, projection, displacement, and identification. The concept of *sublimation* is already somewhat familiar, since a previous discussion focusing on the manifestations of *Eros* and *Thanatos*. In chemistry, sublimation is the process by which a solid substance transforms directly into a gas. Since human beings are natural creatures and the instincts have a completely physiological basis, the emotional energy connected with an experience, once repressed, can undergo the same process. Psychologically, sublimation is the process by which the emotionally charged energy connected with an experience is repressed and later resurfaces in a different, usually more socially acceptable form. For instance,

---

[4] Freud never gave systematic exposition to the defense mechanisms. For that achievement, his daughter, Anna Freud deserves credit. See her *The Ego and the Mechanisms of Defense* (New York: Routledge – Taylor & Francis Group, 2018).

consider a man who finds a woman attractive. His ultimate desire is to engage in sexual congress with her. However, social stability demands the postponement of such actions, which requires that the instinct be repressed. It later resurfaces in the form of a love letter written to the woman. Or, it may take the form of sending the woman flowers. Courtship rituals, thus, comprise the sublimation of the sex drive. The same applies to the drives of violence and aggression. Once repressed, such drives resurface in the form of a desire to watch violent films or contact sports.

Projection occurs when one sees one's characteristics in the behavior of others. Usually, the attributes projected are those that the subject finds undesirable. For instance, consider a man who has a crush on a female associate. These feelings make the man uncomfortable, hence are repressed. They later resurface in the form of the belief that one of his friends fancies the same woman. He sees his own attributes in someone else, divesting himself of the quality and eliminating the tension it caused.

Displacement compares to both projection and sublimation. It is the process by which energy is deflected from its intended object to a substitute, usually a safer object. For example, the re-emergence of sexuality during puberty frequently causes tension in adolescents, especially when such feelings are directed toward peers of the opposite sex. To ease the tension, such feelings are repressed and then *redirected*. A teenage boy develops a crush on an attractive but unavailable female celebrity rather than one of his classmates. Since the celebrity is beyond his reach, out of sight, not someone he must confront regularly, such a target promises greater mental security. The same applies to females. Displacement of aggression follows a similar pattern. Suppose an individual is reprimanded by his employer. Obviously, he cannot physically assault his employer and hope to keep his job. Thus, he releases his aggression when returns to his home to verbally abuse his wife and child.

Identification, in some ways, is the opposite of projection. Identification occurs when one assumes the personality of someone else, of which identification with the aggressor constitutes the most common form. Children who are abused at home often become bullies at school. When one is forced to confront a violent force that is beyond one's control, inevitably the experience will cause an extraordinary amount of tension. But if one takes on the personality of the aggressor, one in effect becomes one with the antagonist, thereby eliminating the tension. Showtime's acclaimed series *Dexter* showcases this defense mechanism brilliantly. The show follows the titular Dexter Morgan, a serial killer who also works as a blood spatter pattern analyst who works for the fictional Miami Metro Police Department. However, Dexter has a very strict code: He only kills people who committed murder but somehow evaded capture. His adoptive stepfather, Harry, himself a homicide detective, taught him this code. Harry adopted Dexter after Dexter witnessed the murder of his mother, during which he was only 3 years old. For most of his adult life, Dexter repressed this memory. That he ultimately became a killer himself reflects a classic example of identification.

Freud applied these principles not only in providing therapy, but also in his critique of religion and culture. Civilization requires the repression of many natural drives and their sublimation into socially acceptable forms. Moreover, religious beliefs are the culmination of many repressed feelings. But should such things be maintained?

Civilization and Its Discontents: While human beings are highly evolved animals, civilization distinguishes them from all other members of the animal kingdom. Civilization represents humanity's success in surpassing their natural limitations and securing protection from the forces of nature. Without civilization, there would be no houses and buildings to shelter us from the cold in the winter or from the heat in the summer. There would be no automobiles, trains, or airplanes to facilitate travel. The printing press made possible the widespread distribution of knowledge and modern technology gives everyone a window to the world. Technology not only improves the quality of lives, but modern medicine extends many lives.

But everything comes with a price. The price of civilization is that many natural desires must be repressed and compromised. Since Freud insisted that the death drive is our strongest instinct, the most natural conclusion to be drawn from his theory is that civilization demands far too great a price from humanity. But even for Freud, returning to a state of nature is not advisable. To flee from civilization would result in total chaos, over which only a savage tyrant could maintain order. Freud's Hobbesian conception of the state of nature coincides with his estimation of humanity's most basic instincts. In Freud's view, two pieces of evidence support such a view. First, the hostility of people prior to the emergence of private property and complex communities testifies to humanity's aggressiveness and voracious appetites. Second, the behavior of young children lends itself as firsthand evidence of humanity's basic cruelty and selfishness.

Nonetheless, Freud noted that civilization emerged from two crucial factors: (1) the necessity of work, and (2) the power of love. First, civilization required people to band together and pool their resources. The greater the amount of people in a group, the greater the chances of survival. Second, not only is sex necessary for human beings to procreate, but families provide a sense of security and stability for people. People can more easily meet their basic physiological needs with the aid of a family, and children learn to become functional members of a community.

Justice is also necessary for the survival of civilization. Freud contends, however, that it emerges from primal taboos, an idea that he advances in *Totem and Taboo* by applying his psychoanalytic theory to the theory of human evolution, according to which humans used to be gorillas. These animals lived in small groups and the leader had the privilege of sleeping with the females. This custom carried over into the development of humanity from gorillas, in which the father of a family had the privilege of sleeping with the women of his clan. His sons, however, became jealous. Hence, they lured him away from the group, killed him, and consumed his remains. Later however, they felt tremendous guilt. The repression of this guilt later resurfaced in the form of taboos against incest, thus, giving rise to the conventions of social justice.

The survival of civilization requires the continued repression and sublimation of those drives that could threaten it. For all its discontents and the frustrations that its continued existence requires, the loss of civilization would have far greater consequences for humanity, especially since civilized human beings are a far cry from their primal ancestors. But is religion necessary to sustain civilization? Freud's answer is a resounding, "NO!"[5]

Freud's Critique of Religion: Like the convention of justice, religious beliefs emerged from repressed feelings as well. Freud argues that this process happens over three stages. First, human beings experience extreme fear and awe at the power of the forces of nature. The sound of thunder, the devastating power of lightning, tornadoes, and earthquakes not only threaten the safety of humanity, but accentuate human finitude. Our cousins in the animal kingdom are stronger and far more self-sufficient than humans. Moreover, just the experience of the vastness of the cosmos, the stars illuminating the night sky, and the seemingly boundless ocean is itself sublime. These experiences culminate in what Freud calls an "oceanic feeling," the feeling that we are one with nature. If we are a part of nature, then it is less threatening.

Second, human beings are also naturally idol-making creatures. Not only do we conceive of ourselves as one with nature, but we personify

---

[5] For the full argument of Freud's *Civilization and Its Discontents*, most translations are reputable, but I'm partisan to Norton's 2010 reprint edition, edited by James Strachey. The bulk of the argument takes place between Chapters III and VI.

those forces. In our minds, they take on human characteristics with power magnified beyond our own. The ocean becomes a God, as do the sun and the earth. The personification of the forces of nature affords us more control over them, further reducing the terror they evoke by making them more familiar.

Freud's analysis thus far echoes previous thinkers. His unique and final contribution consists in applying his psychoanalytic theory to religious beliefs. Freud claims that when we were young, we felt the same fear that we do as adults. The oceanic feeling associated with religious experience parallels the experience of infant who lives undifferentiated from the rest of the world. But as children, we had a father to protect us. Hence, as adults, we project the image of a father onto the universe itself, the basis for the idea of God. Not only will this God protect us while we are alive, but he will reward us for our suffering in the afterlife. Even death itself need not be feared.

Religious beliefs Freud insists are *illusions,* which contrast with *delusions.* The former may or may not be true, whereas the latter are indubitably false. Illusions always carry the intent of wish fulfillment but, most of the time, turn out to be false. Freud concludes, therefore, that religious beliefs are probably false. Ideal happiness is no more than a fantasy, a pale reflection of the happiness we wish we could obtain in this life, just as Feuerbach argued before him. Moreover, the standards of religion are impossible to follow. Consider the Christian mandate to love one's neighbor as oneself. Freud insists that such a maxim is psychologically unrealistic, given the prevalence of instinctive selfishness and aggression. Human sexuality also is a target of attack by traditional religion. Not only is sex out of wedlock a sin, but even fantasizing about sex is deemed to be sinful. Religion demands that human beings act contrary to their nature. And even if the demands of religion were not so cumbersome, religion did not achieve the goals it intended. The promise of reward for the just and punishment for the wicked hardly succeeds in compelling people to refrain any transgressions.

Thus, humanity will greatly benefit from the elimination of unreasonable and illusory worldviews and the continual willingness to compromise their instincts. Ultimately, Freud pledged great faith in the future success of science, especially due to its achievements in his own time. While Freud judged religion to be illusion, he also concluded that the belief that humanity could obtain from religion what it cannot obtain from science is a far more dangerous illusion.[6]

(III) Psychoanalysis After Freud and Bacon's Idols of the Mind

Whether one accepts his ideas or not, Freud's influence cannot be denied. The psychoanalytic model continues to be applied in modern psychiatry. Nonetheless, it changed drastically after Freud and frequently evolves to this day. Freud had many followers, but two of the earliest were Carl Jung and Alfred Adler. Adler was born and trained in Vienna. He broke with Freud in 1911, unable to accept Freud's fixation with sex. In 1932, he traveled to the United States, where he taught for the last 5 years of his life. He maintained that self-realization or self-worth is at the heart of the human predicament, such that every person needs to strive for perfection in his own way. Mental illness results primarily from the failure to overcome one's innate sense of inferiority. Hence, Adler coined the term "inferiority complex." We spend our lives trying to overcome our feelings of inferiority, seeking power and self-worth. The task of therapy is to help one realize one's potential.

Carl Jung believed that Freud underestimated the power of religion and overestimated the role of sex in one's life and broke with him in 1913. He also rejected Freud's naturalism, as he believed in both God and something like a soul, independent of the body. He maintained

---

[6] *The Future of An Illusion* is still available from Norton's Standard Editions of the Complete Psychological Works of Sigmund Freud Series. While it is relatively short, it is still challenging to read. The bulk of Freud's argument takes place between Chapters III and VI.

that Freud's theory relied far too heavily on the individual uncon-scious but that there also existed a collective unconscious consisting of cosmic archetypes (universal symbols), the meanings of which can be revealed through mythology, literature, and fairytales. The job of the therapist consists in uncovering the collective unconscious. Whereas Freud's theory emphasizes the application of general ideas to specific individuals, Jung's theory moves in the opposite direction. His archetypes of the collective unconscious are comparable to Pla-tonic Forms.

Other famous contributors to the psychoanalytic tradition include Freud's daughter, Anna Freud, Otto Rank, Harry Stack Sullivan, Karen Horney, John Bowlby, and Object Relations Theorists such as Melanie Klein, Margaret Mahler, D.W. Winnicott, and W.R.D. Fairbairn. Prior to Freud's death, he banished many of his followers, including Adler, Jung, and Rank. Freud refused to tolerate criticism in any form. If anyone ever dared to disagree with him, he looked upon the infrac-tion as a betrayal. Hence, Freud's theory affords humanity another monumental "theater" of thought which demands assessment in terms of Bacon's Idols.

Freud and Bacon's Idols of the Tribe: Since Freud's many writings marked historically monumental contributions to psychology and personality theory, in some way, *all of them* address Bacon's idols of the tribe. The potential for such errors is universal, emerging from human nature itself. Freud's theory aimed to uncover the universal basis for human personality and behavior. Nonetheless, Freud's theory specifically addresses Bacon's idols of the tribe in two ways. First, his claim not only that there is an unconscious part of the mind but that this aspect of an individual accounts for most of one's personality, if true, implies that no one can fully understand one's own motivations. In other words, no one can completely fulfill the Delphic Oracle's mandate to "know thyself," at least not without the aid of a therapist trained to expose the roots of one's personality by investigating the unconscious.

Second, Freud's theory of repression and the defense mechanisms give rise to universal tendencies for error that may be interpreted as extensions of the Idols of Tribe of which Bacon wrote. The mechanism of projection provides the most obvious example. For Bacon, people tend to interpret reality as a reflection of their own attributes. Through projection, people see their own attributes manifested in the behavior of others. A similar process occurs with sublimation and displacement. In the former, one finds a way to conform the world to one's desires, albeit in socially acceptable ways. In the latter, the object of one's desires may be found in any item, even one that is inappropriate. With identification, the process is reversed. Overwhelmed by the world, one becomes its mirror, but then imposes oneself on the world, continuing the process of absorption. Victims become the victimizers and cause others to do the same.

Freud and Bacon's Idols of the Cave: Freud's developmental theory and his tripartite conception of the personality – the Id, Ego, and Super-Ego – are the aspects of his thought most relevant to Bacon's idols of the cave. Many people become fixated at specific stages of development, such as the oral stage or the anal stage, and if that happens, one's unique characteristics and behaviors reflect the stage of fixation. Moreover, any one of the three basic structures of personality may become dominant. In people who are balanced, the Ego dominates and effectively balances the demands of the Id, the Super-Ego, and the external world. In some people, the Id overwhelms both the Ego and the Super-Ego. In others, the Super-Ego is dominant. The relationship between these structures dictates an individual's personality. Also, defense mechanisms, even though they are universal, have many variations depending on the individual. Everyone has the capacity for projection, but what one projects onto another depends on the individual. Everyone at some point augmented the mechanism of sublimation, but again, the process varies between individuals. One person may sublimate his sexual drives by writing poetry, whereas another may do so by painting erotic pictures. One person may sublimate his aggression by playing football, while another might simply prefer to watch the game. Lastly, the process of dream analysis, a popular technique among many psychotherapists, supposedly reveals the unconscious wishes of a person. Freud distinguished between the *manifest content* and *latent content* of dreams. The manifest content of a dream consists of the surface images and sensations experienced in the dream itself. The latent content concerns what those images and sensations mean. For example, suppose you dream that you are riding on the back of a Griffin. Suppose that the Griffin represents a friend who helped through a difficult time. The manifest content is the Griffin, whereas the latent content is the friend it represents.

Freud and Bacon's Idols of the Marketplace: A commonly used term is "Freudian slip," a peculiar slip of the tongue. Such slips typically refer to accidental utterances that reveal the unconscious desires of an individual. The unconscious determines our thoughts and behavior. Hence, most of the language that we use and the words we speak have their basis in unconscious motivations. Usually, our language can be controlled through training or through defense mechanisms to countenance our desires in a more socially acceptable way. However, occasionally, the truth "slips" off the tongue! For example, suppose you have a friend who intends to say the word "vase," by really says, "vagina." When you ask your friend to repeat himself, he brushes off the incident as merely a mistake in speech. But according to Freud's theory, such slips reveal the individual's unconscious motivations. Since your friend unintentionally used a term with a sexual connotation, he revealed his unconscious sexual desire. Freud argued that many aspects of language provide clues to the unconscious, including jokes, many of which are of a sexual nature. Free association comprised one of Freud's therapeutic techniques, and it continues to be used by psychotherapists to this day. Basically, a patient will randomly say any words that come to one's mind, automatically and without thinking. The therapist then will write down the words uttered and use them to construct a model of the patient's personality. Supposedly, the words reveal the patient's unconscious.[7]

Freud and Bacon's Idols of the Theater: On the one hand, Freud's psychoanalysis purports to explain virtually all academic exercises and forms of culture as emanating from the unconscious through the mechanism of sublimation, mostly. Why an individual devoted oneself to a specific discipline and developed or adopted any specific theory in that discipline can be revealed through psychoanalysis. More generally, however, while the influence of German philosophy resonates through the writings of Freud, his originality and influence cannot be denied. Not only did he creatively apply the ideas of Schopenhauer, Feuerbach, Darwin, and Nietzsche (who will be addressed in the final chapter), but he also utilizes concepts from classical thinkers such as Empedocles and Epicurus. Freud's concept of the pleasure principle derives mostly from his reading of Epicurus, but his conception of the instincts is not unlike Empedocles's conception of the two forces that sustain the universe – Love and Hate. Love mixes things together while Hate segregates them. The same might be said about Eros and Thanatos. Freud does not merely adopt such ideas but provides a unique synthesis of them that can be used for the good of others. Moreover, his conception of the trinity of personality hearkens back to Plato. For the latter, the individual soul consists of reason, passion, and appetite. Clearly, the Id corresponds to Plato's appetitive, or desiring, faculty. The pattern of correspondence between the others is not so clear. However, I can hazard the following. In Freud's view, it would be safe to assume that the Super-Ego corresponds to reason, since the former operates on principles of ideal values. That leaves the

---

[7] For more on the topics discussed in this paragraph, see the *Psychopathology of Everyday Life* and *Jokes and Their Relation to the Unconscious*, both available from the Norton Standard Editions series.

Ego to match up with passion, the spirited part of the soul, which may be viewed as struggling to resist the temptations of the appetite and follow the dictates of reason. Of course, Plato's conception of these faculties differed from Freud's conception of the structures of personality, but that fact only further testifies to Freud's originality.[8] Finally, Freud's critique of culture and religion establishes his humanistic and progressive vision, his faith that humanity could domesticate its "dark side" for the good of all without the draconian imposition of illusions from traditional religion.

Does Freud Avoid Bacon's Idols? Freud's theory seems vulnerable to Bacon's idols of the tribe in at least two ways. First, Freud's theory purports to account for the origin of ideas, motivations, behaviors, and general personality traits by identifying their roots in an individual's unconscious. However, if Freud's theory is universal and a fact, as he insisted, then it would apply to him as well. If tracing a theory to its psychological basis yields a deflationary effect on it, then the same would apply to Freud's psychoanalysis. Second, Freud recognized his theory as scientific. However, like Marx's, it seems to be unfalsifiable. That is, Freud constructed theory in such a way that nothing can be allowed to count as evidence against it. For instance, suppose that a rival theorist criticized Freud's developmental theory, suggesting that it fails to explain roughly two-thirds of the people in the world. That is, it applies only to people raised in the industrialized west. Hence, Freud's developmental stages are not universal. A defender of Freudian psychoanalysis might respond to this criticism by suggesting that the critic only attacked the theory in the first place because of displaced aggression! On the other hand, a defender might simply propose that if the theory were applied to indigenous people, it would be proven true. Of course, such an attempt to justify the theory might result in its

---

[8] For an alternative account of the parallels between Freud's model of the mind and Plato's model of the soul, see Joel Kupperman's *Theories of Human Nature* (Indianapolis, IN: Hackett Publishing, 2010), Chapter 5.

proponent twisting the data collected in favor of psychoanalysis. It is, thus, always possible for a psychoanalyst to appeal to psychoanalysis itself for justification.

In addition, Freud's critique of religion seems to underestimate many human tendencies. First, the religions of the world indicate that human beings are naturally idol-making creatures. Hence, the tendency of people to personify the forces of nature and project their wishes onto reality does not necessarily conflict with any religious worldviews but may only serve to confirm some of their doctrines. Second, Freud suggests that religious beliefs originate in the desire for wish fulfillment. Specifically, humanity wishes to conquer death and completely overcome the forces of nature. Hence, they invented the idea of an all-powerful protector to do so. However, the God of traditional religions – especially the monotheistic traditions of Judaism, Christianity, and Islam – has great expectations of humanity, expectations that are extremely difficult if not impossible to fulfill. But such a God would be more a source of fear and anxiety than comfort and security. That such a God condemns those guilty of moral failure to eternal torment in Hell makes the idea of such a being even more terrifying. Why would anyone *want* to believe in such a thing? Lastly, even if Freud successfully uncovered the origin of human religious beliefs, that does not mean that such beliefs are false. Moreover, the limitations of Freud's developmental theory would extend to his critique of religion as well. Would the origin of religion be the same for all people universally? And if all people universally believe in a transcendent reality, is that not a signal that there is something more than only the physical world? Maybe or maybe not. But Freud's critique alone certainly fails to provide justification for rejecting religion.

The hypothetical criticism of Freud's developmental theory and its anticipated rejoinder in the previous paragraph illustrate one vulnerability of Freud's theory to idols of the cave. Freud generalized his theory to the entire population without a significant sample of patients on which to base his conclusion. In fact, it is believed that Freud fabricated many of his reports, ascribing dreams and symptoms he experienced himself to imaginary clients. Moreover, Freud originally intended to become a physician and operated on the assumptions of biological naturalism. It would not be an exaggeration to suggest that Freud intended ultimately to locate the Id, Ego, and Super-Ego within the human brain. Even though Freud's theory contains many brilliant insights that no doubt accurately describes a sizeable portion of humanity, Freudians cannot ignore the fact that a literal reading and application of the theory simply amounts to a hasty generalization of unsubstantiated claims.

While Freud himself does not necessarily misuse any terms and while he does not seem to write with the intention of evoking emotion, he stipulates terms to describe aspects of the personality that may not, in fact, exist. The only tangible evidence for the existence of an unconscious portion of the mind consists of dreams and slips of the tongue. But labeling a part of the mind as unconscious leads to the belief that there is such a thing. People have a natural tendency to link words with objects. If there is no obvious corresponding object, usually the imagination will make up one for it! In short, many people became enticed by Freud's theory without knowing with any certainty if its foundations had a concrete basis. Is there really an unconscious part of the mind? Is there really such a *thing* as the Id? Is there really such a *thing* as the Super-Ego? There may be, but not because one author expressed them in words.

Finally, while Freud clearly made several original and instrumental contributions, the "theater" to which the theory seems most vulnerable is naturalism, more specifically, Darwin's theory of evolution. During Freud's life, many intellectuals popularized Darwin's theory, some even embracing it as a fact. Much of Freud's theory rests on the assumption that human beings are highly evolved animals that inherited most of their instincts from distant animal ancestors. If Darwin's theory of evolution is erroneous, then what accounts for the content of the Id?

While a thorough critique of evolution cannot be pursued here, the existence of irreducibly complex organisms such as bacterial flagella and events in the earth's history such as the Cambrian explosion suggest that the step-by-step linear progression implied by Darwinian evolution stands in need of revision. The fine-tuning of life on Earth, furthermore, suggests that the existence of intelligent life could not happen by accident, but implies an intelligent agent who designed our cosmos to bring forth life. If such a being existed, it would not only undermine the evolutionary basis for Freud's psychoanalysis, but his critique of religion as well.

The viability of Freud's theory also depends on the strength of the other philosophical systems from which he borrowed, such as Schopenhauer's idealism, Epicureanism, and causal determinism. Causal determinism is an interesting case for two reasons. First, the principles of quantum mechanics cast a dubious light on the doctrine. Particles at the sub-atomic level seem to behave in unpredictable patterns, which makes it even less likely that mental phenomena are physically determined, that is, if the basis of the mind is the brain, which may not be the case. Second, Freud must allow some room for free will, since the point of his theory is to provide a foundation for therapy to eliminate neuroses. If it is possible to change a person's behavior, then change itself must be possible, which means that not everything is totally determined.

Not only did Freud's thought give birth to an influential branch of psychology, but many of his successors, such as Wilhelm Reich, became part of the Frankfurt School and contributed to the intellectual trends that emerged from Marx, the intellectual giant of the previous chapter. One important parallel between Freud and Marx, in addition to the apparent influence of German philosophy on both, is that they intended to produce scientific accounts of human nature. The thinkers who are the subject of the final chapter – the *existentialists* – will find this approach to be thoroughly incompatible with human nature.

Work Sheets

1. Which two German idealists do you find more appealing and why: Hegel or Schopenhauer?

2. In addition to Darwin and Freud, find at least one other historical figure who reflects Schopenhauer's influence.

3. Discuss how Freud's theory reflects the ideas of at least three of the following: Schopenhauer, Darwin, Feuerbach, Epicurus, Empedocles, or Plato.

4. Did Freud miss any instincts in constructing his theory? That is, do more instincts drive human behavior than only *Eros* and *Thanatos*?

5. Try to remember a dream that you had recently. Distinguish between the *manifest* and *latent* content of your dream. What do you think it means?

6. Observe any three of your own personal behaviors and indicate how each one might reflect a different defense mechanism discussed in this chapter.

7. Research and explain the meaning of the following defense mechanisms: introjection, reaction formation, regression, suppression, and intellectualization.

8. Do you agree with Freud's critique of religion? Why or why not?

9. Watch the first season of Showtime's *Dexter*, especially episodes 1, 8, 10, and 12. Explain how at least three aspects of Freud's theory apply to this series.

10. Find a film or novel and analyze the events in terms of Freud's theory.

Existentialism—Kierkegaard Or Nietzsche? Worship God Or Become Him?

Theoretical inquiry usually proceeds from prior assumptions. For instance, an author cannot construct a *theory of human nature* unless that author first assumes that human beings share a common nature and that such a common nature can be discovered and articulated to others. Suppose also that an author's theory relies heavily on naturalism and the idea that human beings evolved from apes, which in turn evolved from other organisms, all of which sprouted from a common ancestor at some indefinite time in the remote past. The construction of such a theory depends on many additional assumptions about evolutionary biology, the nature of the cosmos, and the amount of time that such things existed. The assumptions making up the theory in question subsume every individual human under its determinations, in which human beings are highly evolved apes. The ends of human beings are determined by that nature and their survival depends on meeting those ends. A second author might propose a different theory, one that relies more on the assumption of the doctrines of a specific religion, such as Christianity. According to this view, God made human beings in his own image, placing them in a privileged position in the scheme of creation with dominion over Earth and other animals. Expecting humanity to augment their talents properly, expecting much from those to whom much is given, God punishes humanity when they fail to meet such expectations. Human beings, thus, are natural creatures with a divine spirit. God, thus, dictates the ends of humanity in terms of the human essence he issues to humanity.

In either case, whether one adopts a naturalistic or a religious theory, the *essence* of humanity precedes the individual. *Essentialism* is the idea that the individual is secondary to the essence, concept, or system that defines him or her. Every theory addressed so far embraced essentialism to varying degrees. For Plato, the universal, transcendent, eternal forms determine what human beings are and how they ought to live. For Aristotle, the nature of a being depends on the type of "soul" that a thing has, which in turn dictates the being's purpose. Human beings have the rational soul, where reason lends itself as the distinctive human faculty. Thus, the final cause of human beings, eudaimonia, must include the augmentation of reason in the life of contemplation. For the Christian philosophers, human nature derives from God and human happiness consists in conforming one's will to the will of God. For Descartes, human beings are primarily thinking things and the human body is sharply distinguished from the mind, even though the two interact. One's purpose in life according to Descartes consists in the achievement of absolute certainty such as that afforded in mathematics and geometry. For Hume, human beings are primarily passional creatures that use reason as instrument in their evaluations. The fact that people have natural inclinations to evaluate the world around them justifies the beliefs on which they operate. For Rousseau, human beings are naturally passional, docile, solitary, and frugal creatures easily corrupted by outside influences. Kant recognized the primacy of the distinctively practical aspect of human reason, not only implying the need for reason to dominate but the need to affirm human spirituality, freedom, the existence of God, and the purposive progression of history. The mandate that humanity affirms that their endeavors are not futile precedes the burden of absolute, decisive proof, be it empirical or rational. Marx's inversion of Hegelian idealism retained the principle that reality constantly changes but also affirmed an ultimate destiny of humanity in a communist utopia. Humans are not merely social creatures, but creatures determined by the social and economic conditions into which they are thrown. One's group, economy, or ideology precedes the individual. Lastly, Freud's psychoanalytic theory, while directed primarily toward individuals, begins with assumptions that base human psychology in unconscious instincts inherited from ancestors who walked the Earth eons earlier. One is a product not only of these instincts but of one's past.[1]

In each case, without fail, essence precedes the existence of the individual. The most basic thesis of thinkers affiliated with the mode of thought called *existentialism* is that *existence precedes essence.* Existentialism, thus, is the mode of thought that emphasizes the significance of the individual as a conscious, experiential subject of a life, rather than a subject assigned a specific, universal essence. The individual person cannot be understood properly through any concept or essence. Inevitably, there are aspects of an individual that elude any generalizations and, thus, essentialism vitiates the meaning of concrete individual existence. An individual's subjective experiences resist easy explanation in terms of any one general theory. Apart from one's own consciousness, in fact, all else constitutes an experience of "the Other," the basis for the profound alienation most people feel, especially in the modern world. The progress of science affords humanity many luxuries, but at the expense of our direct unity with nature. Most people understand nature as beyond civilization and a mere object to be investigated. Humans rarely think of themselves as part of the animal kingdom, revealed by the way they often speak, distinguishing humans from animals rather than from *non-human* animals. In addition,

---

[1] I must grant that the theories of Marx, Darwin, and Freud all are predicated on the idea that reality is unstable. Marx views reality as dialectical. Darwin views the species as constantly evolving and struggling to adapt to their environments. Freud's theory assumes Darwinism and views the instincts as constantly shifting. However, in each case, the individual is defined, at any given moment, by some general concept. For Marx, one is defined by the ideology determined by the dominant class of one's regime. For Darwin, one is defined by one's species. For Freud, one's nature is determined by the affect one's past experiences yield on one's unconscious. Even though a regime, a species, or one's personality can change, what does not change is the principle that *the individual is defined by them.*

modern civilization consists of impersonal institutions that dwarf the individuals who are forced to submit to their regulations to sustain the disenchanted comfort of modern life. We enjoy the fruits of the labor of our ancestors, but in reaping what they sowed we lose any sense of connection with the past and our history. Only when a crisis or catastrophe jeopardizes our mundane security and throws us back onto ourselves to feel the dread of the abyss of the possibility of our own non-existence can we fully embrace the meaning of that existence. For this reason, many authors classified as existentialists – such as the 19th century Danish thinker Soren Kierkegaard and one of his 20th century heirs, the German thinker Martin Heidegger – maintain that dread constitutes the most primal human emotion. Known by the more common designation of anxiety, *dread* differs from *fear* in that a specific, concrete object always triggers the latter. The spider on the wall of your bedroom causes you fear. A rabid dog approaching you causes fear. Since concrete objects trigger fear, the removal of the trigger removes the feeling. Removing the spider removes the fear, as does restraining the dog with a leash. Dread lacks any specific object. One might feel dread about the possibility that a lethal spider is in the room. A freshman about to engage in her first year of college may feel dread about the possibility of not performing well academically. A young professional recently thrust into unemployment dreads the possibility that his future may be very bleak. In each case, *possibility* triggers the emotion. Since possibility is not concrete, dread forces on us the nothingness of our existence, the inevitability of non-existence. One is most aware of the meaning of life when one fully confronts the inevitability of one's non-existence, hence, why the presence of death compels people to reveal their true selves.

In addition to the thesis that existence precedes essence, the idea that *meaning has priority over facts* constitutes a second theme of existentialism. Traditional thinkers understood truth in terms of correspondence with facts that are outside of an individual. For instance, my belief that there is a dog in my backyard is true just in case there really is a dog in my backyard and it is false otherwise. When correspondence fails, coherence affords a secondary criterion by which to assess the truth of a belief. For instance, there is no way for me, at this very moment, to verify whether an elephant is tap dancing at Buckingham Palace. However, since I already believe that elephants neither tap dance, nor visit Buckingham Palace regularly, I can reject such a belief, as it is incoherent with other facts. Truth, thus, is usually understood as something that is outside of us, and we must use both observation and reason to discover it. But observations through sense-experience always lead the individual away from the self, and reason can only apply and develop general definitions and concepts. Facts, however, have no meaning without an individual to interpret them. Without individuals to interpret the world, there would be no science, and without science, there would be no medicine, automobiles, planes, central heat, and air conditioning. Moreover, such developments came about through individual interactions with and struggles against the world. The meaning of experience always influences a person more than the facts beyond the individual. A heated discussion with a friend, from a purely factual standpoint, consists merely of sound waves moving in opposite directions causing vibrations. Further-more, often the meaning of what a person says can change based on the way they say it. Much communication between people is non-ver-bal and, thus, it falls on the individual to interpret the meaning of most social exchanges. Secret codes and passwords rely on relations between people for their meaning. From a purely factual standpoint, natural disasters can be described in terms of matter and motion, while the meaning of such events is inextricably linked with the being and emotions of individuals. To a significant extent, even emotions themselves derive from the way a person chooses to interpret the world. Emotions are not merely physical pleasures and pains that are caused by external forces. When a person feels sorrow, the source of the sorrow cannot be separated completely from the feeling of sorrow itself. The way one sees a situation that causes sorrow also justifies the feeling. The loss of a loved one usually impacts those closer to the deceased than those who shared only a tenuous relation with the departed. One would not become angry with another person for breaking a rule unless one interpreted the rule as being important and inviolable. The meaning of stories, in addition, escapes mere factual descriptions. Many stories that are not factual may still be described as *true.* Even if none of the events of the Greek myths happened, they reveal many truths about human nature and human relations. The same may be said about the stories of any religion, as well as about any literary work of fiction. The meaning of a story outweighs its correspondence to any facts, just as truth transcends mere correspondence between belief and the external conditions independent of experience.

A third theme of existentialism is the idea that *freedom is the defining feature of humanity.* If existence precedes essence, then there is no universal human essence. If there is no universal human essence, then every individual must create their own essence. As the 20th century thinker Jean-Paul Sartre wrote, humanity is "condemned to be free." Sartre's use of the term "condemned" seems counterintuitive. Throughout history, people fought, bled, suffered, and died to achieve freedom from tyranny and oppression. Why, then, is it something to which people are "condemned?" Quite simply, freedom is a source of great burden and insecurity to most people. Since freedom forces one to face one's possibilities, it forces one to confront the nothingness of their existence, since there is, in fact, *no thing* that can provide complete guidance. It forces people to consider the possibility of failure in their endeavors. But failure would not be possible if we were not mortal. Hence, freedom forces us to confront the inevitability of death. Most people, thus, would prefer relinquishing their freedom, giving someone else the power to make choices for them. In his classic, *Escape from Freedom,* Erich Fromm insisted that dictators acquire their power only because people fear freedom so much that they would rather live under the conditions of tyranny than make their own choices.[2]

Just as there are two general theories of the universe – the religious and the naturalistic – there are two groups of existential thinkers, those who believe in God and those who do not. Each group traces back to one of the two pioneers of existentialism. The first, the putative father of existentialism, Soren Kierkegaard, epitomizes religious existentialism. The second, the 19th century German philosopher Friedrich Nietzsche, insisted that humanity must, instead of worshipping God, become Gods themselves!

(I) Soren Kierkegaard (1813-1855)

Danish thinker Soren Kierkegaard lived a short but very fruitful life. Like Marx, Kierkegaard took significant inspiration from Hegel, but unlike Marx, Kierkegaard revolted against the Hegelian system. Hegel's system, indeed, provides a grand unified theory of everything . . . ALMOST! Hegel's theory explains everything except the meaning of concrete, *individual* existence. Kierkegaard believed that Hegel lost himself in his own abstractions. Specifically, Kierkegaard wanted to understand the meaning of his own existence. Ironically, Kierkegaard published most of his own works under pseudonyms, such as Johannes De Silentio ("Silent John") or Johannes Climacus ("John the Ladder," or "John the Climber"). Thus, it is difficult to know Kierkegaard's theory of human nature with any certainty. Nonetheless, the central themes in Kierkegaard's writings include anxiety and the problems of meaninglessness and despair in the lives of individuals. The feeling of anxiety forces one to confront the possibility of the

---

[2] For a more detailed introduction to the themes of existentialism see Chapter 24 of Lavine's *From Socrates to Sartre*. See also Chapter 12 of Pojman's *Who Are We?*, which provides a concise thematic overview of existentialism with several important primary passages from the writings of several authors in the tradition, including Kierkegaard, Nietzsche, Sartre, and Camus.

nothingness of one's existence. Anxiety reveals to us the risk of fail-ure, an unpleasant feeling that people wish to escape. But for Kierke-gaard, the burden of freedom and the risks involved with existence must be faced. For the sake of brevity, I will address Kierkegaard's thought directly through Bacon's Idols of the Mind.

Kierkegaard and Bacon's Idols of the Tribe: Kierkegaard suggests that we all suffer from anxiety even if we are not aware of it, because our anx-iety is subjective rather than objective. The most general Idol of the Tribe of humanity, thus, is to try to escape the feeling of anxiety and the possibility that life is meaningless. The reason that we experience such anxiety is that in our experience of the world, we are simultane-ously alienated from it. As Jean-Paul Sartre, one of Kierkegaard's suc-cessors, observed, my awareness of an object is simultaneously an awareness of something that is "not me." Kierkegaard expressed this sentiment in the following passage:

> Cannot consciousness then remain in immediacy? This is a foolish ques-tion, for if it could, no consciousness would exist. If this immediacy be identical with that of an animal, then the problem of consciousness is done away. But what would be the result of this? Man would be an animal, or in other words, he would be *dumb*.[3]

What separates human beings from other animals is that human beings are differentiated from nature, whereas non-human animals have immediate contact with it. For Kierkegaard, speech and lan-guage introduce the obstacle between humanity and nature, but that discussion is better reserved for the section on idols of the market-place. In the current context, the lack of immediacy to which Kierkeg-aard refers consists of a lack of unity with nature and it raises the "possibility of doubt,"[4] specifically, doubt about the meaning of one's

---

[3] *Johannes Climacus, Or, "De omnibus dubitandum est,"* cited in Donald Palmer, *Visions of Human Nature* (Mountain View, CA: Mayfield Publishing Company, 2000), p. 157.

[4] Ibid, in Palmer, p. 158.

existence. The nature of human consciousness implies freedom, since the experience of oneself is always fragmented and incomplete in some way. Generally, there are three ways that one may attempt to escape the basic anxiety of one's existence.

Kierkegaard and Bacon's Idols of the Cave: For Kierkegaard, there are three stages of existence – the *aesthetic*, the *ethical*, and the *religious*. These stages may also be interpreted as separate spheres, or descriptions of three different types of individuals, based on how they attempt to escape the problem of anxiety and find meaning in life. Those who pursue the aesthetic path principally devote their lives to seeking pleasure. In Freudian terms, such people are governed by something akin to the pleasure principle. Since the term "pleasure" designates many different activities and indulgences, the aesthetic life may encompass a wide variety of people. A typical working-class man who simply wishes to work 40 hours per week, pay his bills, watch television, eat his favorite foods, and occasionally have a romantic encounter constitutes one form of the aesthetic life. On the other hand, an aristocratic man who devotes his life only to the cultivation of higher pleasures, such as the finest cuisines, the finest wines, lavish houses, stylish clothes, and occasional visits to a theater or opera house also lives an aesthetic life. Fundamentally, sensualism governs the behavior of each person. To an extent, the lives of such individuals align closely with those of non-human animals, since their unity with nature does not compel them to experience their existence as problematic in any way. In fact, it is entirely possible that aesthetically inclined people never do so either. However, Kierkegaard, like Plato and Aristotle, insists that human life was not built for pleasure alone, for reasons previously entertained. Pleasure is not only temporary, but it is not distinctly human. Moreover, the actual experience of pleasure usually does not match the intensity that one can imagine or anticipate. Hence, if one devotes one's life to pleasure, one will easily become bored. The only way to sustain a life of aestheticism is constantly to seek out different forms of entertainment. In *Either/Or*, an anonymous aesthetician known only as "A" suggests the "rotation method," in which one creates surprise pleasures. For example, if you enjoy football, stop watching a game at half-time. If you become involved with a woman, stay with her for a limited amount of time, such as 6 months, then move on to another. One might also intentionally provoke the indignation of people, such as when a teenager gets a tattoo or exotic piercings only to rebel against his or her parents. The problem with these methods is that they still provide no true satisfaction. One's actions continue to be determined by others since he only reacts to them. Hence, the life of aestheticism is never truly free and can lead only to despair.

While Kierkegaard gives a detailed account of the aesthetic stage of existence in Volume I of *Either/Or*, he devotes Volume II to the *ethical stage.* However, the "either/or" implied by the title is not necessarily a choice between the aesthetic stage of existence and the ethical stage of existence. Rather, it consists in the choice either to entertain good and evil or to exclude such categories completely. Basically, an individual must choose an *ethos* by which to live. An individual must decide to operate under a law that applies both to himself and other human beings. The principles one lives under consist of relationships that come to define the individual, as opposed to the fragmentary existence of the aesthetic life. One might choose to abide by Christian ethics, by which one must love God and one's neighbors as oneself. Or, one might choose to become involved in specific charity organizations. But whatever one chooses, the world thereafter becomes defined by the law under which one lives, hence, leaving very few grey areas. Every situation presents an "either/or" option based on the dictates of one's ethos. In these situations, an individual either succeeds in following the law or fails, which implies that the individual is either "guilty" or "not guilty." Kierkegaard suggested that marriage presents the paradigm of an ethical life, in which a man and a woman have a defining relationship with each other.

The third stage of existence, the *religious life*, like the ethical life, involves a defining relationship, but with God instead of with other human beings. However, the religious life is wholly incompatible with the ethical life, a separate sphere of existence that requires a *leap of faith*. Since the ethical life is determined by one's relations to other people and institutions which themselves are finite and temporary, the ethical individual may confront problems like those faced by aestheticians. Defined by other people, one is never wholly free. Since human beings can have no definite knowledge of God, God can only be the object of *faith*. In *Fear and Trembling*, Kierkegaard uses Abraham's obedience to God as the clearest example of true faith. God commanded Abraham to sacrifice his son, Isaac. Abraham struggles with the decision but resolves to go through with the sacrifice. However, at the very last moment, the angel of God intervenes, insisting that Abraham proved his faith in God. Reflecting on this story, Kierkegaard asks, "Can there be a teleological suspension of the ethical?" That is, can an individual suspend his ethical judgment and defer to the command of a higher power? Ethically, it is wrong to commit murder, but Abraham intended to suspend his knowledge of the moral law in deference to the will of God. Moreover, he did not make his decision dispassionately. His decision represents a true act of religious faith. Thus, Abraham moved beyond the ethical stage to the religious based on his personal relationship with God. Since one cannot have knowledge of God, the religious life involves insecurity, risk, and confronting dread. Isaac's death not only is a viable possibility in the story of Abraham, but Abraham risks losing the one person he loves the most. Obedience to God, thus, gives life its deepest meaning, consisting not merely in dispassionate conformity to laws and rituals, but passionate love for a higher power.

Kierkegaard and Bacon's Idols of the Marketplace: Recall that humanity is differentiated from nature. For Kierkegaard, people can have only mediated or indirect contact with reality. In his view, "That which annuls immediacy is speech."[5] Once a person acquires a language, one's experience of reality becomes classified under the concepts and abstractions denoted by that language. Because concepts are abstracted from reality, they run contrary to it. The introduction of concepts, that is, implies both a distinction between the real and the ideal and opposition between them. The idea of what a person should be opposes one's actual being and forces one to confront the possibility of approximating that ideal, which, removed from reality, may not be achieved. Non-human animals, on the other hand, have no distinction between the ideal and the real. A dog has no conception of his own being and that of an ideal dog, hence, will never languish under the notion that he is not acting as a dog should act. Language, thus, introduces a distinction between what is and what could be, possibility. Hence, it is through language that doubt emerges as well. The more complex language becomes, the more complex one's possibilities become and the more inclined one is to flee from them.

Because language creates a barrier between the individual and immediate contact with reality, it gives rise to misconceptions about reality, the self, and truth. One might believe, for instance, that because one understands the meanings of the words one uses to describe reality, one has uncovered some deep, absolute truth. Truth, however, as Kierkegaard understands it, is a *subjectivity*. While Kierkegaard does not reject objective truth, he denies that truth can be inferred from abstract thought alone. Truth consists in the way one relates to the world through one's relationships. For example, consider again the story of Abraham. Abraham's relationship with God may be called true because of Abraham's personal struggle and experience followed by his leap of faith. Abraham's decision is a totally authentic and free submission to God's will. It was not a decision based on rational principles or rigorous argumentation. In the same sense, an individual who behaves a certain way

---

[5] Ibid, p. 157.

only to incite the anger of others may be called *untrue*, or *inauthentic*, since the decision consists only in a reaction against others and through it, one betrays one's true intentions. One may also be called inauthentic if one too easily acquiesces to the demands of others simply to please them, such as when an adolescent conforms to the standards of his peers to ingratiate himself to a popular in-crowd. Mere knowledge of a system that is removed from reality and the subsequent application of that system in one's thinking, thus, oppose *truth.*

Kierkegaard and Bacon's Idols of the Theater: As the putative father of the existentialist movement, Kierkegaard rejects all past philosophies as adequate to explain the meaning of individual existence. His rejection of the system of Hegel's idealism constitutes his most notorious revolt against one of the philosophical theaters of his time. In fact, Kierkegaard's distinction between the aesthetic and ethical stages and his critique of the life devoted to aestheticism may be applied to Hegel. Recall that Hegel maintained that history is essentially progressive and that every event in history serves the point of that progress. For instance, slavery allows the slave to use the master as a mirror and discover his freedom. Hence, there is no "either/or" in Hegel's conception of reality and, thus, no true freedom. Individuals and communities are all mere cogs in the wheel of the mind of God.

In addition, Kierkegaard had several misgivings with Christianity in his own time. In *An Attack on Christendom*, Kierkegaard argued that the church reduced Christianity merely to empty rituals practiced only as formalities. His critique of Christianity also represents his thesis that truth is a subjectivity, where grasping truth subjectively through an impassioned act of faith deeply influences and shapes how we live. In his *Concluding Unscientific Postscript*, Kierkegaard tells of two men in prayer. One is a church member who lackadaisically prays to God, while the other is a heathen who prays to the idols of a Pagan religion. In Kierkegaard's view, the heathen, ironically, prays to God, whereas the apathetic church member worships an idol. Truth is discovered through the inward struggle by which one attempts to find meaning in the world, rather than in the external cognitive apprehension of facts.

Before transitioning to the thought of Nietzsche, it deserves to be mentioned that Kierkegaard's conception of truth is the source of much controversy, since his definition of truth implies that all internal passions are true. For example, if one passionately worships Satan, then one truly worships God, and is, presumably, better off than the members of any modern Christian church. Moreover, Kierkegaard's description of the leap of faith as a leap into absurdity seems too extreme an exclusion of rationality. Even if Christianity is mysterious and, in many ways, paradoxical, it is not irrational. Some thinkers, however, regard it as one of the most dangerous errors in human history.[6]

(II) Friedrich Nietzsche (1844-1900)

Like Kierkegaard, Nietzsche focused on the problems of concrete, individual existence, emphasized psychological states, and judged all previous philosophical systems – specifically, Platonism, rationalism, and idealism – as inadequate to explain human individuals and properly address their problems. In addition, like Kierkegaard, Nietzsche philosophies consist not merely in resolving intellectual puzzles. Rather philosophies have psychological effects, the power to enhance or weaken one's life, the power to affect one's health. Kierkegaard was correct in claiming that meaning in life always involves insecurity and risk, but the ability to live by one's own morality requires far more courage than blind acceptance of God's will. Thus, Nietzsche rejected Kierkegaard's religious solution to the problem of meaninglessness. On the one hand, such a solution strips humanity of its

---

[6] For alternative introductions to the thought of Kierkegaard, see Chapter 6 of Donald Palmer's *Visions of Human Nature* and Chapter 11 of Sproul's *The Consequences of Ideas*. Each chapter focuses exclusively on the thought of Kierkegaard and is accessible to students with no prior knowledge of his work.

power. More importantly, in the modern world, total surrender to God is impossible, since *God is dead.* However, human beings must now find the courage within themselves to become Gods in a world without God. To understand Nietzsche's prescriptions, the following themes in his work will be addressed: (a) his style; (b) the death of God; (c) the will to power; (d) the three human types – slave, master, and overman; (e) the mission of Zarathustra; and (f) the eternal return of the same.

Nietzsche's Style: Classical thinkers such as Aristotle, Thomas Aquinas, Descartes, Kant, and especially Hegel (and to some extent Plato), attempted to produce systems to explain reality. For Nietzsche, such efforts result in a double problem. First, it is impossible for any one individual to explain ALL reality. Every individual is limited to their own unique experiences and the meaning one attaches to them. Even the application of logic has limits, since the laws of logic can be applied only to those things conceivable by the human mind. To construct a system that explains reality, one must, in effect, stand *outside* of that system to fully comprehend its coherence. But it is impossible to remove oneself fully from the reality of which one is a part, hence, why Nietzsche wrote, "I distrust all systematizers and stay out of their way. The will to a system is a lack of integrity."[7] Second, Nietzsche privileged a Heraclitean view of reality, in which the world as it is known is unstable, perpetually changing. Thus, imposing any kind of system on reality inevitably misrepresents it. Usually, the system produced captures only the perspective shaped by an individual's social and cultural perspective. To produce a system of reality, one must explain not only the present, but the past and future as well. Nonetheless, both can be understood only through the window of the present. Nietzsche expresses this problem where he writes,

---

[7] Friedrich Nietzsche, *Twilight of the Idols*, Richard Polt (Translator) (Indianapolis, IN: Hackett Publishing Company, 1997), Epigram 26, p. 9.

"Looking for beginnings always turns you into a crab. Historians look backwards; they end up *believing* backwards too."[8] The search for a system of reality results in the simplistic reduction of all truth to that system, hence, making all truth simple, which is "doubly a lie."[9] On the one hand, no one can discover all truth. On the other, the shifting nature of reality implies that no truth is simple. Moreover, suppose that one discovered the complete and total truth about reality. That individual would likely experience profound disappointment, recognizing that one could not make reality any better than it is. Every achievement leads to the loss of the thrill of a chase afforded only by the risk of failure and the allure of mystery: "Once and for all, there's a lot that I don't want to know. – Wisdom sets limits even to knowledge."[10]

Instead of creating a system, Nietzsche found himself much more compelled by *how* or *why* beliefs arise. His work, thus, consists primarily of a series of *deflationary* rather than *formal* critiques of traditional ideas. Even though most metaphysical beliefs cannot be refuted decisively, by uncovering their origin, one can at least weaken them. Nietzsche maintained that the source of many beliefs is psychological. Like one of his predecessors, Freud, Nietzsche maintained that human beings are, at bottom, a kind of animal, subject to instincts and drives that keep humanity firmly rooted in the affirmation of life. Thus, he suggests that belief in God and the morality of Christianity associated with it constitutes a profound error on the part of humanity.

The Death of God: "Is man God's mistake, or is God man's?" Nietzsche seems to pose this question rhetorically in Epigram 7 of his *Twilight of the Idols* (hereafter, *Twilight*), seemingly to imply that God is man's

---

[8] Ibid, Epigram 24, p. 8.

[9] Ibid, Epigram 4, p. 5.

[10] Ibid, Epigram 5.

mistake. Nietzsche's most famous critique of religion occurs in the parable of the Madman in *The Gay Science:*

> Have you not heard of that madman who lit a lantern in the bright morning hours, ran to the market place, and cried incessantly: "I seek God! I seek God!" – As many of those who did not believe in God were standing around just then, he provoked much laughter. Has he got lost? asked one. Did he lose his way like a child? asked another. Or is he hiding? Is he afraid of us? Has he gone on a voyage? emigrated? – Thus they yelled and laughed.
>
> The madman jumped into their midst and pierced them with his eyes. "Whither is God?" he cried; "I will tell you. *We have killed him* – you and I. All of us are his murderers. But how did we do this? How could we drink up the sea? Who gave us the sponge to wipe away the entire horizon? What were we doing when we unchained this earth from its sun? Whither is it moving now? Whither are we moving? Away from all suns? Are we not plunging continually? Backward, sideward, forward, in all directions? Is there still any up or down? Are we not straying, as through an infinite nothing? Do we not feel the breath of empty space? Has it not become colder? Is not night continually closing in on us? Do we not need to light lanterns in the morning? Do we hear nothing as yet of the noise of the gravediggers who are burying God? Do we smell nothing as yet of the divine decomposition? Gods, too, decompose. God is dead. God remains dead. And we have killed him.
>
> "How shall we comfort ourselves, the murderers of all murderers? What was holiest and mightiest of all that the world has yet owned has bled to death under our knives: who will wipe this blood off us? What water is there for us to clean ourselves? What festivals of atonement, what sacred games shall we have to invent? Is not the greatness of this deed too great for us? Must we ourselves not become gods simply to appear worthy of it? There has never been a greater deed; and whoever is born after us – for the sake of this deed he will belong to a higher history than all history hitherto."
>
> Here the madman fell silent and looked again at his listeners; and they, too, were silent and stared at him in astonishment. At last he threw his lantern on the ground, and it broke into pieces and went out. "I have come too early," he said then; "my time is not yet. This tremendous event is still on its way, still wandering; it has not yet reached the ears of men. Lightning and thunder require time; the light of the stars requires time; deeds, though

done, still require time to be seen and heard. This deed is still more distant from them than most distant stars – *and yet they have done it themselves*.

It has been related further that on the same day the madman forced his way into several churches and there struck up his *requiem aeternam deo*. Led out and called to account, he is said always to have replied nothing but: "What after all are these churches now if they are not the tombs and sepulchers of God?"[11]

This passage is replete with metaphors that convey Nietzsche's critique of religion, the history of philosophy, and the future of human culture. That the madman in this passage "lit a lantern on a sunny morning" poses a paradox. Why would anyone need a lantern if they have the light of day? The implication is that without God as a natural source of truth to guide humanity, the burden falls on us to light our own way. Moreover, what does it mean to say that we have *killed* God? How can an omnipotent and eternal being die, let alone be killed by mere mortals? Nietzsche seems to intend to convey the hypocrisy of modern culture in which the idea of God no longer plays a vital role. Even if people mouth the perfunctory prayers and lackadaisically perform the rituals of their religion of choice, they do not honestly and genuinely believe in them. Even those who appear to be the most devout of Christians sit through a Sunday mass only half-listening to sermons they likely heard countless times before, planning for the events of the day that will follow. Perhaps they anticipate visiting a local mini mall and purchasing the latest electronic gadget, or maybe they eagerly look forward to next televised sporting event. The Madman makes explicit the death of the belief in the grand illusion of religion. The proof is in their response to the Madman's pronouncement. Their bewilderment at his words may be understood as both apathy and utter lack of understanding of the gravity of the death of God. That the Earth is now "unchained from its sun" means that the

---

[11] Friedrich Nietzsche, *The Gay Science*, in Walter Kaufman (ed.) (New York: Vintage, 1974), pp. 181–182.

basis for reality and the moral compass of humanity now plunges into a vacuum. The death of God implies that reality is devoid of intrinsic value, leaving humanity to impose values on it. Why would people pretend that there is a God? Because they lack the courage to embrace fully the implications of radical independence with which such an affirmation would confront them.

Perhaps there is another solution, as indicated by the Madman after he smashes his lantern on the ground in frustration. All the churches and religious institutions of the world lend themselves as nothing more than the tombs of God, monuments to a relic whose very being would not matter even if it were real. All the masses, Bar Mitzvah's, First Communions, Confirmations, celebrations of Christmas, Easter, and Ramadan serve as nothing more than recurring funerals. Nietzsche deeply embeds irony into the Madman's proclamation through the very title of the parable. He forces us to question just who is truly *mad* – the eccentric individual whose paroxysmal tirade leaves everyone astonished, or the people in the crowd who seem to care less about this cataclysmic event. Nietzsche's parable of the Madman has many parallels with Plato's allegory of the cave except that the disenchantment of modern people leaves them so enervated that they cannot muster the passion to fight against any threats to their security. At least the prisoners of Plato's cave cared about the images on their wall!

But even if the Madman's audience took physical action against them, it would only be to protect themselves from the trauma of their alleged crime. The "murder" of their alleged creator lies buried, deeply repressed, the perpetuation of religion merely a way to wash the proverbial blood from the hands of humanity. Thus, its implications cannot be fully realized, as the Madman indicates when he claims that he has "come too early." Just as many distant stars burn out before their light reaches Earth, many ages will pass before the meaning of the death of God reaches humanity. In that time, they must evolve into something greater. They must become Gods themselves.

The phenomenon of the death of God need not be interpreted as a purely *atheistic* thesis. That is, the parable of the Madman does not necessarily affirm the claim that there is no God. While it is unclear as to whether Nietzsche believed in God, he certainly did not believe that such an idea could be proven or disproven, given his rejection of systematicity. The parable of the Madman, rather, is meant to suggest that even if there is a God, his existence is irrelevant to human life. But why would such a belief emerge in the first place? On the one hand, the idea of an all-powerful protector who will reward his loyal followers is very appealing. But recall that such a belief may be just as much an anti-wish, since most religions promise eternal punishment for even the most trivial of transgressions in addition to placing the burden of autonomy on people to navigate the murky elements of religious doctrines that are open to interpretation. Nietzsche seems to think that psychological strife leads to an attitude of resentment toward life in general, in addition to the desire for a better world. For Nietzsche, this mentality is both dangerous and circular. It is circular because in order to reject the conditions of life, one must at least be alive. One depends on life in denying it. But the danger of this mentality is that it keeps people from fully embracing life.

Like Epicurus, Nietzsche embraced the *finality* of this world and the instability of reality. Historically, the belief in a transcendent world can be justified only through numerous fallacies. First, the reasons often marshaled to establish that this world is illusory often lend more support to its ultimacy. For instance, the fact that a living, breathing organism has unique attributes of its own that fall short of a universal, eternal essence, traditionally, would justify the belief that it is less real than the idea of humanity itself. But the only item that could possess ALL the key attributes of humanity would be an abstraction. Perhaps someone could create a mannequin that had all the features of the entire human race, but such a thing would not be a real person. Hence, not only do the arguments that deny the ultimacy of the natural world confirm its reality, but also serve to undermine the reality of any transcendent realm. Such a realm is thought to be ontologically basic, real in a more fundamental way than any physical reality. Why? Because the physical world always undergoes change, exists in perpetual state of flux. But if something changes, that is proof of its vitality. The only things that never change either are imaginary works of fiction or artifice, such as replays of old movies, old photographs, or statues. What is more real, a mannequin that does not change, or a living human? The fact that this purported transcendent realm cannot change would only be reason for rejecting its reality. The ability to change indicates life and life affords possibility. But resentment toward life not only sparks the desire for something better, but is in fact a mark of decadence, since it consists in the admission of cowardice and the rejection of the burden of independence embraced by the strong. Specifically, the morality of traditional Christianity arises from resentment over the failures and frustrations endured in this life. Thus, it perpetuates and protects what Nietzsche deemed the slave morality, which fails to affirm life and hinders humanity from evolving. But the key to humanity's evolution will consist in the affirmation of both life and *the will to power*.

The Will to Power: Like Schopenhauer, Nietzsche maintained that the *world as will* is the basis of unreality. However, Nietzsche rejected Schopenhauer's distinction between the world as will and the world as idea or representation. The world as will is the world of appearance, and the world of appearance is all that exists. Nietzsche also embraced Darwin's conclusion that human beings evolved from apes. However, he denied that evolution occurs merely through the process of organisms adapting to their surroundings. Organisms strive to overcome or *overpower* their circumstances. Life, thus, is not merely a struggle for existence but a struggle for *power*.

Why would anyone conceive of reality as a manifestation of a universal will? Epigram 18 from *Twilight* conveys Nietzsche's reasoning: "Those who don't know how to put their will into things at least put a *meaning* into them: that is, they have faith that a will is already in things (principles of 'faith').''[12] In short, everyone shares the universal tendency to search for explanations. If an explanation cannot be found, then, usually, one is invented. A priori, everyone believes that there is a *purpose* behind everything, which implies a *will*. Nietzsche does not intend to impose a system of teleology on reality, rather this passage alludes to the universal implicit assumption that a process of willing drives reality. This shared tendency underlies anthropomorphic ascriptions of human characteristics to non-human organisms, including other animals and plants. People countenance the behavior of non-human animals and the processes of nature with terms that imply willing and purposiveness.

The implicit assumption that there is a will behind things coincides with the assumption that all things strive for *power*. People engage in their choice of activities usually to achieve power in some form. Those who are drawn to athletics usually wish to become physically stronger and dominate others. Politics draws those who wish to ascertain positions of authority. Academia affords its practitioners esteem and recognition, with which privileges and influence are concomitant. Virtually everyone wishes to be beautiful, since beauty affords power over others. Any man or woman who yearns to be more physically attractive does not wish so only because such attributes will facilitate the satisfaction of their erotic desires, but because they come with power over others. Everyone wants to please celebrities. But beneath such cordiality is the desire to share in the power such people have over others. Once accepted into the circle of powerful people, you will have some of that power as well. Even the authors of religious texts assume that people are motivated by the desire for power. Eve ate the forbidden fruit because she wanted to be as powerful as God. And Nietzsche points out in Section 51 of *Beyond Good and Evil*, people admire and worship saintly figures throughout history *because of the power* such figures manifest in self-renunciation.

---

[12] See p. 7 in Polt.

Power, thus, is the motive behind everything. As such, the term "will to power" has three aspects. First, will to power refers to *growth in activity*. The growth and maturation of children makes them stronger, wiser, and generally able to exercise greater autonomy, each quality representing a specific kind of power. Strength signifies the development of physical power. Wisdom consists in the combination of knowledge and comprehensive understanding, through which one can change the world around them. Anything that can produce change requires power, in this case, intellectual power. Being autonomous requires one to make decisions for oneself, which demands that one breaks free of old habits and augments one's creativity, shaping one's own destiny, which demands what earlier thinkers called spiritual power. Nietzsche, thus, would later label such people as "Free Spirits" in his *Beyond Good and Evil*. In part, that the will to power expresses creativity and the extension of one's being contrasts with Darwin's conception of survival of the fittest as mere self-preservation. One does not struggle simply to adapt to one's surroundings, rather one struggles to adapt one's surroundings to oneself.

Second, will to power may be understood as *power over others.* These "others" consist of both other people and one's surroundings. There are three kinds of struggles, or three kinds of fights. First, there are physical struggles. Usually, if one merely tries to alter the natural environment, such a struggle would consist in the sort of physical labor expounded by Marx and, to an extent, Locke before him. Contact sports, combat, and various athletic competitions typically reflect physical struggles. In each case, the goal is to win, which requires overcoming an opponent physically. Second, there are intellectual or cognitive struggles which emphasize intelligence and the ability to think. Games such as chess or debates signify such struggles. More generally, rival armies might try to best each other through strategy rather than physical combat. Athena, the Greek goddess of wisdom, often defeated Ares, the God of war in this way. Usually, the procedure for investigating and resolving crimes takes the form of an intellectual struggle between the detectives and the criminals, popularized in dramatic fashion in films classified as psychological thrillers, such as *Seven, Silence of the Lambs*, and *Saw*. Beliefs manifest themselves through actions. That is, people act on what they believe. The ability to change an individual's mind, thus, equates to changing an individual's behavior. Hence, wars can be won on the intellectual front by shifting focus from armed combat to the arena of ideas. The will to power, therefore, lends itself as the foundation for *rationality*. Descartes, the father of both modern philosophy and modern rationalism, intended to erect a worldview and master nature through reason, a motive emanating from the drive for power. Going back even farther in the history of philosophy, Nietzsche suggests that Socrates appealed to so many of the youth of Athens because he discovered a way to make himself seem superior to the authority figures during his time, seeming always to best them in dialogue. People were fascinated by him not because of his immaculate virtue, but because of the allure of his *power*.[13] Finally, there are *spiritual* struggles. A spiritual war may be fought either against others or against oneself. An individual dedicated to reforming social institutions must contend with threats of violence from his opposers. Such an individual surely will struggle with the notion of apostasy, relinquishing the idealistic basis for his initial purpose and giving up altogether. This individual might also face the temptation to stoop to the level of his opponents and become violent himself.

The idea of a spiritual struggle coincides with the third meaning of will to power, *power over oneself.* On the one hand, power over oneself hearkens back to the prescriptions of the classical virtue theorists, specifically to the virtue of moderation. As Plato suggested, the ability to control one's desires consists in spiritual power distinct from

---

[13] See "The Problem of Socrates," in *Twilight*.

reason. And as Aristotle recognized, the path to virtue is not easy, but requires trial, error, effort, time, and experience. One must have the endurance to prevail, which implies the determination of a powerful will. While Nietzsche would not want to be interpreted as a classical virtue theorist, as he suggests that attributes recognized as virtues usually depend on the perspective of one's culture, he would prescribe the goal of overcoming one's limitations. Frequent and continued exposure to difficult tasks chosen for oneself enhances one's power on all fronts. The ability to abandon dogmatic conventions and determine one's own destiny constitutes the power one asserts in a spiritual struggle of self-overcoming. While fear of failure forces the expression of the will to power within oneself into a dormant state, failure itself, Nietzsche implies can make one more powerful, as Epigram 8 of *Twilight* implies, "What does not kill me makes me stronger." A few passages later, Nietzsche implies that simply *having* a goal can make one stronger: "If you have your *why* for life, you can get by with almost any *how*," (Epigram 12).[14]

While everything is driven by the will to power, not everyone is driven to affirm it. Becoming physically stronger takes effort, time, and comes with the risk of failure and humiliation. The more traveled road seems to be the one by which many flee from such prospects, especially since failure is more common than success. Basically, there are people who join the herd, rule over the herd, or transcend humanity altogether, or, slaves, masters, and overmen, respectively.

Three Human Types – Slaves, Masters, and Overmen:[15] The idea that Nietzsche distinguishes human types implies a paradox, since he may be classified as an existentialist and, thus, would deny universal human essences, except for the will to power which drives all things

---

[14] See p. 6 in Polt.

[15] For a more detailed discussion of Nietzsche's classification of these types, see John Richardson's *Nietzsche's System* (New York: Oxford University Press, 1996). It is best to approach this work after sampling Nietzsche's corpus in addition to some rudimentary secondary literature on the subject.

and implies that it is always possible for one to change one's circumstances. Moreover, each type is linked with Nietzsche's critique of morality and religion. Nietzsche suggested that God is irrelevant to modern culture and that it is the protector of a morality fit only for *slaves*. The desire for security motivates those individuals classified as slaves. Such individuals prefer to join the "herd" and conform to the behavior and standards of others rather than think for themselves. It is easier to follow the pack than to risk failure by breaking free from it. However, to live among sheep, one must be comfortable with one's mediocrity. Hence, one must embrace a mantra that simultaneously neutralizes the pain of one's failure to thrive while elevating one's station in life. The morality of the herd, therefore, privileges the idea that all humans are equal and the virtue of humility. Historically, Christianity succeeded by protecting this morality by fueling the mentality of resentment in addition to a dichotomy between absolute good and evil. Key ideas of Christianity include the Beatitudes from Christ's Sermon on the Mount, such as "Blessed are the *meek*, for they shall inherit the earth" and "Blessed are the poor in spirit, for they will be called the children of God." God not only loves all people equally and rewards those who suffer but reviles and punishes those who thrive – the *Masters*. But the celebration of humility only serves to rationalize one's resentment of those who are stronger: "A worm squirms when it's stepped on. That's prudent. In that way it reduces the probability of being stepped on again. In the language of morality: *humility*."[16]

The *masters* reflect nobility, privilege, and class. Masters consist of the beautiful, the wealthy, and the esteemed. More generally, masters are *leaders*. There are people who act from their own initiative and those who either cannot or will not act unless they are ordered to do so. Masters not only act of their own accord but usually *give* the orders. Typically, masters do not concern themselves with the opinions of

---

[16] *Twilight*, Epigram 31, p. 9, in Polt.

others. Moreover, masters are inclined to expose themselves to difficult challenges that strengthen their will to power. Ironically, they feel pity and compassion for the slaves, hence, care for them. Whereas slaves tend to be followers, masters tend to be leaders. Furthermore, to be a master, an individual must be born a master, born of privilege. Nonetheless, the morality of Christianity prevailed historically as a way for the slaves to exact revenge against the masters.

In *Beyond Good and Evil*, Nietzsche suggests that all civilized forms of morality typically ignore individual differences by generalizing to all people. Herds of humans feel the instinct for obedience at the expense of the "art of commanding." Nonetheless, the construction of civilization required the need of aggressive, strong, and independent individuals who could lead the herd against the unmitigated forces of nature as well as against threats posed by other humans. However, once the structure of society is fixed, its preservation demands the suppression of the courage and creative ingenuity of the individuals that made civilization possible. Instead, the opposite virtues are extolled and rewarded, sedating citizens in a way that not only cultivates the herd mentality of submissiveness and conformity but makes people *desire* it. Christianity helps to sustain the herd instinct epitomized by the slave type by privileging equality over magnificence. In addition, to help contend with the frustrations of daily life, we are all promised eternal reward in a transcendent world to which our spirits will migrate at the end of our existence in this life.[17]

Nietzsche, however, suggests that there is much hope for humanity. Throughout history, the actions of many gifted *Übermenschen*, "over-men," substantially benefited humanity.[18] Such people display extreme *dialectical courage*[19] not only by resisting and overcoming

---

[17] See Sections 197–202 of *Beyond Good and Evil*, Chapter 5, "The Natural History of Morality."

[18] This term may also be translated as "super men," but I chose a different rendering to deflect attention from the famous comic book character who does not quite reflect the meaning of Nietzsche's term.

[19] See Sproul.

dominant paradigms, regimes, and the instinct to conform and obey, but by overcoming *themselves* as well. An *ubermensch*, thus, is neither a slave nor a master. Obviously, since such individuals resist the herd instinct, no overman is a slave. But why are they not masters? For at least two reasons. First, masters typically inherit their privilege or status. One is born beautiful, an heir to a wealthy empire, or perhaps has the right connections. Second, and more importantly, the master type usually will operate within a pre-existing system or paradigm. Masters typically do not attempt to transcend the systems of which they are a part. Moreover, even many people born of privilege display a slave mentality and, thus, are not true masters. Many wealthy youths simply obey the dictates of their parents. Even more frequently, Aristocrats snipe and quarrel with each other and attempt exact revenge on each other for trivial reasons, and often do so in passive-aggressive ways. The character Patrick Bateman of *American Psycho* reflects such an individual, who fantasizes about murdering his colleagues if they happen to possess fancier business cards than he. Another example is the iconic Francis J. Underwood of *House of Cards.* Majority whip of the House of Representatives, Underwood is unceremoniously passed over for appointment to the office of Secretary of State. Hence, he exacts an intricate revenge plot on all who contributed to the decision, eventually becoming President of the United States himself. Such a person should easily be classified as an overman, or at least as a master, right? Not necessarily. Underwood's motivation seems to emanate strictly from revenge. His actions are reactions to other people, almost as though there exists an invisible puppeteer pulling his strings. Nietzsche reflects in Epigram 14 of *Twilight*, "What? You're searching? You'd like to multiply yourself ten times, a hundred times? You're looking for followers? – Look for *zeros!*"[20]

Overmen do not inherit their status. Rather, they decide what they will be and become it. Overmen neither follow the rules of others, nor

---

[20] See p. 7, in Polt.

do they issue directives decided by others. Rather, overmen create their own rules. They construct their own morality and universalize it for everyone. Overmen are truly exceptional individuals, although they are not necessarily wealthy or famous. Often it is difficult to know what constitutes an overman, since it is difficult to discern an individual's motivations. Candidates for the term would include Alexander the Great, Napoleon, George Washington, Bruce Lee, and Barack Obama, among others. Recall that the Madman believed that he delivered his message too early, that humanity itself requires time to evolve before they can understand the gravity of the death of God. In that time, just as man evolved from apes, man must now evolve into overman. Nietzsche provides his own example of an overman through the character of Zarathustra, based on the Persian prophet.

The Mission of Zarathustra – The Revaluation of Values: In Epigram 3 of *Twilight*, Nietzsche wrote, "To live alone one has to be a beast or a god – says Aristotle. But there's a third case: one has to be both – a *philosopher*."[21] In *Thus Spoke Zarathustra*, the titular characters' favorite pets are the snake and the eagle. The character of Zarathustra represents the unity of these two contrary creatures. The first, a snake, is the beast that crawls on the ground closely tethered to the Earth. The second, an eagle, represents a transcendent figure that soars above the earth. Zarathustra, the combination of the two, represents a figure who transcends the Earth while remaining part of it. He represents the evolution of man into overman.

Why did Nietzsche choose Zarathustra as his spokesperson? The historical Zarathustra was a Persian prophet (for the Greeks, Zoroaster) and is important for Nietzsche because he originally established that the central struggle in human life was between two absolutely distinct principles, good and evil, which Nietzsche interpreted in Christian terms as selflessness and benevolence on the one hand and egoism and

---

[21] See p. 5, in Polt.

self-interest on the other. Nietzsche tells us that Zarathustra "created this fateful error of morality." Thus, the burden falls on Zarathustra to first recognize the consequences of this error and then deliver the message that humanity can now live freed from the picture of absolute dualism, but still without primitive moral anarchy or slavish complacency. Zarathustra, thus, is a prophet, who encourages modern Christians to accept their failings and pursue a new way of life.

This new way of life Nietzsche refers to as a total *revaluation of values*. He does not call for a new *system* of morality, but rather for a revolt against the slave morality, the pinnacle of which is Christianity, and exposure of life as nothing but will to power. A key example occurs when Zarathustra encounters a shepherd under attack from a serpent crawling into his mouth. Zarathustra compels the shepherd simply to bite off the creature's head. Traditionally, shepherds are associated with Christianity, specifically with Christ himself, whereas the serpent represents an incarnation of Satan himself. It is possible to interpret this scene from *Zarathustra* as reversing traditional Christian symbolism, in which the serpent represents Christianity, which must be overcome by the shepherd by an aggressive and violent act of will. In addition, Nietzsche calls back to another key scene from *Zarathustra* in Epigram 21 of *Twilight*: "To get into all kinds of situations where no fake virtues are allowed, where instead, like the tightrope walker on his rope, you either slip or you stand, or you get away."[22] This passage refers to a scene in which the titular Zarathustra leaps over the head of a tightrope walker who then falls to the ground and dies. As the man lays dying, Zarathustra thanks him, for he served the purpose of making Zarathustra stronger.[23]

---

[22] See p. 8, in Polt.

[23] To consult the primary source passages of *Thus Spoke Zarathustra* referred to here, see David P. Barash's *Ideas of Human Nature* (Pearson, 1998) pp. 191–196. The selections are taken from Section II of the work. It can be read in its entirety in *The Portable Nietzsche* (Walter Kaufman, Trans.) (New York: Viking Press, 1954). For a thorough overview of the work, see Robert Pippin's "Nietzsche: *Thus Spoke Zarathustra*," in Pippin (Ed.), *Introductions to Nietzsche*, pp. 152–177.

The Eternal Return of the Same: Briefly, Nietzsche's conception of the eternal return of the same may be understood in terms of three philosophical enterprises – metaphysics, epistemology, and ethics. Metaphysically, the eternal return of the same may be understood as an eternal recycling of world events, in which time constitutes an infinite circle. This idea overlaps with the Hindu notion of reincarnation, except that the religious doctrine assumes a forward trajectory of time in which an individual will be reborn into a different life. Moreover, the conditions of that life reflect the work of Karma, in which one is rewarded or punished in some way. Nietzsche's metaphysical conception of the eternal return stipulates that everything that has happened will happen again, regardless of one's conduct. History, thus, is doomed to repeat itself. From the perspective of modern science, specifically the laws of thermodynamics, physical reality unfolds to its limits and then collapses back into itself. Perhaps the metaphysical phenomenon of the eternal return can account for déjà vu.

Epistemologically, virtually everyone embraces the eternal return, either implicitly or explicitly. Recall Hume's critique of causality, in which causal laws consist of inductive generalizations about the future based on past experiences. Such an inclination has its source in the implicit assumption that the past will repeat itself. The same assumptions often are made about the behavior of people that the best indicator of future behavior is past behavior.

Ethically, the idea of the eternal return of the same lends itself as a diagnostic of nihilism. Generally, a nihilist is an individual who believes that life, existence, has no discernible, intrinsic meaning or value. Recall, however, Nietzsche's prescription of life affirmation and the revolt against the slave morality of Christianity and the desire for a better world. For Nietzsche, the desire for a better world fails to recognize the value of life and the superior instincts that keep humanity rooted to reality as the will to power. Thus, if an individual can affirm the eternal recurrence of the events of history and one's own life, then such an individual is not a nihilist. Nietzsche's proposal of the eternal return as a test for nihilism runs parallel to Albert Camus's reflection on the Myth of Sisyphus, a figure in Greek mythology chained to a boulder and condemned eternally to roll it up a hill. Each time Sisyphus came close to the very top of the hill, he would fall to the bottom. Using Sisyphus as a metaphor for human life, Camus insists that we must imagine Sisyphus happy, so long as he can embrace the absurdity of his situation and find meaning in what he does. If humanity can embrace the absurdity of life, then they can create their own meaning and find value in even the most mundane activities. People engage in their favorite activities many times over, whether those activities include watching their favorite movies or television shows, eating their favorite foods, vacationing at their favorite resorts, reading their favorite novels, listening to their favorite songs, taking long walks along their favorite routes, or making love. All things have meaning, but all instances of meaning vary depending on the individual. Once meaning is discovered, life can be affirmed.

Nietzsche and Bacon's Idols of the Mind: One of his last works, Nietzsche intended *Twilight of the Idols* to be an introduction to his thought. Many of the passages referred to above come from the first part of this work, "Epigrams and Arrows," each of which alludes to a prevalent theme in Nietzsche's eclectic and seemingly anti-systematic body of writings. But his inclusion of the word "Idol" in the title is curious. While it does not appear that Nietzsche intended to make any direct references to Bacon, his work directly refers to the play of his associate Richard Wagner, *Twilight of the Gods.* Wagner based his opera on Norse mythology, in which even gods face their death. After a flood submerges the world, it will be reborn out of a few survivors. Nietzsche's pun indicates that the impending "twilight" is of "false gods," hence, the diminutive "götzen" in Nietzsche's title. The subtitle of the book is "How to philosophize with a hammer." In the preface,

Nietzsche indicates that he intends to use his hammer as a "tuning fork" to assess the "eternal idols" under consideration and the "false gods" of Western philosophy.[24] Hence, like Bacon, Nietzsche aimed to diagnose the errors of the history of thought.

Nietzsche and Bacon's Idols of the Tribe: Nietzsche devotes considerable attention to idols of the tribe because emphasizes the psychological origins of beliefs. His critique of religion, morality, and previous philosophies all suggest that Nietzsche had a deeper concern with idols of the tribe than even Bacon himself. Nietzsche's proposal for the exposure of life as primarily will to power may afford a more efficacious prescription for the avoidance of such errors than Bacon, since Nietzsche insists that once humanity embraces the will to power, humans can evolve. In control of their own destiny, humanity can create an entirely new tribe of beings less susceptible to the resentments and desire for security on which traditional morality, which Nietzsche regards as the most profound error, is based. However, in his attempt to deflate traditional ideas and philosophical systems through exposing their psychological origins, the same criticism may be applied to Nietzsche himself. Perhaps his assault on the history of thought had its source in Nietzsche's own resentments. Furthermore, if all prior systems of thought can be undermined once it is shown that they are perspectival, then so can that of Nietzsche. Granted, it is for this reason that he avoided systematizing his own thought, but he certainly wrote as though he discovered universal truth about humanity, especially when he describes the origins of traditional morality and religion in human history. Even scientific theories such as the theory of evolution that purport to explain human origins involve at least a degree of speculation. Are Nietzsche's reflections on history an exception to the rule? Lastly, perhaps, like Freud after him,

---

[24] See Tracy Strong, "Introduction to *Twilight of the Idols*," in Polt, pp. vii–xxviii. See also Aaron Ridley's "Nietzsche: The Anti-Christ, Ecce Homo, Twilight of the Idols," in Robert Pippin (Ed.), *Introductions to Nietzsche* (New York: Cambridge University Press, 2012), pp. 215–239.

Nietzsche misunderstood Christianity. While many people embrace religion due to an infantile desire for security, Christianity demands that people take risks and make good on the talents God gave them. Hence, it does not merely offer security but rewards those who earn it by bearing the burden of freedom.

Nietzsche and Bacon's Idols of the Cave: Nietzsche's distinction between slaves, masters, and overmen, coupled with his psychological analyses, reflect his concern with idols of the cave. What a person believes reflects specific motivations, but all motivations have the will to power as their foundation. Everyone, in some way, wishes to become more powerful. The slaves resent those with true power, so construct an imaginary, transcendent world in which they will be the heroes and their oppressors will be punished. The masters wish to keep their power and reflect the vantage point of privileged status. Many, however, wish to legitimize themselves by carving out their own niche. Nonetheless, most attempts to do are *reactive*, a response to some perceived affront or threat. However, the prescription to become an overman constitutes the only viable way to unshackle oneself completely from idols of the cave, since overmen must overcome themselves and introduce a totally new perspective on reality. In his own way, however, Nietzsche's reflections on the overman may represent everything that he wished he could become. Perhaps Nietzsche viewed himself as a slave. Moreover, his use of the idea of the eternal return as a diagnostic for nihilism may lead one only to indulge their own idiosyncrasies, even those that are self-destructive. Many people who may be described as slaves seem content in their slavery and, thus, would will it to eternity. Paradoxically, if the overman must constantly evolve and expose himself to new struggles, then does not such a mentality *fail to affirm life*? The diagnosis that humanity's greatest obstacle is the slave morality for which the resolution is the affirmation of life and the construction of one's own code seems to entail that no one can will everything and anything to eternity. And if some things should not be willed to eternity, then there must be a way to distinguish those things worth willing from those that are not. But then, some things would have absolute value, which Nietzsche wishes to deny.

Nietzsche and Bacon's Idols of the Marketplace: The most discernible way that Nietzsche addresses himself to idols of the marketplace is through his critique of traditional morality. Nietzsche suggests that the use of terms such as "good," "evil," "right," and "wrong" all countenance the drive for power and feelings of pleasure and pain. Language ushers in the illusion of moral absolutes and, thus, has the potential to preserve the life-denying mentality. Nietzsche understood the power of language, hence why he aimed to uncover their instinctive origin. If something is "good," it causes one pleasure, whereas something is "bad" if it evokes pain in some way. Moreover, those experiences that create in us a feeling of power usually evoke the most pleasure, whereas those that instill a sense of weakness are accompanied by pain. It may be said that the inauguration of the evolution of humanity into a race of overmen begins when "good" and "evil" are replaced with "power" and "weakness." However, Nietzsche himself chooses terms intended to elicit strong emotional responses from his readers. Nietzsche's suggestion that most modern people are slaves comparable to sheep that merely obey the herd, thus, functions as a kind of rhetorical device to motivate action. The same may be said about his condemnation of the decadence of a "life-denying mentality." Moreover, Nietzsche's terminology introduces ideas that are subject to the same criticisms he levies against morality and religion. Merely because one uses the term "overman" does not mean that there can be any such thing. Merely because he reifies the will to power does not mean that everything ultimately reduces to this elusive, mysterious force.

Nietzsche and Bacon's Idols of the Theater: Like Kierkegaard and other thinkers who may be classified as existentialists, Nietzsche rejects all previous philosophies as inadequate to address the problems of individual existence. Nietzsche's rejection of systematic philosophy along with traditional morality and religion reflect his most prevalent and incisive indictment against idols of the theater in the history of thought. For Nietzsche, Christianity is the most dangerous "theater." Nietzsche, however, locates the origin of Christianity within the thought of Plato, judging that Christianity is merely Platonism for the masses. In a key section of *Twilight* titled "How the True World Finally Became a Fiction," Nietzsche traces the development of Platonism into Christianity, followed by the latter's subsequent permutations. This section of *Twilight* represents Nietzsche's summary of the history of the idea of a true, or transcendent world. In short, Plato suggested that the true world can only be achieved by the wise. Christianity does away with the esoteric elitism implied by Platonism and instead suggests that the true world can be achieved only by those who repent of their sins. Kant's philosophy represents the next great step, in which the true world is indemonstrable, but must be postulated for the sake of morality. Positivism represents the fourth step in this process, in which the true world cannot be verified empirically. Thus, we cannot speak about it. Next, the stage of the "New Horizon" emerges in which the idea of the true world becomes metaphysically superfluous, at which point the era of Zarathustra comes to fruition, in which the true world may be recognized as a complete fiction and we can open ourselves to new possibilities.

Since Nietzsche suggested that everyone must create their own worldview and universalize it for all others, his prescription is that each of us creates and lives by our own theater. Moreover, his conception of the eternal return further suggests that each theater consists of perpetual reruns! Despite his critique and rejection of previous systems of thought, he relies heavily on at least three. First, his conception of the will to power borrows heavily from Schopenhauer, even though he rejects the distinction between the world of appearance and the world as will. Second, he clearly embraced part of Darwin's explanation of human origins, the idea that modern humans evolved from apes, although he disagreed with Darwin's linear conception of natural selection. More generally, Nietzsche, like most of his predecessors, privileges the idea that reality is unstable, constantly in flux, which traces back to Heraclitus and naturally leads us to the end of our journey.

Before closing this final chapter, it is worth mentioning that the writings of Kierkegaard and Nietzsche inspired many others now classified as existentialists. Those who continue the theistic trend consist of authors such as Martin Buber, Simone De Beauvoir, and Paul Tillich. Those who continue the atheistic trend consist of Jean-Paul Sartre and Albert Camus. One especially important thinker associated with this tradition is the German philosopher Martin Heidegger. While he claimed to be agnostic, his thought is certainly compatible with theism. But the point of existentialism is that it is up to the individual to choose how to live, just as it is up to the reader to decide to pursue these ideas further.

Chapter 10 Worksheets

1. Find an example from your personal life, history, or any medium of fiction in which the commitment to some form of *essentialism* led to harmful results.

2. Give an example of a story that is not factual but still demonstrates fundamental truth or truths about reality.

3. Explain how Kierkegaard's claim that truth is a "subjectivity" is compatible with the idea of truth as both correspondence to and coherence with reality.

4. Do you believe that the aesthetic, the ethical, and the religious constant different stages of existence that everyone must pass through, or independent spheres of existence each tailored specifically to different types of people?

5. Compare and contrast Kierkegaard's conception of the aesthetic, the ethical, and the religious with Plato's faculties of the soul – reason, spirit, and appetite.

6. Compare and contrast Kierkegaard's conception of the religious life with Kant's claim that we must postulate the existence of God for the sake of morality.

7. Does Nietzsche's conception of the death of God imply that God is necessary for there to be a universal and absolute system of morality? Why or why not?

8. Find at least three examples of activities from your own observations that may be interpreted as manifestations of the will to power.

9. Find an example of what you believe Nietzsche would consider to be a Slave, a Master, and an Overman from your personal experience, history, literature, or any medium of entertainment.

10. Compare and contrast Nietzsche's conception of Slaves, Masters, and Overmen with Plato's three classes of the ideal city.

11. Compare and contrast Nietzsche's Zarathustra with Socrates and Jesus Christ.

12. Explain how Nietzsche's concept of the eternal return of the same applies to at least three of the following areas: philosophy, science, literature, art, theater, history, music, or popular culture.

Finding Common Ground

The end of our journey brings us back to the beginning, where I suggested that one of the difficulties with the study of any subject, including theories of human nature, is not there are not enough theories but that there are so many. My aim, thus, is not to add a new theory but rather to find some common ground between those examined here. While each thinker surveyed had a unique theory of human nature and addressed Bacon's idols of the mind in a distinctive way, each theory in some way reflects the influence of a central thinker—*Heraclitus*. Recall that the two key principles of Heraclitus's thought are (1) the instability of reality, which is constantly in a state of flux, and (2) war, or conflict, is the father of all things, since change occurs between contraries.

Plato tried to establish a basis for permanence despite the flux of the physical world, hence, the transcendent realm of forms. Plato's theory, thus, may be understood as a synthesis of the ideas of both Heraclitus and Parmenides. Nonetheless, the former applies to Plato's theory in the following ways. First, Plato's identification of the faculties of the soul demanded the search for conflict, since conflict implies multiple parts. Second, Plato's allegory of the cave carries the moral that people should resist a dominant paradigm in order to discover ultimate reality. Third, and more generally, Plato's use of dialogue to convey his ideas suggests that the process of dialectic between two characters leads to truth.

Aristotle, like Plato, recognized the importance of both Heraclitus and Parmenides. Since Aristotle tried to ground reality in natural substances, though, his thought seems more to reflect the influence of Heraclitus.

Even though Aristotle identified the Prime Mover as an eternal source of motion, the principle that everything is constantly in motion led him to such an idea. Moreover, Aristotle's account of the human soul emphasizes the unity of matter and form, which may be separated in thought but not in reality. However, the clearest Heraclitean influence on Aristotle appears in his account of virtue and happiness. The process by which one acquires virtue is long and difficult, requiring a lifetime of trial and error in which one tries to find the mean by facing numerous tumultuous situations. Happiness requires virtue, and virtue requires conflict.

Christianity demands that its followers struggle to overcome the temptations of the world. Jacob's struggle against the angel of God led to the creation of the name Israel. Abraham struggled with God's command to sacrifice Isaac. Moses led the Israelites out of captivity against the world's strongest empire in his time. Once freed, the Israelites faced much uncertainty and doubt. Christ had to face the temptations of Satan in the desert and subsequently endured death on the cross so that humanity could be saved. His resurrection shows that without death there can be no life. The teachings of Christ show that ultimate salvation involves insecurity and risk, since God gives talents to everyone without explicit and clear instructions about how to use them. Later Christian philosophers emphasized the incompleteness of humanity. Augustine's description of the great chain of being implies that the finitude of humanity is a kind of evil, since evil is the absence of good. Nonetheless, it is through humanity's awareness of its own finitude that leads us to the infinite, God. Moreover, Augustine understood that God would allow evil in the world because it is the risk God takes in making humans free, and a world with freedom is better than a world without it. Satan, thus, is a fundamental part of God's plan, since he provides the temptations for humans to overcome. Aquinas, too, recognized that humanity's knowledge of God is incomplete and must be mediated through nature or scripture.

Nonetheless, God gave humanity the capacity of natural reason so that they can discover their purpose.

The Cartesian revolution in philosophy began with a rebellion against accepted Christian modes of thought that dominated the Western world for centuries. Using Descartes' method of doubt forces the thinker to cast off the habitual shackles of one's thought and create one's belief-system anew from its very foundations. In his use of this method, Descartes discovered the importance of free will, the primacy of thought, and the distinction and relationship between the mind and the body. That Galileo came under suspicion and spent the remainder of his life under house arrest due to the way he espoused his discoveries about the cosmos establishes the dangers Descartes faced during his time.

Like other thinkers in the modern tradition, Hume's thought developed during a time in which modern science began to replace religion. That Hume published his work long after Newton's discovery of the universal law of gravity and mechanics means that he faced less opposition than the likes of Galileo and Descartes. But it is Hume's bifurcation of the human soul that most reflects the influence of Heraclitus. Recall that Hume described reason as the "slave of the passions," reversing the classical model in which passion must obey the dictates of reason. That only passion can motivate humanity indicates the need for a "gross earthy mixture." Our interactions with the world give rise principles and our passions give rise to morals and the justifications we need to navigate reality. Hume's critique of personal identity also establishes his recognition of the flux of sense-perception and that humanity is forever changing. It is no surprise, thus, that he became an early proponent of pre-Darwinian evolutionary theories.

How could Rousseau be influenced by the idea that "war is the father of all things"? After all, he insisted that human beings are basically good. However, Rousseau recognized that human beings in their modern condition certainly do not manifest the qualities of their original, natural unity and docility. Hence, some historical event changed humanity for the worse. Rousseau understood that despite the initial conditions of human nature, it can still be changed. One of the most basic human attributes is perfectibility, the capacity to improve oneself by making comparisons between oneself and others. But such comparisons usually give rise to conflict, which gives rise to new needs, which give rise to more conflict. If human beings could not be changed in such ways, there would be no need for the rigorous social and education programs Rousseau prescribes.

Kant's system is the result of great synthesis. On the one hand, he combined rationalism with empiricism, recognizing that neither, on its own, can generate knowledge. The dynamic between contraries generate truth, just as birds require wind resistance to fly. That Kant maintained the primacy of *practical* reason demonstrates his understanding that the resolution to perennial ultimate questions often entertained by speculative reason must be tethered to concrete human concerns. The existence of God and the immortal soul, in addition to the postulate of free will, must be affirmed so that we can live moral lives. Nonetheless, the causal laws of science in the realm of nature cannot be denied, hence, the need for a distinction between two realms. Finally, the viability of morality within the realm of nature demands that we view history as progressive and nature as contributing to our development by confronting us with challenges by which we can improve and become stronger.

Hegel's dialectical conception of reality and Marx's subsequent inversion of it practically assume a Heraclitean view of reality. For Hegel, not only does the opposition between the various theses and antitheses and their eventual syntheses throughout history drive reality, but self-awareness implies awareness of others. For Marx, human nature consists in the discovery of creative labor through one's interactions with the natural world. Moreover, social and economic change happen as a result of conflict between classes. Each class, like every item in nature, has the potential for its own negation built into it. The idea that the working class itself must bring about the communist revolution establishes that conflict is a force that gives people meaning.

For Schopenhauer, the will to live is the driving force behind everything and it is essentially antagonistic, aggressive, and destructive. For one thing to survive, another must be consumed. Indubitably, this idea inspired Darwin's conception of natural selection and the idea of the struggle to survive. Also embedded in Darwin's theory of evolution is the denial of the fixity of any species. The kingdoms of the natural order constantly evolve, and if so, then reality is unstable. Both Schopenhauer and Darwin, thus, share Heraclitus as a common intellectual predecessor, as does Freud, for whom the conflict between the life and death instincts drives most human endeavors. The tripartite structure of personality—the id, ego, and super-ego—emerge based on the individual's interaction with the external world. The repression and sublimation of various instincts represent the changes that occur as the result of one's interface with the world, all of which are necessary to sustain civilization. The fact that Freud recognized the death instinct as stronger than the life instinct suggests, moreover, that war is not only the father of all things, but the *goal* of all things as well.

Since all existentialists deny that there exists any universal human essence, all are to a degree committed to the instability of reality and human nature. Specifically, Kierkegaard's suggestion that the invention of human speech creates a barrier between people and the reality of nature introducing doubt and possibilities testifies both to a duality and instability within human nature, hence, why the self must be constructed out of freedom. The aesthetic self can find meaning only by either constantly consuming the resources of the world or through opposition with others. The ethical self can find meaning only by defining oneself in terms of others. Even the highest of Kierkegaard's stages of life, the religious self, can achieve meaning only in relation to the ultimate "other," God, and only through a passionate inward struggle. It is thus, through conflict and confrontation with the anxiety concomitant with life that we can find meaning.

Finally, for Nietzsche, reality is a manifestation of a will to power, which may also be called a will to overpower. Not only is reality unstable, but the force that drives it has conflict built into it. Without conflict, no one can become stronger. And if no one can become stronger, no one can have power. But power is the ultimate motivation of everything. Even the seemingly highest of human aspirations have the ulterior motive of the achievement of power, status, or recognition. Those who cannot achieve power create an imaginary transcendent world in which they are the true heroes while the privileged masters and the exceptional overmen of the world are truly evil and deserve to be punished. Even those who seem to desire perpetual peace, comfort, and security only do so because they fear failure. Such people secretly desire power and entertain a fascination with war and conflict. Everybody wishes to be Zarathustra, but most will never break free of the herd.

So, which of these theories is the *best*? Which of these theories is "the right one"? In short, each one is, in its own way, the best, which seems to imply that each one is, also in its own way, the worst. But I leave it to the reader to determine how. Hopefully the skills and knowledge you acquired if you read this far will serve as useful guides to your inquiry. Perhaps you can create your own theory. No doubt, doing so will be a struggle and perhaps cause conflict within you. But conflict is a force that gives life meaning. Any task that can be completed without struggle is not worth doing. It is because human life is so precious that it is filled with conflict and struggle. Our goal should not be to eliminate conflict, but to ensure that what we achieve in the end is worth the fight.

Selective Bibliography

Adamson, Peter. *Classical Philosophy*. New York, NY: Oxford University Press, 2014.

Adler, Mortimer. *Aristotle for Everybody: Difficult Thought Made Easy*. New York, NY: Touchstone, 1997.

Ariew, Richard, and Eric Watkins, editors. *Modern Philosophy: An Anthology of Primary Sources*. Indianapolis, IN: Hackett Publishing, 2009.

Auxter, Thomas. *Kant's Moral Teleology*. Macon, GA: Mercer University Press, 1982.

Barbour, Ian G. *Religion and Science: Historical and Contemporary Issues*. New York, NY: Harper-Collins, 1997.

Beck, Lewis White. *Commentary on Kant's Critique of Practical Reason*. Chicago, IL: University of Chicago Press, 1960.

Cassirer, Ernst. *The Question of Jean-Jacques Rousseau*. Translated by Peter Gay, Indiana University Press, 1975.

Copleston, F.C. *Aquinas*. Bergenfield, NJ: Penguin Books, 1956.

Cornman, J.W., et al. *Philosophical Problems and Arguments*. Indianapolis, IN: Hackett Publishing, 1992.

Cottingham, John. *Descartes*. Malden, MA: Wiley-Blackwell, 1991.

Crews, Clyde F. *Ultimate Questions: A Theological Primer*. New York, NY: Paulist Press, 1986.

Durant, Will. *The Story of Philosophy*. New York, NY: Pocket Books/Simon & Schuster, 2006.

Eagleton, Terry. *Why Marx Was Right*. New Haven, CT: Yale University Press, 2011.

Ewing, A.C. *A Short Commentary on Kant's Critique of Pure Reason*. Chicago, IL: Chicago University Press, 1996.

Farrell, B.A. "An Outline of Freud's Mature Theory." *The Study of Human Nature*, edited by Leslie Stevenson. New York, NY: Oxford University Press, 2000, pp. 170–184.

Freud, Anna. *The Ego and the Mechanisms of Defense*. New York, NY: Routledge—Taylor & Francis Group, 2018.

Gardner, Sebastian. *Kant and the Critique of Pure Reason*. New York, NY: Routledge, 1999.

Gaskin, J.C.A. *Hume's Philosophy of Religion*. London: MacMillan, 1988.

Gonzalez, Francisco. *Dialectic and Dialogue: Plato's Practice of Philosophical Inquiry*. Northwestern University Press, 1998.

Herman, Richard. *The Cave and the Light: Plato Versus Aristotle and the Struggle for the Soul of Western Civilization*. New York, NY: Random House, 2014.

Gildin, Hilail. *Rousseau's Social Contract: The Design of the Argument*. Chicago, IL: Chicago University Press, 1983.

Kolakowski, Leszek. *Main Currents of Marxism*. New York, NY: W. W. Norton & Company, 2005.

Kreeft, Peter. *A Summa of The Summa*. San Francisco, CA: Ignatius Press, 2011.

Kupperman, Joel. *Theories of Human Nature*. Indianapolis, IN: Hackett Publishing, 2010.

Lavine, T.Z. *From Socrates to Sartre: The Philosophic Quest*. New York, NY: Bantam Books, 1984.

McLellan, David. *Introduction to the Thought of Karl Marx*. New York, NY: Harper & Row, 1971.

_____. *Marxism After Marx*. New York, NY: Palgrave-Macmillan, 2007.

Melling, David J. *Understanding Plato*. New York, NY: Oxford University Press, 1987.

Melzer, Arthur M. *The Natural Goodness of Man: On the System of Rousseau's Thought*. Chicago, IL: University of Chicago Press, 1990.

Neiman, Susan. *The Unity of Reason: Rereading Kant*. New York, NY: Oxford University Press, 1994.

Nietzsche, Friedrich. *Twilight of the Idols*. Translated by Richard Polt, Indianapolis, IN: Hackett Publishing, 1997.

_____. *The Gay Science*, in Walter Kaufman (Ed). New York, NY: Vintage, 1974.

Palmer, Donald. *Looking At Philosophy: The Unbearable Heaviness of Philosophy Made Lighter*. New York, NY: McGraw-Hill, 2013.

Palmer, Donald. *Visions of Human Nature: An Introduction*. Mountain View, CA: Mayfield Publishing Company, 2000.

Pippin, Robert. "Nietzsche: Thus Spoke Zarathustra." *Introductions to Nietzsche*, edited by Robert Pippin, New York, NY: Cambridge University Press, 2012, pp. 152–177.

Plattner, Marc. *Rousseau's State of Nature: An Interpretation of Rousseau's Discourse on Inequality*. Dekalb, IL: Northern Illinois University Press, 1979.

Pojman, Louis. *Who Are We? Theories of Human Nature*. New York, NY: Oxford University Press, 2005.

Pyle, Andrew. *Hume's Dialogues on Natural Religion: A Reader's Guide*. New York, NY: Continuum International Publishing, 2006.

Quine, W.V.O. "On What There Is." *From a Logical Point of View*, edited by W.V.O. Quine, Harvard University Press, 1961, pp. 1–19.

Ranasinghe, Nalin. *Socrates in the Underworld*. St. Augustine Press, 2009.

Rawls, John. "Kantian Constructivism in Moral Theory," in *The Journal of Philosophy*, 77: pp. 515–572.

Richardson, John. *Nietzsche's System*. New York, NY: Oxford University Press, 1996.

Ridley, Aaron. "Nietzsche: The Anti-Christ, Ecce Homo, and Twilight of the Idols." *Introductions to Nietzsche*, edited by Robert Pippin, New York, NY: Cambridge University Press, 2012, pp. 215–239.

Rothman, Tony. *Instant Physics: From Aristotle to Einstein and Beyond*. New York, NY: Ballantine Books, 1995.

Russell, Bertrand. *The Problems of Philosophy*. New York, NY: Oxford University Press, 1959.

——————————. *A History of Western Philosophy*. London: Allen & Unwin, 1961.

Ryle, Gilbert. *The Concept of Mind*. Chicago, IL: University of Chicago Press, 1949.

Sirridge, Mary. "The Treachery of the Commonplace." *Philosophy in The Twilight Zone*, edited by Lester Hunt and Noel Carroll. Malden, MA: Wiley-Blackwell, 2009, pp. 58–76.

Sproul, R.C. *The Consequences of Ideas*. Wheaton, IL: Crossway, 2009.

Stevenson, Leslie, et al. *Twelve Theories of Human Nature*. New York, NY: Oxford University Press, 2013.

Strong, Tracy. "Introduction to *Twilight of the Idols*." Translated by Plot, *Twilight of the Idols*. Indianapolis, IN: Hackett Publishing, 1997, pp. vii–xxviii.

Telotte, J.P. "Through a Pumpkin's Eye: The Reflexive Nature of Horror." *American Horrors: Essays on the Modern American Horror Film*, edited by Gregory A. Waller, University of Illinois Press, 1987, pp. 114–128.

Thomson, Garrett. *Bacon to Kant: An Introduction to Modern Philosophy*. Long Grove, IL: Waveland Press, 2012.

Tiel, Jeffrey. *Philosophy of Human Nature*. CreateSpace Independent Publishing Platform, 2012.

Trigg, Roger. *Ideas of Human Nature*. Malden, MA: Wiley-Blackwell, 1999.

Tucker, Robert, editor. *The Marx-Engels Reader*. New York, NY: W. W. Norton & Company, 1978.

Velkley, Richard. *Freedom and the End of Reason: On the Moral Foundations of Kant's Critical Philosophy*. Chicago, IL: Chicago University Press, 1989.

_____. *Being After Rousseau: Philosophy and Culture in Question*. Chicago, IL: Chicago University Press, 2002.

Wall, Thomas F. *On Human Nature: An Introduction to Philosophy*. Belmont, CA: Wadsworth, 2005.

Whitehead, Alfred North. *Process and Reality*. Tampa, FL: Free Press, 1979.

Wolff, Jonathan. *Why Read Marx Today?* New York, NY: Oxford University Press, 2002.

Wood, Allen. *Kant's Moral Religion*. Ithaca, NY: Cornell University Press, 1970.

Yovel, Yirmiyahu. *Kant and the Philosophy of History*. Princeton, NJ: Princeton University Press, 1982.

Zammito, John. *The Genesis of Kant's Third Critique*. Chicago, IL: University of Chicago Press, 1992.

Zeldin, Mary-Barbara. *"The Summum Bonum, the Moral Law, and the Existence of God."* *Kant-Studien*, vol. 62 (1–4): 43–54, 1971.